Theory, Knowledge, Development and Politics:
What Role for the Academy in the Sustainability of Africa?

Editors

Munyaradzi Mawere & Artwell Nhemachena

Langaa Research & Publishing CIG
Mankon, Bamenda

Publisher:
Langaa RPCIG
Langaa Research & Publishing Common Initiative Group
P.O. Box 902 Mankon
Bamenda
North West Region
Cameroon
Langaagrp@gmail.com
www.langaa-rpcig.net

Distributed in and outside N. America by African Books Collective
orders@africanbookscollective.com
www.africanbookscollective.com

ISBN: *9956-763-64-0*

© Munyaradzi Mawere & Artwell Nhemachena 2016

List of Contributors

Munyaradzi Mawere holds a PhD in Social Anthropology from the University of Cape Town (UCT) in South Africa. Professor Mawere also holds a Master's Degree in Social Anthropology from UCT, a Master's Degree in Philosophy and B. A. (Hons) Degree in Philosophy from the University of Zimbabwe. He is currently Professor in the Department of Culture and Heritage Studies at Great Zimbabwe University. Before joining this university, Professor Mawere was a lecturer at the University of Zimbabwe and at Universidade Pedagogica, Mozambique, where he has worked in different capacities as a Senior lecturer, Assistant Research Director, Postgraduate Co-ordinator and Associate Professor. He has an outstanding publishing record of more than one hundred and twenty pieces of work which include more than twenty-five books and over a hundred book chapters and papers in scholarly journals. Professor Mawere has published extensively on poverty and community development, knowledge studies, political anthropology, science and technology studies (STS), environment and agrarian issues, democracy and African states, coloniality, decoloniality and transformation, African philosophy and political systems, culture and heritage studies. Some of his bestselling books are: *Humans, Other Beings and the Environment: Harurwa (Edible stinkbugs) and Environmental Conservation in South-eastern Zimbabwe* (2015); *Democracy, Good Governance and Development in Africa: A Search for Sustainable Democracy and Development*, (2015); *Culture, Indigenous Knowledge and Development in Africa: Reviving Interconnections for Sustainable Development* (2014); *Harnessing Cultural Capital for Sustainability: A Pan Africanist Perspective* (2015); *Divining the Future of Africa: Healing the Wounds, Restoring Dignity and Fostering Development* (2014); *African Cultures, Memory and Space: Living the Past Presence in Zimbabwean Heritage* (2014); *African Philosophy and Thought Systems: A Search for a Culture and Philosophy of Belonging* (2016); and *Colonial Heritage, Memory and Sustainability in Africa: Challenges, Opportunities and Prospects* (2016).

Artwell Nhemachena holds a PhD in Social Anthropology from the University of Cape Town in South Africa. Dr Nhemachena has studied Sociology and Social Anthropology. He has lectured at several universities in Zimbabwe including the University of Zimbabwe, Women's University in Africa and Great Zimbabwe University before pursuing PhD studies in South Africa. His current areas of interest include Indigenous Knowledge Systems, Environment, Democratic Governance, Social Theory from the South, Decoloniality and Transformation, African Jurisprudence, Human Security, Food Security and Food Sovereignty, Conflict and Violence, Poverty and Development, Science and Technology Studies. He has published on Democracy, Environment, Indigenous Knowledge, Decoloniality, Health, Resilience and Theory.

Mirjam van Reisen is currently Professor of Computing for Society at Leiden Centre for Data Science at the University of Leiden. She is also Professor of International Relations, Innovation and Care at Tilburg University. Professor van Reisen is the Director of Europe External Programme (EEPA) with Africa based in Brussels. She is a member of the Dutch Advisory Council on International Affairs (AIV) and Chair of the Development Assistance Committee (COS). Besides, Professor van Reisen is a member of the Board of Philips Foundation, the Dutch Development Organisations and Transnational Institute. In 2012, Professor van Reisen received the Golden Image Award from President Ellen Johnson Sirleaf. She is an expert on EU-Africa relations and has published extensively on ICT innovation, migration, social security, gender, energy and community development, human trafficking, peace building, diplomacy and international relations, technology and innovation. Some of her books include: *Women's leadership and Peace-building: Conflict, community and care* (2014); *The human trafficking cycle: Sinai and beyond (2014); Refugees between life and death: Human trafficking in the Sinai* (2012); *Window of opportunity: European Development Cooperation after the end of the cold war* (2009); and *EU global player* (2000).

Aboyeji, Adeniyi Justus holds a PhD in History. He presently teaches in the Department of History and International Studies at University of Ilorin, Nigeria. His areas of specialisation cut across economic, diplomatic and military histories, as well as Igbomina Studies. A number of his publications have appeared in indexed journals. He graduated from the University of Ilorin with a B.A (Hons) in History in 2001 and Master's Degree in 2006. His doctoral thesis deals with a seminal aspect of the history of the Igbomina people. Dr Justsus has also taught at Sapati International School, Ilorin and Kwara State College of Education in Oro before he joined his current university.

Ismaila O. O. Amali is from Benue State, Nigeria. He holds a B.Ed (Arts); M.Ed (Guidance & Counselling) from University of Jos, Nigeria; and PhD (Educational Foundations) from University of Maiduguri. He is currently a senior lecturer in the Department of Social Sciences Education, Faculty of Education, and University of Ilorin, Nigeria. He teaches Sociology of Education and other related courses at undergraduate and postgraduate levels. He is a scholar and researcher in the field of Sociology of Education with special interests in the development of indigenous Nigerian and African educational practices. He has supervised many research works and still supervising students at undergraduate and postgraduate levels. He has published in many academic international, national and local journals. He has served in Nigerian Immigration Service before transferring his service to the University of Ilorin, Nigeria in 2006. He is married with children.

Lemuel E. Odeh is a graduate of the Lagos State University Ojo-Lagos in B.A. History and International Studies, an MSc International Relations and Strategic Studies and a Ph.D. in History from the Benue State University Makurdi. His area of research is Diplomatic History & International Economic Relations. He is currently a lecturer in the Department of History & International Studies, University of Ilorin, Nigeria. Some of his publications include Odeh E. L., (2011) *"Sino-Nigeria Economic Relations under the Obasanjo Administration"* in Ilorin Journal of History and International Studies Vol. 2 No. 1 2011, Published by the Department of History and International Studies, University of Ilorin, Ilorin pp. 217-231; Odeh E. L., (2013) *Sino-Nigeria Investments: Prospects and Challenges 1975 – 2010 in Journal of African East-Asian Affairs.* The China Monitor Centre for Chinese Studies, Stellenbosch University, South Africa Issue No. 4 December 2013 pp 24 – 49; Odeh E. L., (2010) "Sino-Nigeria Economic Relations 1990-2008" African Renaissance Volume 7, Number 1, 2010 (US – Africa Relations under Obama) Adonis & Abbey Publishers, pp. 43-56; Odeh E. L., & Aghalino. S. O (2011) *"The Moral Precepts of Chinese Confucianism and the Relevance to the Nigerian Society"* in Ilorin Journal of Sociology Vol. 3 No 1 July, 2011,Published by the Department of Sociology, University of Ilorin, Ilorin p177-183; Odeh E. L., (2012) *"A Comparative Analysis of Global North and Global South Economies"* International Journal of Current Research in the Humanities University of Cape Coast Cape Coast Ghana No. 14 June 2012 p67-82.

CostainTandi is a High school teacher for Advanced level History and Sociology as well as Head of Department (Humanities) at Rufaro High School, Chatsworth, Zimbabwe. He holds a Masters Degree in Development Studies from Midlands State University, Bachelor of Arts 4th year Honours (History) from Great Zimbabwe University, Bachelor of Arts General Degree from the University of Zimbabwe, Graduate Certificate in Education from Great Zimbabwe University, An Executive certificate in Program and Project Monitoring and Evaluation from the University of Zimbabwe and An Executive Certificate in Project Management from the University of Zimbabwe. His research interests include but not limited to Indigenous Knowledge systems, Climate change and Variability, Rural poverty, agriculture and community development.

Ogunbiyi, Olatunde Oyewole studied religion, literary/film theory and criticism, cultural and media studies with particular emphasis in representations of African religion in movies. His research interest covers how the Nigerian film industry, Nollywood, shapes and is shaped by contemporary practices of religious consciousness in Africa and in the Diaspora. He had his B.A. and M.A. Degrees in Christian Studies from the University of Ilorin, Ilorin, Nigeria and his PhD in African Religion from the University of Ado-Ekiti, Ado-

Ekiti, Nigeria. He lectures in the Comparative Religious Studies Unit of the Department of Religions, University of Ilorin, Ilorin, Nigeria.

Nkwazi Mhango is the author of *SaayaUkombozi, NyumayaPazia, Souls on Sale, Born with Voice* and *Africa Reunite or Perish*, a poet, teacher, columnist, Journalist, Peace and Conflict Scholar, and member of Writers' Association of Newfoundland and Labrador (WANL) St. John's NL, Canada. Also, Mhango is an alumnus of Universities of Dar es Salaam (Tanzania) Winnipeg and Manitoba (Canada).

Ògúnlolá Omolayò Dúrótadé was born in a village called Omido in Ìrépòdùn Local Government Area of Kwara State, Nigeria some fifty-six years ago. Dr. Ògúnlolá Omolayò Dúrótadé attended Ará-United Primary School, Àrándùn/Omido, Esìé/Ìlúdùn Anglican Grammar School, both in Kwara State, Federal Teachers' College, Ankpa, School of Basic Studies, Kwara State College of Technology (now Kwara State Polytechnic), Ìlorin, Kwara State, Nigeria for his GCE Advanced Level. He bagged his First Degree B.ed (Hons), Yorùbá at the University of Ìbàdàn, Òyó State, Nigeria, MA Degree in Yorùbá from University of Ilorin, Nigeria and PhD in Yorùbá Literature also from University of Ìlorin, Nigeria. He is currently a Senior Lecturer in the Department of Linguistics and Nigerian Languages, University of Ìlorin, Nigeria. Dr. Ògúnlolá has written a number of texts. They include: ÈyìnÒrò (Prose), OhunOjúwá (Play), Kòsórò (Prose), Ogbón ÌlànàÌkóniní ÈdèYorùbá and Opéyemí Ìgbèyìnádùn (Play), now with the Press. He also has over eighteen home-based, National and International paper articles to his credit. He is married and blessed with children.

Aboyeji Oyeniyi Solomon holds a PhD from the Department of History and International Studies at University of Ilorin, Nigeria. He also holds B.A and M.A Degrees from the same University. For the past decade, Dr Solomon has been teaching in the Departments of History and General Studies in Education at Kwara State College of Education in Oro, Nigeria. At Kwara, Dr Solomon has taught and graduated students with the Nigerian Certificate in Education (NCE) and Graduate Degree Certificates in History. His research interests include cultural history and Igbomina Studies. He has a number of scholarly publications with internationally accredited peer-review journals.

Afolabi Opeyemi Glory is a graduate of Kogi State University, Anyigba with a B.A in History and International Studies and an MA in History from the University of Ilorin, Nigeria with emphasis on Afro-Asian Studies.

Gertjan van Stam is a Research Fellow at the Scientific and Industrial Research and Development Centre (SIRDC) of Zimbabwe. He holds an MTech (cum laude) from Nelson Mandela Metropolitan University (NMMU) in South Africa. Gertjan and his family lived in the rural areas of Zimbabwe and Zambia for over 13 years. His broad academic interests focus on the nexus of society and technology in the so-called periphery with the goal to identify and inspire local talent and engender local capacity for community-led activities.

Tapuwa Raymond Mubaya is a Lecturer and a PhD candidate at Great Zimbabwe University, Faculty of Culture and Heritage Studies. Before joining Great Zimbabwe University, Mr. Mubaya worked for National Museums and Monuments of Zimbabwe (NMMZ) for eight years as the Curator of Archaeology and Head of the Great Zimbabwe Monument Conservation Centre. Currently he is heading the Department of Heritage Studies at Great Zimbabwe University. Mr Mubaya holds a Master of Arts Degree in Heritage Studies from the University of Zimbabwe. He is also a member of the Association of Southern African Professional Archaeologists (ASAPA) and the Zimbabwe Association of Professional Archaeologists and related Disciplines (ZAPAD. His current research interests are focussed on heritage management and conservation, cultural tourism and museums. Mubaya has written and published fourteen articles in internationally esteemed scholarly journals and is the co-editor of the books: *African Cultures, Memory and Space: Living the Past Presence in Zimbabwean Heritage* (2014) and *Colonial Heritage, Memory and Sustainability in Africa: Challenges, Opportunities and Prospects* (2016); and co-author of *African Philosophy and Thought Systems: A Search for a Culture and Philosophy of Belonging* (2016).

Fidelis Peter Thomas Duri is a lecturer in the Department of History and Development Studies at Great Zimbabwe University. He is a holder of a PhD in History from the University of the Witwatersrand in Johannesburg, South Africa. He has published a number of books and articles which focus on environmental history, socio-cultural dynamics, subaltern struggles, African border studies and politics in Zimbabwe during the colonial and post-colonial periods. He has also reviewed and edited a number of scholarly books and articles and is also a member of the editorial boards of international journals such as the *Zimbabwe Journal of Historical Studies* and the *International Journal of Developing Societies.*

Table of Contents

Chapter One

'Blackness,' 'Whiteness' and the Euro-American Socio-economic and Political Exploitation and Theorisation of Africa: An Introduction

Munyaradzi Mawere & Artwell Nhemachena

Introduction

The obsession of Europe and North America with the questions of fame, wealth and status portrayed through skin colour and physical appearance undoubtedly influenced their attitude towards Africa and the African people. The racist European and American theorists from the Global North though they knew that Africa was richly endowed with treasure of all kinds, they mistakenly but deliberately believed that all those riches belonged to them and not to the people of Africa. This is because they believed that they were "the people" – the legitimate owners of all the treasure in Africa regardless of their geographical location being Global North. No wonder why even though in terms of colour definitions the theorists knew that "Africans were chocolate skinned and not black, yet they went a step further to label all Africans 'black people' while labelling themselves white, a symbol of purity" (Mawere 2013: 25). Black colour, though did not truly depict the colour of the African people was imposed on Africa to cement the inferiority complex, negativity and poverty that Africa and the people of Africa have always been associated with since the beginning of theorisation of Africa by the Global North.

The realisation that false labels such as "Black" and "White" continue to be used, regrettably even in the corridors of academia, some decades after the formal demise of colonial administration in many formerly colonised states leaves a lot desired to be done. It is disheartening and worrying such that it prompted us and all the contributors to this impeccable volume into wanting to explore more on the so-called decolonial project and theorisation in and on Africa. The questions that continue to boggle the back of our minds are: If

1

the decolonial project has always been genuine, why little or no attention has been directed towards the theorisation of race and colour? Also, why Africa has not allowed permission to deploy its own methodologies and epistemologies in its contexts, worse still those of the Global North? Why the Global North has, for a long time, looted both natural and human resources from Africa? Why the Global North, for a long time, has always wanted to take the lead in the debates on decoloniality?

Why the world is haunted with problems of racial exploitation and colour?

The Elizabethan European perception and American repulsion of the African people greatly influenced many people in the Global North to think that they were superior and more civilised than all other races. Africans, for example, were considered as primitive, backward, illogical, savages, and uncivilised. Eurocentric scholars failed to see the viability of African cultures and that any perception that associated complexion with the intellect was a misguided, false and nefarious theory meant to subjugate the people of Africa then and forever. This explains why European travellers like Walter Wren got totally surprised when he visited Coast of Guinea in 1566 and see that 'although the people [of Coast Guinea] were black and naked, they were civil' (see William Shakespeare, The Merchant of Venice 11, p. 7) as he did not expect the people of Guinea to have a coherent ethic and cultural fabric. Race and colour were the only two criteria used to determine one's role in history and society. The civil rights movement of the 1960s in the US and across Africa was a clear testimony of the reality that obtained around colour and racial differences the prejudices associated with them. In Southern Africa especially South Africa, Affirmative Action and Black Economic Empowerment are a clear testimony that prejudices on the basis of colour and race have not been totally erased even in today's formerly colonised of Africa as well as in imperial countries of Europe and America.

While the problems associated with racial prejudices in Africa as elsewhere are difficult to solve today, their source from the European and American colonists remain unquestionable. Some of the persisting problems associated with racial prejudices especially with reference to Africa are racist labels such as "dark continent," and "black continent." The Economist headline in 2000 that "Africa is a hopeless continent" is one example. The continued use of the labels "white people" and "Black people" referring to Europeans/Americans and Africans respectively is another case in point. These false and pejorative labels which are still in full use even today after the colonial wave in Africa and beyond clearly show how and why racial prejudices remain a big question worth investigating even today. It remains questionable whether the decolonising process that is purported to have started in the 1960s has been taking place honestly and in earnest. Such observations make many critical scholars believe that Africa is in the phase of neo-colonialism – another form of colonialism which is possibly worse than the one that Africa experienced in the 19th century. Cultural diversity and the fact that Africa is the fatherland and motherland of mankind were both ignored by Euro-American imperialists to avoid contradictions in their preaching of the need of the civilisation of Africa.

Likewise, the question of colour did not only end with skin descriptions but also with "unconstructive" analysis and negative associations. In fact the black colour was associated with evil. Dickson Mungazi in his book *The Mind of Black Africa* (1996) is apt to parade a series of events, associations and personifications associated with blackness. In the United States of America, for example, Black Friday was made to represent the economic collapse of the 1869 and 1873 which were caused by the sudden and rapid decline in the price of gold. Blackmail is even today associated with people involved in serious crime such that they will be more of outcasts in society. Black magic is likewise associated with witchcraft activities. Black Death of the Dark Ages was associated with bubonic plague which killed 25 % of the European population. In many societies that were affected by European colonialism, black cat is associated with misfortune as this is the belief in many European societies. The same applies to black clothes in the aforementioned societies. In Europe, black clothes signify moaning – the presence of a funeral. Today in both Europe and many societies that experienced European colonialism, the significance of black clothes remains the same. Personifications of witches and wizards are all over the world camouflaged in black

3

clothing and never in white clothing. Even the Black Sea was named so due to the heavy fog that normally cloudy itself in the sea making navigation risk and unpredictable during certain times of the year. In the United States of America, the black widow is a name given to one of the most deadly spiders in that country. When the Great Depression started in the United States of America in 1929, the day that marked the depression was named Black Tuesday. In 1921, members of the Benito Mussoloni's Fascist Party were nicknamed the Black Shits as a result of their brutality and atrocities against political opponents of their time. In the 2008 atrocities in Zimbabwe, one politician who was well-known for beating up opposition supporters identified himself as "Black Jesus."

All these examples are a clear testimony that Blackness is associated with evil. It is therefore disturbing, nerve-racking and in fact tormenting to realise the tragic truth that the colour of Black accorded to Africans was deliberately meant to damage the image, persona and reputation of the African people. The million-dollar question that remains mind boggling is: Should we, critical academics and theorists, let such misinterpretations and misrepresentations continue and live for ever?

The genesis of the exploitation and negative theorisation of the other

The exploitation of other races particularly the African race was pioneered by the Portuguese people. The Portuguese opened the floodgates for other European imperialists and later the United States of America. After the collapse of the Roman Empire the now loosely organised nation-states of Europe experienced a tight struggle amongst themselves in a bid to garner power and influence to control trade and commerce in the region. This end of the protracted Roman Empire power since the time of the Caesars also left European nation-states with an obsession for new power to control others' territories. This ignited the European quest for territorial congest and expansion that resulted in the age of exploitation. The Germanic, Vikings and later the Portuguese, British and Italians and Spaniards joined in the hunt for power, influence and wealth from distant lands. The major ambition of each of these nation states was to amass power that would enable them to rule Europe. Two Italians, Nicolo Polo and his brother, Maffeo in their attempt to evade the tricks of the Arab traders who normally acted as middlemen between the Middle East and Europe, made a breakthrough for Europe when they decided to establish a port at the eastern end of the Black Sea to trade directly with China. The Polo brother's establishment of a strong friendship with the powerful oriental chief, Kublai Khan changed both their fortunes and that of Europe. The Polo brothers stayed 10 years and managed to amass large proportions of wealth that lured many other European business people. Some two years after their return to Europe, the Polo brothers travelled again to Khan Empire, now with Nicolo's son, Marco, who as a matter of fact became Kublai Khan's one of his most trusted confidants. On returning to Venice, Europe, Marco published an account of his travels and exploitation in a book he titled "The adventure of Marco Polo." The account contained rich stories of the enormous wealth that distant people had such that it greatly influenced later voyages of exploitation by European entrepreneurs and fortune or fame seekers. It later resulted in colonial imperial adventures and the plunder of African resources and people. Polo's books were translated into many European languages thereby extending their influence beyond Venice. The books inspired later explorers like Christopher Columbus who is believed to have founded the USA in 1492. It should be noted, however, that although Polo keenly observed other cultures, he tended to exaggerate in his descriptions of other cultures of the people he interacted with during his travels.

Henry the Navigator (1394-1460) though navigated no further than North Africa was one other key historical figure influenced by Marco Polo's books. Henry who was the brother of King of Portugal took a leading role in European voyages to Africa such that Portuguese took an early lead in knowledge about exploitation of nations outside Europe. In his quest to understand people of the world, Henry the Navigator established a naval school at Sagres in 1416 where people from all over Europe and Arab world studied geography, navigation, cultures of distant lands, human behaviour, skin colour and cognitive ability.

Some 28 years after Henry the Navigator's death in 1460, the Portuguese sailor, Bartholomew Diaz (1457-1500) arrived at the southern tip of Africa in search of the sea passage to India where he was commissioned to go by King John 11. This was the beginning of the subjection of the African people to asymmetrical relationships with Europe. Diaz's expedition provided valuable information and opinions about Africa such that in 1498, Manuel 1 who succeeded John 11, commissioned Vasco Da Gama (1469 – 1524) to come to Africa and complete the expedition that Diaz started. Diaz had failed his expedition for two major reasons namely hostility of the African people and violent storms at the southern tip of the African continent – Diaz's Cape of Storms, later named Cape of Good Hope. Although Da Gama managed to overcome the violent storms at the southern tip of Africa, he failed to contain the hostility of the African people. This hostility led to Portugal's failure to establish a settlement at the Cape of Good Hope up until 1652 when the Dutch managed to establish settlement there.

The Portuguese, however, used knowledge acquired through Diaz and Da Gama to make more inroads to Africa. Through Da Gama's recommendation, the Portuguese started laying big plans to control both the people of India and Africa together with their wealth under control. The Arabs were, however, unhappy with Da Gama's success especially towards the lucrative spice trading, incited the Hindus to revolt against the Portuguese. The Portuguese also established a military base at the Cape of Good Hope to protect its sailors and trade. This resulted in tension between the Portuguese and the African people. The tension continued up until the 1960s when the Portuguese African colonies entered into war of independence besides that Portugal's trade links with India and Africa was weakened by its annexture by Spain in 1580.

Yet the military tactics adopted by the Portuguese were also employed by other European explorers thereby resulting in a permanent conflict between Europe and Africa. The Europeans became more and more concerned with the amassing of wealth and occupation of territory through force and violence other than establishing good human relationships based on mutuality, thereby giving the Dutch an opportunity to establish themselves at the Cape of Good Hope. The violence and force executed by the Portuguese against Africans also resulted in trans-Atlantic slave trade wave and later colonialism with which Europeans believed were going to dominate the world. In 1575, some 77 years before the Dutch establishment of a settlement at Cape of Good Hope, Portugal claimed Angola on the West Coast and Mozambique on the east coast as its colonies. In 1680, the Portuguese demanded trade concessions from the African people. These included the shipment of large numbers of slaves, copper and ivory to Portugal, though they met serious resistance from African Chiefs such as King Alfonso of Angola (see Shillington 1987: 19).

It should be emphasised that with all its domineering projects, Europe deceived herself to believe that it was now socially, economically and politically in total control of the African mind once and forever. The Portuguese, for example, made themselves to believe they were the wisest of all people on earth. Europeans never believed that one day the African people will rise above situation to be in total control of their land, wealth and destiny as a people.

Condemning the false logic of racism and misrepresentation

Some decades after the whole continent of Africa is free from the bondage of colonialism, at least administratively, it is disturbing that people of the world including Africans themselves continue using the malfabricated labels of blackness and whiteness. It is even more disturbing to realise that many prominent African scholars have done little or virtually nothing to shake and challenge those Eurocentric constructions and misrepresentations of Africa and the African people. This explains the "persistence of resilience of many remnant fronts of injustice, misrepresentations, and misguided theorisation on Africa even today, some decades after the formal demise of colonial administration and inception of the decolonial project" (Mawere 2015: 9) in Africa and the world. This kind of scenario calls for the need to decolonise not only the philosophical foundations of institutions but knowledge and power within those institutions and their people. We remain fervently convinced that "he who fights smoke will never extinguish the fire except if he fights the fire itself.' In the same token, we argue that 'the decolonial process can never achieve a level ground justice in both resource (re-)distribution and conceptual theorisation except if the philosophical foundations that brought the injustices and misrepresentations are dislodged and

7

decolonised first and foremost" (Mawere 2015: 8). There is need to decolonise postcolonial studies, the hidden agenda of coloniality and the decolonial thinking itself. In fact, "we need to go a step beyond the decolonial thinking to rethink the theoretical framework for the decolonial project and determine the suitability of knowledge produced using that framework" (Mawere: Ibid).

A Journey through the Book

This book explores and theorises, through interdisciplinary engagement, the problems, challenges, as well as prospects of Africa coming out of the Global North "manufactured" traps and machinations in issues to do with knowledge production and dissemination and development in Africa. Contributions to this impeccable volume were solicited from scholars with different scholarly background and experiences around Africa and beyond, who have research interests in and on Africa, but with majority of them drawn from southern and western Africa. Yet, while the chapters that constitute this book were produced by scholars with diverse teaching and research experiences and contextual milieus, they all advance the argument that theorisation and solutions to African problems and challenges can better be provided for when approached from within as opposed to out of context and one-size-fits-all Global North-based approach.

Artwell Nhemachena's seminal work in chapter 2, for example, grapples with ways in which Africa has since the colonial era been theorised in terms of animism. He argues that animism was in fact a Western theory that originated from Western preoccupations with teleology including the view, since the advent of Western science, that nature was a polite word for an immanent God. These Western views were subsequently applied to knowledge systems of colonised peoples who were thereby deprived of their own distinct metaphysics and cosmologies. He argues that there is need to unthink this category of animism that has become resilient, with unfortunate results in that it has unhinged the human essence of the colonised.

Munyaradzi Mawere *et al.*'s luminary chapter 3 draws on African indigenous knowledge, as understood through *Ubuntu*, to highlight the inapplicability of Maslow's theory of human motivation. They argue that there is lack of supportive empirical evidence especially in context like Africa and that this shows that the theory of human motivation is not universally applicable. They authors point out that while for Maslow, the individual is the point of reference and the realisation of the individual is the highest goal, in *Ubuntu* African philosophy of humanness it is the collectivity that is prized.

Nkwazi Mhango's chapter 4 focuses on ways in which Africa has, since colonialism, been operating under wrong and misleading education. He argues for the need to decolonise education so that African epistemologies, including African science and philosophy, can be resuscitated. He argues that such African education and philosophy allowed Africa to live without depending on handouts and loans from the so-called developed countries that continue to entrap and exploit Africa.

In chapter 5, Amali et al dwell on social media and how they are used by undergraduate students in Nigerian universities. The authors look at uses of social media, factors that motivate university undergraduates to use social media and factors hampering the students from using social media. They also highlight the downside of the use of social media by undergraduate students.

Costain Tandi *et al.*'s chapter 6 grapples with terms indigenous and endogenous knowledge, and they argue that the terms indigenous knowledge is not as crippled as its critics argue. They further discuss the value of indigenous knowledge on health and medicine particularly in context where western medicine is expensive, unavailable and beyond the reach of the poor majority. Because of its utility, they argue, indigenous knowledge has been resilient over centuries since colonial era.

In chapter 7, Layo Ogunlola examines and evaluates present political system in Nigeria as presented by selected playwrights. He argues that most Yoruba playwrights like traditional poets regard themselves as the conscience of the society in terms of reflecting socio-political, cultural and economic activities of society and advocate for change. He notes that politicians that personalise political offices use threats against playwrights as ways to control them.

Chapter 8 focuses on issues of engineering in Africa. The authors, Munyaradzi Mawere and Gertan van Starm, argue that often technologies imported into Africa are unsuitable for the African contexts. For Mawere *et al*, African practitioners find technologies to be unfit to context, sometimes irrelevant, and in most cases detached from the epistemologies of the indigenous people. Their chapter therefore focuses on techno-social grounding of African engineers.

Aboyeji Adeniyi Justus and Aboyeji Oyeniyi Solomon's chapter 9 delves into the challenges of decoloniality and integration in Africa. They focus on Nigeria in the light of organised crimes, such as terrorism. They argue that terrorism is not unconnected to organisations or "Corporatocracy" that are behind the new global empire including global matrices of power that have looted control from individual African states. Arguing that terrorism is not only perpetrated by the Global South but also by the North, the authors point out that it is only until the battle against neo-colonialism in Africa is fought and won that there will be attainment of laudable integration and decoloniality.

Chapter 10 is authored by Ogunbiyi Olatunde Oyewole who focuses on African religion and representation in selected movies. Ogunbiyi argues that as a result of depiction of African religion as worthless and destructive, many Africans have come to detest African religion, its culture and worldview. The Africans who have come to detest African religion prefer foreign religion rather the indigenous one. Ogunbiyi argues that foreign religion such as Christianity portray, in movies, African religion as weak yet movies produced in favour of African religion show that it is acceptable to some people within the Yoruba and beyond.

Munyaradzi Mawere's chapter 11 takes us through matters of conservation in Zimbabwe. Arguing against the 'danger of a single story', he critiques colonial and postcolonial monoconservation. Drawing data from a community in Zimbabwe, he argues for multiple conservation epistemologies including collaboration among different conservation knowledge forms to foster justice and sustainable conservation.

Chapter 12 authored by Amali focuses on education and religion as sociological tools for sustainable development in Nigeria. Amali argues that though education and religion ought to serve as instruments of social solidarity for any society, in Nigeria religion has at times caused insecurity because some citizens lack understanding of various religious doctrines. Amali notes that there are various sects ravaging Nigeria, and as if this is not enough, Christianity and Islam try to disconnect people from their traditional religion, which they believe unholy, ungodly and fall outside the purview of true religion. For Amali, education and religion should jointly help to promote peace, and appropriate social order required for national development.

In chapter 13, Mawere and Mubaya argue for the need to rehabilitate detention camps that played a key role in the liberation of Zimbabwe. They point out that the detention centres serve as centres of national unity and identity yet some of the detention centres are in states of neglect.

Fidelis P T Duri's chapter 14 takes us through colonial land husbandry measures and African responses. While noting various ways in which Africans responded to colonial land husbandry, Duri argues that colonial land husbandry would not have failed had its administrators integrated some of the indigenous knowledge systems and factored in the involvement of African communities as willing participants in a dispensation free of racial discrimination in the access to natural resources.

Lemuel *et al* dwell, in chapter 15, on impact of religion on socio-political and economic development in China and Nigeria. They argue that the Nigerian government has failed to put an end to Boko Haram which has claimed responsibility for several terrorists' attacks. In the chapter, authors link the religious conflict in Nigeria to religious conflicts in China, and argue that the religious conflicts are a result of "frustration aggression" on account of religious restrictions and the influence of western education in China and Nigeria respectively.

References

Mawere, M. 2013. *Lyrics of reason and experience*, Langaa Publishers: Bamenda.

Mawere, M. 2015. 'Indigenous Mechanisms for Disaster Risk Reduction in Africa,' Paper Presented to the *2015 EDITION OF THE DZIMBAHWE ARTS FESTIVAL (DAF) ACADEMIC*

SYMPOSIUM, (1-3 October 2015*),* Great Zimbabwe University: Zimbabwe.

Mungazi, D. 1996. *The mind of black Africa,* Praeges Publishers, London.

Shillington, K. 1987. *History of southern Africa,* Longman: Essex, England.

Chapter Two

Animism, Coloniality and Humanism: Reversing the Empire's Framing of Africa

Artwell Nhemachena

Introduction

The charity case, in spiritual, material, ideological, ontological, and epistemic senses, into which Africa has been reduced by empire needs to be destroyed and channelled to the dustbin of oblivion if Africa is to make African-defined progress in its manifold dimensions. The charity-case-Africa is not only evident in material terms whereby Africa has been reduced to a rubbish dumping ground or to the wasteland of empire; charity-case-Africa is also evident in contemporary modes of epistemic "charity" by empire where Africa became a theoretical and epistemological dumping ground for disused, defunct ideas that are shunned by empire even as the same empire produces them for use elsewhere. Such defunct ideologies and epistemologies that empire produces for export to Africa include liberal economic reforms (what Samir Amin [2004] calls "liberal virus"), conceptual frameworks such as Economic Structural Adjustment Programme and contemporary efforts to foist "animism" on Africa and other parts of the Global South (Garuba 2013; de Castro 2013). Animism, for instance, has been produced and used by empire in history to justify enslavement and colonisation of Africans while ESAP was used to impoverish the African states after colonialism. Via such defunct ideologies and epistemologies, Africa has become a wasteland of empire where empire not only harvests hapless African minds, through facades of inclusion, for empire's ideological experiments: Africa has also been constituted into a wasteland where African bodies are harvested and used by empire in medical, social, political and economic experiments couched as "charity" to Africans when in fact Africans are guinea pigs for global pharmaceutical, political, economic and other such experimental adventures. Purveyed as charity, the toxicity of ideologies and epistemologies of empire are effectively hidden to the senses of Africans suffering neural fatigue after centuries of being force-fed by empire with material and ideologies suitable only for wastelands. Much as empire often recycles old apparels including human hair of the dead (Nyamnjoh and Fuh 2014), from empire's centres to the peripheries often in the name of charity, empire also recycles under the guise of charitable newness colonial ideologies such as "animism" from the centres of empire to the peripheries.

The imperial defunct ideology of animism is being raised and resuscitated so that it again haunts postcolonial Global South that is becoming too bold to bother empire with postcolonial reclamations of restitution and reparations for historical dispossessions and exploitation. Indigenous people are increasingly reclaiming reparations, restitutions and repossessions of their resources in various places such as Australia, New Zealand, South Africa, Zimbabwe, Canada, United States of America (Mubaya and Mawere 2015; Adhikari 2010; Moyo 2008; African Media Agency 2015; Ray 2013; United Nations 2007; Susskind *et al* 2008; Ministry of Aboriginal Affairs British Columbia 1995; Dust 1995). In the midst of empire's troubles about how to resolve these claims by indigenous people, empire is resuscitating colonial ideologies of animism and pretending to be conceding to indigenous knowledge, by way of epistemic charity, so as to swallow indigenous people using that bait. The colonial/imperial ideologies of animism assume that indigenous people are hardly distinguishable from animals and that therefore the indigenous people have no entitlement to property rights as well as to human rights (Jacobson 2000; Adhikari 2014; McDonald 2014; Harring 2014; Gordon 2014; Barta 2014; Ryan 2014). Apart from this presumption, animism presumes that indigenous people have never had scientific knowledge of their own, no industries and no religion except abundance of superstition. In this regard, animism is used by empire to render indigenous people as racially expendable, exploitable and dispensable others. Through this pejorative labelling of the indigenous people as indistinguishable from animals, slave traders and (neo-)colonists (of bodies and minds) have sought to legitimise and justify their ill treatment, killing and dispossession of indigenous people that are then hunted like animals (Mail Online 7

September 2015; S V Crossberg (440/07[2008] ZASCA 13 [2008] 3 All SA 329 (SCA); Frank 2006; Churchill 2004; McDonald 2014; Gordon 2014; Adhikari 2014; Ryna 2014). Thus after being portrayed as indistinct from animals, indigenous people were shot at and had dogs set on them without recourse to law courts (McDonald 2014: 53); sometimes the indigenous people so labelled were not only shot at but also poisoned such that they died *enmasse* in colonial genocides such as those recorded in Australia and Namibia (Ryna 2014: 207; Olusoga et al 2011: 71, 72, Magubane 2007, Jacobson 2000). Even in the contemporary era, indigenous farm labourers are shot at in Africa followed by pleas in courts that the three-metre-range killers ("White" farmers) were not able to distinguish the African labourers from animals like baboons (see for instance, South African case S V Crossberg (440/07[2008] ZASCA 13). This recent court case, in which African farm-labourers were depicted as baboons and then shot at, underscored continuities of colonial portrayals of Africans as indistinct from animals. Similarly, Mawere (2014) notes cases in South Africa where African school pupils were dehumanised as 'white' teachers and School principal derogatorily addressed them as baboons, monkeys and kaffirs. Also the massive exploitation of Africans and their subjection to structural violence show the disregard which apartheid mind-sets have for human Africans even as apartheid and colonial minds have increasingly paradoxically pretended to show more concern for African animals or nature than for African human beings.

While Africans struggled for and are claiming, via Pan-Africanism and African Renaissance, humanisation including through ownership of their resources (Nabudere 2013: 73; Buntu 2013: 88, 89; Mbeki 2000: 77), empire is via animism, seeking to reverse the humanisation of Africans suffering the bitter-after effects of (neo-)colonial dehumanisation. Instead of reversing their age-old Western antihumanism the West seeks to perpetuate the slave and colonial era antihumanism (to Africans) via recycled colonial notions such as animism and posthumanism. For this reason critical African scholars have raised concerns about the resilience of colonial education, calling upon African universities not to continue excelling at irrelevance, not to force-feed students with intellectual "toxic" waste and to begin studying and understand Africa on its own terms

(Nyamnjoh 2012). Nyamnjoh (2012: 145), for instance, argues: "There is little discourse on Africa for Africa's sake, and the West has used Africa as a pretext for its own subjectivities, fantasies and perversions". The suggestion to study and understand Africa first on its own terms is easily and uncritically dismissed as an invitation to celebrate African essentialism and exceptionalism. There is little patience with anything African even by Africans"

Posthumanism and animism are intended to sidestep African worries about human suffering and legitimise purported imperial concerns for environmental issues (see Bryant 2012). Instead of considering equality between coloniser and colonised, the empire is seeking to conflate indigenous people with animals via insidiously packaged ideologies of animism. Instead of humanising Africans by acknowledging, as recently called upon by African delegates in Durban, that slavery and colonialism were crimes against humanity with serious effects that require reparatory compensation (Nesbitt 2004:361), empire is determined to further dehumanise the indigenous people of the so-called the periphery. Empire is not only taking flight by physically pulling out of Conferences where demands for humanisation of indigenous people are made. As Nesbitt (2004: 361) notes of some imperial countries, empire is also taking ideological flights by trying to foreclose reparations and restitution through misrepresentations in terms of animism. Instead of resolving the demands for reparations and restitution conventionally, by restoring the identities, cultures, religions, languages and lands (Buntu 2013: 88; Prah 1993, 2011) empire is minded on preventing the suits for reparations by distorting, via animism, pollution of African epistemologies and identities. Empire can continue to rule and dominate over Africa only if the Africans are mired in confusion and crises of identity, culture, epistemology, polity, economy and so on. Thus states such as France, England, Australia, New Zealand, Canada, United States of America, Portugal and Germany that are besieged with reparations law suits (Nesbitt 2004: 361) seek, much as during the slave trade and colonial eras, to confuse and dominate claimants by animalising them through liquidating their traditions, substituting their languages for the claimants', destroying the cultures of the claimants as was done for Indigenous people in America and Canada (Churchill 2004).

Empire is well aware that it is easier to rule over a confused and crises ridden world and this is evident not only in the colonial inducement of crises through dispossessions of land, livestock, cultures, societies, polities, languages, epistemologies and exploitation as cheap labour. It is also evident in crises, some of which often appear as charity, induced via (neo-)colonial ideologies and interventionism. Like victims of infectious possession by divisive demonic spirits (see Ong 1988; Behrend 1999a, 1999b; Colson 1971; Gelfand 1959) Africans have fallen one after the other in whirlpools of confusion and crises of various kinds including of identity induced by imperial and (neo-)colonial ideologies, that have come to "animate" countless mediums in Africa. This imperial addictive urge to possess people in the peripheries has unfortunately been ignored by scholarship that assumed that empire merely seeks to possess material resources when in fact its possessiveness, even as it demonises African modes of possession, includes possessing people via ideological apparatuses of capture. While some in Africa celebrate demonisation of African cultures, polities, societies, languages, epistemologies, and reclamations of colonially dispossessed resources, recovery of these African institutions promises to humanise Africans. Africans cannot be fully human without their own cultures, societies, polities, economies, epistemologies and resources, and so celebrating destruction of these institutions amounts to celebrating "animalisation" and self-destruction.

One way to corrupt identities, confuse, demobilise and dominate claimants for reparations and restitution is to portray them as lacking basic elements that characterise human society including lacking concepts of property, commerce, law, government, industry, art, social institutions, philosophy or God (McDonald 2014: 52). Another way, as Churchill (2004) notes about genocide of Indians in North America, is to destroy and corrupt their institutions on which they rely to make claims for restitution and reparations. A third way in which genocide of indigenous people, portrayed by (neo)colonists as animals, was practised by Europeans in North America and this involved causing epidemics such as smallpox for instance by deliberate infection through smallpox infested blankets being sent as trade goods (Harring 2014: 279). And in Australia the genocide of indigenous people by Westerners was by giving Aborigines, also portrayed by colonists as animals, poisoned bread such that they died in their numbers. So apart from being used to discursively dispossess indigenous people in specific ways (Veracini 2014: 291), animism was used to decimate indigenous people by poisoning their food. The use of chemical and biological agents including poisoning of food, drinks, clothes, water, and injecting with poisons (Gould and Folb 2000; 2002; Simmons 2012) have not only characterised apartheid, that still exists at both local and global scales, but they also underlie contemporary concerns about transnational capital feeding the world with genetically modifies food that Westerners are paradoxically shy to consume (Rootes 2003; Natural Society September 19 2015; BBC News 13 January 2015 www.bbc.com/news/world-europe-30794256). Part of the problem in the (neo-)imperial genocidal practices is the uncritical embrace of postmodernist and poststructuralist theoretical pretensions including celebrations of invasions and *hybrid infected bodies as postmodern bodies* (see Halberstam and Livingston 1995). The postmodernist injunction to dedifferentiation and erosion of binaries, as I will argue below, entails the inability to distinguish between what is poisonous and what is not poisonous. These claims suited apartheid genocidal tendencies and they would sit well with contemporary posthumanism/antihumanism as well as animism.

The contemporary modality of empire for confusing indigenous people is to portray them as having animist ontologies, to attribute to indigenous knowledge the category of animism which category is not only erroneous but mischievous (Asante et al 1996: 289; Nchojied 2015; Bullock 1927; Gelfand 1970; p'Bitek 2011; Opoku 1978, Fontein 2006; Stanner 2005; Rattray 1927; Parrinder 1967; Nhemachena 2015). While empire often pretends to be visiting Africa with loads of epistemic charity (Nanda 2003) including in the form of animism, which it would want indigenous Africans to believe is an indigenous category, attentive African scholars have not taken the bite at empire's hook. Asante *et al* (1996: 289), for instance, argue that: "Animism is not an adequate description of these [African] religions and it is better for the term to be abandoned once and for all". Similarly Nchojied (2015: 259) argues that: "They [Westerners] saw Africans worshiping on waterfalls, near rivers and under trees and they thought that they were animistic. African scholars who are closer to reality have different explanations for what they [Westerners] describe as 'animism'. For Africans, God is transcendent". In other words, these scholars point to the need as Ndlovu-Gatsheni (2013: 26) argues for a decolonial turn that inaugurates a new thinking about strategies and tactics of opposing coloniality of power, coloniality of knowledge, and coloniality of being that are constitutive of global imperial designs in place since the colonial encounter of the fifteenth century. Such a decolonial turn is traceable to various responses and resistances to such inimical processes as the slave trade, imperialism, apartheid, neo-colonialism, neoliberalism and even globalisation (Ndlovu-Gatsheni 2013: 256), and so it is necessary to be always mindful and trace the genealogies of ideologies such as animism that have for long been constituted and used by empire to dominate others.

There is a lot of evidence to show that animism has not been an African idea or practice but that animism is a Western construct in so far as it conflated God with nature. As early modern Europe denied the existence of God, they increasingly began to think in terms of what they called secular science that embraced teleology which is the doctrine that nature, much as human beings, intrinsically has its own purposes (Artigas 2001). They began to think in terms of naturalist metaphysics that had no place for God and so instead of acting on God's purpose nature was viewed as having its own purpose (Kincaid 2013). Nature began to be considered by Europeans as the polite word for God (Evensky 2003) and so God began to be considered, by Europeans subscribing to such teleological thinking, to be immanent in nature rather than to be residing in Heaven and exercising Heavenly transcendence. Missionaries, travellers and colonial European scholars writing about Africa and other places outside Europe began to portray other people in terms of animism that had taken root in Europe. So James Frazer (1926) and many other Europeans began to export their European animism to territories about which they wrote: they also portrayed the territories as having no notions of God even if they actually knew about God well before contact. The territories were erroneously portrayed as having animism described as the lowest and most primitive religion where all objects of nature were considered to have souls just like human beings. Frazer (1926) erroneously portrayed some inhabitants of those territories as worshiping nature rather than God, and other inhabitants were portrayed as "worshiping" ancestors (portrayed by Europeans as demons rather than saints [see Comaroff and Comaroff 2005]) rather than God. It is unfortunate that all these scholars did not bother to see amble evidence that the inhabitants had notions of and worshipped the Heavenly God, who was known by different names, centuries before European contact (Ntholi 2006; James 1957; Parrinder 1967; Crawford 1967; Gelfand 1959; Muphree 1967; Setiloane 1976). The portrayals of Africa as animistic and as having no religion, no notion of God, no science, knowledge, industries, societies and polities are paradoxical especially in the light of evidence that Africa is the cradle of humanity and also the cradle of Egyptian and other civilisations from which paradoxically early European philosophers learnt (Okumu 2002; George 2009; Onyewuenyi 2006; Gann et al 2000; Asante 2000), and in the light of evidence that even Old Testament prophets received their revelations of the sovereign Heavenly God while in Africa.

Anxious to conquer and subdue the entire world, Europeans have sought to legitimise their projects by erroneously assuming that the rest of the world is flat and already prostrate, waiting for Westerners to (re-)occupy and rule over. They have ignored the indigenous property ownership regimes (Moyana 1984; Schofeleers 1979; Matikiti 2007). Besides, they have pre-empted various forms of modernity that existed prior to colonialism (Taiwo 2010). They have exploited and distorted various forms of science in the Global South (Chirikure 2010; Hardin 1994) and they have distorted the various ways in which indigenous people distinguished between nature and culture (Jahn 1961; Stanner 2005). Assumptions of the ideology of animism, that human beings in the pre-colonial territories were indistinguishable from animals, served the Europeans' purpose. Westerners could, via animistic assumptions depict themselves as the only indisputable human beings with entitlement to rule the entire world including territories of other human beings that they depicted as indistinguishable from animals. The ideology of animism further legitimised the enslavement and colonisation including dispossession, violence and exploitation of other human beings that Europeans considered indistinguishable from animals. Further the ideology of animism in its assumption of flatness legitimised

Europeans disregard of the supremacy of God, and attendant moral laws, that they in any case wrongly assumed to be absent among the inhabitants of the territories they colonised. The poisoning of the inhabitants such as in Australia where aboriginal people were given poisoned bread in the genocide that almost cleared them is explicable in terms of the ideologies of animism that portrayed Aborigines as animals to be trapped, poisoned and killed without regard to humanity, ethics, laws and morals. The continued destruction of the cultures, societies, polities, religions, laws and economies of other people have roots in animist ideologies that depict those other people as indistinguishable from animals, hence as having no worthy societies, cultures, polities, laws, religions and economies. The contemporary portrayals and assumptions of the superiority of Western cultures, societies, polities, economies, laws, religions and languages have roots in animist ideologies that devalorise, trivialise and destroy the institutions of other inhabitants of the world portrayed in terms of animism. The sad thing is that these Western assumptions have been inculcated in the territories such that some of the inhabitants themselves have come to accept and live by the assumptions that they are like animals without worthy cultures, societies, languages, polities, economies, laws and religions.

The exhortations to inhabitants of the territories to abandon their cultural, social, political, religious, economic and legal institutions in favour of individualism that is erroneously considered better and liberating, is one chimera that Africans need to unthink and reverse for good. Though Westerners are often portrayed as individualistic, this is on critical examination, a façade because if Westerners really intended to be individualistic, they would not have carried their cultures, social, political, economic, religious, legal and linguistic collectivism with them to other parts of the world. They would not have carried their own cultures and other institutions including to territories whose inhabitants are paradoxically exhorted by the Westerners to abandon their own cultures, social and political institutions in the name of individualism. The collectivism that Westerners demonstrated at the Berlin Conference convened to partition Africa among themselves need not be forgotten by scholars that depict Westerners as individualistic. Westerners equally were not individualistic when they colonised territories of other people in the names of Western Kings and Queens many of which institutions still exist in the West that has paradoxically destroyed similar Kingdoms and Queendoms everywhere else. Similarly the collectivism Westerners demonstrated in colonising, dominating and suppressing inhabitants need not be forgotten. The collectivism Westerners demonstrated through alliances, to the extent that they even enlisted Africans, to fight in World Wars I and II need not be forgotten. All these instances demonstrate that one has to be cognisant of one's culture, society, religion, polity, law, language and economy. Conversely it demonstrates that when Africans are exhorted to abandon their culture, society, laws, religions, languages, polities and economies; they are in effect being treated as or being animalised by empire. Individualism particularly tied to greediness does not humanise but it animalises and also Western culture, social and political institutions are badly placed to humanise Africans. Witness the recent slighting of the lives of blacks in the heart of the empire, which empire cannot easily relinquish tendencies to animalise others including those that it has invited to be its converts (Gunning 2015). In other words, empire invites inhabitants of peripheries to participate as less than fully human converts in empire's culture which they, as vassals, are neither allowed to depart nor to fundamentally change. Even as empire often pretends to celebrate hybridity it can only tolerate hybrids that it has the monopoly to create and that do not threaten its own sensibilities for it is also concerned with maintaining purity at the centre of empire.

So hybridity is a mechanism of dispossession including at the level of identity yet it is also an after-effect of dispossession such as in the case of those who came to be derided as Bushmen: some indigenous people who had been dispossessed of their livestock by colonists became hunter-gatherers and the same colonists paradoxically derided them as Bushmen. In the contemporary era Africans dispossessed of their cultures, social, political, linguistic, legal, economic and religious institutions have similarly been animalised by being converted into (neo-)scavengers not only for material means of survival but for empire's identities, cultures, social, legal, political and economic institutions.

The ideology of hybrids has come to be emphasised in recent theories but little critical examination of the contexts and meanings of hybridity has been done particularly in the context of coloniality, transformation and deformation at the peripheries. In most recent theories, hybridity has come to be interpreted in some scholarly works as an imperative to bridge binaries between nature and culture, and between the West and the rest. However, lacking are efforts to think beyond mimicry of Western notions and ideologies such as animism, binaries and hybridity.

This chapter critically interrogates the notion of "animism" in relation to coloniality and to African struggles for humanism after centuries of colonial dehumanisation. It argues that recent scholarly efforts to portray Africans in terms of "animism" effectively reverse the humanism that Africans have struggled to regain since the colonial era. The chapter argues that "animism" is a recycled colonial ideology with similar agendas as colonialism: it effectively denies the humanism of Africans, perpetuates coloniality and therefore it is a tool for the realisation and sustenance of the old empire that other scholars have hypocritically described as "new empire".

Binaries, hybridity and animism

Some recent theories, following upon postmodernist theoretical explications on dedifferentiation, have problematised binaries particularly Cartesian binaries as responsible for polarisations and conflicts in the world and as responsible for the nature-culture binaries but how they sit in African contexts has not been properly examined. It is necessary to critically appraise these Western theories in Africa so that the tragedy of uncritical visitations of neoliberalism and other Western concocted harmful theories coated in synthetic jewels is not repeated. In Africa where inhabitants have been dispossessed and exploited, the worry is not so much about Cartesian binaries than about reclaiming possessions, restitution and reparations. To expect Africans to worry more about Cartesian heritage (Western heritage) than about their own heritage, disinheritance and concerns is in fact to repeat the old colonial animistic practices where Africans were expected to be the beasts of burdens for colonists and empire. Indeed when Africans and other scholars in the Global South are made to carry the theoretical and epistemological burdens of Westerners, they are assuming the roles of beasts of burdens in the old colonial animistic sense and this is the tragedy of many African universities that remain beholden to empire. For this reason scholars like Nyamnjoh (2012: 79) have argued: "The African ethnographic elephants mean little on their own terms in a game in which they are externally defined and confined exogenously, even when supposedly involved in the crafting of their stories. What if the elephants could speak back or were allowed to study themselves and to shape the world with their knowledge and ways of knowing?"

The worry in Africa is not principally, or entirely, about erasing binaries but about the failure of (neo-)colonialists and (neo-)empire to distinguish between human African beings and animals; it is about (neo-)empire and (neo-)colonists' conflation of human African beings with animals as a way in which they justify and legitimise their colonial projects of dispossession, enslavement and exploitation of others. Colonial wars of liberation did not emanate from worries about Cartesian binaries but about the concrete need for repossession, restitution and reparations. In any case the theories of Cartesian binaries seem not to have always impacted on Western empirics of colonisations as Westerners collaborated among themselves as much as they enlisted their victims to assist them. This connotes the Westerners did not always live by Cartesian ideologies. In fact when British colonists dispossessed Africans by animistically naming the colonial territories after British personalities or persons such as Cecil John Rhodes after whom colonial Zimbabwe was named as "Rhodesia". There were also schools (which still exist in independent Zimbabwe) named after Rhodes and other British persons like "Queen Elizabeth", "Prince Edwards", "Allan Wilson", "Lord Malvern" and so on. The famous indigenous *Mosia Tunya* (the smoke that thunders) was expropriated from indigenous Africans by the British via colonial animistic conceptions that resulted in it being named "Victoria Falls", after the British Queen Victoria. The significant issue here is that colonialists were animistic so as to dispossess Africans: animism is evidently a colonial category serving as a mechanism of dispossession and so it cannot be argued to be an apparatus for contemporary liberation struggles of Africans. Thus if colonists paid as much fidelity to Cartesian binaries, they would not have named these physical or natural areas after their personalities in ways that suggested that they animistically failed to distinguish between the persons and natural areas/features. The failure by colonists to distinguish between natural features and their persons are still evident in that they address animals and territory as "she" presuming that there is absence of distinctions between people and territory. If colonists were as rooted in binaries and dichotomies, then logically they would have left Africa and the Global South alone rather than trick, trap and enmesh them into empire's matrix of power. The problem between Africa and the West, should not be misdiagnosed as merely binaries, it is not a problem of binaries but one of exploitative, dispossessive entanglements. What (neo-) colonists always lived up to was the dispossession, enslavement and exploitation of inhabitants of other parts of the world, often conflating them with animals rather than distinguishing them as human beings. In this sense, it can be argued that the worries in slave riots and rebellions were not simplistically about Cartesian dualisms but by the failure by slave owners to distinguish between human beings, that they enslaved, and animals. The problem of binaries is, therefore, undoubtedly a Western problem because in Africa the problem is conversely failure to distinguish between human beings and nature including animals.

Bridging binaries, crossing borders and border linkages are not in themselves heralds of peace particularly in a context where empire has historically crossed its borders and the borders of others in order to execute its imperial projects including the slave trade. Of course this is not merely historical given empire's contemporary readiness to cross borders and stage its expansionist wars veiled as humanitarian wars or responsibility to protect (see Boyle 2013, Ndlovu-Gatsheni 2013). Empire has, through the slave trade and colonial projects, been always anxious to export its own problems to territories on the periphery. Insightful scholars like Hornborg (2009) have therefore noted that capital and empire pretend to support indigenous people and their knowledge when in fact they intend to "*swallow the noble savage*". Hornborg's argument is apt in view of the fact that indigenous people have crossed may borders, cultural, social, political, economic, religious, linguistic and identity matrixes in the hope of the better life promised by empire but all they have gained, after abandoning their own spaces to cross into empire's terrain, have been increasing imperial avarice. If capitalism and empire are apparatuses of capture, they capture and enslave on the baits of promises for sham freedom and liberation that are repackaged from time to time, to enable empire and capital to take flight from each load of their mess in the world.

The ways in which empire and capital exhort bridging binaries, crossing borders and border linkages are nothing strange to indigenous African people who have their own age old idioms and proverbs covering such activities. The Shona people of Zimbabwe have a game that children often play in the clear winter evenings and in the song is a phrase *"Garwe heri sadza, swederera* (Crocodile, here is food, move closer). The game is used to demonstrate how the cunning can offer baits to their intended victims in order to induce them to move closer so that they get swallowed by the cunning predator. Apart from being a game where children enjoy the fun in the winter moonlight, the game teaches children to be sceptical of things that may appear on the surface to be good. It teaches them to think more than twice before linking up, or before crossing borders as it were, so that they reflect on possibilities that await them when they eventually cross borders. In the world, invitations to cross borders are replete with dangers of human trafficking, of being kidnapped, of being enslaved and robbed in the *terra incognita* that one steps into. In short the Shona game underlines the fact that the borders are frontiers, where there are shifting sands, uncertainties and where dangers lurk particularly in light of the history of dehumanisation of others after they were placed within frontiers (Weaver 2006), now renamed borders.

In a contemporary world where Africans and other inhabitants of the global south have struggled for humanisation it would not make sense to continue to theorise their lives in terms of animism, that is, in terms of the assertion that there are no distinctions between them and animals. It would equally not make sense to theorise the lives of human beings, struggling for humanisation, in terms of posthumanism (Wolfe 2010) that is interpreted by others as antihumanism, as prioritising nature rather than the humans struggling for humanisation. But animism, posthumanisim and notions of cyborgs (Clark 2003) all have the effect of collapsing human beings with nature, with other things, that is, they celebrate hybridisation via other terms. But how might this celebration of

26

conflation and hybridity be understood in the context of broader projects of empire and capital that sponsor such ideologies and theorisations? One way to examine it is by considering how empire and capital instituted and celebrated animism in territories, to legitimise and justify enslavement and colonisation. The erroneous underlying assumption of animism is, as noted above, that the other people are indistinct from animals. The empire's celebration of hybridity can also be understood in terms of assumptions, in hybridity speaking to animism, that humans are indistinguishable from animals and plants hybrids. In fact the celebration of hybridity by empire and colonists can be understood in view of how historically colonists had hybridised livestock looted from Africans (Palmer 1977) in ways that masked their identities making it difficult for dispossessed Africans to identify and reclaim their livestock. The celebration of hybridity by empire and capital can also be interpreted in terms of ways in which it confound African identities making it difficult for Africans to mobilise one another and reclaim not only their lands, but also their culture, societies, polities, economies, religions. So hybridity like animism is in the service of empire's projects of subjugating, justifying and pacifying colonised others in the periphery that are depicted as not so pure or to be not indisputably human.

In a contemporary context where Africans and other indigenous people are not only threatening to delink from empire (Amin 2004, 2011) but also reclaiming their resources including land as well as restitution and reparations, empire is making efforts to remind them that the indigenous people are its hybrids and cyborgs portrayed as inextricably linked to empire. Empire is downplaying and opposing the autonomy of indigenous people by depicting them as hybrids. Depicting them as hybrid is intended by empire to weigh them down with burdens of animality, including with the sense that like animals they are not entitled to their own autonomous institutions including language, economy, culture, politics, society, culture, law and religion. In a context where Africans and other indigenous people are suing and threatening to sue empire for enslavement, colonial expropriations, dispossessions and genocide, empire is busy trying to depict them as not indisputably human beings with human rights claims against it. Therefore empire has increasingly come to celebrate animism, deconstruction, and hybridity in the peripheries. In the light of celebrations of hybridity, animism, deconstruction and cyborgism in the peripheries, it would be interesting to consider how empire would reconcile these with its claim to universalise human rights. Since a hybrid can as well be less than human, how would human rights be applied where hybrids are assumed to exist? Since in animism no distinctions are drawn between human beings and animals, how then would human rights be applied? Since a cyborg is a symbiont of human and machine, how would human rights be applied where human beings are depicted as cyborgs or posthumans? The point here is that while those in the Global South believed that empire gave them human rights, empire in fact was busy animalising them by considering them hybrids, and in term of animism; the net effect was that human rights effectively belong to empire that is deemed to be purely and undoubtedly human.

The problem lies with the fact that in its hypocrisy, empire often claims to liberate and emancipate while it in effect enslaves, colonises and dominates. On one hand it claims to humanise or to grant universal human rights while on the other hand it depicts and treats others in terms of animism, hybrids, cyborgs or posthumans, that it imposes on them. The problem is that in empire's hypocrisy it claims to grant universal human rights while in effect it resists indigenous claims to the human dignity of owning and repossessing their resources that colonists looted and robbed. The problem lies too in the fact that empire paradoxically exhorts indigenous people to fight *for their human rights* when in fact empire has not humanised the indigenous people with the dignity of repossessing their resources or getting restitutions and reparations from colonists some of whom sponsor empire's contemporary projects. In view of the hypocrisy of empire, the challenge is for those that it portrays as animals and hybrids to consider whether they are not merely enrolled via various instruments as empire's shock absorbers, when empire's "fundamentalistic monopolistic rights to own the world are threatened". While empire promotes the view among indigenous people that human rights can still be substantially realised without reverting ownership of resources, empire's resistance to restitute and repay in effect shows that one becomes less than human without repossession and ownership of one's resources. It shows that only animals survive entirely on gifts and donations, human beings need to own and control the resources besides.

The fact that indigenous people are often exhorted by empire to work as shock absorbers for empire's grand project of owning the entire world is clear when one considers ways in which much, if not all, of the deconstructionism empire encourages is of indigenous people's institutions including culture, society, polity, language, law, economies. Much as during the trans-Atlantic slave trade era when slaves were considered most useful after shedding their cultures, social, religious, linguistic and other attributes, the postcolonial global order requires indigenous people to shed their cultures, languages, social, religious and other attributes. Where they are allowed to keep aspects of their cultures, languages and religions they can only do so as hybrids of empire lacking purity and lacking the liberty to delink no matter how much they yearn for decoupling from empire. It is effectively a world in which, in a metaphorical sense, divorce is not allowed no matter how abusive the relationship is.

One of the greatest paradoxes of empire is that even as it promotes deconstruction of the institutions of indigenous peoples, empire resists being deconstructed via claims for restitution and reparation; it resists deconstruction of its "global" economies that it purveys as not subject to alternatives. As poststructuralist and postmodernist theories of the 1960s show (Bertens 2008: 91, 103), their theorists were careful to emphasise textual, cultural, political and social deconstruction in the peripheries, to the virtual exclusion of deconstructing economies. After independence in many post-colonies, economies remained in western hands and so theorists arguing from Eurocentric locus of enunciation could not have promoted the deconstruction of the economies in the sense of meaningfully devolving ownership of them to Africans or other indigenous people. In spite of the fact that decolonial wars of liberation were about repossession of resources looted by colonists, poststructuralist and postmodernist theories shifted attention away from deconstruction of colonial materialities, redirecting energies instead to deconstruction of cultural, social, textual and political indigenous institutions. Similarly, in spite of the fact that decolonial wars of liberation were about repossession of resources by indigenous peoples, empire entrenched via independence constitutions, such as the Lancaster House Constitution for Zimbabwe, colonial ownership of resources. The deconstruction of everything else except the economy is encouraged in the guise that such deconstruction falsely entails emancipation and freedom. Similarly some contemporary scholarly thinking in terms of animism is a way to sidestep demands for restitution and reparations by indigenous people who are minded instead on humanisation. Thinking in terms of animism is presented as liberating and emancipating for empire even if it does not speak to the demands of indigenous peoples who clamour to be granted the human dignity of owning their resources rather than be collapsed together with animals. Thinking in terms of animism facilitates coloniality over inhabitants of the periphery as it does over their environments.

Coloniality, animism, and the environments in the south

Imperial thinking in terms of animism and hybridity enable the constitution of zones of perpetual frontiers, in the peripheries, where everything including ownership of resources and identities is depicted in hegemonic epistemologies as contestable and up for grabs. Considered against a background where the broader processes of colonisation were marked by the creation of frontiers that enabled colonists to invade other territories, animism and hybridity are antithetical to the autonomy and liberation of the Africans. Empire has contrived seemingly new ways of depicting the targeted territories and peoples as savages, barbarians, as authoritarian, autocratic, as uncivilised, backward and therefore as empty, without human essence, open and waiting for the betterment by (neo-)colonists. In a world where empire seeks to justify and legitimise its new expansionist wars, on the façade of humanitarianism and protectionism, empire readily assumes that everyone else is less than human and that empire, posing as the only epitome of humanity, has the prerogative to protect everything else near and far. For this reason, it is in empire's service to resuscitate colonial ideologies of animism and hybridity that aid its presumptions of flatness in the rest of the world, assumed to have disputable human identities. Such zones are assumed by empire to be frontiers with unsettled identities, chaos, permanent crises and anarchy, even if some of the crises are generated by empire (Boyle 2013). While empire often pretends to bewail chaos, anarchy and crises at the peripheries most of the crises emanate from empire that has a long history of exporting its own problems, crises and anarchy to other parts of the world and then using these crises to secure its foothold via interventionism and protectionism. If the world did not have problems, empire would be hard-put to justify its presence, for this reason empire adores the presence of problems in other territories to the extent that when there appear to be no problem it does not hesitate to create some or to create images of there being problems.

So in spite of the fact that empire thrived on the bases of corrupting not only economies but societies, cultures, religions, laws and polities of the peripheries, in empire's media emphasis is on alleged corruption by the peripheries that have also become the beasts of burdens for (neo-)colonial/(neo-)imperial global corruption. In spite of empires' having foundations in protectionism, patrimonialism, and patriarchy on a broader "global" scale, what is emphasised in empire's media are the adversities in the alleged patriarchy and patrimonialism of the periphery that has also become the beasts of burdens for empire's hidden patrimonialism and patriarchy on a world scale. Despite the fact that ancestors of the Westerners, now depicted by empire as saints, perpetrated genocide, lootings and robberies, in the peripheries (Schmidt 1992: 37-39; Rodney 1972) it is paradoxically the ancestors of the peripheries that are labelled in Western media as evil and demonic even if they were victims rather than perpetrators in the colonial encounters. Thus African ancestors are converted by empire into beasts of burden for the faults and evils of imperial ancestors: African ancestors are animalised by empire while the same empire superhumanises its own ancestors into sainthood.

So negativity linked to chaos and crises is always portrayed as characterising the peripheries not necessarily because the peripheries are negative but because empire seeks to retain them as frontiers, as zones of indeterminacy, uncertainty and as zones where inhabitants cannot be certain, assertive and autonomous. Consequently, the resuscitation of animism and the celebration of hybridity in the peripheries are meant to blow up claims of autonomy, of sovereignty, of repossession, of reparations and restitutions. The resuscitation of animism ideologies is meant to generate frontiers on the identities of the inhabitants of Africa and with these frontiers reverse African confidence, to foster diffidence instead of confidence among them. Thus empire seeks not only to portray African environments as contested but it also seeks to portray African identities as contested so that Africans perpetually live on the frontiers of uncertainty about their environments and identities while empire retains the privilege of certainty, stability, autonomy, sovereignty and humanity.

Assumptions of stability, autonomy and determinacy at the centres of empire and conversely openness, instability and absence of autonomy in the peripheries date back to John Locke (Parekh 1995). Locke presupposed that it was only the peripheries, and not the centres, which were open and colonisable. Inhabitants of peripheries, were arrogantly depicted as indistinct from animals, the inhabitants were deemed not to have property rights, their cultures, social, political and other institutions were deemed to be disputable. These centuries old depictions by Locke find residence in some contemporary theorisations that depict the Africa and the Global South as flatness, openness, fuzziness and ambiguity (Deleuze and Guattari 1994, Best, n.d: 177). In spite of these depictions of indigenous people as animals, as illiterate, as having no notions of property and as immature, empire would still want us to believe that the contracts it presumably signed with "immature" chiefs of indigenous people were legitimate. Contemporary portrayals of the peripheries as unstable, indeterminate even if sometimes it is empire that brews crises in them, are serving to justify views that peripheries are still frontiers open to colonisation. For this reason, the inhabitants of the territories considered to be frontiers are advised to demilitarise even as empire is busy militarising for the planetary domination. Instead of abandoning erroneous colonial animistic assumptions that indigenous people were immature and childlike, empire has in fact reinforced such perceptions in the contemporary era where it assumed that it alone has the maturity and the right to militarise and even develop nuclear weapons: the rest of the world is considered immature and their militarisation, which in some cases does not even involve nuclear armaments, is treated by empire with disdain. In this sense portrayals in terms of frontiers are meant to facilitate dispossession, prevent repossession, and to justify coloniality in territories of other peoples. Frontiers are by definition territories that are free for all except for the indigenous inhabitants that empire portrays and treats as disputably human even if in terms of ethics and morality their humanity surpasses that of their enslavers and colonisers.

The contemporary theorisations in environmentalism in terms of openness, transparency and accountability erroneously presume that empire is indeed a champion of openness, transparency and accountability when contrary to openness, it is still busy enclosing the wealth it looted from the peripheries. The contemporary theorisations on corruption erroneously assume that empire genuinely detests corruption when it is still busy corrupting everything from cultural, religions, social, political, economic and identities of inhabitants of the peripheries. They ignore the fact that empire is the last to support genuine transparency and accountability since it is still investing efforts in hiding what it looted and robbed from those that are reclaiming repossession and ownership. Uncritical contemporary theorisations in terms of liberal democracy erroneously assume that empire genuinely supports liberal democracy when in fact it stands ready to condemn and sanction those in the peripheries that take the liberty to repossess what colonists looted and robbed. In spite of its appearance as liberation and emancipation, Western liberalism is in fact meant to pre-empt and prevent liberation and emancipation of inhabitants of the peripheries from (neo-)colonial historical dispossession. In this sense it is a façade of liberation that hides its chains and mechanism of enslavement using ideologies.

The quandary of how to simultaneously liberate the pest and its victims is at the core of empire's route of pushing the indigenous other towards negativity as its way of guaranteeing its own peace and freedom to dispossess and continue to exploit the territories of others. As indicated above, during the trans-Atlantic slave trade and colonialism empire chose to push the enslaved to negativity in the sense of treating them not as human beings but as indistinct from animals. Empire also chose to push the colonised other to negativity in the sense of considering them as empire's opposite, as uncivilised, savages, barbarians, as having no institutions, having no notions of God and as having no laws, polities and so on. In post-independence era empire chose to push the indigenous other to negativity by considering them to have no human rights histories even if paradoxically colonists were treated humanely by indigenous people right from the first moments of contact. Sometimes the imperial colonial efforts to portray the indigenous other as negativity bordered on absurdity in that while on one hand Africans were portrayed as *Bushmen with no houses* and living in the bush, they were also portrayed as the negativity of Europe in that they *kept women bound to households*. Even as Africans were portrayed as Europe's negativity in terms of having *no schools and universities* there have been portrayed as Europe's negativity in *not allowing women to go to school*. Even as Africans have been portrayed as Europe's negativity as having *no industries* they have been characterised as negativity in *not allowing women to go to work*. Even though Africans have been portrayed as the negativity of Westerners in having *no notions of ownership of property* they have been portrayed as negativity in *denying property rights to women*. Even if Africans have been portrayed as negativity of westerners in *not having notions of property ownership*, they have been paradoxically portrayed in negativity as *taking women to be property*. Though Africans have been portrayed as having *no notions of industry and property*, they have been depicted in negativity as *having had slaves similar to those used in Western plantations and industries*. Anxious to keep to itself, in the logic of monopoly, the image of absolute imperial purity as contrasted with Africa depicted by empire as monopolising negativity in terms of absolute impurity, empire has created inconsistencies in its narratives.

For the above reasons, negativity has increasingly become empire's way of socially, culturally, politically, religiously and economically "castrating" the indigenous other in metaphoric as well as actual senses. The logic, as Patrick Manning (1993) has noted of "de-gendering" slaves, was as foundational to *animism* as to the *slave trade* in which slave women and men were often forced to perform task that they would have left to others or for which they would have enlisted draught power. In other words African families, communities, nations, regions and continents have been so pervaded by images of negativity, some artificially contrived by empire, that not only the African self but also the African other has become lived as negativity often without hope of realising positivity except by cognitive voyages out of Africa. Much like slave trade thrived on the basis of weeding slaves out of their social, cultural, political, economic, religious and linguistic institutions in order to render them more vulnerable and dependent on new masters, empire does the same. Empire thrives by weeding indigenous people out of their institutions and by pretending to offer undefined welcome into the new imperial culture where indigenous people are expected to effectively serve as deculturated imperial slaves.

The coloniality of weeding people out of their cultures is best captured by Frantz Fanon's (1963) observation that during the colonial era the African subject was welcome by colonists as an individual and not as bearer of African cultural, social and political imprints. But this divestiture from own cultural, social, political, economic, linguistic and religious imprints was ancillary, to as Fanon (1963) proceeds to note, the treatment of the Africans, shorn of their institutions, as animals. The upshot of this is that while empire purports to humanise Africans or indigenous people by exhorting them to abandon their own institutions and adopting instead imperial garb, this in fact replicates the colonial animalisation of indigenous people. It is in fact animalisation rendered a veneer of humanisation, for by losing one's institutions one acquires only the negativity of an animal that empire is so anxious to create so as to generate its beasts of burdens, which are often made to appear as blessings. If burdens appear as mere burdens no one would take pleasure in carrying them for someone else: the pleasure in carrying imperial burdens therefore lies in them appearing as blessings from empire.

The animalisation of indigenous people during the slave trade and (neo-)colonisation underlines the fact that empire has always run short of real animals to bear its burdens. Such animalisation of human beings also allows us to analyse as façade empire's recent ideologies of African "animal rights" and the so called "rights of nature" defined with little, if any, cognisance of indigenous African environmental practices. While paradoxically oblivious of its tramplings on the human rights of Africans, empire seeks to do public relations by pretending to be concerned genuinely about African environments even if it means neglecting the African people. Hardpressed by challenges of numerical minority of its "orphans" in the peripheries, empire seeks to play its politics by increasingly foregrounding African environments, depicting them animistically as persons and using them as its political cloaks. So, since the years of decolonisation from the 1960s one notices empire increasingly digging in its heels through environmentalism including conservationism and ideologies of deep ecology in territories outside empire's centre.

While ideologies that depict Western NGOs as the best in conserving environments appear to be postcolonial in post-independence Africa, such ideologies in fact perpetuate the colonial ideologies of "civilisation" as they continue to assume that indigenous people are ignorant even about how to conserve their own environments and immediacies. While recent ideologies trying to depict nature as persons, just like indigenous human beings, appear in the mould of liberalism they also mask empires hidden political-economic efforts to dig into indigenous environments. They mask the fact that empire would not readily personalise nature including animals when it has dearth of beasts of burdens. The empire's efforts in this regard can properly be understood in terms of numerical minority status of its orphans in Africa and its anxiety to neutralise African majority decisions to reclaim their resources by presenting a façade of alternative environmental personhood, in the western liberal sense. The attempts to present the environment as persons just like human beings facilitate empire's ideologies of animism, hybridity and they generate indeterminacy, foster chaotic and anarchic identities in the "frontiers" of the peripheries. These outcomes help empire to firm up its grip on the indigenous peripheries that have increasingly been "pestering" empire with claims of restitution and reparations for colonial dispossessions, exploitation and violence including genocide.

There are signs that empire is concocting a second "neoliberal" regimen disguised as extension of "liberal" democracy to the environment when in fact it is meant to help empire evade the claims for reparations, restitutions and repossession by indigenous people that were colonially dispossessed and exploited. Like the preceding "neoliberalism", the new "neoliberalism" will be intended to weaken African and other states in the peripheries. The new "liberalism" will be intended to challenge African state sovereignty over the environments in the territories of indigenous African people. While it will appear as "liberalism", perhaps couched as "rights of nature", it will in effect be rights of empire that poses as the self-appointed godfather over environments in the peripheries. So the upcoming "liberalism" is designed to ideologically deliver nature and environments in the peripheries to empire and this is the sense in which the recent arguments that there is no nature and culture in the peripheries (Strathern 1980) should be understood. It will strengthen the hold of empire over the peripheries even as it weakens the hold of local African states and indigenous people over their own resources. Like the preceding "neoliberalism" it will unleash suffering, crises and chaos in the indigenous peripheries while delivering bounties of stability, sovereignty and autonomy to empire's centres. In other words, it is intended to deterritorialise and reterritorialise the peripheries with the net effect not only of dispossessing and further impoverishing of indigenous people but it also has an antihumanist posthumanism that treats the indigenous other as indistinct from animals, and thus enjoins them to be resilient or die out.

So, as it has come to be realised that western "neoliberalism" was not ultimately meant to bring prosperity and development to the indigenous peoples, empire's contrivance with environmental "neoliberalism" is not ultimately meant to better the indigenous people. Empire will rely on adulterating of indigenous knowledge with a view to swallowing up indigenous knowledge scholars and people into empires' nefarious project. As pointed out above, empire pretends to be against sovereignty in general when in fact it is merely against the sovereignty of other states including indigenous people over their resources. While empire is critical of local state sovereignty, it asserts its own sovereignty directly and via Western backed civil society organisations including Non-Governmental Organisations that often serve as empire's public relations servants. Empire can only strengthen its sovereignty by trampling on other people's sovereignties. This is why empire is against the sovereignty of African states that have been summarily depicted as failed, weak and corrupt as precursors to replacing them with organisations and institutions set up by empire and that have since independence been operating as parallel governments, though defined as nongovernmental. While empire is critical of "land invasions" by indigenous people reclaiming their land, it is lacklustre when multinational corporations engage in new contemporary land grabs in Africa. As shown below, contemporary proponents of animism (Stengers 2010) in fact celebrate the invasions and intrusions by the western Greek goddess of witchcraft they call *gaia* that would want to replace African forms of religion including God, ancestors as well as replace Christian and Islamic religions. Although "global" institutions are named in ways that presuppose they are for the whole world, they in fact refer to and are manned and controlled by Western states and institutions serving western interests. Thus the terms "global" and "world" are often fig leaf coverings to hide empire's brute exclusive selfishness hidden in pretences of inclusive liberalism.

It should be underline that by using concoctions of animism, empire seeks to swallow the "noble savage" in a project effectively meant to further empire's planetary domination. The empire's notion of "rights of nature" independent of African human beings facilitates empire's rights including its right to own, control and speak on behalf of nature in other people's territories just as it has sought to speak on behalf of its (neo-)colonial subjects. Even as it argues that indigenous people and their states in the Global South (Smith 2011) should let go of sovereignty over nature, empire is gearing up to bolster its sovereignty over other people' territories worldwide. In the animistic projects presented by empire, it is not nature that litigates but it is human beings at the centre of empire who want to arrogate to themselves the monopoly to litigate purportedly on behalf of nature when in fact they will be furthering their own ends of planetary domination over resources including those in other people's territories. From the history of colonisation including colonists' gospel of "civilisation", it is clear that empire's bondage always comes in the good but vacuous names of freedom, emancipation and liberation. Similarly empire's gospel of "inclusion" effectively manifests as empire's intrusions and invasions hidden under the loin cloths of freedom, liberalism and democracy.

Inclusive or intrusive involvement? Reversing empire's animist framing of Africa

While proponents of animism argue that it is, as a relational ontology, inclusive they also conceptualise it in terms of *gaia*, the

Greek goddess of witchcraft that is obviously not an African but a Western goddess. This repeats the history of colonisation of African religions and epistemologies. It repeats the history of colonisation in the sense that it perpetuates the erroneous assumption that Africa has always been empty of its own religions (including belief in God) and epistemologies. In this way it is understandable when the proponents of animism point out that the *gaia* they write about is an "intrusive" force (Stengers 2015; Smith 2011) but perhaps it should be added that it is an intrusive colonial force repeating the history of colonisation in Africa and the other parts of the world. The point here is that there cannot possibly be intrusiveness without there being some kind of violations, colonisation and therefore an intrusive *gaia* is a colonising one yet the proponents do not bother to go this far in clarifying their points. *Gaia* is according to the proponents of animism an intrusive goddess of witchcraft that visits punishment on Africans and the Global South for industrially polluting and rapaciously exploiting the environment, even if the Africans do not own the industries that pollute the earth. In this sense, the *gaia* is not a goddess of justice or morality but one of blind indiscriminate, immoral punishment without cognisance of innocence or proportionality. In this way it is a goddess that sacrifices the poor, including the innocent poor for the offences and for the stomachs of the rich: it is a goddess that sacrifices the poor for their crimes of constituting "excess mouths for the dispossessive rich to feed" (Pignarre and Stengers 2011). It is for this reason that Pignarre and Stengers (2011: 19) argue, supporting sacrifice of the impoverished, that "…in the spaceship Planet, with its limited resources, there is no pity for jokers, rebels, mutineers-and if there is a shortage there is no pity for excess mouths to feed and for the weak".

In its purported indiscriminate punishment, the *gaia* is a Western goddess that has no principles of accountability and transparency. Of course the depiction could be mere attempts by rich regions of the world, that have already declined to sign Protocols for Climate Change, to evade responsibility for greenhouse effects by passing the buck to their goddess that they depict as faceless and hence unaccountable. History indicates that colonists had tendencies to introduce diseases such as anthrax, botulism, smallpox as well as using biological and chemical weapons during years of colonial subjugation and liberation struggles (Simmons 2012; Gould and Folb 2000, 2002; Feuerman 1990) and then explain them on the basis that it was God who was angry with Africans' resistance to colonisers. Contemporary literature also shows that some powerful countries have technologies that produce bacteria, such as *Yers in Pestis* that causes pneumonia plague, and stocks of other biological and chemical weapons some of which are not easy to detect (Sanger 2009: 419-29) and these can well be used by human beings who then attribute the effects to the actions of their *gaia* goddess of witchcraft. Gaia proponents do not inform us how their goddess *gaia* treats rich states that refused to sign international protocols to reduce greenhouse emissions. If *gaia* does not consider these inequalities in the world and the dominance of some over others, then *gaia* is as irresponsible as what indigenous Africans call *chikwambo/tokoloshe* or goblin. In African indigenous cosmology, ancestors are sensitive to inequalities, to morality and ethics, to distinctions between the innocent and the guilty, to proportionality in punishment. In this sense, some may quibble that the African ancestors and God are not postmodern enough to dedifferentiate and bridge binaries between the innocent and the guilty but it is in the interest of justice and fairness to draw such distinctions or binaries. In African indigenous knowledge an irresponsible thing is not a goddess or even an ancestor but a goblin and giving good names does not necessarily transform the evil into angels, it does not dedifferentiate them.

Vitriolic attacks on God and on Christ by proponents of animistic *gaia* some of whom openly support AntiChrist, including advocating for sorcery and witchcraft (Deleuze and Guattari 1987; Matt 2013; Bryden 2001; Stengers 2012: 7, 8) run counter to African indigenous religions, metaphysics, and epistemic pronunciations. Logics of coloniality have always been against indigenous African religions that were for indigenous people a resource to oppose not only colonialism but also to oppose witchcraft (Nyathi 2001, Anderson 1995). The logics of coloniality have always involved supporting witchcraft through legislation favourable to the practice (Nyathi 2001). The colonial legislation was viewed as supporting witchcraft (Ashforth 2005, Zimbabwe Criminal Law Codification and Reform Act 2004). However, proponents of animistic *gaia* are not only avowedly AntiChrist but they are also posthumanist in the sense of being antihumanist (Bryant 2012) and some of them advocate for human beings to become animals (de Castro 2013). In Africa which is founded on *Ubuntu* and *Chivanhu* (see Nhemachena 2014; Jahn 1961; Samkange and Samkange 1980) it is inconceivable that a human being can actually aspire to become an animal in the sense promoted by proponents of animism and posthumanism. Rather in *Ubuntu* and *Chivanhu* indigenous people aspire to be human beings and to be treated as human beings rather than to become animals or be treated as animals or even to be classified as animals (see also Mawere 2015).

The failure to distinguish between nature and human beings, that is, animals and human beings, as proponents of animism and posthumanism advocate, is central to (neo-)colonial projects. Conrad's portrayal of colonists' expeditions into Africa as "penetration to the most ancient core of the European mind and hearing the incomprehensible yells of the savages" (Cox 1989: 79) underscores the personalisation, in the form of a feminine, of Africa by colonists invading it. Conrad's characterisation of adventures down the Congo in terms of "Freudian voyage into the wilderness of sex" and his characterisation of the movement as "not one of penetration and withdrawal only" (Cox 1989: 50, 58) show the deleterious effects of animistic perceptions of Africa by colonists. Failure to draw distinctions between animals and human beings have also resulted in some women being forced to have sex with animals to humiliate and sexually exploit them as well as for purpose of "satanic rituals" (Adam *et al* 1995; Ngosa 2011). Walker (1979: 120) cited in Adam *et al* (1995: 65), for instance, notes a woman stating thus: "He would tie me up and force me to have sexual intercourse with our family dog...He would get on top of me, holding the dog, and he would like hump the dog, while the dog had its penis inside me".

Other cases show that the failure to draw distinctions between animals and human beings have resulted in some husbands taking turns with dogs to forcibly have sex with their wives. In other instances colonists who did not distinguish between human beings and animals forced African women to have sex with dogs. Adams *et al* (1995: 65) cite Russell (1990, xii) who note a woman as stating that her husband purchased a large dog and trained it to have sex with her as he watched for his own arousal. Auma-Osolo (2013) noted cases in which African women in various British colonies and protectorates were put at the mercy of European colonists who incited their dogs to have forced sexual intercourse with the women: this Auma-Osolo (2013) links not merely to abnormality but to "Satanism" by the colonists. Similarly, Van Onselen (1977: 175, 1984, 15) cited in Epprecht (2013) noted a colonist in Zimbabwe who in mid-1890s forced men to have sex with each other. Although he notes some colonists as forcing their employees to have homosexual intercourse and also sex with animals, Epprecht (2013) argues that it was men's physical experience of strong orgasm that forced them to have sex with other men and with animals. But there were also instances in early years of Zimbabwean independence where some frustrated by Zimbabwe gaining independence forced their African maids to have sex with dogs.

While these failures to draw distinctions, including between human beings and animals, are celebrated by postmodernists and poststructuralists, by proponents of animism and posthumanism, they have the effect of dehumanising people. Of course when capitalists advocate for the erosion of such distinctions they do not mention how they intend their own industries such as the growing pornographic industry to benefit massively when they show human beings having sex with animals. They do not mention the benefits, of failure to distinguish the real human beings from animal, or human being from machine, for capitalists who create and boost their markets for their dildos and other sex machines after destroying human relations, and replacing them with human-machine, human-animal synergies. Equally when proponents of empire summarily demonise African indigenous institutions, they do not mention the benefits that they intend to accrue to empire, to which Africans are often encouraged to take refuge, in terms of creating a pool of cultural, social, political, economic, religious and linguistic slaves for the empire.

If everything in Africa is a person as proponents of animism would have it, then it follows logically that they want to assume that there are no persons in Africa. The proponents of animism therefore repeat, in a different way, the old colonial depictions of colonial territories as *terra nullius* or empty and unowned places. Through such depictions of Africa as *terra nullius* (virgin land), empire hopes to forestall claims for repossession of colonially looted land by indigenous people. Depicting everything as a person is, in effect, a way of repeating the colonial assumptions that indigenous human beings and persons in those territories have no essence of humanity and of personhood; it is a way of saying they are no different from things that colonists and empire have looted. The worry is that the repetitions of colonial assumptions of animism and *terra nullius* come at a time when there are concerns about the "new scramble" for Africa (Southall 2009) and when some in the West are keen to establish "new empire" (Hadt and Negri 2000). Thus empire's apparent [epistemic] charity is in fact a trap to draw indigenous people closer and in Hornborg's (2009) phrase, "swallow the noble savage": the "charity" is intended not to decolonise but to perpetuate epistemic, including indigenous institutional asphyxiation.

How Africans can resist animalisation if they uncritically assume that empire is all about benevolence is cause for epistemic concern particularly where Africans are striped off not only of their identities but of their cultures, social, political, linguistic, economic and religious institutions? Like all stripings, be they physical or otherwise, striping indigenous people of their institutions amounts to taking away their dignity as much as it fails to reckon distinctions between them and bare animals. Like during the slave trade and colonialism, the trick for empire has been to make the striping of the indigenous people appear as benevolent as possible even as it actually is intended to create multiple forms of bondage. The challenge is that some indigenous people have become so used to the synthetic taste of being culturally, socially, politically and economically stripped by empire such that they do not realise even when it amounts to indecent exposure. So empire continues following colonial logics, to strip and expose indigenous people even as it expects them on threats of sanctions to cover themselves using ill-fitting imperial institutional garbs that simultaneously serve as their badges of subservience. With regard to African women and men, empire paradoxically claims to promote gender equality while it is very busy feminising and battering the broader African context within which the men and women live. They feminise and batter African indigenous institutional contexts even as they claim to champion gender equality. The question then is

43

how one can claim to promote gender equality when one is at the same time feminising and battering the broader context within which African women live? Put differently, how can one claim to be "championing freedom or liberty for fish" when one is busy poisoning the aquatic context within which the fish live?

Conclusion

If empire was a partner in "animistic" relationships with the rest of the world, it is a partner that demands the stripping and exposure of the other without itself conceiving chances of it also being stripped off and exposed in turn. In all this, one sees the resilience of empire's old logics of "penetrating" the others without conceiving the chances of it also being "penetrated" and stripped by the other. The old missionary logics of "penetrating" Africa that they considered as *terra nullius* belonging to no one (Schmidt 1995) are very much still in the marrow of empire which continues to gnaw at the institutions of others hoping not only to dispossess ideologically but also hoping to retain in perpetuity material it dispossessed the indigenous people. And of course empire knows that the first effective way to colonise is to invade and "penetrate" and so it has "penetrated" the peripheries physically, ideologically, metaphysically, culturally, economically, politically and linguistically in the process rendering the "penetrated" territories inside-out. Equally the mental and ideological "penetration" rendered some indigenous minds inside-out. Through contemporary propositions by proponents of animism to conceive the world as without inside and outside, one is yet to witness the birth of many other inside-outs that have lost sensitivity to "penetration" even if it tears their tissues and fabrics inside-out. What Africa needs therefore is a process where it is not conceived and treated as inside-out but where its inside is as clear and visible as empire would hope its own to be even projecting into the world. African humanism needs to clearly project into the world to forestall the mischief of confusing African human beings with animals. Let Africa humanise Africans, and be patient with empire to allow it time to become human by reversing its dehumanisation of others. Empire cannot humanise others before it has become human enough, and as posthumanists referred to above posit, empire animalises others, and sometimes it does this even as it claims to be humanising them.

44

References

Adam, C. J. and Donovan, J. Eds, 1995. *Animals and Women: Feminist Theoretical Explorations*. Duke University Press: Durham and London.

Adhikari, M. 2010. *The Anatomy of a South African genocide: The Extermination of the Cape San Peoples*, University of Cape Town Press: Cape Town.

Adhikari, M. 2014. 'The Bushman is a Wild Animal to be Shot at Sight: Annihilation of the Cape Colony's Foraging Societies by Stock-Farming Settlers in the Eighteenth and Nineteenth Century,' In: Adhikari, M. Ed, *Genocide on Settler Frontiers: When Hunter-Gatherer and Commercial Stock Farmers Clash*, Claremont: Juta and Co Ltd, pp. 32-59.

African Media Agency (AMA), 31 March 2015, African Leaders Call for taking Ownership of Resources and using them effectively. africanleadership.co.uk/Africa-leaders-call-for-taking-ownership-of-resources-and-using-it-effectively.

Amin, S. 2004. *The Liberal Virus: Permanent war and the Americanisation of the World*, Monthly Review Press: New York.

Amin, S. 2011. *Ending the Crisis of Capitalism or Ending Capitalism*, CODESRIA: Dakar.

Anderson, D. M. 1995. 'Revealing Prophets.in Johnson,' D. H., and Anderson, D. M., eds. *Revealing Prophets*, James Currey: London, pp.1-27.

Asante, M. K. *et al.*, 1996. African Intellectual Heritage: A Book of Sources. Temple Press: Philadelphia.

Asante, M. K. 2000. *The Egyptian Philosophers: Ancient voices from Inhatep to Akhenaten*, African American Images: Chicago.

Ashforth, A. 2005. *Witchcraft, Violence and Democracy in South Africa*, University of Chicago Press: Chicago.

Artigas. M. 2001. *The Mind of the Universe: Understanding Science and Religion*, Temple Foundation Press: Pennsylvania.

Auma-Osolo, A. 2013. *Why Leaders Fail and Plunge the Innocent into a sea of Agonies: The danger of Abnormal Politics Vol I*. Trafford Publishing: British Columbia.

Behrend, H. 1999a. *Alice Lakwena and the Holy Spirits War in Northern Uganda 1986-97*, James Currey: Oxford.

Behrend, H. 1999b. *Spirit Possession, Modernity and Power in Africa*, James Currey: Oxford.

Bertens, H. 2008. *The Basic Literary Theory, 2ⁿᵈ Edition*, Taylor and Francis: London and New York.

Best, U. n.d. 'Gnawing at the Edges of the State: Deleuze and Guattari and Border Studies,' Berg E., n.d. *Routing Borders Between Territories, Discourses and Practices*, Ashgate pp. 177-189.

Boyle, F. A. 2013. *Destroying Libya and World Order: The Three-Decades U.S Campaign to Terminate the Gaddafi Revolution,* Clarity Press Inc.: Atlanta.

Bryant, L. R. 2012. Questions for Flat Ethics, Hosted by the Philosophy Department at University of Texas Arlington 18 October 2012: 1-23.

Bryden, M., 2001. 'Introduction,' In: Bryden, M. (ed) *Deleuze and Religion*, London: Routledge: 1-6.

Bullock, C. 1927. *The Mashona (The Indigenous Natives of Southern Rhodesia,* Juta and Co: Cape Town.

Buntu, A. O. 2013. 'Perspectives on African Identity in the twenty first Century,' In: Bankie, B. F. and Mchombu, K., eds, *Pan-Africanism, African Nationalism: Strengthening the Unity of Africa and its Diaspora*, Beracah Printing Enterprise: Windhoek. pp 75-91.

Churchill, W. 2004. *Genocide by any other name: North American Indian Residential Schools in Context,* In: Jones, A. Ed, *Genocide, war crimes and the west: History and complicity,* Zed Books: New York, pp. 78-115.

Clark, H. 2003. *Natural Born Cyborgs: Minds, Technologies and the Future of Human Intelligence,* Oxford University Press: Oxford.

Colson, E. 1971. *The Social Consequences of Resettlement: The Impact of the Kariba Resettlement upon the Gwembe Tonga,* Manchester University Press: Manchester.

Comaroff, J. and Comaroff, J. 2005. 'The Colonisation of Consciousness,' In: Lambek, M. Ed, *A Reader in the Anthropology of Religion*, Blackwell Publishing: Oxford, pp. 493-510.

Cox, C. B. 1989. *Conrad: Heart of darkness Nostromo and Under Western Eyes,* Macmillan Education Ltd: Hampshire.

Crossberg, S. V. (440/07[2008] ZASCA 13 [2008] 3 All SA 329 (SCA), 2008 (2) SACR 317 (SCA) 20 march 2008) Supreme Court of Appeal of South Africa.

de Castro, E. 2013. 'Economic Development and Cosmopolitical Reinvolvement: From Necessity to Sufficiency,' In Green, L. ed, *Contested Ecologies: Dialogues in the South on Nature and Knowledge*, HSRC Press: Cape Town.

Deleuze, G. and Guattari, F. 1987. *A Thousand Plateaus: Capitalism and Schizophrenia*, University of Minnesota Press: Minneapolis.

Dust, T. M. 1995. *The Impact of Aboriginal Land Claims and Self-Government on Canadian Municipalities: The Local Government Perspective*, An Intergovernmental Committee on Urban and Regional Research Project ICURR Press. Toronto, Ontario.

Epprecht, M. 2013. *Hungochani: The History of Dissident Sexuality in Southern Africa*, 2nd Edition: McGill-Queen University Press. Montreal.

Evensky, J. 2005. *Adam Smith's Moral Philosophy: A Historical and Contemporary Perspective on Markets, Law, Ethics and Culture.* Cambridge University Press: Cambridge.

Fanon, F. 1963. *The Wretched of the Earth,* Grove Press: New York.

Fayemi J K, 1998, The Future of De-militarisation and Civil Military relations in West Africa: Challenges and Prospects for Democratic Consolidation, *Afr.Polit. sci* (1998) vol 3, No 1: 83-103.

Feuerman, S. 1990. *Peasant Intellectuals: Anthropology and History in Tanzania*, The University of Wisconsin Press: Madison.

Fontein, J. 2006.*The Silence of Great Zimbabwe: Contested Landscapes and the Power of Heritage*, University College Press: London.

Frank, E. 2006. *Negotiating Futures in the Time of AIDS: Contests over Inheritance in Southern Province, Zambia*, PhD Thesis: Indiana University Press: Bloomington.

Frazer, J. G. 1926. *The Worship of Nature*, MacMillan and Co Ltd. London.

Garuba, H. 2013. 'On Animism, Modernity/Colonialism, and the African Order of Knowledge: Provisional Reflections,' In: Green, L. Ed. *Contested Ecologies: Dialogues in the South on Nature and Knowledge.* HSRC Press: Cape Town, pp. 42-51.

Gelfand, M. 1959.*Shona Ritual with Special Reference to the Chaminuka Cult*, Juta and Co: Cape Town.

Gelfand, M. 1970.Unhu-The Personality of the Shona, *Studies in Comparative Religion* Vol 4, No 1, www.studies in comparative religion.com.

George, G. M. J. 2009. Stolen Legacy: Greek Philosophy is Stolen Egyptian Philosophy, *The Journal of Pan African Studies ebook.* www.sacred-texts.com/afr/stle/stle05.htm.

Gordon, R. 2014. 'Vogelfrei and Besitzlos, With no Concept of property: Divergent Settler Responses to Bushmen and Damara in German South West Africa,' In: Adhikari, M. Ed, *Genocide on Settler Frontiers: When Hunter-Gatherer and Commercial Stock Farmers Clash.* Juta and Co Ltd: Claremont. pp 108-133.

Gould, C. *et al.* 2000. The South African Chemical and Biological Warfare Programme: An Overview, *The Non-Proliferation Review Fall-Winter* pp 10-23.

Gould, C. *et al.* 2002. Project Coast: Apartheid's Chemical and Biological Warfare Programme, Geneva: *United Nations Institute for Disarmament Research.* Centre for Conflict Resolution: Cape Town.

Gunn, L. H. *et al.* 2000. *Africa and the World: An Introduction to the History of Sub Saharan Africa from Antiquity to 1840*, University of America Press, Inc.: Maryland.

Gunning, F. L., 2015, Ferguson and Faith: Sparkling Leadership and Awakening, Chalice Press: Missouri.

Hadt M and Negri A. 2000. *Empire*, Cambridge, Massachusetts: Harvard University Press.

Halbestam, J. and Livingston, I., 1995. Introduction: Posthuman Bodies, in Halberstam J. and Livingston, I. Eds, *Posthuman Bodies, Bloomington and Indianapolis*, Indiana University Press: Bloomington.

Hansen, H. B. 1995. The Colonial Control of Spirit Cults in Uganda. In Anderson, D. M. and Johnson, D. H. Eds. *Revealing Prophets*, James Currey: London, pp.143-163.

Hardin, S. 1994. Is Science Multicultural? Challenges, Resources, Opportunities, Uncertainties, *Configurations* 2.2: pp 301-330.

Harring, S. L. 2014. Dispossession, Ecocide, Genocide: Cattle Ranching and Agriculture in the Destruction of hunting Cultures on the Canadian Prairies, in Adhikari M. Ed, *Genocide on Settler*

Frontiers: When Hunter-Gatherer and Commercial Stock Farmers Clash, Juta and Co Ltd: Claremont, pp 259-285

Hornborg, A. 2009. Zero-Sum World: Challenges in Conceptualising Environmental Load Displacement and Ecologically Unequal Exchange in the World System, *Journal of Comparative Sociology* 50 (3-4): pp 236-261.

Jacobson, M. F. 2000. *Barbarian Virtues: the United States Encounter with Foreign Peoples at Home and Abroad 1876-1917*, Hill and Wang: New York.

Jahn, J. 1961. *Muntu: The New African Culture*, Grove Press Inc: New York.

James, E. O. 1957. *Prehistoric Religion: A Study in Prehistoric Archaeology*, Thames and Hudson: London.

Kincaid, H. 2013. Introduction: Pursuing a Naturalist Metaphysics, in Ross, D. *et al.*, Eds. *Scientific Metaphysics*, Oxford University Press: Oxford.

Kumu, A. J. 2002. *The African Renaissance: History, Significance and Strategy*, Africa World Press: Trenton.

Levtzion, N. 1973. *Ancient Ghana and Mali: Studies in African History*. Methuen and Co Ltd: London.

MacDonald, J. 2014. Like a Wild Beast, He can be God for the Catching: Child Labour and the 'Taming' of the San along the Cape's North-eastern Frontier, C1806-1830, in Adhikari M, Ed, *Genocide on Settler Frontiers: When Hunter-Gatherer and Commercial Stock Farmers Clash*, Juta and Co Ltd: Claremont. pp 60-87.

Magubane, B. M. 2007. *Race and the Construction of the Dispensable Other*, UNISA: Pretoria.

Mail Online 7 September 2015 www.dailymail.co.uk/news/article-3225116/oregon-police-chief-retires-fellow-officer-accuses-responding-racis.

Manning, P. 1993. *Slavery and African Life: Occidental, oriental and African slave trades*. Cambridge: Cambridge University Press.

Matikiti, R. 2007. Environmental Management: Karanga Ecotheology in Charumbira Communal Lands, *Swedish Missiological Theme*, 95 (3): pp 217-226.

Matt, L. 2013. Memoirs of a Sorcerer, Notes on Giles Deleuze-Felix Guattari Austin Osman, Spare and Anomalous Sorcerers Academia.ed.http://www.academic.edu/18/993/memories-of-a-sorcerer-notes-on-Giles-Deleuze-Felix-Guattari-Osman-Spare-and-anomalous-sorcerers.

Mawere, M. 2014. *Divining the future of Africa: Healing the Wounds, Restoring Dignity and Fostering Development*, Langaa RPCIG: Bamenda.

Mawere, M. 2015. *Humans, Other Beings and the Environment: Harurwa (Edible Stinkbugs) and Environmental Conservation in Southeastern Zimbab*we, Cambridge: Cambridge Publishers.

Mbeki, M. 2000. Issues in South African Foreign Affairs Policy, *Souls*, Spring.

Mbiti, J. S. 1970. *Concepts of God in Africa*, SPCK: London.

Ministry of Aboriginal Affairs, Province of British Columbia, 1995. Summary Report: Social and Economic Impacts of Aboriginal Land Claims Settlement: A case Study Analysis, Federal Treaty Negotiations Office, Government of Canada.

Moyana, H. 1984. *The Political Economy of Land in Zimbabwe*, Mambo Press: Gweru.

Moyo, S. 2008. *African Land Questions, Agrarian Transitions and the State: Contradictions of Neoliberal Land Reforms*, CODESRIA: Dakar.

Mubaya, T. & Mawere, M. 2015. 'Orphans in a Strange Land': Controversies and Challenges in the Repatriation of African Cultural Property from European Museums,' In: Mawere, M. *Et al.* (Eds), *African Museums in the Making: Reflections on the Politics of Material and Public Culture in Zimbabwe*, Bamenda: Langaa Publishers.

Muphree, M. W. 1969. *Christianity and the Shona*, The Athlone Press: New York.

Nabudere, D. W. 2013. Towards a New ethos in Human Relations, in Bankie, B. F. and Mchombu, K. Eds, *Pan-Africanism, African Nationalism: Strengthening the Unity of Africa and its Diaspora*, Beracah Printing Enterprise: Windhoek.

Nanda, M. 2003. *Prophets Facing Backwards: Postmodern Critiques of Science and Hindu Nationalism in India*, Rutgers University Press.

Natural Society, September 19 2015, Activists in Kenya Protest against GMO Food Introduction, NaturalSociety.com/activist-in-kenya-protest-against-gmo-food-introduction/

Nchoji, P. 2015. 'The Anthropology of Africa: Challenges for the Twenty First century,' In: Mbuy T. H. Ed, *African Traditional*

Religion as a Socio-Cultural Background of the African of the Third Millennium, Langaa RPCIG: Bamenda.

Ndlovu-Gatsheni, S. J. 2013. *Coloniality of Power in Postcolonial Africa: Myths of Decolonisation,* CODESRIA: Dakar.

Nesbitt F N., 2004. Coming to Terms with the Past: The Case for A Truth and Reparations Commission on Slavery, Segregation and Colonialism, in Jones A., ed, *Genocide, War Crimes and the West: History and Complicity,* New York: Zed Books, pp 361-379.

Ngosa, K. 2011. *Satan's Best Kept Secrets: His Nefarious Schemes and Deepest Fears Unveiled,* IUnierse rev: Bloomington.

Nhemachena, A. 2014. *Knowledge, Chivanhu and Struggles for Survival in Conflict Torn Manicaland, Zimbabwe,* PhD Thesis, University of Cape Town.

Nhemachena, A. 2015. 'Indigenous Knowledge, Conflation and Postcolonial Translation: Lessons from Fieldwork in Contemporary Rural Zimbabwe,' In: Mawere, M. and Awuah-Nyamekye, S. eds, *Between Rhetoric and Reality: The State and Use of Indigenous Knowledge in Postcolonial Africa,* Langaa RPCIG: Bamenda, pp. 59-108.

Ntholi, L. S. 2006. *Contesting Sacred Space: A Pilgrimage Study of the Mwali Cult of Southern Africa,* Africa World Press Inc.: Eritrea.

Nyamnjoh, F. B. 2012. 'Potted Plants in Greenhouses': A Critical Reflection on the Resilience of Colonial Education in Africa, *Journal of Asian and African Studies,* 47 (2): 129-154.

Nyamnjoh F B., 2012. Blinded by Sight: Divining the Future of Anthropology in Africa, *Africa Spectrum,* 47(2-3): 63-92.

Nyamnjoh, F. and Fuh, D. 2014. Africans Consuming Hair, Africans Consumed by Hair, *Africa Insight: Development through Knowledge* vol 44 (1) June 2014: pp 51-68.

Nyathi, P. 2001.*Traditional Ceremonies of Amandebele,* Mambo Press: Gweru.

Okot p'Btek. 2011. *Decolonising African Religion: A Short History of African Religion,* Diasporic Press: London.

Oliver, H. H. 1981. *A Relational Metaphysics,* Morton Nijhoff Publishers: London.

Olusoga, D. and Erichsen, C. W. 2011. *The Kaiser's Holocaust: Germany's Forgotten Genocide,* Farber and Farber Limited: London.

Ong, A. 1988. The Production of Possession Spirits and the Multinational Corporation in Malaysia, *American ethnologist* Vol 15, No 1: 28-42, http://www.jstor.org/stable/645484, accessed 22/8/2008.

Onyewuyenyi, I. C. 2006. *The African Origin of Greek Philosophy: an Exercise in Afrocentrism*, University of Nigeria Press: Nsukka.

Opoku, K. A. 1978. *West African Traditional Religion*, FEP International Private Limited: Accra.

Palmer, R. 1977. *Land and Racial Domination in Rhodesia*, University of California Press: Berkeley.

Parekh, B. 1995. Liberalism and Colonialism: A Critique of Locke and Mill, in Pieterse, J. N. and Parekh, B. Eds, *The Decolonisation of Imagination: Culture, Knowledge and Power*. Zed Books: London and New Jersey.

Parrinder, J. 1967. *African Mythology*, Paul Hamlyn: London.

Pignarre, P. and Stengers, I. 2011.*Capitalism Sorcery: Breaking the Spell*, Palgrave MacMillan: New York.

Prah, K. K. 1993. 'African languages, the Key to African Development: A Critique of Ideas in Development Thinking,' In: Von Troil M., ed, *Changing Paradigms in Development-South, East and West: A Meeting of Minds in Africa,* Uppsala: Nordiska Afrikainstitutet.

Prah, K. K. 2011. 'Culture: The Missing Link in Development Planning in Africa,' in Keita, L. Ed, *Philosophy and African Development: Theory and Practice*, CODESRIA: Dakar.

Ramose, M. B. 1999. *African Philosophy through Ubuntu,* Mond Books: Harare.

Rattray, R S. 1927. *Religion and Art in Ashanti*. Clarendon Press: Oxford.

Ray, A. J. 2013. *Reclaiming History, Land and Rights: A Comparative Examination of Land Restitution in Australia, Canada, New Zealand, the United States and South Africa*, Cape Town Paper, 23 March 2013, Pp. 1-34.

Rodney, W. (2012[1972] *How Europe Underdeveloped Africa*, CODESRIA: Dakar.

Rootes, C. Ed. 2003. *Environmental Protests in Western Europe,* Oxford University Press: Oxford.

Ryan, L. 2014. No Right to the Land: The Role of the Wool Industry in the Destruction of Aboriginal Societies in Tasmania (1817-1832) and Victoria (1835-1851) Compared, in Adhikari M, ed, *Genocide on Settler Frontiers: When Hunter-Gatherer and Commercial Stock Farmers Clash* Juta and Co Ltd: Claremont.

Samkange, S. J. T. and Samkange, T. M. 1980.*Hunhuism or Ubuntuism: A Zimbabwe Indigenous Political Philosophy,* Graham Publishers: Salisbury.

Sanger, D. E. 2009. *The Inheritance: the World Obama Confronts and the Challenge to American Power,* Transworld Publishers: London.

Schimdt, A. 1995. "Penetrating Foreign Lands: Contestation over African Landscape: A Case Study from Eastern Zimbabwe, *Environment and History* vol I, No 3 p 351-376.

Schmidt, E. 1992. *Peasants, Traders and Wives: Shona Women in the History of Zimbabwe, 1870-1939*, Baobab: Harare.

Setiloane, G. 1976. *The Image of God among the Sotho Tswana,* AA Balkema: Rotterdam.

Simmons, D. 2012. *Modernising Medicine in Zimbabwe: HIV/AIDS and Traditional Healers.* Vanderbilt University Press: Nashville.

Smith, M. 2011. *Against Ecological Sovereignty: Ethics, Biopolitics and Saving the Natural World,* University of Minnesota Press: Minneapolis.

Stanner, W. E. H. 2005. Religion, Totemism and Symbolism, in Lambek, M., Ed, *A Reader in the Anthropology of Religion*, Oxford: Blackwell: Oxford. P 90-98

Stengers, I. 2012. Reclaiming Animism, *efflux Journal Number 36-July 2012,* pp 1-10.

Susskind, L. E. and Anguelovsk, I. 2008. *Addressing the Land Claims of Indigenous Peoples, Programme on Human Rights and Justice*, Massachusetts Institute of Technology Programs. http://publicdisputes.mit.edu/sites/default/files/documents/indigenous_peoples.pdf.

Taiwo, O. 2010. *How Colonialism Pre-emptied Modernity in Africa,* Indiana University Press: Bloomington, I N.

Thompson, C. 2009. The Scramble for Genetic Resources, in Southall R and Melber H., eds, *A New Scramble for Africa? Imperialism, Investment and Development,* University of KwaZulu Natal Press: Scottville. Pp 299-323.

United Nations, 2007. *Indigenous People-Lands, Territories and Natural Resources*, United Nations Permanent Forum on Indigenous Issues.

Veracini, L. 2014. 'Seeing Receding Hunter-Gatherers and Advancing Commercial Pastoralists: Nomadisation, Transfer, Genocide,' In: Adhikari, M. Ed, *Genocide on Settler Frontiers: When Hunter-Gatherer and Commercial Stock Farmers Clash*, Juta and Co Ltd: Claremont. pp 286-304.

Weaver, J. C. 2006. *The Great Land Rush and the Making of the Modern World 1650-1900*, McGill-Queen's University Press: Quebec.

Wolfe, C. 2010. *What is Posthumanism?* University of Minnesota Press: Minneapolis.

Chapter Three

Maslow's Theory of Human Motivation and its Deep Roots in Individualism: Interrogating Maslow's Applicability in Africa

Munyaradzi Mawere, Tapuwa R. Mubaya,
Mirjam van Reisen, Gertjan van Stam

Introduction

In Social Studies the theory of Abraham Maslow on human motivation is considered a seminal work. Frequently, Maslow's theory of human motivation is cited as a general description of the priorities of what humans need and want. There is no doubt that Maslow's reasoning, particularly his theory of hierarchies of needs and motivation has proven helpful within the contexts of perspectives on growth and even equality, as Maslow emphasised the potential of every human being. In Maslow's thinking, the 'individual' is seen as the most important actor, and his/her individual agency supersedes other motivations of action (Maslow 1943). As a humanistic psychologist, Maslow believed that every person has a strong desire to realise his or her full potential, to reach a level of 'self-actualisation'. He was the founder of the new movement of humanistic psychology that reached its peak in the 1960s, and whose main point was to emphasise the positive potential of human beings (Schacter *et al.* 2012). His thinking has deeply influenced the paradigm of the development agenda, both in theory and in practice, and set the foundation for moral thinking on individual entitlements.

Maslow's theory was perhaps more a programme than a theory and practitioners have lamented that the theory is not aligned with realities. As Graham and Messner (1998: 196) summarised, there are generally three major criticisms directed to Maslow's Theory of Motivation:

(a) there is scant empirical data to support the theoretical model

(b) the studies assume human beings are similar and that the theory universally applies, and

(c) applications or validation of the theory do not concern themselves with a theory of motivation but rather with theories of job satisfaction.

This criticism is supported by many other scholars (c.f. Nadler *et al.* 1979) in the field. The author and former philosophy professor, Sommers, and practising psychiatrist, Satel, asserted that, due to lack of empirical support, Maslow's ideas have fallen out of fashion and are no longer taken seriously in the world of academic psychology (Sommers and Satel 2005). Despite such fundamental criticism, the work remains standard literature in management studies and other fields and is part of standard curricula and textbooks for secondary education students. This chapter adds to the existing criticism of the theory, but from an African perspective.

This chapter problematises a lack of empirical evidence, especially from other contexts, such as those of Africa, and hence questions the claim of 'universality' of the theory of Human Motivation. House and Aditya (1997) demonstrated in their study of leadership from over 3,000 studies that 98% of the empirical evidence for theoretical development is rather distinctly American in character. Although Maslow's theory is taught as an explanatory universal model, Maslow's theory is not validated in contexts or environments other than those where the theory was created. This validation outside of a western framework is important, given that Maslow's theory emerged from an American cultural setting, characterised by individualism. In this cultural context, the individual is the point of reference and the realisation of the 'individual' is the highest goal.

The question of whether Maslow's theory of human motivation is universally applicable is important, as much of the world that Galtung refers to as "the Periphery" does not resonate with putting the 'individual' as the focus of human motivation (Trompenaars and Hampden-Turner 2011). In many parts of the world, it is *the group*, or *the community*, and 'the attributes the group reflects upon its members' that are central, and considered worthy to be pursued. In Southern Africa, for example, the philosophy of Ubuntu is at the centre of all human sphere, whether economic, religious, political or cultural. In Ubuntu, it is the group and not individuals that motivates daily endeavours, design, and behaviour (Mawere 2014; Khoza 2005; Mawere and Mubaya 2014; Mbiqi 1994; Nyamnjoh 2015; Ramose 2009; van Stam 2014).

This chapter is an attempt to provide some suggestions of motivational realities in Southern Africa, as a caution for positioning and applying Maslow's theory as a universal theory. In many indigenous cultures in Southern Africa, the group and the moderating role of cultural factors influence human motivation, as opposed to Maslow's individual as the determining force. The chapter concludes that the theory of Maslow is not applicable to many settings in Africa, in the past or even today. The claim for universality of the model proposed by Maslow is therefore questioned and its universal application is discredited. This conclusion calls for further interaction with the subject of human motivation outside of Maslow's framing, by contextualising such theory(ies) in space and time.

Maslow's Theory of Motivation

The starting point for Maslow's theory is the question: 'What motivates behaviour?' According to Maslow, our actions as human beings are motivated in order to achieve certain needs. Maslow first introduced his concept of a hierarchy of needs and motivation in his 1943 paper *"A Theory of Human Motivation"* and his subsequent book in 1954, *"Motivation and Personality."*

Maslow introduced a new area of attention in the field of psychology. While psychological theories and schools of thought were dominated by psycho-analysis and behaviourism, psychology focused heavily on problematic behaviours. Maslow on the other hand was more interested in learning and understanding what motivates people. He was also much interested in comprehending what people do, in order to achieve what makes them happy. As a humanist psychologist, Maslow believed that people have an innate desire to be self-actualised: that is, the desire to be all they can fully be. Yet for Maslow, in order to achieve these ultimate goals of what people really want to be, a number of more basic needs must be met, such as the need for food, safety, love, and self-esteem, among others.

While this theory is generally known as the hierarchy of needs, he never displayed his theory as a pyramid (Eaton 2012). Depicted in terms of a pyramid, however, the lowest levels are made up of the most 'basic needs', while the more 'complex needs' are located at the top of the pyramid. The needs at the bottom of the pyramid are basic physical requirements including the need for food, water, shelter, and warmth. But for people to move on to the next level of needs, which are mainly for safety and security, the lower-level needs have to be met first. This is one reason why, Maslow explains, as people 'progress', their needs become increasingly psychological and social to the extent that the need for love, friendship, and intimacy become more important than any other needs. Yet as we go even further from this level of the pyramid, the need for personal esteem and feelings of accomplishment become more important than those at the lower-levels.

Maslow's five levels of the hierarchy of needs

Maslow (1943) distinguishes five different levels of needs, to which he assigns different levels of relevance: "if I may assign arbitrary figures for the sake of illustration, it is as if the average citizen is satisfied perhaps 85% in his physiological needs, 70% in his safety needs, 50% in his love needs, 40% in his self-esteem needs and 10% in his self-actualization needs" (Maslow 1943: 388-389). If we were to draw a diagram (a pyramid for that matter) to represent the hierarchy of needs as explained by Maslow, the physiological needs would need to represent a much bigger piece of the pyramid. The five different levels in Maslow's (1943) hierarchy are as follow:

Physiological Needs
Psysiological needs include the most basic needs that are vital to survival, such as the need for water, air, food, and shelter. As Maslow believed, these needs are the most basic and instinctive needs in the hierarchy because all needs become secondary until these physiological needs are met. Maslow added that most of these lower level needs are probably fairly apparent. This is because everyone, as

long as s/he is human, needs food and water to survive. We also need to breathe and maintain a stable body temperature. Besides eating, drinking, and having adequate shelter and clothing, Maslow also suggested that the other important physiological basic need was sexual: reproduction.

Security Needs

Security needs include the desires for safety and security. Security needs are important for survival, but they are not as demanding as the physiological needs. Examples of security needs include a desire for steady employment, health care, safe neighbourhoods, and shelter from the environment. These needs become a bit more complex at this point in the hierarchy as they are considered 'higher' than physiological needs. And when the more basic survival needs have been fulfilled, people begin to feel that they need more control and order to their lives. People begin to concern themselves with safety in terms of where they live, financial security, physical safety, and staying healthy.

Social Needs

Social needs include needs for belonging, love, and affection. Maslow described these needs as less basic than physiological and security needs. Relationships such as friendships, romantic attachments, and families help fulfil this need for companionship and acceptance, also involvement in social, community, or religious groups.

Esteem Needs

When the first three needs have been satisfied, esteem needs become increasingly important. Esteem needs include the need for things that reflect on self-esteem, personal worth, social recognition, and accomplishment. At this point, it becomes important to gain the respect and appreciation of others. People have a need to accomplish things and then have their efforts recognized. People often engage in activities such as going to school, playing a sport, enjoying a hobby, or participating in professional activities in order to fulfil this need. Satisfying this need and gaining acceptance and esteem helps people become more confident. Failing to gain recognition for accomplishments, however, can lead to feelings of failure or inferiority.

Self-actualising Needs

Self-actualising needs assume the highest level of Maslow's hierarchy of needs. Self-actualising people are self-aware, concerned with personal growth, less concerned with the opinions of others, and interested in fulfilling their potential.

Criticism against Maslow's theory over the years

From the fame that Maslow's theory has gathered over the years, it is clear that Maslow's contribution to psychology was momentous. Yet, while some research shows some support for Maslow's theories, most research has not been able to substantiate the idea of a needs hierarchy. Wahba and Bridwell (1976), for example, reported that there was little evidence for Maslow's ranking of these needs and evenless evidence that these needs are in a hierarchical order.

As Nadler and Lawler (1979), Denning (2010), and Rutledge (2011) point out, other criticisms of Maslow's theory note that his definition of self-actualisation is difficult to test scientifically. Maslow's research on self-actualisation was also based on a very limited sample of individuals, including people he knew, as well as biographies of famous individuals that Maslow believed to be self-actualised, such as Albert Einstein and Eleanor Roosevelt.

Based on psychological research of human coping mechanism, Graves (1970) provided an alternative theoretical perspective on human behaviour. He described an open system of theory on values. His theory was worked out in "Spiral Dynamics" by Beck and Cowan (2005). The theory was used in South Africa, validating the theory during turbulent times and beyond. Graves recognised units of cultural information, so called 'memes,' spreading from person to person. Beck colour-coded the memes in a spiraling hierarchy of motivations for behaviour:

    i.   tribal, safety driven (beige)
    ii. exploitive, power-driven (red)
    iii. authority, order-driven (blue)
    iv. strategy, success-driven (orange)

v. social, people-driven (green)

vi. systems, process-driven (yellow)

vii. holistic (turquoise).

The lack of a perspective that human beings function in groups has been addressed by Pinto (2000), a Dutch scholar studying Intercultural Communications. He calls for a revision of Maslow's pyramid to address the motivation of people in group-settings. He points to the emergence of group-focus arising due to economic circumstances, religious influences, peer-groupings, or individual choices. He proposes a different motivational hierarchy relevant for such settings: (i) primary needs; (ii) group pleasing, (iii) good name and, (iv) honour.

These criticisms reveal the absence of congruence and agreement in the sequencing of human needs, like the progression as proposed by Maslow: there is strong indication of variations in labelling and sequencing of needs fulfilment in different contexts.

Alternative propositions approach Human Motivation from different (academic) perspectives. However, positing the heuristic nature of (a simplification of) Maslow's Theory of Motivation continuous to be taught. This is problematic, especially in communal societies like those in Africa. Therefore, there is need for a dialogue informed by inputs from alternative paradigm and epistemological positions.

Dialoguing with Maslow: From an African perspective

In South Africa, while studying the facets of local entrepreneurship, Hart, Jacobs, Mangqalaza (2012) and their team at the Human Sciences Research Council found that rural communities mention a different set of motivations for economic action. Respondents deem 'quality of life' and 'group harmony' as their prime motivations for behaviour. This aligns with Sheneberger and van Stam's (2011) exposition of the consistence of motivation for particular economic (inter)action in rural Zambia, the so-called 'relatio-economy'. Weijland (2014) described the mechanics of this motivation through the mathematics of an 'economy of giving', after witnessing such behaviour in rural Africa.

There is much evidence of strenuous and discordant situations due to motivational variances. This subjects and exposes Maslow's theory to the spotlight. One is left with no option but to question and test whether the theory works in alternate contexts. Such studies are remarkably low in number. As an example, in their multi-national study, Tay and Diener (2011) showed there is a weak alignment with Maslow's thinking, but strong indication that societal conditions influence the sequencing of fulfilment of basic, security and psychosocial needs.

However, it seems Maslow's concepts and theories have enjoyed more comfort than they deserve, not only in the contexts in which they were produced. We agree with Graham *et al.* (2015) that the underlying asymmetrical relations in the politics of knowledge production and dissemination are accelerated by a lopsided geography of information.

Bigirimana (2001) and Gibson (2011) have independently shown the distinct differences in motivation of people in post-independence leadership positions in Africa versus the motivation of the indigenous population. In previous works, van Stam (2013; 2014) showed the variance in African contexts (and motivation) within the academic realm and the importance and substantiality of orality. Further, in the field of activism, there is a whole range of literature depicting the colonisation effect of Western framing of realities (derived upon schema provided by Maslow, among others). For instance, from their Canadian setting, Alfred and Corntassel (2005) link human motivation with land, language, freedom, diet, and indigenous resurgence.

More than 10 years of Action Research in Southern Africa, in ever-evolving cycles of planning, action, observation and contemplation, provides the input for this paper to substantiate the incompatibility of Maslow's thought within the indigenous African context. Observations took place during many different circumstances of the authors. These roles were mostly in parallel and sometimes consecutive:

- national and international academics, researchers, educators and professors
- technical director in a foreign-funded medical research institute

- advisors to leading individuals in professional institutes in Africa and further afield
- leaders and volunteers in a professional bodies
- social entrepreneurs and executive director of rural co-operative.

We have endeavoured to unearth indigenous, practical motivations. Work focused on rural areas in Southern Africa (with a focus on Zambia) and less in the urban areas. With most of the African population living in the rural areas, views espoused in rural areas were regarded as the most significant and culturally grounded.

Sensitivity towards the enshrined forms of information and knowledge transfer (see for example, van Stam 2013), the collaborativity in communities (Matthee *et al.* 2007), and the interaction with local stakeholders (Kroczek *et al.* 2013) constituted the research grounding within various social contexts (institutes), co-operative activities (practices) and human qualities (virtues). Each of these entities applies ethics models and acts upon moral judgments, informed by ethics based upon respective world-views. Ubuntu is an African philosophy of humanness that emphasises the virtues of sharing, peace, unity and harmony in society (Mawere 2014; Mawere and Mubaya 2014). It represents a view on self as in co-living with the other.

Ubuntu involves empathy and focuses on wholeness of the conglomerate, whether a household, family, or community of any sort. It acknowledges that facts are relational/contextual, and incorporate many components, and transfers everything into an embodiment in people (holism). Ubuntu is a metaphor that embodies the significance of human solidarity and stands explicitly against inequality or isolating individualism (van Stam 2014). Within Ubuntu, all interactions are oriented towards the common ground, the community, the family, the birthed relationships, and in relation to the physical land. The latter is congruent with African Science, where three facets of existence are taken into account: the physical, the spiritual, and the interaction between the two (Chimakonam 2012).

In indigenous African interactions, reality is approached equal to a *commons* (cf. Trancoso et al. 2015). The prime motivations for interactions are *relationships* and *community*. These can be witnessed during elaborate greetings and inquiries into family well-being,

63

affirming respect and aiming to (re-)establish and confirm relationship on a continuous basis.

Our observations can be summarised through a list with variations in emphasis between an Ubuntu tradition and Western tradition, augmented, dualistically presented in Table 1.

Ubuntu Tradition	Western Tradition
Relatio	Ratio
Who	What
Community	Individual
Responsibilities	Rights
Relationships	Goods
Character	Credentials
Member	Actor
Paradox	Consistency
History	Future
Orality	Literacy
Authority	Power
Proven	Emerging
Reactive	Proactive
Paradox	Consistency
Elaborate	Concise
Existence	Essential

Table 1: Emphasis dissimilarities in Ubuntu and Western tradition

Most analytical tools for cultural differences come from the seminal works of Hofstede, Hall, Kluckholn, Strodtbeck, Carbaugh, and Trompenaars. It must be noted that all these experts emerged from a Western background. As the list of diverge emphasis in traditions (like Table 1) can be of any length in our diversified world, and will change over time, these kinds of lists basically show contemporary differences in cultural codings. For an explanation of underlying reasons, the enshrined norms and values should ideally be informed by indigenous sources. Such input is greatly needed, especially in assessment of the underlying structures, and their effects in the field of Human Motivation. These inputs show how Maslow's Theory of Motivation does not align with, nor includes concepts of human motivation in an African setting. African epistemology, like Ubuntu, however does provide for such input. If a harmonized, globally valid Theory of Motivation would exist, we contend such can be deducted only through an intellectual journey allowing for diversity.

Findings in the African context

Nakazibwe (2015) shows how rational decision-making on priority needs by women farmers follows very different logics than the one provided in commodity chain thinking. It also points to the need to look at how human motivation manifests itself in gender and the politics surrounding gender issues. Nakazibwe shows how women prioritise a commodity, not because of an individual desire for profit that can be made but because of the access to group processes that it gives and the information, exchange, support mechanisms, and cultural approval derived from this. An example is pastoralist decision-making to sell title deeds after group land division because the land and cattle belongs to the pastoralists anyway so the value of the individual title deeds does not exist in this logic. From the researchers' observations in the lived reality of Southern Africa, the following African components of Human Motivations can be derived, in no particular order:

i. Pursuit of relationships,
ii. Strengthening of community,
iii. Acknowledgement of authority,
iv. Sharing and avoidance of shame.

It is fundamental to point out that absence of the satisfaction of these needs in an African perspective leads to inertia, which can be either active or passive. Active inertia is executed in non-actions, like withholding of – or denying access to – information, exclusion or ex-communication, while passive inertia includes numbing of expressions and/or actions which eventually leads to isolation.

In conformity with Maslow's reasoning for certain conditions which are immediate pre-requisites to needs satisfaction, the following constructive behaviours are observed in the African context:

i.   Expressed permission, grounded in lasting relationships,

ii.   Tangible production, with sustainable achievements through commendable actions in the community,

iii.   Capacity development, building abilities in communities within existing structures of authority,

iv.   Honourable representation, through recognition of wholesome conglomerate of people, resources and ecology.

Discussion

Communications and negotiations on commons are hampered by Western-centric mix of theories (among which is Maslow's pyramid), ethics models and their hermeneutic and existential interpretations. Murphy and Ellis (1996) in *"On the Moral Nature of the Universe"* describe a helpful layering of sciences, each layer building abstraction with the input from the layer below, or by piercing apart aspects of the levels above. The aforementioned scholars describe a Science of Ethics spanning the social and applied sciences. This model provides guidance on how to deal with a mix of ethical models that influence motivation for human behaviour emanating from different world views.

It is only recently in the West, in the late modern period (ca. 1900-1990) that the concept of pure individual power has emerged, that sanctifies the view that one can do as one likes with one's person and one's property (Murphy and Ellis 1996: 1596). This view has been adopted in - and subsequently propagated by – the West. It is this concept of power of the individual that is a precept in Maslow's thought. His thought emerges from a focus on the individual, and her/his agency, ultimately expressing him/herself in "a fullest (and healthiest) creativeness" (Maslow 1943). The authors observed that the approach to motivations framed within an individualistic view on the reason of activities (as proposed by Maslow) is unsuitable for understanding genuinely social processes like the African epistemology as set in Ubuntu which does not provide moral grounding for self-renunciating efforts.

General examples of a communal-agency are African sayings like "It takes a community to raise a child", implying that even for the most basic needs (the physiological needs in Maslow's reasoning), a balance is sought in agency vested in community and individuals. Therefore, a motivation to engender community can be seen as among the most basic needs. As Africa is an environment with abundance of resources (Unwin 2008), the fulfilment of primary needs is seen as a collaborative venture of communities, individuals and the spiritual realms.

The dominant Western view shown by Maslow represents an external influence in proceedings, ethics and judgments in Africa. For instance, 'pure sciences' employ Maslow's contextually-loaded conceptions of human nature, such as assumptions about the intrinsic egoism of individuals, conceptions of human dignity, or more broadly, views on human good or human flourishing. Therefore, African practitioners' interaction with Western academics is hampered (van Stam 2014). Maslow's precepts and philosophy are not in line with the African precepts and philosophy as an African-based epistemology recognises leading concepts of interdependence, interconnectedness, reconciliation, collectivism and solidarity. These concepts are inherently non-egoistic.

The African reality and resulting 'pyramid' can be seen as perpendicular to Maslow's reasoning. Where he describes the freedom for the individual, for instance, for inquiry and expression, in the African context such freedom must be regarded from a community perspective. In Maslow's thinking, the outset is an individual (and her/his needs), after which the community could be seen as the total sum of the individuals it contains. From an indigenous African point of view, however, the outset starts with the community, after which an individual can be regarded as a particular derivative of the community.

The researchers observed that behaviour and characteristics can be well understood, developed, and evaluated within a social context. In many parts of Africa, however, these understandings with the social context are significantly different from those derived through a Western schema. What will count as a virtue rather than a vice or morally indifferent characteristic, however, is determined by the needs of social practices and by the location of those characteristics within the whole of the community's life story.

This discordant situation calls for diversified perspectives on appropriate means of interactions in the world, and guidance on misinterpretations of events. Maslow's theory leads to an approach that often regards human interaction as the negotiation of resources, as if all resources are owned by an individual entity and its dissemination needs to be pursued through a process of negotiation. In the African context, the process is mostly approached from a different perspective, as human interactions are foremost meant to establish relationships. When discussion on sharing of resources occurs, the perceived governing authority over the resource is considered to offer resource-sharing as a means of strengthening the relationship.

The result of the negation of the variance in human motivation is often personal and economic damage, domination, and systematic oppression.

The absence of recognition of a large variety of motivations of human behaviour gives rise to domination by hegemonic (and individually oriented) power, which in turn fuels inequality and social injustice. In the interactions between the Western economic and its social (Maslow) view of realities, and African economic (Relatio) and social (Ubuntu) view of realities, the predatory view – where a win-lose situation is acceptable – seems to dominate in the present.

Conclusion

Each culture and subculture judges human behaviour according to its own norms and values. Maslow's theory of human motivation is a widely accepted theoretical framework which grounds the development of other motivational theories. These theories are presented to be universal and to apply everywhere. However, these academic frames are grounded in one particular set of cultures only: the Western ones. We show the theory is not applicable in many parts of Africa.

Our work shows that in many Africa settings, motivation is derived from the pursuit of relationships, the strengthening of community, the acknowledgment of authority, sharing of resources, and the avoidance of shame.

We conclude that Maslow's theory of Human Motivation does not represent a universal motivational theory. To facilitate better understanding of expectations and interpretations of realities, it is good to critique Maslow's thought by people embedded in non-

Western contexts. It is equally important for those raised within Maslow's settings to understand the concepts of human motivation in other contexts and cultures. This chapter has demonstrated that while Maslow's theory might be considered seminal work, the theory is not applicable to many African contexts owing to the huge differences in ideology, philosophy, and cultural orientation.

References

Alfred, G. T., & Corntassel, J. 2005. Being indigenous: Resurgences against contemporary colonialism, *Government and Opposition, 40* (4): 597–614.

Beck, D. E., & Cowan, C. 2005. *Spiral Dynamics: Mastering Values, Leadership and Change*, Malden, MA: Wiley-Blackwell.

Bigirimana, S. S. J. 2001. Cultural Duality Leadership and Nation Building in Africa, *Chiedza, Arrupe College Journal*, 29-47.

Chimakonam, J. O. 2012. *Introducing African Science Systematic and Philosophical Approach*, Calabar: Author House.

Denning, S. 2010. *The Leader's Guide to Radical Management: Reinventing the Workplace for the 21ˢᵗ Century*, San Francisco, CA: Jossey-Bass.

Eaton, S. 2012. Maslow's Hierarchy of Needs – Is the pyramid a hoax? Retrieved August 12, 2015, from https://drsaraheaton.wordpress.com/2012/08/04/maslows-hierarchy-of-needs/

Gibson, N. 2011. *Fanonian Practices in South Africa*, Palgrave Macmillan: New York.

Graham, M. W., & Messner, P. E. 1998. Principals and job satisfaction, *International Journal of Educational Management, 12*(5), 196–202.

Graham, M., Sabbata, S. De, & Zook, M. A. 2015. Towards a study of information geographies: (im)mutable augmentations and a mapping of the geographies of information (in press), *Geo: Geography and Environment*.

Graves, C. W. 1970. Levels of Existence: An Open System Theory of Values, *Journal of Humanistic Psychology, 10*(2), 131–155.

Hart, T., Jacobs, P., & Mangqalaza, H. 2012. *Rural Innovation Assessment Tool (RIAT) Key Concepts in Innovation Studies*, Pretoria: HSRC.

House, R. J., & Aditya, R. N. 1997. The Social Scientific Study of Leadership: Quo Vadis? *Journal of Management*, 409–473.

Khoza, R. 2005. *Let Africa Lead: African Transformational Leadership for 21st century Business*, Sunninghill: VezuBuntu.

Kroczek, A., van Stam, G., & Mweetwa, F. 2013. Stakeholder Theory and ICT in rural Macha, Zambia. In *5th Annual International Conference on ICT for Africa (ICT4Africa), 20-23 Feb 2013, Harare, Zimbabwe*.

Maslow, A. H. 1943. A theory of human motivation, *Psychological Review, 50*(4), 370-396.

Maslow, A. H. 1954. *Motivation and Personality*, New York, NY: Harper & Row.

Matthee, K., Mweemba, G., Pais, A., van Stam, G., &Rijken, M. 2007. 'Bringing Internet connectivity to rural Zambia using a collaborative approach,' In *IEEE/ACM International Conference on Information and Communication Technologies and Development (ICTD2007), 15-16 Dec 2007, Bangalore, India*.

Mawere, M. 2014. *Environmental Conservation through Ubuntu and Other Emerging Perspectives*, (2014), Langaa RPCIG Publishers: Bamenda.

Mawere, M., & Mubaya, T. R. (Eds.). 2014. *African Cultures, Memory and Space: Living the Past Presence in Zimbabwean Heritage*, Langaa: Bamenda.

Mukuka, G. S. 2010. *Reap What You Have Not Sown. Indigenous Knowledge Systems and Intellectual Property Laws in South Africa*, Pretoria University Press: South Africa.

Murphy, N., & Ellis, G. F. R. 199. *On the Moral Nature of the Universe* (Kindle), Fortress Press: Minneapolis.

Nadler, D. A., Hackman, J. R., & Lawler, E. E. I. 1979. *Managing Organizational Behaviour*, Boston, MA: Little Brown.

Nakazibwe, P. 2014. "To offer a glass of millet-milk, is to offer you my peace': The relational relevance of food in organizing community peace in Uganda," In M. van Reisen (Ed.), *Women's Leadership in Peace-Building: Conflict, Community and Care*. Trenton, NJ: Africa World Press.

Nyamnjoh, F. B. 2015. Incompleteness: Frontier Africa and the Currency of Conviviality, *Journal of Asian and African Studies*, 1–18.

Pinto, D. 2000. *Eennieuwperspectief*, Amsterdam: Vossiuspers AUP.

Ramose, M. B. 2009. 'Ecology through Ubuntu,' In M. F. Murove (Ed.), *African Ethics: An Anthology of Comparative and Applied Ethics*, University of KwaZulu-Natal Press: South Africa.

Rutledge, P. B. 2011. Social Networks: What Maslow Misses. Retrieved August 12, 2015, from https://www.psychologytoday.com/blog/positively-media/201111/social-networks-what-maslow-misses-0.

Schacter, D. L., Gilbert, D. T., & Wegner, D. M. 2012. *Psychology* (Second Edition), Palgrave Macmillan: New York.

Sheneberger, K., & van Stam, G. 2011. Relatio: An Examination of the Relational Dimension of Resource Allocation, *Economics and Finance Review*, 1(4), 26–33.

Sommers, C. H., &Satel, S. 2005. *One Nation under Therapy: How the Helping Culture Is Eroding Self-Reliance*, St. Martin's Press: New York.

Tay, L., &Diener, E. 2011. Needs and subjective well-being around the world, *Journal of Personality and Social Psychology*, 101(2), 354–365.

Trancoso, S., Utratel, A. M., & James, G. (Eds.). 2015. *Commons Transition: Policy Proposals for an Open Knowledge Commons Society*, P2P Foundation: Brussels.

Trompenaars, F., & Hampden-Turner, C. 2011. *Riding the Waves of Culture: Understanding Cultural Diversity in Business* (Second Edition), Nicholas Brealey Publishing: London.

Unwin, T. 2008. On the richness of Africa. Retrieved August 29, 2011, from http://www.gg.rhul.ac.uk/ict4d/workingpapers/richness.pdf.

Van Stam, G. 2012a. 'Is Technology the Solution to the World's Major Social Challenges?' In *IEEE Global Humanitarian Technology Conference (GHTC 2012), 21-24 Oct 2012, Seattle, WA, USA*. IEEE.

Van Stam, G. 2012b. Oral Budgeting in rural Macha, Southern Province, Zambia. *Anthropological Notebooks*, 18(3), 41–46.

Van Stam, G. 2012c. *Towards an Africanised Expression of ICT*. (K. Jonas, I. A. Rai, & M. Tchuente, Eds.) *E-Infrastructures and E-*

Services on Developing Countries, 4th International ICST Conference (AFRICOMM 2012) 12-14 Nov 2012, Yaounde, Cameroon, Revised Selected Papers, Berlin, Heidelberg: Springer.

Van Stam, G. 2013. Information and Knowledge Transfer in the rural community of Macha, Zambia, *The Journal of Community Informatics*, *9*(1). Retrieved from http://ci-journal.net/index.php/ciej/article/view/871/979.

Van Stam, G. 2014. 'Ubuntu, Peace, and Women: Without a Mother, there is no Home,' In M. van Reisen (Ed.), *Women's Leadership in Peace-Building: Conflict, Community and Care*, Africa World Press: Trenton, New Jersey.

Van Stam, G., & van Greunen, D. 2014. Review of an African Rural Internet Network and related Academic Interventions, *The Journal of Community Informatics*, *10*(2). Retrieved from http://ci-journal.net/index.php/ciej/article/view/985/1095.

Wahba, M. A., & Bridwell, L. G. 1976. Maslov Reconsidered: A Review of Research on the Need Hierarchy Theory, *Organisational Behavior and Human Performance*, (15), 212–240.

Weijland, W. P. 2014. Mathematical Foundations for the Economy of Giving, *Cornell University Library*, Retrieved from http://arxiv.org/ftp/arxiv/papers/1401/1401.4664.pdf.

Chapter Four

Toxic and Hegemonic Education: "Development and Underdevelopment by Copying and Concealing"

Nkwazi Mhango

Introduction

> *"According to the unanimous testimony of the Ancients, first the Ethiopians and then the Egyptians created and raised to an extraordinary stage of development all the elements of civilization, while other people especially the Eurasians were still deep in barbarism,"* Amélineau cited in Diop, (1989).

It is not exaggeration to note that Africa –since the inception of colonialism –has been operating under wrong and misleading education. This can be seen on how Africa has been viewed as a backward continent full of miseries and dependence. All started when African education and ways of doing things were altered. Arguably, toxic and colonial education espoused by the West or our former colonial *masters* has ruined our lives. After over fifty years of political or flag independence, Africa has the duty to itself which is to deconstruct and decolonize the current regime of education in place. Africa is taught almost everything including things that it used to teach others such as interconnectedness, interdependence, equality and human rights. This cannot go on. African academics need to make their case. It boggles minds to note that Africa has always been recipient as if it is inhabited with brainless creatures. Maanga (2015) notes that:

> It is culturally and academically frustrating to see that some heroes and heroines in the African history are purposely left out in some historical accounts. Worse still, foreign writers and some brainwashed local historians blow trumpets of alien masters, sometimes at the expense of local champions (p.1).

What pains even more is the fact that when colonial monsters misconstrued, and thereby misrepresented Africa's history, they did so purposely by intentionally suppressing all beauties and truths found in the said history. Yet they came shamelessly calling their twisted history a body of knowledge while it actually was, and still is, a body of lies. Time for reclaiming Africa's robbed and lost glory has now arrived after some brave African academics embarked on the journey of self-reinvention. Mhango (2015) suggests that African academics should take on what he calls "foul-smelling trickery" of demonizing Africa.

This being said, this chapter aims at challenging other African academics to join hands and decolonize our education systems. It is from this drive that the author of this chapter invites all African academics from a range of disciplines to offer their expertise all aimed at academically emancipating Africa from intellectual dependence and *infancy;* if I may use the terms. Is it fair for example for Africans to be taught about humanity or human rights while they are the ones who practically showed Europeans how these two concepts work? Under the concept of Ubuntu, every human being was presumed to be a human regardless her or his race, gender or economic status. Didn't colonial monsters violate this philosophy when they enslaved and colonized Africans? Kunene (1996 cited in Makgoro, 1998) notes that, "Ubuntu is the very quality that guarantees not only a separation between men, women and the beast, but the very fluctuating gradations that determines the relative quality of that essence" (p. 2).

In this chapter, we are trying to show how Africa was not lagging behind as colonial monsters alleged after writing a pseudo history of Africa Maanga (op cit) notes. We seek to challenge the current grand narrative epistemologically as a catalyst of embarking on positive change aimed at emancipating Africa so as to contribute to the world's affairs instead of remaining a passive consumer. The major argument we make here is that knowledge is a God-given tool that enables any society to function in its own environment. So, deconstructing and decolonizing the current education regime is a sine qua non for African academics especially those who are conscious of the true meaning of education. Despite being a racist John Dewey noted an important thing. Dewey (2004) notes that "There is the standing danger that the material of formal instruction will be merely the subject matter of the schools, isolated from the subject matter of life- experience (p.13). Dewey underscored the weakness of the Western superimposed education to others. We can see this in global warming, arms race, conflict, exploitation, capitalism and colonialism. The writings are all over the place, so to speak. Nyerere (1967) poses a question, "'what kind of education?'… Rejected simplistic imitation of Western forms and levels of education, on the grounds of both limited economic resources and the different political economic contexts in which children were growing up (p. xi). This is very telling in terms of how our current education regime is wanting. Nyerere speaks from the practical point of view. Under his leadership, Tanzania tried to do away with colonial education with the aim of resolving the problem of colonially induced divisions and military coups in East Africa.

Aughey and Morrow (1996), Bloomfield (1996), Fitzduff (1996 cited in Byrne 2001) espouse the need of embarking on "education for mutual understanding, and prejudice reduction" [Sic] (p. 339) in addressing the problems of Northern Ireland. His aim is to effect "change in perception promoted by education and reconciliation have to proceed alongside structural reforms to prevent a return to dominant relationships" (Jeong, 2005, p.4). Arguably, this approach needs to be taken universally to address the anomaly in post-colonial era in former colonies whereby local elites have become a new group of colonizers or homegrown colonialists. Adeyimi & Adeyinka (2003) seem to concur with Byrne inveigling us to understand that education should be functional in the environment of those receiving it. They argue that, "With few exceptions, if any, traditional educational practices in pre-colonial Africa were predominantly utilitarian [...]. It was a participatory kind of education in which people learned through imitation, initiation ceremonies, work, play, oral literature etc. (p. 432). According to Adeyimi and Adeyinka, African education was more of problem-solving, and practicable than theoretical. And if you look at it critically you make sense of it. Why, for example, should one strive to know the type of the soil in the moon while he or she does not know her own body or the soil of her own planet and farm? The practicability and usefulness of utilitarian African education was evident in the fact that one person carried many function at one time. For example, an herbalist was the same doctor,

75

leader, artist and pharmacist whereby under Western education such roles need more than three people. One person would have knowledge of herbs, he or she would go to the forest to identify and collect them. Coming back home from the forest, the same person (African doctor) would process the herbs, prescribe and distribute them after listening to a sick person and do some diagnostic works. The same person would fully participate in other activities of the day. Also, for such multifaceted activities aimed at helping the society, African medicine people did not charge much as is the case currently yet many African skills were demonized and destroyed so as to force Africans to depend on expensive western medicines. Ironically, while Europe was groaning in diseases such as smallpox and bubonic plague, Africans with their despised education were so healthy that Europeans envied them and decided to enslave them on the basis that they were stronger than Europeans. There are many traditional healers who cure injuries especially bone fractures without taking any x-ray or metal gadgets. In Dar es Salaam, sometimes in 1990s people who were referred to orthopedists for amputation were smuggled out of hospitals to be cured by traditional healers in cases where western-trained expert doctors failed. Evidentially, such practices still prove how the utilitarian nature of Africa education practically works. Mawere (2011) notes that, "There is monumental literature by philosophers like David Hume, George W.F. Hegel, Immanuel Kant, Lucien Levy-Bruhl and Diedrich Westermann that describe Africans as 'tabula rasa', a people with no reason/rationality; hence without a history and worse still philosophy" (p.1). It nauseates and goads whoever comes across such nonsense not to mention how it boggles the mind, and abhors the rationale of the-called modernity –which, essentially, denotes Western ways of doing things –that keeps maintaining the same stance even when things have changed to empirically show that Africans had knowledge, science and philosophy just like any other community. Mhango (2015) argues that nobody can export knowledge to another. Instead, everybody can export and import some skills but not knowledge. He, too, goes further arguing that no society has its unique self-dependent skills. For, all societies on earth have been copying from; and lending some skills, science and technologies to each other since time immemorial.

African education

We argue that African education was based on the African environment, African culture and socialisation. This is because what Adeyimi and Adeyinka (Ibid)propose is what African education system used to be before the coming of colonial toxic education system that left Africans tarnished, confused and typically stereotyped as ignorant and backward. The above statements give us a clue of how African or *traditional* education (as it is sadly called) was, and the way it benefited the society. There was no joblessness or desperation for those who acquired this sort of education. African society did not have any prejudice with the colonialists when they arrived. Even when they butchered African education systems Africans did not immediately react with counter-violence. Instead, through what African societies thought would be mutual understanding; they welcomed colonialists and their ways. However, the double-faced colonialists did not reciprocate. Also, this testifies to the fact that wherever there are human beings there is knowledge however different it may seem from others. To understand how Africans functioned well before the introduction of colonialism and its toxic and hegemonic education, we need to firstly appreciate the fact that they had their ways of educating one another suitable to their needs, time, and environment. Thus, it is noteworthy to interrogate the type of education Africa had instead of denying, ignoring or oversimplifying its existence. African or *traditional* education system was intended deliver results quickly due to the needs of the time. I think to try to force African education system to look like Western is to miss a point given that the two societies lived in different environments and their needs and goals were different too as were their education systems. Even Muslim world's education from which Western education loaned was not the same as the latter. Bakari (1997) claims that:

Although much of African history had been passed down by oral traditions, there were many scripts which gave clues to ancient African epistemology. They included the three scripts of ancient Egypt: hieroglyphic, hieratic, and demotic; Meroitic and Coptic scripts of Nubia; Sabean and G'eez scripts of Ethiopia;

the Toma and Vai scripts of Liberia; and the Mum script of Cameroon (p.3).

True, African education system might have concentrated more on praxis than theories and written epistemological niceties, and of course, complexities to make it sound like or compete with the hegemonic Eurocentric one. Some people might wrongly translate education as the art of writing and reading only while it is more than that. However, this is not the case with many African societies. Despite the fact that there are some that had their own scripts as we will prove later, Africans –despite having scripts –did not espouse the art of writing as their only means of representing their views and knowledge due to cramming almost everything that was vital for their survive and livelihood. One would argue that Arabs had more advanced written knowledge than Europeans who scoped many inventions from them. Apart from Africans, other societies such as Eskimos did not institutionalize the use of written means of education and communication due to the way they kept their history and information as Irving (1953) note: "The Eskimo preserves his names without writing or museum to serve his memory" (p.35). For example, close-knit societies did not need writing skills or say to read identity card for its bearer to be recognized due to the fact that everybody knew everybody. Thus, identification was based on knowledge and connection of another than on carrying Identity cards which can be seen as a weird thing today. Again, if we ask ourselves why we have to carry identity cards, we might understand why other did not carry them. Firstly, with a small population, whereby everybody knows everybody, there was no need to have to carry an ID. Secondly, trust among people knowing one another is likely to be higher than big centres or cities where it is impossible to know all citizens. So, we need to appreciate that carrying IDs is not a sign of advancement but the necessity of time and lifestyle in a certain environment. Here the population dictates what to use for identification. Why should carrying and reading from IDs that can be read be viewed as advancement and education while being able to recognize almost all members of the society is not?

Interestingly, despite having no script, the same Eskimo were able to memorize and differentiate many things such as many names of snow whereas Westerners just call it snow? To me, having many names for the same things has some scientific underpinnings even if the said concept is not recorded anywhere except in the head and minds of the user. This is striking. Irving (1953) notes, "The Eskimo preserves his names without writing or museum to serve his memory" (p.35). You cannot underestimate such a people with such unwritten and complicated ways of keeping records. Martin (1986) was astounded to find that Eskimo have many words for snow as she notes, "Eskimo languages are credited with some variable number of unique words for snow and are compared to English, which has but one" (p.418). The same applies to types of birds whose names were associated with snow. Thus, she warned scientists not to force their conceptualization of the same birds onto Eskimos. Those were their birds living in their environment. They thus knew them well and nobody would teach them how to name them. However, just like Eskimo's naming of snow, "primitive" and "underdeveloped" African education systems as colonialists like to derogatory it –may be wrongly conceptualized, it still had some many important aspects that we cannot gainsay. It is argued that through their education, Africans were able to live peacefully without states as Lonsdale (1981:139) cited in Zartman (1994) notes, "Most Africans did not actually live in states until colonial rule fastened Leviathan's yoke upon them. Indeed the most distinctively African contribution to human history could be said to have been precisely the civilized art of living fairly peaceably together not in state" (p.62). Such argument makes sense given that the said states were superimposed on Africa and ended up dividing Africans. It is obvious that Lonsdale does not hide his ignorance about how African empires or kingdoms, and nations were made. Africans had their system of ruling based on kingdoms and communities all depending on what a society chose to govern itself. Education that can lead to peaceful life is more important than the one that leads to chaos and violence however "civilized" and "advanced" it may wrongly and arrogantly purport to be as the current hegemonic education is. However, Lonsdale wants to show how peaceable African societies were, he seems to still labour under the same colonial mentality of praising the state without underscoring the fact that the said state were superimposed on Africa. Lonsdale world view as far as states are concerned is hugely contorted and revolves around European concept of nation. Despite all weaknesses in Lonsdale's statement, he admits that Africans were peaceful before the coming of colonial monsters. Africans lived in nations which Europeans wrongly narrowed down to kingdom such as Mwenemutapa, Buganda, Bunyoro-Kitara, Asante, Songhay, Luba-Lunda and many more. To Africans, the so-called kingdoms by Europeans were but nations just like Queendoms like Britain and Holland are. It is sad that many academics fail to appreciate the concept of nation (among others) in African context compared to European one due to do undermine the orality of many African epistemological concepts. This is why we encourage African historians to document this history in order to bring to the fore many concepts African philosophy has that are not well known currently.

To do away with the current academic toxicity, rigidity and crudity, worthy education needs to dig deeper down history and come up with the true history of the world so that stereotyping of one society and another could be ended as means of creating equality and equity aimed at reducing tensions that degenerate cultural conflicts whose results have been the rise and surge of terrorism currently. It defeats the meaning of academia when one epistemological sources or setting is seen as better than or superior to others. Sometimes, it boggles the mind to find that half-baked and doctored findings such as despising and demonizing African history are accepted as researches while true research would not alter the findings. Instead, as per the rule, true research has to present the facts as found *mutatis mutandis* but not otherwise. You wonder to find that the so-called enlightened European elites are the same that called other civilizations uncouth or savages and whatnot something that has produced many conflicts especially after those originating from these cultures or societies realize the hoax behind the current history written by the current hegemonic grand narrative of the west that demonizes others especially Aboriginal people in various parts of the world. Such a desire to decolonize education system is especially indispensable now. In addressing this anomaly in this chapter we are going to use questions, storytelling and other means to show the importance and the needs of decolonising the current education.

To avoid being regarded as anachronistic or parsimonious, we will touch on both sides namely the colonizers and the colonized in order to forge a new and mutual relationship aimed at addressing this matter intellectually, truthfully, and honestly for the good of our world. More importantly, through decolonizing education, as practitioners, professionals and academics, we will be able to clearly and transparently deal with some ills especially in the areas not represented by the current educational regime as enacted by colonialists to suit their needs, interests and problems. We thus need to start by revisiting the history of the victims of colonial education. The decolonization of education gives us an impetus for seeing things the way they are instead of looking at them the way the lenses of toxic education dictate us to do. We will be able to see a clear picture of the conflict we want to address for the good of the whole world. We stand to learn from a new version of decolonized education. And this is important given that we will be able to erase all anomalies, bigotry, lies and fabrication the current regime has inculcated in many people especially its prescriptive nature as opposed to elective, utilitarian and observatory approaches under a new regime of decolonized education. Again, this is a challenge of its kind given that we are dealing with an established system posed to gain from its existence even if it means to achieve that through victimizing others as it has been the case since its introduction to the world. Normative as it may seem education needs to turn a page and focus on how to objectively treat those anomalies marring it due to its nature of drawing from many discipline which also are mudded by bigotry, lies, fabrication and stereotypical things as we will show later. We essentially will base our findings and questions on history among others. History will play a great role to prove the point that Indigenous people who were, and still are affected by the current regime of toxic education, indeed, had their own functioning systems based on their education. We understand that the current regime of education has failed due to the fact that it has created more problems than solutions. Such problems can be seen on many faces such as the increase of violence, poverty, exploitation, ecological degradation consumerism and whatnot. New deconstructed education based on the needs of all in the world, will be nourished by our desire to live in a just, equitable, equal and peaceful world. So, whatever is argued in this chapter, however it might be regarded or misconstrued, is aimed at finding the truth by facing reality in order to successfully make the case that might attract, provoke or make some feel guilty. In so doing, many African academics will create the need of embarking on the journey of decolonizing education as harbingers for decolonization of other fields shall it succeed.

African society before colonialism

Importantly, if we explore or consider African society before the coming of colonialism, we find that the society was functional thanks to this type of education. When we ponder on education, we need to avoid Western mentality-cum-tunnel vision of wanting everything to look the way they want or the way they perceive it. People have different lenses and understanding of things based on who they are and why they look at these things. Mountains for an Eskimo might have different meaning from an African living nearby huge and tall mountains such as Kilimanjaro, Kenya or Ruwenzori. The same applies to snow. As you can see, African education, as well as indigenous education in various areas, was utilitarian. It enabled the members of the respective societies to function in their environment swiftly according to the needs of the day. This is why colonial governments did not have to bother to bring workers or a contingent of experts to carry out their day-to-day function. If there was a lack of workers or people to carry on day-to-day business of the government, obviously, the colonial governments would have imported their workers from home countries. This did not happen, and it proves beyond any doubt that colonies had what it takes when it comes to deliver services. How did they produce such workers that made government function swiftly and normally if they were not educated? To say that Africans were not educated or enlightened is an insult. For, no people or society can function without knowledge. This is what differentiates humankind and animals. Dependence on colonially-trained workforce started during colonial era and went on even after African countries gained independence. Zvogbo (2006) argues that, "Colonial education systems in the developing world were designed during colonial times to support colonial capitalism. After independence few internal mechanisms have been put in place to ensure that genuine reforms occur in education," (p2).

If African education was unworthy or did not exist where did such people acquire their education and skill? This speaks volume as far as competence and applicability of their knowledge and education were. How could colonial governments bother to bring their workers while indigenous were there to carry on all types of jobs that made colonial governments function well? Sadly though, this is not appreciated. This was done – *sui generis* and deliberately in order to undermine traditional education system to sound as if it did not exist, and if it did, it was irrelevant and useless. How would colonial governments appreciate and credit such an African system that saved them money and time that would be spent on importing workers in foreign lands out of Europe while it even failed to appreciate an already advanced system of education in their colonies? Lanning and Mueller (1979) note in their book *Africa Undermined* that Africa was technologically at par with others in some areas. They disclose:

> For many centuries before the arrival of Europeans, minerals were produced in Africa by Africans for Africans. The scale of techniques of mining and metal working were clearly comparable with those both in Europe and in the great Eastern civilizations of India and China – until towards the end of the seventeenth century (p. 27).

Also see Parrinder and Parrinder (1976) who prove how Africa was morally and religiously ahead of other societies. Lanning and Mueller note that when Dr. David Livingstone arrived in Africa, he was stunned to find that iron technology in Mozambique was way far more advanced than Britain's whose products of iron seemed "rotten" comparably. Where did this go and who felled it? Again, if the most "civilized" nation of the world Britain, at the time, admits this, how will it lead others in its deceit evidenced in colonialism and colonization? Ironically, despite its backwardness, African traditional education did not endorse crimes such as colonialism, exploitation and environmental abuses. What of the Western "advanced" education? The history of colonialism, slavery and neocolonialism speaks volume everywhere and elsewhere.

Britain that had many colonies, for example, is renowned for not appreciating others. This lugubrious behaviour did not only apply to

Africa but also others including her European cousins in Northern Ireland. Britain will nary admit that Northern Ireland was as developed as Britain was before it invaded and occupied it. If you want to kill a dog just give it a bad name. Indeed, colonial academy did not only give Aboriginal people a bad name but also demonized them in every aspect mainly on their education system as pillar of their knowledge. As if that was not enough, it gave them toxic education that perpetuated colonialism even after the colonial masters left the colonies. They were called savages, barbarians and all bad names just because of their ways of life, culture and – of course – their land. If this is not corrected, identity-based conflict are likely to emanate from them especially at this time Africans and other Aboriginal people are more aware of chicanery than immediately after colonialism.

The straw that broke camel's back for Africa came when the colonizers decided to disingenuously write their history as a way of telling their stories. In telling the story of pre-colonial Africa and other colonized areas, colonial writers and spin doctors – no doubt – purposely ignored the contribution Africans made in their continent. Such has been the plight of almost all Aboriginal people in the world. For example, it took time for the United States to admit that it learned the art of confederacy from Aboriginal people of Americas who used this system to rule themselves as sign of democratic system. History has it that the confederacy we evidence today in Canada and the US were copied from Iroquois. "The standard works on the American constitution and the articles of confederation do not credit American Indians with having contributed to their origins" (Payne 1996, p. 605). Despite hiding and avoiding this reality, it is still there. If there is anything hegemonic and toxic colonial education is good at is none other than copying and concealing that it copied such toxic education is good at demonizing others as it glorifies itself. Amélineau cited in Diop (1989) notes:

> I then realized, and realized clearly, that the most famous Greek systems, notably those of Plato and Aristotle, had originated in Egypt. I also realized that the lofty genius of the Greeks had been able to present Egyptian ideas incomparably, especially in Plato; but I thought that what we loved in the

Greeks, we should not scorn or simply disdain in the Egyptians. Today, when two authors collaborate, the credit for their work in common is shared equally by each. I fail to see why ancient Greece should reap the entire honor for ideas she borrowed from Egypt (n.p).

Diop (Ibid) goes on saying, "According to the unanimous testimony of the Ancients, first the Ethiopians and then the Egyptians created and raised to an extraordinary stage of development all the elements of civilization, while other people especially the Eurasians were still deep in barbarism" [Sic](n.p).

Consecutive American governments tried to conceal it for years but they lastly decided to come out of the closet and admit how they copied confederation science from Aboriginal people of Americas they used to refer to as savages. Who is actually savage between the one who copied and concealed and the one who allowed another to copy and share? I am wondering. What if this type of governance that Aboriginal people of the Americas used was continued without interference? Maybe, many conflicts resulting from the aped-confederacy and constitutions would not have occurred. Maybe the US would not have participated in dirty politics all over the world. Maybe the US would not have perpetrated and supported apartheid for many years. Maybe, the world would have more security and democracy today than it currently has. Why don't we go back and scavenge what is left to see how it can help us to forge ahead in decolonizing the current Eurocentric education system?

It is only in Africa where the mummified bodies that have endured the punishment of the element for thousands of years are found in Egypt. King Tut is a living example of how Africa was advanced scientifically. Remember king Tut ruled Egypt before it was conquered by modern times Arabs who destroyed the nose of the mummies in order to erase African heritage. Those who deem Africa uncivilized tried to *arabize* everything that has to do with ancient civilization in Egypt. Again, they forgot one fact that pyramids were not only in Egypt. The Encyclopaedia of Ancient Myths and Culture (2003) notes that "there are in fact remains of about 80 pyramids in Egypt, while there are well over 100 later, less substantial ones in the Sudan," (p.512) not to mention the great houses of stones of

Zimbabwe. Essentially, Western science scooped from Egypt so as to come up with temporal embalmment that cannot be equated with the mummification of Egypt. So, too, you can look at how Africa helped others especially the current hegemonic regime of knowledge. No standing building whatsoever today can scientifically be equated with the pyramids. Western science scooped from Egypt so as to come up with temporal embalmment that cannot be equated with the mummification of Egypt. So, too, you can look at how Africa helped others especially the current hegemonic regime of knowledge. No standing building whatsoever today can scientifically be equated with the pyramids.

According to the Independent, 22 October 2011, AlKaraouine in Fez, Morocco – founded in 859 AD and considered the world's oldest, continually-operating university, and Cairo's Al Azhar University (975 AD), were established in Africa and they are predated by a Buddhist university of Nalanda. And this is not the end of Africa's footprints on science. The Egyptian pyramids and the mummies in them are another stunning mystery that up till now has never been solved. Arguably, there is no modern-scientifically advanced building on earth that is at par with the pyramids. So, too, the chemicals that were applied on the mummies have never been deciphered. Belmonte (2001) notes that "Hieroglyphic in the tombs of nobles and workmen offers little information about the pyramids themselves, about how they were built, or about the corpus of beliefs surrounding it" (p. 4). Essentially, the pyramids are still mythological and cosmological wonders to the modern world of advanced science. What makes these pyramids a hard nut to crack for modern scientists is the fact that there is no evidence of whatever type of machinery that used to mount mega blocks of rocks on top of one another. As for the mummies, Smith (1914) urges that:

> Egyptian practices of embalming influenced the history of European medicine and European customs in manifold ways; to mention only one instance, by familiarizing the popular minds through twenty centuries with the idea of cutting the human body, Egypt made it possible for Greek physicians of Ptolemaic ages to begin for the first time the systematic dissection of human

body, with popular prejudice forbade in all other parts of the world (p.190).

Smith (Ibid) goes on saying that Egypt "exerted the most profound influence not only upon the development of anatomic knowledge, but provided foundations upon which fabric of modern science has been built,"(p.190). Those accusing Africa of being backward scientifically without underscoring such findings must have their knowledge and motives called to question. Brandt-Rauf and Brandt-Rauf (1987) cite Kahun, Edwin Smith, Ebers, Hearst, Erman, London, Berlin, and Chester Beatty who note that there are eight major ancient Egyptian medical papyri or volumes dating from 1900BCE to c 1200BCE (p.68). Ironically, those papyri are given European names but not Egyptian or African names to show how European scientists and historians are good at copying without offering any attribution to the original authors of the volumes. Brandt-Rauf and Brandt-Rauf (Ibid) note that behind those stunning discoveries there was one of African famous scientists and administrator, Imhotep whom Risse (1986) calls, "the first figure of physician to stand clearly out from the mists of antiquity" (p. 622). Here we are talking about Imhotep, a scientist. There are famous writers who helped Romans to conquer the world such as Quintus Septimius Florens Tertullianus, St. Augustine of Hippo (jus bellum iustum), to mention but a few. Arguably, Western countries did not only copy from Africa and other ancients civilization that predate Western one but robbed them as Bidgood argues that , "These artefacts and products are now deposited in the Economic Botany Collections of the Royal Botanic Gardens, Kew, UK together with plant-based handiwork from all over the world" (p.311; Also see, Gates Jr, 1999).

African science and philosophy

When it comes to how African science created things, Horton comes up with a stunning argument to indicate that even modern religions copied from African philosophy and the view of the origin of the world. Horton (1967) notes that:

A central characteristic of nearly all the traditional African world-views we know of is an assumption about the power of words, uttered under appropriate circumstances, to bring into being the events or states they stand for. The most striking examples of this assumption are to be found in creation mythologies where the Supreme Being is said to have formed the world out of chaos by uttering the names of all things in it (p.157).

Ironically, when foreign religions came with the same idea they copied from Africa about the creation. If you take the Bible, and the Quran, for example, you find that there is nothing new in their theology. This is why they used swords and crusades to spread their religions. They know there was nothing new Africans did not know about their faiths. When I consider Genesis, 1:1 or the Quran Surat 41, verses 9 to 12. The Genesis 1:1 says, "In the beginning God created the heavens and the earth." The Quran Surat 41 says, "Do you verily disbelieve in Him Who created the earth in two Days? And you set up rivals with Him? That is the Lord of all that exists." The distinction I find is that African God was unique in the sense that there was no reference based on gender creation. African God is neither he nor she.

Another evidence to substantiate that Africa was not impotent and backward as the grand narrative has maintained is the fact that when invaders arrived in Africa and other places they claimed to conquer, they found that there were organized, and partly in some places had advanced empires, states and institutions which fiercely resisted the occupation. This is why colonialists had to depend on weapons, lies, pitting people against others to succeed. Education was for practical purposes based on the environment one faced in his or her day-to-day life. Education was for self-reliance and self-actualization as a society. African education was about humanity that allowed Africans to trust colonialists they thought were as civilized and trustworthy as Africans were. Indeed, this type of education was more helpful, multipurpose, and more practical than colonial one. Africans used to learn about their environment and the way they could utilize it well and peacefully and function well as they did before the coming of colonial monsters. Practically, Africans were educated, and their education enabled them to function without depending on other countries like it is currently due to the introduction of toxic western education aimed at subduing and exploiting them. Freeman-Grenville (1957) notes that, "since 1955 the writer has had access to, or obtained information of, thirty-two unpublished hoards, site finds, and private collection of coins of medieval times and earlier, found in Tanganyika, Zanzibar, Pemba and Kenya" (p.151). What evidence will one need more than this to substantiate that assertion that Africa was uncivilized, underdeveloped and backward is but malicious and a hoax aimed at undermining her so that she can lack self-confidence, and thus, submit herself for West to exploit as the current grand narrative maliciously and wrongly espouses through Eurocentric education?

Before the coming of invaders, African societies were divided in administrative strata whereby every member of the society had the role to play in the society and his or her contribution was appreciated. There was no chaos or vacuum at all save the existence of normal competitions among states. For instance, in Asante, Buganda, Mwenemtapa and elsewhere, some well advanced and strong empires were in existence and their interests basically were to equally trade with the foreigners thanks to having many resources such as timber, minerals and animal products. You cannot call such people or societies backward or underdeveloped. If these empires were underdeveloped or backward –as Western historians and thinker like to assume – then there would not have been anything whatsoever for Western invaders to benefit from or do with such societies. When they came to Africa – for example – they found that some skills and institutions such as iron smelting, salt making, cloth making, and bargaining (business management) had already taken shapes for many decades if not centuries. How were Africans – for example –able to trade with India, China and Middle East before doing so with Europe if they were such underdeveloped and backward if we face it?

However "primitive" –as it is always referred to –such an education system enabled African to live without depending on handouts and loans from the so-called developed countries whose development resulted from exploiting and plundering Africa wantonly. Arguably, uncontaminated and self-reliant Africa –of that time –was better than the ever-dependent African of today. The major questions one can ask are: How much wealth did colonial thieves plunder from Africa for all decades they colonized her. How much land did settlers grab from Aboriginal people of Americas and Australia? How many innocent people –who opposed the whole project –were killed and how much would they have contributed to the wellbeing and development of their people and the world in general? How much energy was sapped from colonized people so as to make colonial master colossally rich? Again, one may wonder. What does this have to do with decolonization of education? If we critically explore the milieu of conflicts Africa faces today, we will agree that most of them are about the distribution, and possibly, redistribution of resources. Many African countries found themselves facing civilian wars based on the distribution of resources as it currently is in the Democratic Republic of Congo (DRC) where many violations of human rights have been going on for long time. Though passive as it may seem or kept under the carpet, all the same, many conflicts existing currently in Canada are about land disputes between the Aboriginal people and settler government. The case is clear that the distribution of resources has become a very good source of conflict in Africa. This becomes a case due to the fact that most of elite group colonial education produced –that is in power – has either embarked on dividing people along class and other vices, corruption and unfair distribution of resources or kept supervising the interests of colonial masters in their countries. Berman (1998) argues that:

> The accumulating weight of evidence shows that African ethnicity and its relationship to politics is new, not old: a response to capitalist modernity shaped by similar forces to those related to the development of ethnic nationalism in Europe since the late nineteenth century, but encountered in distinct African and colonial circumstances (p. 308; Also, see Posner 2005).

Berman argues that colonialism introduced what he calls the 'politics of the belly' (ibid 309) whereby "ethnicity" as social constructed to suit the division of Africans so that they could be used by the colonizers easily without spending much money on army or security apparatuses. This culminated in the introduction of 'divide and rule' championed by Lugard in modern Nigeria. Lugard wrote an influential book The Dual Mandate in British Tropical Africa (1922) whose policies seem to be an extension of Pale Ireland that was totally rejected so as to be exported to Africa where it worked well for the benefit of British colonialists (Christopher 1988, p. 233). One would ask: Why Africans accepted this rule if they were united? No society is made of angels or devils. Africa, at that time, had her own baggage resulting from normal day-to-day relationship based on competition. Essentially, the urge for commerce had a lot to do with the colonization almost all over the world even if for Africans trusting foreigners uncritically is the major cause of their miseries resulting in colonialism. Desire for trade is the same in the Americas even Asia. People wanted new item such as guns and other belongings they deemed fit for their consumption or use. So, when the colonial monsters came to Africa exploited this weakness the same way they did wherever they colonized. Remember. Before the coming a full-fledged colonial government, missionaries, explorers and traders had already spied the continent so as to put her under the influence of their home or mother governments that paid for all explorations. Therefore, it must be understood, Africa and other countries that were colonized, not because of their candour or disorganization. It was because of competition that existed among empires and societies. This is a normal thing. First of all, when colonizers came, Aboriginal people trusted them thinking they were well intended the same way they were. They welcomed generously and humanely everybody who visited them hoping that their guests would reciprocate equally and humanely. Sadly though, the people thought would be like them ended up being different. Apart from betraying their trust, the newcomers abused, misused, and violated the generosity and goodwill that were extended to them. Funny enough, this abuse based on better-than-thou mentality has been going even after colonialism. Remember. Indigenous societies did not practice any form of racism save for those who seemed to go against the norms of the society were reprimanded and regarded as an anomaly. This is why when shrewd and corrupt colonialists, missionaries, merchants and explorers came to those areas were accorded warm welcome thinking they were like their hosts. Therefore, Africans extended their warmly welcome to their guests hoping that they would do business and establish strong ties for the benefit of both parties. Just like modern governments like to invite investors, African states of that time did the same. Kelsall (2008) notes, "Before the arrival of Europeans the African continent was home to a rich diversity of political formations, out of which, with some caveats, a broad evolutionary pattern of increasing complexity and scale can be discerned" (p. 225). If African "traditional" education was primitive and premature as many Western spin doctors allege, how would she be able to establish such complicated systems of administration as Kelsall underscores? Ironically, up till now, whenever a foreigner goes to Africa, is more welcome than an African going to foreign countries. When I look at how Africans and other immigrants risking their lives to reach Europe that exploited them so as to become rich, I re-conceptualize how the situation was when colonial agents came to Africa. I see an antithesis to Africa's and other Aboriginal people's true generosity and upholding of human rights and equality. Kelsall makes a strong case to prove that Africa was organized in complex empires that knew the concept of commerce and international relations.

African administrational successful story

However African empires or administrational institutions those empires had, they functioned well. Arguably Buganda and Kitara kingdoms (as they were then known) were highly advanced compared to some European fragmented territories. Johannssen (2006) notes that:

> At the time the first Europeans arrived in East- Africa, the Buganda kingdom had a well-developed government. Not only did this create a strong attachment between the king and his people, but the Buganda kingdom also maintained a strong position towards the other regional kingdoms in the area" (p.2).

This speaks volume vis-à-vis the Dark Continent and all other garbage thrown at Africa as far as civilization and advancement are concerned. The kingdoms of Africa, as Johannssen argues, were mature and advanced enough so as to have all institutions we see today. They had their high courts, parliament, armies, ministries of various affairs, and above all, awareness of the existence of other kingdoms they traded and cooperated with. Bourdillon (1991: 13 cited in Nhemachena 2014) discloses why such kingdoms were successful noting, "Yet scholars writing about Africa have argued that a picture of the pre-colonial period as feuding chaos is incorrect as there were networks of trading links which could only have been possible in a situation of some stability, "(p.19). Nhemachena (Ibid) shows how African kingdoms resolved conflicts. These kingdoms were advanced. Even when the first missionaries arrived in Uganda they were mesmerized by the orderliness and advancement so as to equate the king of Baganda (Kabaka) with their godly Adam as Green (2010) notes:

> Especially since the 1760s, when the then Kabaka created a new initiation rite brought Kintu more prominence, Kintu has held a prominent place among the Baganda as both the mythical first man – early missionaries had no problem equating him with Adam of the Genesis story – and as the first Muganda" (p.5).

You cannot call such a person who boggled the minds of missionaries savage, uneducated or unenlightened otherwise you must include other white savages who equated this king with their Adam. What difference is there as far as the concept of kinghood is concerned between Buganda and Great Britain whose first rulers (The house of Stuart) came to power in 1707-1714? Remember. We are talking about Buganda where, according to Du Bois (1947) the first primitive stone tools known as pebble tools were found earlier than any place on earth (p.89).

Another point that proves the existence of organized states with their education machinery is the fact that many African countries were colonized after signing agreements. There is no way one can sign an agreement without having representatives or knowledge to understand at least the process regardless whether it was right or wrong. However in many areas Africans did not know the contents of the said agreements, at least they were aware of a foreign way of entering agreement. The detriment of this action was the fact that written agreements were foreign things to Africans. This is why in conflict resolution, prescribing signing the agreement after mediation can sound colonial to some communities especially whose freedom was robbed by colonialism. Again, by not using written agreements for African societies, it should not override the fact that some African societies –just like any others in Europe –had their scripts as indicated above. Signing agreement re-traumatizes those whose lands were taken through written agreements. These former victims are always suspicious of those who invite them for written agreements.

Colonialism is essentially a violent project. It repressed where it should have fostered, tamed instead of inspired and enervated rather than strengthened. It succeeded in making slaves of its victims, to the extent that they no longer realize they are slaves, with some even seeing their chains of victimhood as ornamental and the best recognition possible (Nyamnjoh 2012: 3).

Apart from being a violent project, colonialism was an exploitative and degrading project that superimposed its ego, altered some realities and fabricated some information to suite its agenda. In fact, colonialism was crime beyond robbery or piracy. For, colonial governments used weapons to rob from Aboriginal or Indigenous people. They robbed everything for many years wantonly. They robbed them almost everything including their story and history. Colonialism through using its toxic education committed all sorts of crimes from theft; murder to genocide in some places such as Namibia and Rwanda where the seeds it left behind –through toxic education, of course – led to the 1994 genocide. If one can summarize colonialism, I think it is supposed to be referred to as a crime against humanity. The right thing –if African countries had united strategic plans –is nothing but to force all who benefited from colonialism to redress those they colonized. So, too, colonialism may be referred to as a crime against environment due to the fact that it contributed a lot on destroying traditional ways of preserving environment by introducing an environmental-degrading system we currently are facing based on its toxic education that promotes individualism and consumerism instead of addressing environmental problems. This is where the shortfalls of the so-called modern education can be vividly seen. It was able to use its advanced science to produce chemicals that are now making the land barren in many places not to mention experimental machines that are now polluting our world. Colonialism through its toxic education is the causal root of many conflicts we evidence currently in former colonies. It created a turmoil which ended in a quagmire whose prolongation is basically conflicts evidenced in many former colonies. For example, the whole colonial period in some countries evidenced illegal introduction of new people in the populations of the colonies. In East and South Africa, for example, Indians were brought purposely to sabotage Africans, and they were made to believe that they were better than Africans based on their race.

British racist tendency is known all over the world. Hurlbert (2011) notes, "the assimilation of non-European [in Canada] was immigrants was considered a much greater problem because they were deemed to be racially inferior to White people" (p.101). Hurlbert argues that racism still exists in Canada and those suffering are Aboriginal people and immigrants. Again, who sowed this seed of racism? The answer is simple, British colonial government. Linking this to Indians in East Africa British racist regime made them middle men in almost everything as noted, "[f]or Africans, Indians were the shopkeepers on the other side of the counter who bought low and sold high, extracting African wealth between the margins" (Burton, n.y: 6). The "middlemanship" mentioned here is not the normal one we all know. It is a superimposed role aimed at exploiting one community as it is carried on by another community to benefit colonial economies. Indians were brought by British colonial government purposely to exploit and discriminate against Africans. Bocock (1971) notes that, "Most of the Indians in Tanzania came after 1918 when Tanganyika was put under British administration after the defeat of Germany, who had formerly ruled the territory," (p.367). Here we can trace the origin of the coming of Indian immigrants to Tanganyika (thereafter referred to The United Republic of Tanzania after union of Tanganyika and Zanzibar in 1964). Despite being brought to carry on economic sabotage –as it was in other African countries including South Africa – Indians went on staying in the country after it acquired her independence in 1961. The new government accepted them as Tanzanians however, they still maintained cultural and colour exclusion and seclusion altogether. Essentially, British project of exporting people to other countries was not only practiced in Africa. Based on their exploitative and toxic education, British destroyed many societies by displacing people. In India subcontinent, Tamils were exported to modern Sri Lanka which evidenced many decade civil wars between Tamils and Sinhalese who regard themselves as the right owners of the country. So, it can be said that the exportation of populations during British colonial era has created many conflicts up till now. So what can we do to address this situation? I think we need to encourage the differing sides to integrate and regard others like human beings like themselves, admitting that what makes them fight is not their fault but that of the colonizers especially through toxic education. To go on discriminating, segregating and fighting one another is in itself a colonial legacy-cum-mentality they are supposed to fight.

After independence, there has been existing tensions between these newcomers brought by colonial masters. Since they were brought – in most cases – they (Indians) have lived a secluded life as it was started by their masters. They are – up till now – regarded as the most racists on earth, even more than their masters. It is easy – for instance – in Dar es Salaam the biggest and multicultural city of Tanzania to see African and European couples but not a single Indian and African couple despite living together for generations. Due to toxic education, despite the said people being the citizens, still discriminate against their hosts whom they blackmailed and exploited in conjunction with their masters. Bocock notes this anomaly that, "Many of the norms and folkways surrounding marriage among the Khoja Ismailis are derived from their membership of a caste," (ibid). Bocock goes on observing that these Ismailis can marry non-Isamils provided that the children born in this marriage become Ismailis. Again, this non-Ismail can be anybody except an African. Is it the same mentality of avoiding Africans for fear of diluting Indian purity? For even the situation in South Africa has been the same ever since prominent people like Mahatma Ghandi stood against apartheid system not to defend all south Africans but his colleagues Indians who were brought by British colonial government in 1860. Bocock observes:

In Tanzania, as elsewhere in East Africa, the Khoja Ismailis are a clearly identifiable community, living in their own Ismaili housing estates in a city like Dar es Salaam, and are among the wealthiest groups and the most modern in outlook" (ibid 368).

To know how the relationship based on colour purity assumption is in east Africa – and possibly –Africa as a whole looks like currently, this quote may tell it well, "In Tanzania, if they could, they would throw them out like they did in Uganda. In Madagascar, if they could, they would throw them out … In China, they hate them …South Africa. They don't like them," (Shupak, p. 108). Although Shupak's observation can be taken lightly even ignored, it still tells that something is not well whether we like or not. In other words, Shupak avoids living in a state of denial; instead, he faces it so that we can appreciate that there is a conflict resulting from racism and exclusion that needs us to take some measures to manage it. These are the things right education need to address but not create and condone as it was for colonial education. If anything, such conflicts – however they may be ignored – are likely to cause problems in the future. As professionals and academics, it is easy to state categorically that we need to address the issue of racism and doing so must be embedded in the type of education we offer to our people. Racism is likely to be a good source of conflict especially in poor countries were those dispossessed will take on those privileged as it once happened in Uganda when Idi Amin expelled Indians in 1972 as the then disgruntled Ugandans cheered him despite his act being inhumane.

Essentially, Amin exploited the weakness of racism and already pent-up hatred against Indians to expel them. In 1990s in neighbouring Tanzania there arose a politician who instigated Africans to kill Indians if Britain and India would not take them so that their blood would reach India and awaken their colleagues. He called Indians gabacholi or thieves. Such fissure is noted, "In Tanzania, however, political elites have been and remain divided over whether to use civic exclusion of the Asian racial minority as a means of fostering national unity among the 'black majority," (Aminzade 2003, p.44). Aminzade goes on tracing the nexus of racism in Tanzania observing, "racial inequality in Tanzania is rooted in decades of racist British colonial policy that constituted Asians" (ibid 46). There is no way British colonial can deny its role in sowing the seeds of racism which, at any time, may result into conflict in many

African countries where Indians still discriminate against their hosts. African education would not have allowed such a relationship. Ask the current education based on materialism what it says about such racism. It is likely to be silent due to the fact that it has thrived based on abusing and discriminating others as it is in the case of writing pseudo history of Africa by colonialists. Slowly, this move went under. Again, what is an upshot of this? In the near future, far-right parties will win many elections in Africa just as anti-immigration and ultranationalist parties are doing in Europe currently. I argue that the difference is that in Africa chaos will be inevitable thanks to tribalism, ethnicity and all sorts of division colonial masters introduced through their education and administration. This is obvious given that most of elites such education produced are not well educated in humanity but in materialism and selfishness. One may argue that this is why Africa has always remained corrupt and poor even after acquiring independence over fifty years ago.

Decolonizing current education

Another example, we currently are evidencing a section of population in Western countries aligning with terror and fundamentalist groups after either being discriminated against or marginalized. This cannot go on without academics doing something. From this tenet, I postulate that we should embark on starting programs especially designed to cover and tackle racism in order to avoid conflicts resulting from this crime of racism. This can be achieved through decolonizing education. So, for African scholars especially, practitioners and stakeholders in particular to address such colonial settings may help to reduce the tensions even to avert future conflicts based on race or ethnicity. This can only be done through decolonizing education regime we currently have all over the world that has always sought to nourish and support the colonial status quo sui generis. We need to avoid special treatments to one group as opposed to others. The other day I was reading about the role of civil society, and, as a Western concept, if it must be exported to Africa. I found that the history of civil society is hand in hand with the "modernization of economy" (Paffenholz 2010, p.4) which is lacking in Africa. So, too, I noticed that traditional African civil societies that used to carry the same role of taking on the high and the mighty were excluded in defining them as civil society. Again, when it came to Asia vis-à-vis the same concept, Paffenholz notes, "Asian values are unique, thereby making Western concept of civil society less applicable in Asia," (ibid 13), unique to what? Aren't African values unique too? Is this why – for instance – British colonialists brought Indians to Africa because they were special as they still think and feel in some countries? Paffenholz goes on saying that, "Under colonial regimes, civil society organized mostly along lines of ethnicity and religion—thus the philanthropic engagement by Buddhist groups in Myanmar, Christian groups in the Philippines, and Muslim groups in Indonesia and Malaysia," (ibid pp. 13-14). Is the argument that one can make is why African civil society excluded? Is it because of being African or what if at all almost all African civil society was organized around ethnicity? Is it excluded because it lacks the element of "appointed" or neo-religions? We need the type of education that can take on such mentalities and deconstruct them.

The same treatments can be seen on the way the West deals with dictators in Asia and Middle East compared to Africa. Dictatorship becomes an issue in Africa but not in China, or other Middle East dictatorships. Why? Isn't this racism done systematically in the international community? The decolonization of education seeks to fully and trustworthily address such anomalies in order to avoid avoidable conflicts in the world. Isn't this systemic and structural violence in the international superstructure?

Essentially, colonial education imposed what Plato would call, "ill-structured teaching situation" (Rud 1997, p.7), (which inflicted inexplicable disability in the heads of its recipients). Under "social cubism" Byrne and Carter (1996) colonialism altered the life of the people in colonies demographically, economically, politically, religiously, historically and psycho-culturally. In doing so, colonial education system represented Aboriginal people as hallow and inept.

In the psyche and conceptual framework of the colonizers the colonized people had nothing intellectual whatsoever to offer. This is sad and bad. The role of colonized people was only to receive whatever colonial education system offered without even the right to question however bad it was. This reminds us how Aboriginal people and their ways were referred to as barbaric and pagan. It reached at the point where people were afraid and ashamed of using their vernacular language, and their names altogether. Some were denied the right to use their medicines. Their ways were abused and their land defecated on. Sadly, such anomalies went on unabated for many years so as to leave behind irreparable and disastrous effects on Aboriginal people. In destroying the wellbeing of Aboriginal people, colonial education made sure that everything was altered and doctored. The economies of Aboriginal people were invaded and toppled while their political institutions were banned or replaced by colonial governments. Their natural and true religions were replaced by the introduction of Christianity and Islam. Their names were abolished through baptismal or conversion. Their history was rewritten to favour the narratives of colonizers full of lies and fabrications. According to some authors, Africans were not supposed to be part of foreign religions. Barkun (1990) notes that "Blacks, according to Wesley Swift, were part of Lucifer's rebellion against God, serving as troops transported to earth "from other planets in the Milky Way," (124). Had all Africans understood such doctrines and rationales, it obviously becomes difficult to know how they would react.

A history written by a victor in the game of deceit will of course demonize or demean the loser. This is how the history of Aboriginal People was misrepresented to suit the needs of the victor. In so doing, colonial masters and their agents who masked themselves under religion made sure that they destroyed everything worthwhile so as to keep on exploiting and abusing their victims. When it comes to psycho-cultural wellbeing of Aboriginal people, colonial masters made sure that they robbed everything that gave them an identity and sense of uniqueness. They changed the names of their hallmarks such as lakes, rivers and mountains. They also changed their names through Christianization of Islamization. They banned them from using their names. They saw to it that the true identity of Aboriginal people is lost so as to carry artificial and colonial one. It was a disaster so to speak. By changing their identity, Aboriginal people ended up with a pseudo identity that would not help to identify themselves as they did before. Through religion and education, Aboriginal people lost almost everything including their value as human beings. Instead of identifying themselves as who they truly were, they started identifying themselves as Christian, Muslims, British, French,

Portuguese and Spanish all depending on who colonized them politically or religiously. Other colonial masters went as far as dictating to their victims who were their siblings and whom they should associate with. Ironically, when I remember how many times I heard the word Paris in Congolese music, I know how they sing more Paris than their places. This is why today in Africa, for example, there have been scuffles between Muslims and Christian who are naturally brothers and sisters. They subscribed to artificial and new colonial identities so as to end up hating one another wantonly and pointlessly. Such hatred and confusion are causing a lot of unnecessary conflicts between the two. This move aimed at blinding Africans from not asking essential questions after suffering gravely under colonialism, slavery and imperialism such as: Why didn't our torturers see us as brothers and sisters when they sold us to slavery or colonized us? Why are we equal today after you have exploited, sold, abused and misused us? Such a danger can be experienced, for instance, when African countries meet at the African Union conferences. When they need to do something, or appoint an official for certain role, they find themselves divided along colonial lines namely Anglophone or francophone lines. Currently, there is another danger emanating from religious background whereby Christians and Muslims compete in the making of the constitutions of their countries. Had our education been overhauled, such a people would appreciate that what connects them naturally is bigger than their religions or colonial identities. Academic toxicity can be seen almost in everything former colonies do. Take, for example, the current crop of African elites especially rulers. To them, better education for them and their offspring is in their colonial masters' countries. Recently, even African terrorist groups pledged their allegiances to Arab terrorist groups but not vice versa! This shows a dire need of overhauling our education system in order to suit our needs and values instead of being good consumers of toxic and foreign doctrines.

I evidenced cultural rot resulting from the introduction of divisive foreign religions when Kenya was writing her new constitution. Muslims wanted Kadhi Courts (Islamic courts) to be enshrined in the constitution while Christians refused. The situation is the same in neighbouring Tanzania which is writing her new constitution. In all these two scenarios, nowhere the citizenry is agitating for something African or traditional. This is because they have already lost their identities thanks to colonial education and religions so as to see one another as an obstacle that needs to be fought. They have created what Byrne and Irvin (2001) call "enemy image" (p.44) which serves as an impetus for more enmity and division wantonly. Instead of becoming a "community of fate" (ibid 10) they end up becoming "enemies of fate" (my own). Instead of fighting for better constitutions, the citizenry end up haggle over things that would not address their true identities and needs. Sometimes, such confusion ends up producing radicals from both sides. Christian-Muslim divide is a very good example of how colonial-sired hatred would be entrenched in the society so deeper that the protagonists think about destroying one another instead of reconciling. Try to imagine. If the duo were truly religious in African sense, no way they would hate one another this way. What do you expect of Christians and Muslims whose doctrines are always in a collision course? Again, aren't they all Africans and sometimes from the same communities in the same country? Much time and money are spent on unnecessary differences instead of working together to address other issues that impact them equally such as economics and politics. Politicians on their part seize this opportunity to plant a seed of division. Kenya evidenced such a sharp and dangerous division that culminated in the 2007/2008 chaos that left hundreds dead. Even on 3rd April 2015 when al-Shabaab, a Somalia-based terrorist group, attacked Garissa University, about 147 Christian students were separated from Muslims and were shot at point blank. Such chaos erupts; apart from tarnishing the image of the country in question destabilizes its economy. Again, when this happens, the same colonizers who sowed the seed of division and mistrust either come in as mediators or just laugh at them so as to come and teach them how to behave. You can see this in Rwanda after genocide. Many Western countries which sowed the seeds of destruction or those who supported those who sowed the seeds of destruction offer aid and other help which end up misdirecting the victims from pursuing the real causal system. What's more, even when it comes to helping such countries from self-inflicted wounds, the international community discriminates against them. This can be seen on how quickly or late they act or how much they offer compared to other affected countries out of Africa.

How long did Aboriginal people languish in ill-structured teachings even after the world declared to have entered in the age of civilization and advancement as it was in Africa, Australia, Canada and US and other Western nations and in their colonies where Aboriginal people, despite such grandiose announcement went on suffering from archaic and rudimentary treatment by the so-called civilized and advanced nations? Aboriginal people were denied the voice and rights to decide how they would like to live. They are totally left out in their countries, and they just depend on the mercy of the governments. This needs to change. And if anything, without changing the status quo, conflict resulting from lack of voice, identity and other rights will be rampant as it currently is in Americas. Under the current education system, Aboriginal people are lost and ignored and nobody sees it this way. Why? Because the current education system makes people selfish and blind so as not to see wanton suffering other people are in.

In Tanzania and Kenya, Masai for many years were the only people left out of the Western capitalist market due to adhering to their culture. But recently, they were lulled out of their world in the name of modernization. Instead of looking after their animals, they were made to believe that urban life is a sign of development. They thus left their animals starting adopting "modern life". Now Masai are leading community in guarding shops and houses something that degrade them and sabotage them culturally and economically. They are now poorer than they were out of capitalistic system of exploitation. They have subscribed to the current grand narrative so as to lose their culture and wealth based on pastoralism. Essentially, Masai were the only people that used to attract many tourists from West. Sometimes in Kenya, there was a tug of war between Masai women and white women they accused of snatching their husbands. As I am writing, the pride and uniqueness of Masai have become history. They no longer eat their foods that enabled them to run tens of miles looking after their herds in the wideness of East Africa as it used to be before they were subsumed in the modern capitalist culture. After losing their ways of life based on their culture and environment, Masai are now in correctional facilities in these countries due to trying to reverse the situation by involving themselves (though not all) in crimes so as to generate capital and go back home to buy some cows. Currently, there is a conflict between Masai and town dwellers in many places in two countries. The trust the society used to place on Masai is virtually long gone and their situation is worsening day by day. What was thought to be either a passing fad or cloud has come to stay as Masai lose more and more of their identity. Masai are not alone. They are many more Indigenous community losing almost all over the globe. Arguably, this is going to cause a lot of problems however nobody can stand in the way of domination hidden in change. Again, such changes should be constructive as far as conflict resolution is concerned. It is only by and through decolonized education that will help the governments to address the problems such people face. One important question one may ask is: Why has this phenomenon happened? Masai have been robbed of their lives and culture so as to be exploited by the capitalist market that seeks to exploit everybody all over the world through consumerism and pop culture exported by Western propaganda machinery. The modernity seen in Masai and other people that are becoming preys to Western consumerism is nothing but perilous encounter. It is like dancing with the devil so to speak. If something is not done to decolonize the current way of doing things drawing from colonized education which produced colonized leaders, some people are facing Armageddon and conflicts resulting from it will never be avoided.

Behind cultural imperialism

Behind this cultural imperialism spearheaded by African regimes in conjunction with their Western masters and other issues and questions are supposed to get the answers from academics based on decolonized education which, if possible, in the course of trying to usher peace in the world by addressing power-crazy conflicts and imperialistic urge to subdue others that are going on in various places of the world. You can easily and swiftly prove this occurrence by looking at how Africa and other colonized societies still ape what former colonizers have to offer. All power-craziness we see in many parts of the world are meant by individuals aiming at having hands on resources that the West and China want. By having control of these resources they will be able to enter in a marriage of a consumer and supplier even if it means to be done through shedding the blood of innocent brothers and sisters of theirs. Had they received decolonized education; leaders would not allow such self-destruction wantonly and pointlessly.

If anything, education, as a field, has always endeavoured to better the lives of those receiving it and their societies. Being a violent project as Nyamnjoh (2012) notes above, the world evidenced all signs and remnants of colonialism need to be eradicated wherever they are. If this is achieved either through individual or structural deconstruction, peace is likely to be more realized than it is currently. When Nyamnjoh postulates that colonialism is a violent project, he encompassed everything that colonialism brought to colonies. This becomes especially true due to the fact that colonialism did not come into being to benefit anybody except colonizers. Even within their circles, women were left out. They were colonized in their own countries just the same as men and women in colonies were colonized and brutalized not to mention being exploited and degraded. Violence of colonialism bears he hallmarks of greed and ignorance of the rights of others provided they are not part and parcel of the project. Again, how come some colonial carryovers are still living on even after colonialism was abolished? Are white women as equal as their counterpart men? Whether colonialism was abolished or not is subject to dialogue. As far as conflict resolution studies field is concerned –thanks to multidisciplinary nature and approach – it allows dialogue almost at all level and all time during conflict. The field makes conflict something dynamic so as to allow intervention of any kind at any time.

Nyamnjoh goes on arguing that colonial education turned those who received it into shadows of themselves, more of zombies, especially, those who and their communities did not benefit from it as a society. If there is anything they knew it was nothing but to strive to become like their masters. You can see this on their manners of doing things such as dress code, and the way they speak and where they want to go. In Africa, for example, those whom Britain colonized like to go to London, those colonized by France make Paris their pilgrimage centre. It goes on for those colonized by

105

Portuguese, Spanish and others. They all adore and revere the capitals of their colonial masters. Truly educated people under worthy and decolonized education would improve their capitals and give them whatever attract them in colonial capitals they like to ape and visit. They go for their tertiary education there. Even the rulers hide their loot there too and the champions of rule of law, good governance and human rights do not refuse to keep such dirty monies stolen from poor people. p'Bitek notes how many colonized elites became zombies. "And they dress up like white men, as if they are in the white man country" (p'Bitek 1966: 45). To sum up this face of colonialism we must ask a question: How does education come into this? Education comes into this scenario because what colonialism produced and left behind need to be deconstructed. And this cannot be possible without deconstructing and decolonizing our education system as we go back to salvage the regime of education we had before the coming of colonialists. We need to do so simply because, at that time, we lived without depending on handouts and whatnots from the West as it currently is.

Colonialism and colonization had no boundary from thuggery and robbery. They destroyed many lives, cultures and civilization. To them the words coexistence, interconnectedness and oneness did not exist. It is only today they realize the mistake they committed so as to look back and talk about the interconnectedness of the world as one family. This is a good move if it is not done in a wrong way by having classes and one grand narrative to rule others as it has always been. However Western society with its individuality has tried to spread to others coming from collectivistic societies, it has failed. We need a community more than an individual however everybody is an individual. Africa and many other Aboriginal people got their power and energy from their interdependence as opposed to individuality. This does not mean that Aboriginal people did not have difference of conflict. Again, the scale of their differences and conflicts did not lead to mass murder as it was in WWI and WWII or other colonial and capitalist related wars the world evidenced in past decades.

Although colonizers have maintained silence, lies and denial, they destroyed the world due to their greed and myopia embedded in incompetent education. You can see this in the fact that after enacting slavery, colonialism and imperialism, the same masters discovered how weak and inhumane these mechanisms were. Today when the world is changing economically, the same masters are trying to befriend those leading in this wave of social and economic changes. For example, they once ruled China and India. Today when these two humongous nations are acting as the engines of world economy, without forgetting Africa that supplies almost everything, the same folks are changing tacks by becoming more humanistic than colonial and imperialistic as they have always been. They know too well that if those nations follow their example of colonizing others, they will not survive. Again, to avoid going back to using financial and scientific muscles to colonize others, we all need to speak the language of interconnectedness and interdependence in which every society will decide how to be ruled. There must be laws that empower the hoi polloi to easily kick out the hoity toity whenever they mess without waiting for them to finish their terms in office as it currently is. Even the most powerful country on earth, the US, today does not want to travel the way European colonial masters did. The messes the US and its allies created in Afghanistan, Iraq and Libya seem to have impacted heavily on them. For as Mearsheimer (2014) underscores it, "America is likely to behave toward China much the way it behaved toward the Soviet Union during cold war" (p. 161). This means that the current grand narrative will seek more legality and tenacity to survive. This cannot let go on if we learned a lesson from cold war era that put the whole world in the way of harm wantonly. Truly educated academics need to reign in to tell the status quo that such move is unfeasible and counterproductive. The solution to this power tragedy lies on cooperation rather than competition. Understandably, we need to equip ourselves with a new type of decolonized education that seeks to accommodate all grand narratives of the world. We need to negotiate our future in a peaceful and constructive manner if we aspire to have a peaceful and developed world. Therefore, decolonizing the way we impart knowledge to our people will not only help the current grand narrative, but it will also help the whole world to avert unnecessary miseries such as exploitation, poverty and conflicts resulting from toxic and colonized education based on individualism instead of collectivism.

Essentially, how we view a conflict depends on the lenses we use. Equipped with colonial education, many actors in many countries suffering from violence tend to see things differently. For example, corrupt rulers see their interests while the *hoi polloi* see a different thing so as to create a conflict. Domestic elites spend public money on private and personal matters as it was for the Democratic Republic of Congo (DRC) dictator Mobutu who bought many villas and mansions in Belgium, US, France, Switzerland and Argentina, to mention but a few, while the majority is dying in abject poverty. Again, those beneficiaries of looted money –despite some of them being the champions of human rights and good governance – did not do anything let alone raising their voices. All the same, the victims of this theft did not challenge the silence of those countries which pretend to care about the rights of others while they actually are the movers and shakers as far as plundering causing harm is concerned.

In sum, we urge that the current education system has totally failed to address important issues such as environmental threats, equality, equity, justice, rights and general human wellbeing. To reverse this situation, we need to deconstruct and decolonize the whole regime if not overhauling it. The surest of doing so is taking on education before other disciplines. With pragmatic and utilitarian education, the world is able to move forward. Paranoid education as it is espoused by Western countries due to the fear of unknown becomes more a problem that a solution. Despite many technological gains, Western education still wants compared to the regimes of education it killed. This can be seen on arms race currently. What do arms do apart from killing humans? Do we need to keep on arms race or think otherwise? When we espouse the decolonizing of education we are truly and sincerely geared by such destruction. As we argued in the beginning, no humans can function without knowledge or education in their surroundings. Given that the world has become a very small village –whose headman or headwoman is unknown –changes in African education system will have effects all over the world the same way colonial and toxic education has always have reverberations all over the world. Changing, deconstructing or decolonizing the current education is not the matter of choice but necessity. This is noteworthy due to imminent problems caused by colonial education the world is now facing. Let us make this clear that when we espouse the decolonization of the current colonial education, we are aiming at reaping benefits not for a certain people, but instead it is for the entire mankind. I know this may sound ridiculous for colonial minds. Again, why should Western countries burden their tax payers for appropriating their money to help third world countries while they truly know that the latter lived for many centuries without depending on the former? The answer is simple, the West does not help poor countries as it has always maintained. Instead, it is robbing them due to their ignorance colonial education inculcated in them. This is very clear. Again, when we consider the fact that the oppressed will never be oppressed forever, those oppressing them need to take note and work with them to alleviate the situation.

References

Achebe, C. 2000. *Home and Exile*, New York: Anchor.

Achebe. C. 1958. *Things fall apart*, Portsmouth, NH, and Oxford, England: Heinemann.

Adeyemi, M. B. and Adeyinka, A. A. 2003. The Principles and Content of African traditional Education, *Educational Philosophy and Theory*, 35(4): 425-440.

Aminzade, R. 2003. "From Race to Citizenship: The Indigenization Debate in Post-Socialist Tanzania." *Studies in Comparative International Development*, 38 (1): 43-63.

Bakari, R. S. 1997. "*Epistemology from an Afrocentric Perspective: Enhancing Black Students' Consciousness through an Afrocentric Way of Knowing.*"

Barkun, M. 1990. Racist Apocalypse: Millennialism on the Far Right, *American Studies*. 31 (2): 121-140.

Belmonte, J.A. 2001. On the Orientation of Old Kingdom Egyptian Pyramids, *Journal for the History of Astronomy Supplement*, 32: 1.

Berman, B. J. 1998. Ethnicity, Patronage and the African State: the Politics of Uncivil Nationalism, *African affairs* 97(388): 305-341.

Bocock, R. J. 1971. "The Ismailis in Tanzania: a Weberian Analysis." *The British Journal of Sociology*. 22(4): 365-380.

Brandt-Rauf, P. W., and Brandt-Rauf, S. I. 1987. History of Occupational Medicine: Relevance of Imhotep and the Edwin Smith Papyrus, *British journal of industrial medicine* 44 (1): 68.

Brantlinger, P. 1985. Victorians and Africans: The genealogy of the Myth of the Dark Continent, *Critical Inquiry* 12 (1): 166-203.

Burton, E. 2013. What Tribe Should We Call Him? *The Indian Diaspora, the State and the Nation in Tanzania since ca. 1850*, 13 (25): 1-28.

Byrne, S. and Irvin. C. L. 2001.Reconcilable Differences. Turning Points in Ethnopolitical Conflict, *The Global Review of Ethnopolitics*, 1 (1): 87-109.

Byrne, Sean. 2001. Consociational and Civic Society Approaches to Peacebuilding in Northern Ireland, *Journal of Peace Research* 38 (8): 327-352.

Christopher, A.J. 1988. 'Divide and Rule': The Impress of British Separation Policies, *Are*a, p.233-240.

Dewey, J. 2004.*Democracy and Education*, Courier Corporation: USA.

Diop, Cheikh Anta. 1989. *The African Origin of Civilization: Myth or Reality*, Chicago Review Press: Chicago.

Du Bois, W. E. B. 1947. *The World and Africa: An Inquiry into the Part which Africa Has Played in* World History. New York, Viking P.

Fishman, J. A. 1968. "Nationality-Nationalism and Nation-Nationism," Chicago Review Press: Chicago.

Freeman-Grenville, G. S. P. 1957. Coinage in East Africa before Portuguese Times, *The Numismatic Chronicle and Journal of the Royal Numismatic Society* 17: 151-179.

Goodhart, M., Ed. 2013. *Human Rights: Politics and Practice*. Oxford University Press: Oxford.

Green, E. 2010. Ethnicity and Nationhood in Precolonial Africa: The Case of Buganda, *Nationalism and Ethnic Politics* 16 (1): 1-21.

Hurlbert, M. A, Ed. 2011. *Pursuing Justice: An Introduction to Justice Studies*, Fernwood Publishing.

Irving, L. 1953. The Naming of Birds by Nunamiut Eskimo, *Arctic* 6 (1): 35-43.

Jeong, H. 2005. *Peacebuilding in Postconflict Societies: Strategy and Process*, Boulder, CO: Lynne Rienner.

Johannessen, C. 2006. *Kingship in Uganda: The Role of the Uganda Kingdom in Ugandan Politics*, Chr. Michelsen Institute.

Kelsall, T. 2008. Going with the Grain in African Development? *Development Policy Review* 26 (6): 627-655.

Lanning, G., and W. M. M. 1979. *Africa Undermined.* Penguin Books.

Makgoro, Y. 1998. Ubuntu and the Law in South Africa, *Potchefstroom Electronic Law Journal/Potchefstroomse Elektroniese Regsblad* 1 (1).

Martin, L. 1986. "Eskimo Words for Snow": A case study in the genesis and decay of an anthropological example, *American anthropologist.* 88(2): 418-423.

Mawere, M. 2011. Epistemological and Moral Implications of Characterization in African Literature: A critique of Patrick Chakaipas Rudo Ibofu (love is blind), *International Journal of English and Literature.* 2 (1): 1-9.

Mearsheimer, J. J. 2014. "China's Unpeaceful Rise," *The Realism Reader.* 105 (690): 464.

Mhango, N. N. 2015. *Africa Reunite or Perish.* Langaa RPCIG, Cameroon.

Nhemachena, A. 2014."*Knowledge, Chivanhu and Struggles for Survival in Conflict-torn Manicaland,* PhD thesis, University of Cape Town.

Nyamnjoh, F. B. 2012. "Potted Plants in Greenhouses': A Critical Reflection on the Resilience of Colonial Education in Africa, *Journal of Asian and African Studie.* 0021909611417240.

Nyerere, J. K. 1967. Education for Self-reliance, *The Ecumenical Review,* p.382-403.

"Oldest University on Earth is Reborn after 800 Years." *Independent,* 22 October, 2011.

Paffenholz, T. Ed. 2010. *Civil Society & Peacebuilding: a Critical Assessment,* London: Lynne Rienner Publishers.

Parrinder, E. G, and Edward Geoffrey Parrinder. E.G. 1976. *African Traditional Religion.* Greenwood Press.

Payne, D. G. 1996.Voices in the wilderness: *American nature writing and environmental politics,* UPNE.

p'Bitek, O. 1973. *Song of Lawino,* Nairobi: East African Publishing House.

Posner, D. N. 2005. *Institutions and ethnic Politics in Africa,* Cambridge University Press.

Risse, G. B. 1986. Imhotep and Medicine--a Reevaluation, *Western Journal of Medicine* 144 (5): 622.

Rud, A. G. 1997. Use & Abuse of Socrates in Teaching, *Education Policy Analysis Archives* 21: 20.

Rutgers, M. R. 2009. The Oath of Office as Public Value Guardian, *The American Review of Public Administration*.

S Maanga, G. 2015. Rewriting Chagga History: Focus on Ethno-Anthropological Distortions and Misconceptions, *Global Journal of Human-Social Science Research* 15 (12).

Shupak, G. (n.d). The Shadow Class Was Condemned to Movement": Globalization and class-consciousness in The Inheritance of Loss, *Global tensions, Global Possibilitie.* p.107.

Smith, G. E. 1914. Egyptian mummies, *The Journal of Egyptian Archaeology.* 12 (2): 189-196.

Zartman, I. W. 1994. *Multilateral negotiation* 27 (3): 1-10.

Zvobgo, R. J. 2006. *After school, Then What? Government and Private Sector Intervention in Youth job Training in Zimbabwe*, Mambo Press: Gweru.

Chapter Five

Drives, Derivatives and Deterrents of Social Media Usage among University Undergraduates in Nigeria

Amali, I. O. O; Akintola, M; Bello, M. B, & Yusuf, A

Introduction

In the early days of university establishment in Nigeria, undergraduates socialise and interact using traditional media such as Telegram, Telex, Newspaper, Radio, Television, and so on. However, there has been a rapid shift from the practices of that era and to this contemporary period. One of the major factors labelled as the driver for this shift is social media (Orlu-Orlu & Nsereka, 2014). Social media has been described as a concept which connotes digital, interactive, integrative, global, communicative, participatory and collaborative in the sharing of information, knowledge and ideas among users and characterized mostly with internet proliferation, particularly, the second version of world wide web (web 2.0; Onah & Nche, 2014). Sawyer (2011) explained the global attribute of social media as the provision of context where individuals across the world can communicate, exchange messages, share knowledge and interact with each other regardless of the distance that separates them. This has made social media increasingly popular element of individual's daily lives in today's western dominated society.

In this vein, Ekeanyanwu and Kalyango (2013) tagged social media as the ninth wonder of the world and Olaniran (2014) christened it a revolutionary medium of global socialization for dismantling previously existing man-made obstacles to information dissemination and sharing. Adaja and Ayodele (2013) identified social media as drivers of social change, organizational and national development and remarked that one of the major advances of the 21st century is the discovery and emergence of social media which has facilitated the creation of different platforms for social interaction. Onah and Nche (2014) unequivocally asserted that the world is yet to experience something more phenomenal than the prodigy of social media. Osahenye (2012) denoted the qualities of social media as an unstoppable power which is contagious and have outreaching impact. Onah and Nche (2014) made reference to the fundamental aim of social media as the enhancement of communication through the acts of socializing, offering great and seemingly limitless benefits. Social media use web-based technologies to transform and broadcast media monologues into social dialogues and support the wide circulation of knowledge and information and transform individuals from content consumers to producers.

The presence of social media has led to overload of all kinds of information, both positive and negative, raising concerns not only in Nigeria and Africa but also the world, particularly, third world countries, to numerous problems associated with social media use. As a result of this, social media leaves users, particularly, university undergraduates vulnerable to its addiction (Ajewole & Fasola, 2012) while others tend to abuse its usage for self-aggrandizement, amusement, and control. Due to university undergraduates' exuberant and adventurous nature that characterizes that period, some of them lack the ability and capacity to thoroughly negotiate and sift media contents (Eshiet, 2014). In this vein, Onah and Nche (2014) outlined some moral issues but not limited to the following that have arisen from the abuse and addiction with social media as cyber-prostitution, internet crime, pornography, indecent dressing and sexual harassment, violence, loss of sense of sacredness of human dignity and life, individualism, social alienation, African hospitality and neighbourliness, impatience and quick syndrome. Fears are also growing that social media is been used as a platform to recruit terrorists.

Adegbilero-Iwari and Ikenwe (2014), and Onah and Nche (2014) noted that social media is a derivative of new form of information tool and clarified that it differs from the old form of information tool in many ways, including quality, sophistication, reach, speed, efficiency, frequency, accuracy, usability, reliability, cheapness, immediacy, portability and permanence as it allows interaction among its users in which they create, share, exchange information and ideas in virtual communities and networks. McQuail (2010) added that old form of information tool is essentially one-directional while social media is essentially interactive. Uwem, Enobong and Nsikan (2013) pointed out that social media comprise of several platforms on which a range of activities take place for socialization among individuals, groups and communities. These platforms include Facebook, twitter, WhatsApp, Instagram, skype, LinkedIn, Google+, YouTube, Hi5, Badoo, Eskimo, Nairaland, and others.

Several studies have been carried out to ascertain Nigerian university undergraduates' presence on social media (Edegoh, Asemah & Ekanem, 2013; Asemah, Okpanachi & Edegoh, 2013; Otunla, 2013; Ezeah, Asogwa & Obiorah, 2013; Ajewole & Fasola, 2012). They revealed that social media has become a constant presence and almost indispensable part in the lives of the average Nigerian university undergraduates. Onah and Nche (2014) did not find this development among university undergraduates as overwhelming because it is generally acknowledged that youths (undergraduates) by their nature are more disposed to social communication technologies. An opinion that was corroborated by Asogwa and Ojih (2013) who labelled today's youths as the most wired and connected generation in human history. Ulrich and Harris (2003) had earlier introduced terminologies like Net Kids, Generation X, Generation @, Adultescents, Tweenagers, Netizens to describe contemporary youths globally.

Nnamonu (2013) elaborated that while the internet, that is, worldwide wide (www), is the chief host of social media, the youths (undergraduates) are the most predominant clients. Tapscott (1997) postulated that children of the information age would be micro-monsters and web-sharks whose cognitive process as hand-eye coordination and functional observation would be such that their levels of ability and skills would far surpass those of their parents and teachers. Nche (2012) also added that social media usage has become common among the youths that it has become unfashionable not to engage oneself at least in one of the social networking sites. Hence, the socialization patterns of undergraduates have dramatically and rapidly evolved, as social media is now solely depended upon for all forms of social interaction.

Sociologists of education are inundated on the influence of social media but the interest of this study centres on the factors that drive university undergraduates to use social media. This implies the motivation or the aim of using social media among university undergraduates. Also, this study probed the derivatives of social media usage among university undergraduates, investigated the benefits and gains university undergraduates get from the use of social media. Lastly, this study examined the deterrents of social media usage, highlighted the constraints or challenges university undergraduates face in the use of social media, and its implication for the Nigerian society.

Statement of the Problem

Though, the influence of social media have been well documented in various studies of Ajewole and Fasola (2012), Orlu-Orlu and Nsereka (2014), Olaniran (2014) to pique interest of researchers. Yet, it can be stated based on recent studies of social media that its evolution is an uncharted territory for researchers and depicts lack of understanding, as findings revealed contrasting results. For instance, Asemah, et al (2013) examined the relationship between social media and academic achievement of students in universities in Kwara State and found that social media negatively affect university undergraduates' academic performance. However, Camilia, Ibrahim and Dalhatu (2013) contrastingly hypothesized that the frequent use of social media by students of tertiary institutions has no effect on their studies. Hence, as educators and researchers seek to understand social media, it is essential to understand the drive, derivatives and deterrents of university undergraduates to use social media, to facilitate in-depth studies on social media. This has been duly explained in the last paragraph of the previous section. Thus, this study examined university undergraduates' drives, derivatives and deterrents in the use of social media in Kwara State.

Research Methodology

This study is a descriptive qualitative survey research. The population of this study consisted of all undergraduates in universities in Kwara State. The target population for this study was all 3rd year level undergraduates from two sampled universities out of four universities in Kwara State, Nigeria. Different sampling techniques were used at different stages of sampling in this study. Purposively, the universities in Kwara State were categorized into public and private ownership. Hence, University of Ilorin and Al-Hikmah University were randomly selected for both public and private ownership respectively. Proportionate sampling technique was adopted in the selection of 387 respondents from the two sampled universities to ensure fair representation in the sample size because the undergraduates' population in the universities are not equal.

A researchers'-designed questionnaire with a content validity which was ascertained by experts in the field of this study who (scrutinized the items) made possible alteration and suggestions, was used to elicit the needed data for this study. Test-retest reliability method was used with a sample of 110 respondents in Kwara State University, Malete, within three weeks interval. The scores of the first test were correlated with the second test, using Pearson Product Moment Correlation coefficient and a reliability index of 0.87 was obtained. The data obtained from the 387 sampled respondents was used to answer the four research questions raised for this study. The researchers analysed the responses, using percentage, mean and standard deviation, and bar chart was used to illustrate the results.

Answering Research Questions

Research Question 1: How many social media accounts do most university undergraduates use?

Data collected from the respondents was used to answer research question 1. The responses were analysed by researchers, using percentage and bar-chart, and the output of the analysis was presented in Table 1 and Figure 1.

Table 1: Number of Social Media Accounts Used by University Undergraduates

NO. OF SOCIAL MEDIA ACCOUNTS USED	RESPONSES	PERCENTAGE (%)
One	24	6.2
Two	59	15.2
Three	117	30.2
More than Four	187	48.3
TOTAL	**387**	**100**

Figure 1: Number of Social Media Accounts Most University Undergraduates Use

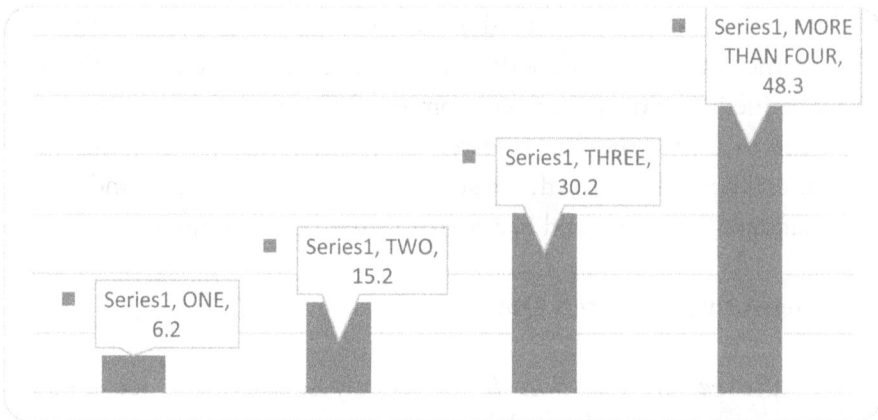

Table 1 and Figure 1 indicate that out of 387 respondents, 30.2% and 48.3% had three and upward social media accounts. 6.2% and 15.2% respondents had one and two social media accounts respectively. This implies that most university undergraduates have more than three social media accounts which is a reflection of their dependence on social media.

Research Question 2: What are the factors that drive university undergraduates to use social media?

Responses to the questionnaire were gathered to answer research question 2. Mean rating and standard deviation were used to analyse collected data and presented in Table 2.

Table 2: Factors that Drive University Undergraduates' to Use Social Media

DRIVING FACTORS	RESPONSES	MEAN	ST. D	RANKING
Reunite with Old Friends	184	1.99	.088	1st
Collaborative Learning	170	1.95	.216	2nd
Connect with New Friends	148	1.93	.264	3rd
Fun and Leisure	125	1.92	.272	4th
Informed on Global Events	119	1.88	.327	5th
Ease Boredom	118	1.84	.362	6th
Entertainment Gossip & Gist	113	1.78	.416	7th
Music/Movies	101	1.76	.429	8th
Religious Propagation	94	1.74	.440	9th
Work and Study	86	1.71	.455	10th
Curiosity	60	1.70	.461	11th
Networking & Business	47	1.69	.462	12th
Political Engagement	31	1.68	.468	13th
Humanitarian Causes	29	1.62	.487	14th
Dating/Flirting	19	1.56	.497	15th
Others	3	1.52	.500	16th

Table 2 illustrates that Reunite with old friends had a mean score of 1.99 and ranked highest among the factors that drive university undergraduates to use social media. Collaborative learning had mean score of 1.95 (2nd), and connect with new friends had mean score of 1.93 (3rd) were the major driving factors. Humanitarian causes and dating/flirting were the least driving factors. This implies that educational and social drives which embody collaborative learning, reunite with old friends and connect with new friends are the factors that motivate university undergraduates to use social media.

Research Question 3: What do university undergraduates derive from the use of social media?

Responses to the items in the questionnaire were collated and used to answer research question 3. This was analysed with mean rating and standard deviation and the result was presented in Table 3.

Table 3: University Undergraduates' Derivatives from Social Media

SOCIAL MEDIA DERIVATIVES	RESPONSES	MEAN	ST. D	RANKING
Reunite with Old Friends	207	1.99	.072	1st
Connect with New Friends	178	1.94	.237	2nd
Informed on Global News	159	1.90	.301	3rd
Academic Study Groups	130	1.88	.327	4th
Fun and Leisure	109	1.88	.327	4th
Ease Boredom	106	1.82	.383	6th
Gossip & Gist	105	1.76	.429	7th
Music/Movies	101	1.74	.440	8th
Religious Propagation	94	1.73	.445	9th
Work and Study	69	1.73	.445	10th
Networking & Business	47	1.72	.450	11th
Humanitarian Causes	47	1.66	.473	12th
Political Engagement	39	1.59	.493	13th
Flirting	23	1.54	.499	14th
Others	2	1.47	.499	15th

Table 3 revealed that reunite with old friends had mean score of 1.99 and ranked highest among university undergraduates' derivatives from social media. This was followed by connect with new friends with mean score of 1.94 (2nd), informed on global events had mean score of 1.90 (3rd), both collaborative learning and fun and leisure share similar mean score of 1.88 and ranked 4th. Thus, the first 5 ranked university undergraduates' derivatives from social media are reunite with old friends, connect with new friends, information on global events, collaborative learning, and fun and leisure. This implies that university undergraduates gain social and educational derivatives from the use of social media.

Research Question 4: What is the deterrents university undergraduates face in the use of social media?

Research question 4 was answered through the collection of data from the responses to the questionnaire administered. Mean rating and standard deviation were used to analyse data and the output of the analysis was presented in Table 4.

Table 4: Deterrents University Undergraduates face in the Use of Social Media

DETERRENTS	RESPONSES	MEAN	ST. D	RANKING
Erratic Network	223	1.99	.072	1st
Epileptic Power Supply	179	1.97	.159	2nd
Expensive Airtime/Data	145	1.97	.174	2nd
Lack of Time	71	1.93	.251	4th
Online Trolling/Abuse/Bullying	48	1.91	.291	5th
Faulty Device	26	1.82	.388	6th
School Regulation	12	1.63	.485	7th
Parental Ban	10	1.54	.499	8th
Others	2	1.42	.495	9th

Table 4 reveals that erratic network was the 1st ranked deterrent, with mean score of 1.99 while epileptic power supply and expensive airtime/data both had mean score of 1.97 and shared the 2nd ranked position. This implies that these 1st three ranked factors are the major deterrents university undergraduate face in the use of social media. On the other hand, school regulation with mean score of 1.63, parental ban with mean score of 1.54, and other factors with mean score of 1.42 fall within 7th, 8th and 9th rank respectively, are rarely seen as deterrents among university undergraduates in the use of social media.

Discussion of the Findings

In the output of the analysis, it was revealed that majority of university undergraduates have more than three social media accounts. This finding is in line with Holliday (2014) who observed that the use of social media has become more fragmented and decentralized. He explained that unlike in the past when most users, especially those that started with Facebook, would use a particular social media account for all their social needs, in recent years, with the launch of more social media platforms, offering specialized services, users are more inclined to use a cluster of different social media accounts. This implies that an undergraduate might use WhatsApp to inform course-mates about changes to examination timetable, use Instagram to share pictures of campus events and twitter to monitor the news and whisper/confess relationship secrets to followers. Holliday (2014) noted that a one size fits all social media account is no longer the preferred choice of users, especially university undergraduates. Africa Practice (2014) corroborated the above that numbers show Facebook is losing active users (logged in and engaged) to other social media accounts such as WhatsApp, Eskimo, WeChat, 2go and so on in Nigeria and other African countries. In a nutshell, the high numbers of accounts show that university undergraduates depend so much on social media.

One of the findings of this study indicated that educational and social drives are the factors that motivate university undergraduates to use social media. This finding was in consonance with Guy (2012); Aniemeka (2013) and Lupton (2014) who found that learners enjoyed and appreciated both the social learning experience afforded by social media and supported themselves in their learning, enhancing their own and other students' experiences. It confirms that university undergraduates' use social media as a powerful tool for both education and social life because it is used as a way of bringing together learners of all ages to collaborate on various activities and projects. Although, Idakwo (2013), Olaniran (2013) and Asemah, et al. (2013) findings were in contrast, as they found that social media negatively affect university undergraduates' social and educational activities. But Micaiah (2014) and Aniemeka (2013) countered that the infusion of social media in teaching and learning might curb the negative effects of social media and further enhance its positives.

Another finding of this study revealed that university undergraduates gain social and educational derivatives from the use of social media. This finding is in agreement with Otunla (2013), Micaiah (2014), and Lupton (2014) who found that learners enjoyed and appreciated the social learning experience afforded by social media, using it to support themselves in their learning, social lives, and enhancing their own and other students' experiences. It further confirms that university undergraduates use social media, among other things to build networks of like-minded people to stay connected, share knowledge, information and social experiences. However, Ajewole and Fasola (2012), Adenubi, Olalekan, Afolabi and Opeoluwa (2013), Edegoh, Asemah and Ekanem (2013), Noah, Oyeyemi and Adeyemo (2014) found out that social media usage is a detriment to social relationship and educational activities. They observed that social media promotes individualism, social alienation, immoral vices and so on which are anti-thesis to the hospitality and communalism of the African culture while also distracting students from their academic activities, leading to poor academic performance.

From the last finding of this study, it was gleaned that erratic network, epileptic power supply and expensiveness of airtime/data are the deterrents university undergraduates face in the use of social media. This finding is in support of Yacob (2011) who found erratic power supply as one of the factors affecting Information and Communication Technology (ICT) use by academic libraries in Southwestern Nigeria. In the same vein, Ikpe and Olise (2010), Atsumbe, Raymond, Enoch and Duhu (2012) observed that high cost of airtime and poor power supply hinder the use of e-learning infrastructures in Federal University of Technology, Minna. In addition, Ikpe and Olise (2010) and Adomi (2006) discovered that low level technology penetration which results in erratic network is seen as one of the challenges to media relation practice in Nigeria and an inhibition to the use of mobile phones among students of Library and Information Science, Delta State University.

Sociological Perspectives

This section is a necessary theoretical exercise on the global phenomenon of social media and education, and involves quite a number of variables which demand an expository understanding through tripartite theories of postmodernism, social reflexivity and technological determinism. No sociologist would approach the study of social life without making a choice from the pool of perspectives available. Nor would the information drawn from such a study be of use to people in their daily lives unless the perspectives from which the study is approached and the ways in which that perspective differs from others are known.

The theoretical approach is eclectic in nature which serves as foundation for this chapter. Reason for this eclectic approach is in recognition of the variant perspectives on issues and the evolution of ideas, hence, one sociological theory may not suffice but different theories may add substance to the debate. Openstax College (2013) explained that sociological theory is constantly evolving and should never be considered complete. Calhoun (2002) considered old or classic sociological theories as still important but new sociological theories build upon the work of their predecessors and added to them. As it is often argued that knowledge does not exist in vacuum, these theories provided the explanation for the observable phenomenon of social media in this chapter.

Technological Determinism

Both Giddens (2013) and Aina (2013) acknowledged that the modern society now live in an 'information age' which is characterized with the evolution in modern technology. Technology is defined by Nolan and Lenski (2006) as cultural information about how to use the material resources of the environment to satisfy human needs and desires. In recognition of the place of technology in our contemporary era, sociologists advanced a suitable concept to define it, known as technological determinism theory. Technological determinism theory was expanded and interpreted by Marshall McLuhan in 1962, who assertively stated that technology shapes or influences the way people think, feel and act and also determines how society organize themselves and operates (Baran, 2010). It explains the way in which technology is employed to drive social change. Asogwa and Ojih (2013) cited Croteau and Heynes who explained that technological determinism is an approach that identifies technologies, or technological advances, as the central causal element in processes of social change. Sociologists understand that technology itself does not necessarily cause social change but it does make provision for the acquisition of new capacities and impose restriction in its own form (Kombol, 2014).

In reference to this chapter, social media has often been described as the technological form of global socialization which brings about social change. In recent years, the use of social media has increasingly influenced the form of global socialization. Asogwa and Ojih (2013) maintained that with every innovative technology, society will change in order to adapt to the technology which explains the different reasons for individuals, especially university undergraduates' gravitation towards social media. However, African scholars like Abanyam (2013) lamented that Africa is witnessing the effects of western technology with its occupying blessings and curses. He accepted that Africa lags behind in accelerating appropriate indigenous technological knowledge to solve African problems because of the excessive exploitation of African resources by the colonial masters, corruption of her leaders and relegation of African knowledge.

Hence, Africa depend on western technology, a situation tagged, 'dependency syndrome' which throws up another enormous challenge on African society. Asogwa and Ojih (2013) observed that the attitude and behaviour of university undergraduates' on social media platforms underscores the postulation inherent in technological determinism, i.e. changes in communication technology inevitably produce profound changes in both culture and social order. This supports the assertion of Abanyam (2013) that western technologies such as social media are not congenial to African context and have rather helped to erode African values to zero mark. This theory shows the negative use of social media by university undergraduates to suit their different idiosyncrasies.

Postmodernism Theory

Scholars have posited that technology has accelerated the society and it has now entered a new era, known as postmodern era where all old ideas in society became antiquated and recycled (Haralambos & Holborn, 2013). Some sociologists posited that human societies have passed through certain broad phases of development, distinguishing between pre-modern and postmodern societies (Haralambos & Holborn, 2013). Proponents of postmodern theory such as Jean Baudillard, Jean Francois Lyotard, Bogard, Binkley, and so on, posited that media technology with its correlate, social media, have destroyed human relationship to the past and created a chaotic empty world (Giddens, 2013; Haralambos & Holborn, 2013). Haralambos and Holborn (2013) maintained that all societies have always been characterized by changes, increasing pace of change, making it difficult for individuals to retain a single, unified sense of what to do and what not to do. In the process of acceleration to postmodern society, alien ways of life such as fraud, prostitution, and perversion of injustice, not known in pre-colonial era were inculcated into the Nigerian society. For this reason, some African scholars like Ahule (2012) have warned against the full embrace of postmodern values: "Nigerian value system have metamorphosed from its collective orientation to take on a western form. Instead of African form, values congruent with western society have come to dominate, and rather than solidify the Nigerian, it degenerate him" (Ahule, 2012: 6).

Haralambos and Holborn (2013) described postmodern society as an era where the media have become increasingly important in societal live. Giddens (2013) emphasized this point on postmodern theorists' argument that rather than economic forces shaping society as postulated by Marxist theorem, social life is influenced, above all, by signs and images, hence, social life is dominated by the mass media which is manifested with social media in recent times. Cultural ideas are being integrated across the globe with western culture becoming dominant because of its technological superiority which has taken control of knowledge and information. Abanyam (2013) raised the assumption that the control of the West has over knowledge and information influence on other cultures mainly through social media.

Thus, university undergraduates who are the largest group using social media in Nigeria have the tendency to imbibe and exhibit attitudes which are antithetical to the establishment of university education in the country. African scholars like Abanyam (2013) contended that university graduates now possess certificates without societal value to complement with, bribery and corruption is now the norm, nudity and indecent dressing is the new cool, indiscipline and disorderliness becomes the order of the day, get-rich-quick syndrome pervades, honour and regard only goes for material worth, because Nigerians seem to have lost their social integrity in a bid to meet up with postmodern society. This has led to opposition to the use of social media by some scholars.

Social Reflexivity Theory

Anthony Giddens developed another theoretical perspective on the contemporary changes in the world and metaphorically reckoned that we live today in a 'runaway world', a world marked by new risks and uncertainties. Giddens (2013) suggested that the notion of trust should be placed alongside that of risk, as trust refers to the confidence we have either in individuals, institutions or activities. This can be explained that African forms of trust seemed to be dissolved which is the effect of western controlled society, depicted by social media. Orlu-Orlu and Nsereka (2014) narrated that university undergraduates of the pre-1970s while at home on their long vacations, would go to nearby schools to mentor the younger ones free of charge.

In those days, newspaper vendors were said to drop heaps of their newspapers and magazines at designated points on university campus and depart for other parts of the city, on their return in the evening, they would meet accurate amounts of money for papers taken away in their absence by undergraduates and no papers were stolen nor was any money missing (Orlu-Orlu & Nsereka, 2014). This can hardly be realized in today's age where individual lives are influenced by people they have never seen or met and who may be living on the far side of the world. Social reflexivity is well pronounced in today's western dominated society and social media era. It refers to the fact that as social beings, individuals have to constantly think, reflect on current circumstances which gives room for modification to suit current situations. In this vein, social reflexivity brings to the fore the dynamism of societies, rather than be static due to custom and tradition, members could follow established ways of activities in innovative fashion.

The social reflexive theory softened the negative response on social media and brings to the fore the understanding on the opposition to the use of social media and the hue and cry over its negative social implication which Valenzuela, Park, and Kee (2008) explained: "Moral panic is a common reaction to new forms of communication…The story with social media is not different. Unsafe disclosure of information and addiction, are few of the concerns raised about the use of social media" (Valenzuela, *et al* 2008: 3).

Appraisal

The social reflexive theory aligns with the position of Orlu-Orlu and Nsereka (2014) that university education is the reflection of the western dominated society. Rather than blame social media for the resocialization and desocialization of university undergraduates, it should be realized that the Nigerian society had long deferred from its traditional culture and imbibed and succumbed to the western culture as enunciated in the postmodern theory. This is an indication that social media as a tool is not the problem, as it is merely a medium and a reflection of the people who use it and the innovators who designed it to advance western domination of the human society. Scholars have noted that the African traditional value is declining which is a serious problem as vices ranging from indecency, dishonesty, corruption, impatience, non-caring attitude of both the young and the old now prevail in our society which present the problem of value conflicts in our society (Bello, 2009). We are living in an age where the societal values are individualistic and materialistic, an apparent state of anomie.

Yet, this is not a recent development as Anadi (2008) cited Maduakor (1983) who lamented on the absolute lack of social order and discipline in Nigeria in the late 1970s and early 1980s:

There is clear manifestation of indiscipline in every facet of Nigeria life. Many believe that the present single problem facing Nigeria today is loss of social values. Indiscipline is seen in our hatred of order, and the enthusiasm with which we welcome the urge to scramble and stampede, our money-mania, our attitude to work, our readiness to cheat and embezzle, our short-cut mentality, our lack of respect for the dignity of human life, our eagerness to devise means of circumventing the law, our lack of patriotism, and complete absence of inner control in our social make-up. In fact, the list is inexhaustible (Anadi, 2008: 36).

Let us persist with the 1980s literatures and observe the similarities with current era. Mustapha (1983) acknowledged that in the period of the 1980s, everyone was materially conscious that everything which was not evaluated in terms of Naira (Nigerian currency) or any material gain was not worth to be recognized. He added that it went to the extent that personal merit would not serve you as much as money would. Decades later, Omonijo, Uche, Rotimi and Nwadialor (2014) corroborated that individuals worship money in Nigeria, the value we place on the life of fellow citizens is low and that informs our choices as a nation. Since money appears the greatest thing in life, Nigerians embezzle public funds and resort to theft. Money dictates who is respected and it is immaterial what others do to become wealthy. Killing of fellow citizens are carried out at the slightest provocation because we place little or no value to life. Anadi (2008) quoted further gory social image and the hopelessness in the social state of the nation as highlighted in the communique of the National Conference on Moral Education (NCME, 1982): Nigeria, a nation which is at the cross-roads of socio-economic development, is in a state of social crisis. Everywhere, and in all walks of life, Nigerians exhibit unhealthy attitude, lack of commitment to a viable social base and the consequent lack of social integrity (Anadi, 2008: 37).

Obasanjo (1999) professed openly that in Nigeria, honesty is disregarded, indolence is extolled, probity is derided, waste and ostentation are paraded, justice is sold to the highest bidder, hard work is ridiculed and service, is to self and nobody else. Abogunrin (1986) earlier expressed that the general lament is that honesty, kindness, dedication to duty, hospitality and respect for human life have become things of the past in Nigeria. Today, our major ethical problems include armed and pen robbery, embezzlement of public funds, bribery and corruption, greed and dishonesty, indolence and negligence of duty, political violence and murder, cheating, profiteering and fraud, cyber-crime, indecency among the youths, among others.

Social deficiency has spread to all nooks and cranny of the nation, no sector in Nigeria is clean from this menace, a picture which was vividly captured by Orlu-Orlu and Nsereka (2014) thus:

> *Our Country seems to be slipping out of social reach. Our legislature is lethal in wasting public funds. The judiciary is jaundiced in its judgements. The executive is exacerbating corruption in the land by not genuinely enforcing anti-corruption measures. The public service is being overthrown by the craze for embezzlement of taxpayer's money. Worse still, pre-mature sex, sex perversion, sex abuse and assault, commercial nudity, lesbianism, sodomy, violence and godlessness among teenagers and youths are on the increase* (Orlu-Orlu & Nsereka, 2014: 40).

Uche (2014) observed that the menace of corruption, a corollary of social crass plaguing the Nigerian polity has slowly permeated the university system such that corrupt practices of diverse forms are perpetrated by university staff and students. Olasehinde-Williams (2006) identified academic dishonesty as one of the major challenges of the University and Nigerian education system in general, due to the fall-out of social crass. Kanu and Ursula (2012) pointed out that social laxity is the harbinger of unethical practices in the Nigerian educational system which has seriously undermined the provision of quality education in the country.

Omeje and Eyo (2008) observed that a significant and positive relationship exist between the social system of university undergraduates and the standard of university education and pointed out that the social system of university undergraduates is the system entrenched by the society. This can be gleaned from the continued colonization philosophy of most African universities which has failed to transform the university system to reflect the African society. Elendu (2012) discussed Nigeria debased social system as exemplified in the quest for money, age cheating, unpatriotism, religious sentiments and inclination (against African traditional religion), lack of time consciousness, favouritism, and mediocrity syndrome, among others and its influence on behaviours and attitudes towards national development. Pemede and Viavonu (2010) investigated the aggressive tendencies and violent behaviours of Nigerian students which result in cult and gangster activities, an epitome of social decadence affecting socio-academic development.

Omede (2011) looked at indecent dressing as a dress pattern that is common among students of higher institutions of learning in Nigeria, particularly the female ones and discovered that fading social values, among other reasons lead students to dress uncultured. In similar vein, Kullima, Kawuwa, Audu, Mairiga and Bukar (2010) identified decay in societal values as one of the common factors responsible for the prevalence of sexual assaults on female students. In the study of social organization of internet fraud among university undergraduates in Nigeria, Tade and Aliyu (2011) pointed out that studies on internet fraud have been biased to the emergence of yahoo-boys subculture while neglecting the importance of the structure sustaining it. In its findings, it was revealed that internet fraud in tertiary institutions is socially organized and highly networked, and is often specialized and sustained by informal networks. This involves nefarious networks of fellow fraudsters and bank staffs, a result of unemployment and unbridled corruption and social decadence in the society.

In Kpangban, Ajaja and Umudhe (2012), students identified crave for paper qualification as the major reason for examination malpractice which is hinged on the culture of certificate glorification of the society. The social analysis of malpractice impeding development of education sector in Nigeria by Omonijo, et al (2014) described decadence of different forms such as lawlessness, perceived as normal part of social life, irrespective of academic qualifications; disorderliness which was the cause of painful death and several injuries of some applicants in the Immigration Service Aptitude Test tragedy; lack of discipline and decorum shown by the political class, including lawmakers; impatience and get-rich-quick syndrome; offensive and abusive language; flagrant display of arrogance and self-centredness common among Nigerian elites; misplaced priorities by losing the values of hard work, respect for elders, truthfulness, honesty, contentment, humility, patience and other social virtues.

Thus, Orlu-Orlu and Nsereka (2014) pointed out the remark of immediate past Governor of Anambra State, Peter Obi in his response to the Cynthia Osokogu murder case (referenced as the dark side of social media in Nigeria – Church {2012}) epitomized the erosion of values in the society, adding that what Nigeria needed most was value-re-orientation and ethical rebirth. Peter Obi's comment earned an ally across the Atlantic from Barak Obama, President of United States of America who cautioned on the casting out of social media like an evil spirit when reacting to the hate video on Prophet Muhammad uploaded on social media. Obama enjoined society to come to terms with the pervasive power of social media, and as such, channel it towards positive results.

However, this chapter argued that the distrust of social media is not centred on the tool as Obama expressed but on the innovators and the users of social media who conceived the idea as an opportunity to further the western domination of the human society. Most African scholars who are against the use of social media understand that the media is not the problem, as it is merely a medium, but it is the users and creators have used this medium to promote individualism, social alienation, immoral vices and so on which are antithetical to the hospitality and communalism of the African culture.

The way forward

The findings of this study become necessary to complement the efforts into how social media and education can co-exist and be beneficial. Hence, understanding social media and its dynamics will help in using it and mitigating its downsides. In conclusion, this study contends that negative use of social media may be on the horizon because of the lack of relevant knowledge and understanding. It is believed that a vivid understanding of the efficacy of the climate of the use of social media would serve as a pragmatic approach and also assist in instituting a positive use of social media among university undergraduates for the Nigerian society. In view of the findings of this study, it was suggested that universities should transform its philosophy to reflect the Nigerian society rather than western domination. Importantly, universities should be mindful and conservative in the adoption of social media in teaching and learning as some elements may be at the detriment of the Nigerian society.

In this vein, universities should promote academic research on suitable social media platforms for academic practice such as lecture delivery, submission of assignments, term papers, review sessions, tutorials and collaborative learning. Universities are also implored to incorporate appropriate social media platforms in academic practice to provide both lecturers and undergraduates with dynamic teaching and learning opportunities. Universities should engage undergraduates on social media to cease the initiative and enhance the use of social media for indigenous use in the Nigerian society.

In addition, government should endeavour to solve the poor power situation to end the frustration of social media users while network providers should work assiduously to improve the low level network penetration for reliable network access. Also, network providers should be mindful of economic class of the country to provide packages that can be affordable to the people. Lastly, government should ensure business organisations (telecom operators, social media owners) in the country operate within the realm of conducive environment through stable power supply and reasonable taxation.

References

Adaja, T. A. & Ayodele, F. A. 2013. Nigerian youths and social media: Harnessing the potentials for academic excellence. *Kuwait Chapter of Arabian Journal of Business and Management Review*, 2(5), 65 – 75. Retrieved from
http://www.arabianjbmr.com/pdfs/KD_VOL_2_5/8.pdf.

Adegbilero-Iwari, I. & Ikenwe, J. I. (2014, February). New media in old media: The Nigerian case. *Paper presented at the IFLA International Newspapers Conference on Start Spreading the News, Salt Lake City, Utah*. Retrieved from

http://www.ifla.org/files/assets/newspapers/SLC/2014_ifla_sl
c_adegbilero-iwari_ikenwe_-
_new_media_in_old_media_slides.pdf.

Adenubi, O. S., Olalekan, Y. S., Afolabi, A. A., & Opeoluwa, A. S.
2013. Online social networking and the academic achievement of
university students: The experience of selected Nigerian
universities. *Information and Knowledge Management*, 3, 5, 109 – 116.
Retrieved from
http://www.iiste.org/Journals/index.php/IKM/article/downlo
ad/5611/5723

Adomi, E. E. 2006. Mobile phone usage patterns of library and
information science students at Delta State University, Abraka,
Nigeria. *Electronic Journal of Academic and Special Librarianship*, 7(1).
Retrieved from
http://southernlibrarianship.icaap.org/content/v07n01/adomi
_e01.htm

Africa Practice. 2014. The social media landscape in Nigeria 2014:
The who, the what and the know. Nigeria. *Africa Practice*.
Retrieved from
http://www.africapractice.com/wp-
content/uploads/2014/04/Africa-Practice-Social-Media-
Landscape-Vol-1.pdf

Ajewole, O. O. & Fasola, O. S. 2012. A study of social network
addiction among youths in Nigeria. *Journal of Social Science and
Policy Review*, 4, 62 – 71. Retrieved from
http://www.cenresinpub.org/pub/September%20Edition%202
012/JSSPR/Page%2062-71_969_.pdf

Aniemeka, E. O. 2013. *Social media and entrepreneurship education:
Pedagogical implications of computer mediated communication in higher
learning in Africa* (Doctoral dissertation, Graduate School,
Greenleaf University, Melbourne). Retrieved from
http://www.greenleaf.edu/pdf/emmanuel_osita_aniemeka.pdf

Asemah, E. S., Okpanachi, R. A., & Edegoh, L. O. N. 2013. Influence
of social media on the academic performance of the
undergraduate students of Kogi State University, Anyigba,
Nigeria. *Research on Humanities and Social Sciences*, 3(12), 90 – 96.
Retrieved from

http://www.slideshare.net/AlexanderDecker/influence-of-social-media-on-the-academic-performance-of-the-undergraduate-students-of-kogi-state-university-anyigba-nigeria

Asogwa, C. E. & Ojih, E. U. 2013. Social networking sites as tools for sexual perversion among students of university of Nigeria, Nsukka. *New Media and Mass Communication*, 9, 27–38. Retrieved from http://www.iiste.org/Journals/index.php/NMMC/article/view/4165

Atsumbe, B. N., Raymond, E., Enoch, E. B., & Duhu, P. 2012. Availability and utilization of e-learning infrastructures in federal university of technology, Minna. *Journal of Education and Practice*, 3(3), 56-64.

Camilia, O. N., Ibrahim, S. D., & Dalhatu, B. L. 2013. The effect of social networking sites usage on the studies of Nigerian students. *The International Journal of Engineering and Science*, 2(7), 39 – 46. Retrieved from http://www.theijes.com/papers/v2-i7/Part.3/F0273039046.pdf

Edegoh, L. O. N., Asemah, E. S., & Ekanem, I. B. 2013. Facebook and relationship management among students of Anambra State University, Uli, Nigeria. *International Review of Social Sciences and Humanities*, 6(1), 205 – 216. Retrieved from http://www.irssh.com/yahoo_site_admin/assets/docs/24_IRSSH-638-V6N1.334175822.pdf

Ekeanyanwu, N. T. & Kalyango, Y. 2013. Rethinking international news flow and communication in the era of social media influence. *The Nigerian Journal of Communication*, 11(1), 139 – 164. Retrieved from https://www.academia.edu/4883500/Rethinking_International_News_Flow_in_the_Era_of_Social_Media

Ezeah, G. H., Asogwa, C. E., & Obiorah, E. I. 2013. Social media use among students of universities in south-east Nigeria. *Journal of Humanities and Social Sciences*, 16(3), 23 – 32. Retrieved from http://www.iosrjournals.org/iosr-jhss/papers/Vol16-issue3/C01632332.pdf

Guy, R. 2012. The use of social media for academic practice: A review of literature. *Kentucky Journal of Higher Education Policy and Practice*, 1(2), 7. Retrieved from http://uknowledge.uky.edu/kjhepp/vol1/iss2/7/

Haliso, Y. 2011. Factors affecting information and communication technologies (ICTs) use by academic librarians in Southwestern Nigeria. *Library Philosophy and Practice.* Retrieved from http://unllib.unl.edu/LPP/

Holliday, K. (2014, March 28). Why chat apps are the next 'breed' of social networks. *CNBC.* Retrieved from http://www.cnbc.com/id/101517922

Idakwo, L. 2013. *The use of social media among Nigerian youths.* Retrieved from www.slideshare.net/goldlami/the-use-of-social-media-among-nigerian-youths2

Ikpe, E. H. & Olise, F. P. 2010. The era of new media technologies and the challenges of media relations practice in Nigeria. *Journal of Communication*, 1(2), 59-68.

Lupton, D. 2014. *Feeling better connected: Academics' use of social media.* Canberra: News & Media Research Centre, University of Canberra. Retrieved from http://www.canberra.edu.au/about-uc/faculties/arts-design/attachments2/pdf/n-and-mrc/Feeling-Better-Connected-report-final.pdf

McQuail, D. 2010. *McQuail's mass communication theory* (6th Ed). London: John Letterman.

Micaiah, W. 2014. *Social media awareness in Nigeria education.* Retrieved from http://www.slideshare.net/statisense/social-media-awareness-in-nigeria-education

Nche, G. C. 2012. The social media usage among Nigerian youths: Impact on national development. *International Journal of Advancement in Development Studies*, 7(5), 18–23.

Nnamonu, T. (2013, June 29). Social media and youth development. *Wise Counsel.* Retrieved from https://teeceecounsel.wordpress.com/2013/06/29/social-media-and-youth-development/

Noah, A. O. K., Oyeyemi, S. O., & Adeyemo, E. A. 2014. An appraisal of social change through social networking: Focus on individualism. *Nigerian Journal of Sociology of Education*, 8(1), 54–62.

Olaniran, S. 2014. Social media and changing communication patterns among students: An analysis of twitter use by university of Jos students. *Covenant Journal of Communication*, 2(1), 40 – 60. Retrieved from http://journals.covenantuniversity.edu.ng/cjoc/published/May 2014/Samuel.pdf

Onah, N. G. & Nche, G. C. 2014. The moral implication of social media phenomenon in Nigeria. *Mediterranean Journal of Social Sciences*, 5(20), 2231–2237. Retrieved from http://mcser-org.ervinhatibi.com/journal/index.php/mjss/article/viewFile/3970/3886

Orlu-Orlu, H. C. & Nsereka, B. G. 2014. Social media as a bastion for correcting moral ills in Nigeria: A focus on educational decadence. *New Media and Mass Communication*, 22, 38 – 49. Retrieved from http://www.iiste.org/Journals/index.php/NMMC/article/view/11078

Osahenye, K. (2011, February 25). The social media challenge. *The Guardian*, pp. 52.

Otunla, A. O. 2013. *Internet access and use among undergraduate students of Bowen University Iwo, Osun State, Nigeria.* Library Philosophy and Practice (e-journal), paper 964. Retrieved from http://digitalcommons.unl.edu/libphilprac/964

Tapscott, D. 1997. *Growing up digital: The rise of the net generation.* New York: McGraw Hill.

Sanusi, B. O., Adelabu, O. & Okunade, J. K. 2014b. Adapting social media for formal learning in Nigeria: Challenges and prospects. *Arabian Journal of Business and Management Review*, 3(9), 22-30. Retrieved from http://www.arabianjbmr.com/pdfs/OM_VOL_3_%289%29/5.pdf

Sawyer, R. 2011. The impact of new social media on intercultural adaptation. *Senior Honours Projects.* Paper 242. Retrieved from http://digitalcommons.uri.edu/srhonorsprog/242

Ulrich, J., & Harris (Eds.) 2003. *GenXegesis: Essays on alternative youth (sub) culture.* Madison: University of Wisconsin Press.

Uwem, A., Enobong, A. & Nsikan, S. 2013. Uses and gratifications of social networking websites among youths in Uyo, Nigeria. *International Journal of Asian Social Science*, 3(2), 353 – 369. Retrieved from http://www.aessweb.com/pdf-files/353-369.pdf

Chapter Six

Indigenous Knowledge or Endogenous Knowledge? An Examination of Health Care in Zimbabwean Communities

Costain Tandi & Munyaradzi Mawere

> *We are going to emancipate ourselves from mental slavery because whilst others might free the body, none but only ourselves can free the mind (Marcus Garvey 1937).*

Introduction

Over eighty percent of the world's population depend on indigenous healthcare-based medicinal plants (Mawere 2011; Nhemachena 2015). In Africa in general and Zimbabwe in particular, indigenous knowledge of medicinal plants has been used since time immemorial for treating and curing various complications and ailments. This living reality attests to the fact that health care in the Zimbabwean communities can be achieved by harnessing the untapped benefits embedded in the indigenous knowledge systems. The World Health Organisation (WHO), as it clearly stipulated in its 2003 Report on sustainable development, recognises the immense and prominent contribution of indigenous medicinal knowledge owing to the fact that sustainable development rests on a health population.

Rural communities in Zimbabwe have been well known for using indigenous knowledge on medicinal plants for medicinal purposes (Sigauke, Chiwaura and Mawere 2014). Indigenous medicinal knowledge to date is practiced by different groups of people and cultures across the board for the prevention and treatment of diseases depending on the belief systems, needs, and values of the society in question. There is a wealthy of information on indigenous medicinal knowledge existing in Zimbabwe although it is not well documented. It is quite genuine to make a standing observation that since the dawn of colonialism in Zimbabwe as elsewhere on the continent the use of traditional medicine has diminished owing to the introduction of Western medicine. Nevertheless, the deployment of medicinal plants in primary health care remains the oldest system that has stood the test of time. The introduction of Western medicine and culture bred and precipitated a "cultural – ideological clash" which eventually culminated in asymmetrical power relations that impacted negatively on African traditional health care system. Indigenous knowledge systems were denied the opportunity to systematise themselves and develop in their own direction.

Since independence from the whims and caprice of colonial administration in Zimbabwe as elsewhere in Africa, the call for traditional medicine is fast increasing. This owes to the fact that Western medicine that was orchestrated to substitute traditional medicine is very expensive, often unavailable, and beyond the rich of the poor majority, most of whom live in abject poverty. This work is an attempt to challenge the Government and the Ministry of Health in Zimbabwe, local communities and other interested stakeholders to sustainably harvest plant species from the forests given that natural resources are continually declining while health care needs are rising. On this note, the attempt is ultimately meant to influence policy and the government of Zimbabwe to come up with sustainable context-based laws to conserve and promote indigenous medicinal knowledge. The study deploys descriptive survey method and critical analysis of literature to advance the argument that the use of indigenous medicinal knowledge in the prevention and treatment of diseases cannot be underestimated. Basing on evidence on the ground and literature across cultures, indigenous medicinal knowledge is, therefore, a phenomenon that should be promoted in post-colonies and other such communities across the world.

Background to the use of traditional medicine

As stipulated in the United Nations Declarations on the Rights of Indigenous Peoples (UNDRI), indigenous peoples have the right to their traditional medicines and to maintain their health practices, including the conservation of their vital medicinal plants, animals and minerals. Indigenous individuals also have the right to access, without any discrimination, to all social and health services" (UNDRI 19: Article 24).

Yet, there has been acrimonious debate on the nature and contribution of indigenous knowledge such that other scholars like Hountondji (1997) and Turnbull (2000) have suggested the change of the term "indigenous knowledge" to "endogenous knowledge" which they argue is more flexible, receptive, and acknowledge modifications or change through time. Hountondji and Turnbull argue that the term 'indigenous' implies stasis and immovability besides it being derogatory. Their view has, however, been challenged by Mawere who argues for the maintenance and promotion of the use of the term 'indigenous knowledge.' As Mawere (2014a: 12) puts it:

> I do not understand indigenous knowledge to be derogatory and static or to be equal to immovable knowledge as scholars like Hountondji and Turnbull argue respectively. Contrary to these scholars, I argue that the term indigenous knowledge is never static and derogatory if understood from an African perspective: it is only from the perspective of the colonialist or of those who have been brainwashed that one may think that the term indigenous knowledge is derogatory, immovable, and/or static.

Mawere further argues that IK has never been local, static, and immovable as Eurocentric scholars would want to put it given the reality that indigenous people have always been crossing borders, mingling with people of other societies, and sharing their ways of knowing yet they remained indigenous. For him, the term "endogenous knowledge" deny indigenous peoples their knowledge forms as it accommodates outsiders at the expense of those who know their knowledge form even better.

From what Mawere tells us, there is no point in us dropping off the concept of indigenous knowledge for endogenous knowledge. We concur with Mawere that the argument by some scholars that "indigenous" implies partiality and the local as opposed to the whole and the global is not only false but pejorative. It is, as Mawere further argues, insidiously meant to prejudice and denigrate the indigenous peoples especially those of Africa to ensure that they remain dehumanised and indeed in a whirlpool of confusion. The argument is in fact frivolous and evil intended. Following Mawere's argument above we advance that the proposed change of terminology from indigenous knowledge to endogenous knowledge is meant to mask the identity of the former and a mechanism of dispossession to dispossess Africans of their knowledge forms. This attempt to dispossess Africans of their worthwhile possessions is nothing strange to Africa. During trans-Atlantic slavery, African bodies, knowledge forms, and material wealth were forcibly taken away from Africa. The same scenario prevailed during colonialism when Africa was dispossessed in many respects ranging from governance, the polities, legal systems, economic systems, languages, material wealth, religion, human capital, knowledge forms, and cultural capital. The ultimate aim of dispossessing the African peoples was to delink them, in the name of hybridity and modernity, from what is typically and rightfully theirs. Besides, the dispossession of the African peoples of their concepts and terminologies was meant to limit their autonomy such that they remain inextricably linked and dependent on their former masters. Once all this has been revealed, even against the will of Eurocentrists and the empire, one wonders why the deconstruction of "indigenous knowledge" to "endogenous knowledge" is necessary. Many other critical questions arise: Why deconstruction is concentrated on the Global South (or the so-called peripheries) and not the Global North or the so-called empire? Is it that the Global North terminologies, polities, cultures, economic systems, political systems, knowledge forms, languages, religions, and cultures are pure such that they don't need deconstruction? Why is it that the deconstruction project concentrate on trivial issues such as the deconstruction of non-offensive terms like indigenous knowledge leaving out offensive terms such as "white people" and "black people" especially in this world where in reality there are no white and black people? There is no doubt, therefore, that the current deconstruction project is a way to sidestep demands for deconstruction of slavery and colonial injustices as well as offensive terms conjured by Eurocentricists. Yet, anti-colonialists and critical scholars of repute warn us against self-enslavement and being bearers of uncritical minds. Munyaradzi Mawere, for example, suggests how the decolonial project can achieve positive results if used critically and cautiously when he argues that "he who fights smoke will never extinguish the fire except if he fights the fire itself. The decolonial process can never achieve a level ground justice in both resource (re-)distribution and conceptual theorisation except if the philosophical foundations that brought the injustices and misrepresentations are dislodged and decolonised first and foremost" (Mawere 2015c: 8). On the same note Marcus Garvey would want us to challenge any narrative that is Eurocentric, oppressive and exploitative thus he declares in a speech in Nova Scotia: "We are going to emancipate ourselves from mental slavery because whilst others might free the body, none but only ourselves can free the mind" (Marcus Garvey 1937). So, who is going to emancipate us, if not ourselves, from hegemonic epistemologies and terminologies? Who shall free us, if not ourselves, from foreign languages, cultures, terminologies, political systems, religions, and economic systems, among other such forms of colonially-biased oppression and exploitation?

Basing on the critical analysis we offer here and those reasons proffered by Mawere, we maintain that there is need to uphold and promote the continual use of the term IK. We further argue that indigenous knowledge in general and traditional medicinal knowledge in particular is an issue of concern in academic circles in Zimbabwean communities and beyond. This has largely been because in its attempt to disarm Africans of their dignity and humanity the colonial government despised indigenous knowledge as unscientific, illogical, local, outdated, and anti-development (Mawere 2015a). However, it is piteous and nerve-racking to note that there is a public outcry in most Zimbabwean communities that the so-called Western medicine is not meeting and addressing their health needs and concerns as expected. International organisations such as WHO have moved away from the colonial standpoint of denigrating indigenous health-care system to supporting the equal use of traditional medicine in meeting the health care needs of indigenous communities across the world. Such organisations realise the obtaining reality in many indigenous communities around the world that the introduction of Western medicine since the inception of colonialism has never been able to fill in the gap in health system created by colonial administration in many communities of the world. This owes to the fact that Western medicine, unlike African traditional medicine for example, poses a plethora of problems which include but not limited to shortage of manpower in hospitals, unaffordability, and its inability to handle other forms of ailments such as those that are spiritually and culturally influenced. Put differently, African Traditional Medicine (ATM) is socially and culturally irrelevant in many contexts such as those of Africa. Closely linked to the above reflection is the fact that Western-imposed development models, theories and experiments in Africa have largely failed mainly because they were exceptionally based on Western reductionist and positivist epistemologies which do not take into account African knowledge systems and values. As Sandra Harding (2001: 48) contends:

> Development was from its beginnings conceptualized as the transfer of Northern sciences and technologies and their standards of rationality and objectivity to the South. Yet the greatest effects of this process have been to create de-development and mal-development for the sixty or seventy percent of the world's citizens who are economically and politically most vulnerable. Development policies have primarily served to develop elites in the North and their allies in the South.

In concordant with Harding, Masoga and Kaya (2007: 154) argue that:

> This situation arises from the fact that the prevailing development paradigm has pressed the distinction between developed and underdeveloped into a dichotomy between good and bad. The underdeveloped societies of Africa including their people are treated as though they have neither validity nor integrity and may be violated at will. Their validity lies in repudiating what they are in order to be reconstituted into something new and better.

Contrary to the Western-imposed proposals, it is a platitude that Traditional Medicinal Knowledge (TMK) such as herbal medicine has been used by many Zimbabwean communities since the pre-historic era to meet their health care needs. According to the World

Health Organisation, over eighty percent of the people in developing countries continue to enjoy the use of traditional medicine for their health care needs. Masocha (2002) opines that traditional medicine continues to be handed down orally from generation to generation and kept without any written records. The continual deployment of TMK is adequate proof to demonstrate the resilience of African traditional institutions despite the colonial onslaughts and Western concocted theories they suffered in the guise of civilisation as colonial administration established its roots in the territories. The deep seated relations between IMK and the indigenous peoples is greatly influenced by the long age enmeshments and ties between the peoples of the territories and their ways of knowing and health care. Such knowledges should be studied on their own right, without using Euro-American epistemic lenses if at all we are to register real development and advancement in both medicine and science in general. This *volte-face* is important as development in any society requires adaptation, changing, refining, self-introspection, and in some cases abandoning traditional ideas and ways. It also involves giving out and borrowing values from other cultures. It is on the basis of this realisation that Masoga and Kaya (2007: 157) argue:

It is therefore, important that Africa must be truthfully studied on its own terms and to satisfy its people's needs through indigenous approaches. The philosophy and theory of truthful knowledge about Africa challenges all African researchers, academics and practitioners to unmask western ideologies about their continent, expose exploitation, injustices and explore local knowledge systems that promote values which facilitate an agenda of social emancipation and equity among all sections of societies, women, men, children, youth, disabled and HIV/AIDS victims.

This African traditional way of healing has its roots in African culture and cosmology. Simmons (2006) and Nhemachena (2015) support the use of traditional herbs and medicine arguing that it comes from external sources that is ancestors or healing spirits, therefore, important for the health and wellbeing of most people in the Zimbabwean communities. Zimbabwe, as part of the global world in general and WHO in particular endeavours to achieve health standards that allows its citizens to have a productive life (Bannerman 1983:7). The WHO provisions stipulates that access to health care is a basic and universal human right which remains a dream in most Zimbabwean communities where seeds of ill health are a common feature owing to the socio-political and economic climate. In the context of acute shortage of drugs, qualified health personnel, cash and other basic commodities (Nhemachena 2015), indigenous knowledge especially in traditional medicine is the only available option to save people from the menace of ill health.

According to Raschke and Cheema (2007), after years of denigrating and marginalising IK as inferior, backward, illogical, savage and an obstacle to development or ungodly, its potential in addressing challenges like human health problems remains recognisable in both many communities around the world. There is need for the extension of affordable, ideologically and culturally acceptable health care system to impoverished societies. Western medicine has failed to address the health needs of Africans. Therefore, indigenous knowledge must play a central role in the health care system in order to narrow the cultural gap in the conceptual appreciation of health and illness in Zimbabwe. Zimbabwean health sector can only be transformed if indigenous knowledge is recognised as an aspect to take a dominant position in the health care system.

Understanding indigenous knowledge and indigenous medicinal knowledge

The conceptualisation of indigenous knowledge (IK) is highly contested in academic circles such that its interpretation remains a battle-field open to academic missiles of all forms. Nevertheless, scholars seem to agree that IK is a complex, multifaceted and multi-dimensional phenomenon that explains the practices of knowledge forms of people of a particular geographic location. This understanding resonates with Eyong's (2007) conceptualisation as he notes that IK is holistic in nature and encompasses several disciplines like anthropology, development studies, geography, agricultural economics, information science, and human health as these relate to the people of a given geographical space. For other scholars like Dei (1993), IK can be understood as the epistemic saliency of cultural traditions, values, belief systems, and worldviews that in any indigenous society are imparted to the younger generation by community elders. Dei (1993) further notes that IK is the product of the direct experience of nature and its relationship with the social world: it is knowledge that is crucial for the survival of society in question. Such knowledge constitutes an indigenous informed epistemology. As Eyong (2007) elaborates, IK is a worldview that shapes the society's relationships with surrounding environments. Indigenous knowledge, thus, is based on cognitive understandings and interpretations of the social, physical, and spiritual worlds of a given society. It includes concepts, beliefs, perceptions and experiences of local peoples and their natural and human-built environments. Wane (2008) links indigenous knowledge with colonialism. He opines that IK is a form of resistance against colonialism and the dominance of Western culture and hegemony. His understanding resonates with Altieri (1995) who argues that IK is that knowledge which has refused to die despite onslaughts and threats of colonialism over time. Indigenous knowledge (IK) is, therefore, the knowledge of local (or indigenous people) of a given geographical space acquired from experimentation with locally available materials and subsequent consolidation of the outcome of the experimentation as a legitimate way of knowing. This connotes that IK is dynamic such that it undergoes modifications to respond to the changing needs and aspirations of the indigenous people. It is experiential and subjective because it is engrained in personal and direct experience (Dei 2000b).

We should be quick to point out that the concept of indigenous knowledge has its origins in the indigenous perspective or worldview. No wonder Simpson (2000) argues that indigenous knowledge can be distinguished from other forms of knowledge in that it is holistic, cyclic, and the relationship between humans and the spiritual world is relevant. Besides, indigenous knowledge implies that there are many truths based on individual experiences and sacredness of land and life. With this, it can be noted that using different perspectives to assess indigenous knowledge may be problematic as it may appear "irrational", "unscientific" and "accidental". These misconceptions, misunderstandings, and misrepresentations of IK based on differences in worldview have led to the denigration and caricaturing of indigenous knowledge as illegitimate way of knowing.

Basing on the various interpretations of the concept of IK as those underlined above, Simpson (2000) has argued that there is need for numerous definitions to accommodate its multi-disciplinary and adaptive nature. It can assume different definitions depending on the context and discipline. On this note, scholars seem to agree that IK is local knowledge of the indigenous people that have originated locally and naturally and has enabled people to manage their environment (Mapara 2009; Mawere 2014a, 2014b; Melchius 2001). Yet owing to the ubiquity in literature and interpretations of indigenous knowledge, Mawere's (2015a, b) definition of IK will be used for the purpose of this study. Mawere (2015a) interprets IK as a set of ideas, beliefs and practices that has been used by its people to interact with their environment and other people over a long period of time. Mawere further notes that indigenous knowledge, just like Western science, is scientific given that it also involves observation, trial and error, as well as experimentation. Mawere, thus, is against those who label indigenous knowledge as unscientific, illogical, superstitious, and backward.

It is worthwhile to note that within the realm of IK are many other forms of knowledge based on disciplinary fields such as agriculture and medicine, among others. The concept of Indigenous Medicinal Knowledge (IMK), for example, derives from IK. As the concept of IK itself, IMK has its roots in the pre-historic times. This knowledge, according to Chigodora et al (2002), has been treasured in the hearts and minds of indigenous communities and has been kept in great secrecy and closely guarded. It has been interpreted differently by different scholars. Chavunduka (1998:39), for example, related IMK with inheritance owing to the fact that the living people are the ones who continue to use and possess the knowledge. On a similar note, Muxhanga (1999:42) argues that IMK is knowledge accumulated by the local population over a long period of time. For him, this knowledge encompasses the way people deal and manage their immediate environment.

However, Chigodara et al (2007) links Indigenous Medicinal Knowledge with poverty as they note that most of the people who use traditional medicine in the rural areas are poor, that is, those who cannot afford to pay for the expensive medicine prescribed in hospitals and private doctors. It is on this note that some scholars have argued for the need to seriously consider the promotion and deployment of homemade frameworks, theories and models. Mawere (2014b), for instance, argues for the need of Africans to create and use context-based theories and home-grown concepts. Likewise, Nhemachena (2015) challenges African scholars not to merely apply theoretical and conceptual frameworks that are Eurocentric to Africa but to critic them and expose their weaknesses. He gives an example of some ailments like spiritual attacks which he argues that they do not require Western doctors to deal with for the latter cannot diagnose them. The arguments advanced by Mawere and Nhemachena are germane to Mamdani's who argues against Enlightenment which he says is exclusively European such that it excludes Africa as it does most of the world. For this reason, among others, Mamdani (2011) urges the African university to rethink its function and to carry out research that seeks to answer questions that have been formulated inside the continent in terms of both location and historical perspective.

Theorising Indigenous Knowledge Systems

The theoretical framework of this work is anchored on the perspective that indigenous knowledge systems (IKS) are a legitimate way of knowing: it is as legitimate as Western science or any other form of knowledge that one may think of. This is contrary to the Eurocentric perspective that views IKS as a form of knowledge based on trial and error while Western knowledge is science characterised by experimentation (Melchers 2001). Besides, it is important to note that IKS is a unique body of knowledge which does not need any validation from Western scientific knowledge (Mawere 2014a). Neither does it need verification by Western science given its uniqueness and context-based effectiveness. As noted earlier, all this does not mean to say that IK do not involve experimentation as Western science. No wonder, Eyong (2007) argues that IKSs were developed by experimentation though not documented and the knowledge systems were legitimised and fortified under suitable institutional frameworks, culture, and practices. They have been transmitted from generation to generation to enable indigenous people to survive and manage natural resources and ecosystems surrounding them like plants, animals, and water sources. We underline here that African IKS and Western scientific knowledge are both legitimate ways of knowing operating at different perspectives or worldviews such that it is misguided and overzealous to glorify one knowledge system at the expense of the other.

According to Warren and others (1991), IK is unique to a given culture and forms the basis of decision making in the management of natural resources and health care. It differs from Western scientific knowledge owing to the fact that it is moral, ethically-based, spiritual, intuitive, holistic, and has a larger social context (Barkes *et al* 1995:283). Besides, unlike Western science which focuses on the intellect and senses, indigenous science stresses the significance of intuition. This is one reason why Milburn (2004) argues that IK permits knowledge bearers to exist peacefully with each other and the environment and is anchored in traditional teachings, empirical observation and spiritual insight. The high prevalence of ailments in Zimbabwean indigenous communities has been largely attributed to the disruption of the cultural identity, spiritual life, environment quality, stability of local economies and political institutions which promote indigenous knowledge in the health care system. Das (1996:24) argues that traditional medicine is largely embedded in the culture and belief system of local people hence it is indigenous. The distinguished features of traditional medicine rest in its ability to focus on the whole patient as compared to Western medicine that concentrates on the specific biological aspects of diseases. This resonates with Nhemachena's (2015: 97) argument in favour of traditional medicine when he laments that "modern medicines that most Zimbabweans trust very much come from the roots and barks of trees, from plants, from forests, though they are then processed into capsules or tablets". With this, it can be deduced that traditional medicine responds well to the patient's ideology and belief system. According to Nchinda (1976:134), traditional medical system has quite a number of merits, especially with regards to aspects of accessibility, availability, acceptability and dependability. It is, therefore, interesting to note that although the use of traditional medicine seems to be losing value as most Zimbabwean communities have become more Christianised and westernised so to speak, in times of distress even the most devoted African Christians and westernised Zimbabweans tend to depend on it. As Mawere (2011) and Nhemachena (2015) observe, about eighty per cent of the population in developing countries especially Africa rely on traditional medicine for their health care needs. This is because indigenous medicine or what we call "soul-body medicine" tends to treat sick people in their totality by providing answers to the "why" question often asked by indigenous African patients. The holistic nature and culture-based approach to traditional health care is a significant aspect of indigenous medicinal knowledge which differentiates it from Western medicine.

Anyinam (1987) observes that at independence most Zimbabwean communities shunned Western medicine in favour of traditional medicine such that the period was characterised by a gradual revival of self-image as well as socio-cultural identity. This was because of the availability, accessibility, acceptability, and adaptability of traditional medicine. Besides, traditional medicine plays a prominent role in the curing and curbing of numerous psychological needs in the traditional system which remains unmet in the Western medical fraternity (see Kirkland 1992:10). More so, in formerly colonised societies such as those of Africa, it can be noted that Western medicine is and has become expensive and therefore in a bid to curb its ever rising costs, a return to traditional medicine remains a pre-requisite.

African-based beliefs on health and illness

In most African communities in general and Zimbabwean communities in particular, the belief system encompasses continuity between the living and the dead. Nhemachena (2015) stipulates that the ability to use medicinal plants implies a moral relationship with ancestors or the healing spirits and or God without whose support, the herbs remain valueless. This means that good health and sickness entail a balance between a person and his relationship with ancestors. According to Gumede (1990:41), being health is a token for good behaviour and the reverse is equally true for sickness. This resonates with Stangard (1986) who observes that Africans believe that a person's wellbeing largely depends on his/her relationship with the society. On the same note, Karim *et al* (1995:5), observes that peaceful co-existence with the society, family, and environment promotes health and wellbeing such that sickness is an indication of lack of harmony between a person and his/her immediate social environment. This observation cohere with the WHO's (1978:13) Report that sickness is a result of an imbalance or disequilibrium of men in his total ecological system. This stands in sharp contrast with the Western perspective of sickness which sees disease as doctor-oriented and mechanistic.

Thus, as highlighted above, the African conceptualisation of disease is in quite contrast to that of the West. African conceptualisation of disease is morally and spiritually linked such that any disease or ailment is traced to a particular moral or spiritual cause. With this understanding in mind, it might be important to briefly explain how illness and disease are normally classified in both Western and African contexts.

Karim and others (1994:6) differentiates between natural and supernatural causation of sicknesses:

"Natural" causation

This denotes sickness with a specific, recognisable and predictable cause. This form of sickness occurs periodically as part of normal life, is fleeting in nature, and resolve completely. Examples are coughs, colds, and slight fever, stomachache and headache ailments. They abruptly respond to both Western and traditional medicine. If the symptoms continue and fails to respond to ordinary treatment then the ailment is automatically regarded as an abnormal phenomenon such that reasons for its occurrence must be established. As Karim (1994:56) reminds us the African cultural belief system addresses the "who" and the "why" question of an individual health, hence the significance of the ancestral spirits must be appreciated.

While this category of causation, to some extent, applies to African contexts, Western-biased perspective of causation seems to dominate this terrain. This is because in Western contexts diseases and ailments are often traced to natural causes such as pathogens of some sort, and never traced to a supernatural cause as in the case of African-based context.

Supernatural causation

This refers to culture-bound illnesses that are perceived to be governed by natural laws and the prescription is bound up with the African traditional notion of health and sickness. Chavunduka (1994:69) classifies sickness into cultural and social categories. Examples of such sicknesses are those associated with menarche, child birth, miscarriage and death. Besides, there are also cases of spirit possession and bewitchment where sorcerers, witches or jealous people may place harmful objects in the path of an enemy resulting for example in stroke or other forms of illness (Karim *et al* 1994:6).

Knowledge of indigenous plants and their uses in Zimbabwean communities

Indigenous peoples in most Zimbabwean communities possess a wealthy of information about plants that have a multi – purpose use in their localities. These multi-purposeful plants are used as food and medicine for curing various ailments. This can be illustrated in table 1 below:

Table 1: Showing indigenous medicinal plants and type of ailments they cure

Botanical name/Indigenous name	Plant part used	Ailment treated	Preparation of dose
Mutamba/ Strychnos Spinoser/ Klapper apple	Barks; Leaves	Immune boosting, Stomach-ache, diarrhea, gastro-intestinal problems, venereal diseases like syphilis and gonorrhea, pneumonia, bronchitis, rushes, skin problems, irritation. Caffeine in leaves can help breathing in premature babies. Also used to treat bleeding as well as chest problems and genital warts. Fruit is nutritious supplement of food for rural communities.	The dose is orally administered by boiling fresh barks in water and drink. Besides, the unripe fruit is broken, opened, mixed with water and boiled. Allow the infusion to cool and apply to the genital area.

Muroro/ Annona Stenophylla	Roots	Chest pains, Sexually transmitted diseases such as gonorrhea and syphilis	Roots are crushed and put in a glass of water and drunk
Mubikasadza / Rhus Dentata	Leaves	All Stomachache problems such as diarrhea, dysentery. They also help in the treatment of ulcers	Leaves are harvested and whilst still fresh are chewed and the sap is swallowed
Mubvumira/ Karkia/ Aiminota	Barks	Used to treat diseases such as cholera, dysentery, diarrhea, typhoid and also constipation.	The bark is collected from the eastern and western sides of the trunk. It is crushed, mixed with water and drunk. Besides the bark can be dried, crushed and the powder is mixed with porridge and ate.
Mupfura	Roots	Sore eyes	The roots are crushed and then boiled. There steam is then directed into sore eyes.
Mugan'acha/ Lannea discolour	Fiber extract; Roots	Duration of menstrual flow; Sore eyes as eye drops	The fiber extract was crushed and mixed with water and drunk in the Zimbabwean communities since time immemorial to

			reduce the duration of menstrual flow. Besides the roots extracts were crushed and directed into sore eyes as eye drops.
Mubhanana / Entandorag	Fruit peels	Genital warts	The peels of the fruit are burnt, mixed with Vaseline and applied to the genital area twice a day after bathing.
Mumango/Mangifera Indica L.	Barks	Diarrhea; Dysentery	The barks of the tree have an anti-bacterial, anti-inflammatory, anti-fungal and anti-viral property. The bark extract are crushed, mixed with water and drunk.
Gavakava / Aloe Feroc	Leaves	Tuberculosis	The leaves are crushed and put in a glass of water. The mixture is drunk.
Munyii/Berchemia	Barks; Roots	Nose bleeding; Flue and colds; Skin itching; Abdominal pains	Bark extract are crushed, mixed with water and drunk. The roots are also chewed and sap swallowed for curing

			abdominal pains.
Mukute / Sygium Cordatum	Barks	Tuberculosis	The bark is stripped off from the eastern and western side of the trunk and crushed. It is mixed with water to make a decoction and drunk.
Ruvavashuro / Indigofera/Stetiflora	Roots	Diarrhea	Roots are crushed, put in a glass of water and the mixture is drunk after a while.
Tsangamidzi / Zingier / Affinale	Roots	Stomach pains	A small piece of root was chewed and the sap swallowed.
Zumbani / Lippria/Javanica	Leaves and twigs	Coughs/ Colds	Leaves and Twigs are boiled in water; the infusion is taken as tea.
Murwiti / Dalbergia/ Melanoxylon	Barks	Asthma	Leaves are dried and used to make a cigarette that is smoked.
Mutodzvo/Leonotis/Leonarus	Leaves	Ulcers	Fresh leaves are taken, chewed and the sap is swallowed
Munhengeni / Ximerna/ Americana L.	Barks; Leaves; Roots	Backache; Unstable pregnancy; Constipation; Cultural bound syndrome;	Barks are crushed, mixed with a glass of water and the decoction is drunk.

		Fertility impotent; Gonorrhea	Leaves are chewed and the sap is swallowed. Roots are crushed, put in a glass of water and again the mixture is drunk.
Mubvamaropa/ Pletocarpus	Bark Fruits; Roots	Bleeding, coughing, leg pain, infertility in women, sore eyes	Barks are collected from the eastern and western sides of the tree, crushed and mixed with water and drunk. The fruits are crushed and directed into sore eyes. The roots are crushed and mixed with water and the decoction is drunk.
Muzeze / Peltotophorum	Fruits; Roots	Sore eyes; Diarrhea; STI; Syphilis; Toothache	Roots or fruits are crushed, mixed with water and the decoction is drunk.
Munzvirumombe / Vangueria/ Infansta/Burch	Roots	Diarrhea	Roots are crushed, put in glass of water and the mixture is drunk.
Mutunduru /Garciana/ Buillensis	Fruit	Aphrodisiac for men	Ripe fruit is eaten
Muvanga/ Arcacia Karoo	Roots	Gonorrhea; Syphilis	Clean roots with water and

				dry them. Crush the roots and then mix with water. The mixture is drunk three times a day.
Musvosve / *Macaranga*/ *Cayonisis*		Roots	Aphrodisiac for men	Take the roots, clean and dry them. After that grind the roots to a powder and mix with porridge.
Mutsubvu/*Mukubvu*/ *Papayas*	*Vilex*	Leaves	Colds	Dry the leaves and use them to make a cigarette and smoke.

Source: *Field research and the botanic garden of Zimbabwe (December 2015)*

Role of traditional belief systems in protecting indigenous medicinal plants in Zimbabwe

In the Zimbabwean communities, the indigenous people do not approve the planting of medicinal plants because of their belief that indigenous plants lose their curative properties when cultivated. However, they have devised their own indigenous ways of harvesting and protecting indigenous medicinal plants to ensure their sustainability. This shows that our forebears were environmentally sensitive when harvesting medicinal plants.

Traditional methods of collecting medicinal plants used by herbalists

In most parts of the country, the indigenous people developed some myths surrounding the collection of different herbs and tree barks for medicinal purposes. It was, for example, traditionally believed that bark from a tree should only be collected for medicine provisions. Besides, it was collected from the east- and west-facing parts of the trunk. Bark taken from the north and south faces was believed to be ineffective for medicinal purposes. We reveal here that collecting barks from the east and west faces of the tree ensured that the plant, although ring-barked, was not completely destroyed but reserved for future use. The tree, for instance, could still have access to sunlight such that it could easily photosynthesise and recover from the ring-barking stress.

Since the pre-historic era, it was again traditionally encouraged that when collecting roots for medicinal use, not all the plant's roots were collected. According to Mavi and Shava (1997), this would allow the plant to feed from its remaining roots and survive. It was believed that if part of a plant was collected for medicinal use and as a result that plant perished, then the patient being treated using that medicine would also dies.

It was strongly believed that the collection of bark, roots and leaves from a plant that showed signs of having been collected from by another *n'anga* (traditional healer) was prohibited. It was believed that when an *n'anga* used a plant to treat a patient, the patient's disease was transferred into that plant. When another *n'anga* subsequently used the same plant to treat a patient, the disease of the previous patient would be transferred to the new patient. This belief ensured that the plant recovered from the effects of collection.

A traditional healer we interviewed for this research, for example, pointed out that whenever an *n'anga* collected annuals for medicinal use they had to leave behind some individuals of the species at the collection site. It was believed that if a species was completely destroyed in a particular area, then the patient to whom the medicine from the species was administered would also die. By leaving behind some representatives of the collected species, localised rare species were protected from extinction.

Lastly, seeds were rarely used for medicinal purposes. When they were used, it was usually as a lucky charm placed in a pocket or hung around the neck. This limited use of seeds allowed the perpetuation of plant species through seeding. This shows that our ancestors were aware of the dangers of the extinction of medicinal plants.

Challenges and threats to indigenous medicinal knowledge

There is widespread concern that indigenous medicinal knowledge is fast disappearing in most Zimbabwean communities. This owes to high levels of illiteracy peculiarly prevalent in most communities. Besides, some factors that have spearheaded the fast disappearance of indigenous medicinal knowledge include idea robbery (or plagiarism) as well as cultural barriers. The practitioners of indigenous knowledge in Zimbabwe are not well recognised and this to some extent has led to the vanishing of indigenous medicinal knowledge. Owing to large scale urbanisation which has led to global warming and deforestation, a lot of indigenous medicinal plants have been either destroyed or their use forgotten. This has in turn led to the disappearance of indigenous medicinal knowledge. Other factors that have threatened the indigenous medicinal knowledge are the fast changing life styles as well as the disintegration of the traditional joint family system.

In addition, the decline in the use of indigenous medicinal knowledge in some societies can also be attributed to globalisation, change in technology, overpopulation, breakdown of traditional land tenure and marine tenure systems, loss of indigenous control of areas and resources, and changes in worldview due to factors such as urbanisation and loss of intimate contact with land (Berkes and others 1985). Besides, colonialism again eroded indigenous knowledge systems as well as a wealth of knowledge about food habits, health and illness. The erosion of indigenous knowledge in health care and the whole area of traditional pharmacology and its preventive cures have been implicated in the prevalence and spread of chronic diseases among the indigenous communities in Zimbabwe.

The way forward

It is important to note that indigenous people in most Zimbabwean communities have a wealth of knowledge on usage of medicinal plants in their respective areas. They can provide adequate leads for scientific validation of their indigenous knowledge and be helped to create databases of this important indigenous knowledge.

Besides, it is a worthwhile venture to capture and store indigenous knowledge from the Zimbabwean communities that for a long time have acted as custodians of traditional wisdom by creating videotapes of illiterate practitioners of indigenous knowledge.

More so, custodians of indigenous knowledge may need to be given some form of incentives and encouraged to divulge and publicise their knowledge in the interest of the society in much the same way Western science has done.

Lastly, we recommend the establishment of some inroads and linkages between universities and people at the grassroots, partnership between local communities, research institutions, pharmaceutical companies and other industries is essential for the promotion of indigenous knowledge. In fact, there is much room in a country like Zimbabwe to move away from hegemonic epistemologies and health care systems and foster indigenous wisdom and knowledge systems.

References

Ali, A. 2011. Trends and challenges in traditional medicine in Africa, *Journal of traditional complementary and alternative medicines (AJTCAM)*, Published online: 10.4314/ajtm.v8555.

Altieri, M. A. 1995. *Agroecology: The science of sustainable agriculture*, IT Publishers: London.

Anyinam, C. 1987. Availability, accessibility, adaptability: Four attributes of African ethno-medicine, *Journal of Social Science and Medicine* 25: 803-811.

Bannerman, R. H. 1987. Traditional medicine in modern health care, *World Health Forum* 3: 8-26, 90-94.

Berkes, F.; Folke, C. & Gadgil, M. 1995. Traditional ecological knowledge, biodiversity, resilience and sustainability: In C. A Perring's, K. G. Maler, C. Folke. S. S. Holling and B. O. Jansson (Eds) *Biodiversity conservation and economic development: The policy problem*, Kluwer Academic Publishers: Netherland.

Dei, G. 1993. Rethinking the role of indigenous knowledges in the academy, *International Journal of Inclusive Education*, 4 (2): 111-132.

Chavunduka, G. L. 1994. *Traditional medicine in modern Zimbabwe*, Harare: University of Zimbabwe.

Chigodora, P., Masocha, R., Mutenheri, F. 2007. The role of indigenous medicinal knowledge in the treatment of ailments in rural Zimbabwe: The case of Mutirikwi communal lands, *Journal of Sustainable development in Africa* Vol 9, No 2.

Das, M. 1996. Traditional medicine: Perspectives and policies in health care development, *Development Southern Africa* 7:351-358.

Gumede, M. V. 1990. *Traditional healers: A medical PR actioner's perspective*, Black Shows: Cape Town.

Eyong, T. C. 2007. Indigenous knowledge and sustainable development in Africa: Case study on central Africa, *Centre for development research* (ZEFa): Germany.

Garvey, M. 1937. *Speech against slavery*, Menelik Hall, Sydney: Nova Scotia.

Harding, S. 2001. Multiculturalism and Postcolonialism: What difference does it make to Western Scientific Epistemology? *Science Studies* 1/2001, pp. 45-54.

Houtondji, P. 1997. Endogenous Knowledge: Research Trials, Dakar: CODESRIA

Karim, A. S. S.; Ziqubu-Page, T. T., and Arendse, R. 1994. Bridging the gap: Potential for health care partnership between African traditional healers and biomedical personnel in South Africa, Report of the South African medical research council, South African medical research council, *South African Medical Journal Insert*, December 1994: South Africa.

Kirkland, J., Mathews, H. F.; Sullivan, C. W.; and Baldwin, K. (Eds), 1992. *Herbal and magical medicine: Traditional healing today*, Duke University Press: Durban.

Mamdani, M. 2011. The importance of research in a university, Mahmood Mamdani Makerere Institute of Social Research, 2011-04-21, Issue 526. Available at: http://www.pambazuka.org/en/issue/526.

Mapara, J. 2009. Indigenous knowledge systems in Zimbabwe: Juxtaposing Post-Colonial theory, in Journal of Pan African Studies, 3 (1) 139-155

Masocha, M. *et al.* 2002. *Identification of medicinal plants used in the treatment of abdominal diseases*, Price Press: Harare.

163

Mavi, S. and Shava, S. 1997. Traditional Methods of conserving medicinal plants in Zimbabwe, Botanic gardens conservation international, Vol 2 (80

Mawere, M. 2015a. Indigenous knowledge and public education in sub-Saharan Africa, *Africa Spectrum*, 50 (2): 57-71.

Mawere, M. 2015b. *Humans, other beings and the environment: Harurwa (edible stinkbugs) and environmental conservation in southeastern Zimbabwe*, Cambridge Scholars Publishers: Cambridge.

Mawere, M. 2011. Ethical quandaries in spiritual healing and herbal medicine: A critical analysis of the morality of traditional medicine advertising in southern African urban societies, *Pan African Medical Journal*, 2011, 10: 6.

Mawere, M. 2014a. *Environmental conservation through Ubuntu and other emerging perspectives*, Langaa Publishers: Bamenda.

Mawere, M. 2014b. *Divining the future of Africa: Healing the wounds, restoring dignity and fostering development*, Langaa Publishers: Bamenda.

Mawere, M. 2015c. 'Indigenous Mechanisms for Disaster Risk Reduction in Africa,' Paper Presented to the *2015 EDITION OF THE DZIMBAHWE ARTS FESTIVAL (DAF) ACADEMIC SYMPOSIUM,* (1-3 October 2015*),* Great Zimbabwe University: Zimbabwe.

Maxhlanga, J. C. L. 1999. "The role of indigenous knowledge systems in the development of Mozambique;" In Matowanyika, J. Z. *Hearing the crub's cough: Perspectives and emerging institutions for indigenous knowledge systems in land resources management in southern Africa*, IUCN Regional office for Southern Africa: IUCN.

Melchius, G. 2001. *Biodiversity and conservation*, Science Publishers, Inc: Enfield.

Milburn, M. 2004. Indigenous nutrition: using traditional food knowledge to solve contemporary health problems, American Indian Quarterly (28) 411-434

Nchinda, J. 1976. Health problems in rural communities, Zimbabwe, *Social Science and Medicine* 29: 927-932.

Nhemachena, A. 2015. Sensing Presences: Health, Illness and Resilience in Contemporary Rural Zimbabwe, *The Journal of Pan African Studies*, vol.8, No 8, November 2015.

Raschke, V. & Cheema, B. 2007. Colonization, the new world order, and the eradication of traditional food habits in East Africa: Historical perspective on the nutrition transition, *Public Health Nutrition*, 11 (7): 662–674.

Sebua, S. S. & Martin, J. 2011. Ethnobotanical survey of medicinal plants used by Bapedi traditional healers to treat erectile dysfunction, *Journal of Medicinal Plant Research* Vol 7 (7):349 -357.

Sigauke, J., Chiwaura, H., & Mawere, M. 2014. 'Connoisseurs of traditional medicine: The use and efficacy of traditional medicine in pregnant women's health care,' In: *African cultures, memory and space: Living the past presence in Zimbabwean heritage*, Langaa Publishers: Bamenda.

Simmons, D. 2012. Modernising Medicine in Zimbabwe: HIV/AIDS and Traditional healers, Nashville: Vanderbilt University press.

Simpson, L. 2000. 'Anishinaabe ways of knowing,' In: Oakes, R. Riee, S. Koolage, L. Simpson & N. Schuster (Eds), Aboriginal health, identity and resource, (pp. 165-185), Winnipeg, Manitoba, Canada.

Staugard, F. 1986. *Traditional health care in Botswana, in the professionalisation of African medicine*, edited by Last, M. and Chavunduka, G. L., Manchester University Press: Manchester.

Steinhauer, E. 2002. Thoughts on an indigenous research methodology, *Canadian Journal of Native Education* 26, 69.

Turnball, D. 2000. *Masons, Tricksters and Cartographers: Comperative studies in the sociology of scientific and indigenous knowledge*, London: Routledge

Wane, N. 2008. Mapping the field of indigenous knowledge in anti-colonial discourse: A transformative journey in Education, *Race, Ethnicity and Education*, 11(2): 183-197.

Warren, D. M., Slikkerveer, J. & Brokensha, D. 1991. *Indigenous knowledge systems: The cultural dimensions of development*, Kegan Paul International: London.

UN .2008. United Nations Declarations on the Rights of Indigenous Peoples, UN

WHO .1978. *The promotion and development of traditional medicine*, WHO Technical

Report Series, Geneva.

Chapter Seven

Yoruba Playwrights and Politics in Nigeria: An Examination of Selected Yoruba Written Plays

'Layò Ògúnlolá

Introduction

The large geographical expression that metamorphosed into an entity christened Nigeria by 1914 has indeed come of age. Since her birth in 1914, Nigeria, the most populated "Black" Country in the world, with two protectorates namely the Northern and Southern protectorates, amalgamated by Sir Frederick Lugard. Sixteen years earlier, Flora Shaw, later married to Lugard, first suggested that the several British Protectorates on the Niger be collectively known as Nigeria (Kirk-Greene, 1956). a land of diverse and multiple ethnic nationalities endowed with good climate, fertile soil for agricultural activities and rich mineral resources had weathered and is still weathering different crises socially, politically, religiously and economically to survive as corporate entity.

Before the amalgamation of 1914, no place would be defined as the Nigeria society but by 1914, there developed the Hausa/Fúlàní, Ìgbò and Yorùbá societies with existing ethnic boundaries which were altered during the period of the colonial rule (Ike 2000, p.2). Although the creation of Nigeria was as a result of European ambitions, it would be wrong to assume that its people had little history before its final boundaries were negotiated by Britain, France and Germany in the twentieth century. Like it was in other nations at the time, Yorùbá society had its own system of government as an ethnic group. The system was based on king's ownership of land as explicated in Marxism. Under this system, the King was the head of the political, religious, economic and social administration of his domain. For instance, as the head of judiciary, all cases, no matter the magnitude, ends with the king's verdict. Whatever the king said was binding on both the prosecutor and the defendant.

167

Like in some African countries like Zimbabwe and Tanzania, the local constitution provides for checks to curb excessive use of power by the king. (See Posselt, 1935, Spierenburg, 2004), the Ọba's council such as the Òyọ́mèsì in the Old Òyọ́ Empire were there to checkmate the King's misuse of power. Their roles could be likened to that of the present day Houses of Assembly and Representative who rather than checkmating the President's misuse of power are themselves corrupt, autocratic and despotic.

Today, the situation in Nigeria has changed. Yorùbá say *"ibi tí a bá pè ní orí, a kìí fi ibè tèlè"* literally meaning "it is improper to walk with one's head on the ground". This infers that a leader/elder should not be underrated or insulted. Such saying is no more respected among the Yorùbá. The kings and community leaders in general have lost this value and this is not doing the society any good. The traditional rulers of today, are prepared to mortgage the sacredness of their throne to the highest bidder. They bestow chieftaincy titles on the rich regardless of the source of their wealth. It is this corruption-ridden society that forms the themes of the two selected plays under study.

This implies that some factors such as Western Animism have disturbed African Indigenous knowledge as we shall see later in this work. In the arduous task of building a virile and egalitarian Nigerian society, successive Nigerian leaders since independence (military and civilian), had mapped out plans and strategies that have not seen the light of the day because of exigency and lack of clear vision of the type of Nigeria of their dreams.

Àláọ́ (2006, p. 248) notes that democratic principles as exercised before and even after independence show that many of the Nigerian politicians are yet to be politically matured. This political immaturity was responsible for series of political crisis over the motion for self-government by Late Chief Anthony Enahoro in 1953, Kano riot of 1953, census crisis of 1962. Other political crises were the Action Group crisis of 1962, Federal election crisis of 1954, the Western Nigeria election crisis of 1965, the general election crisis of 1983 as well as the annulment of June 12, 1993 presidential election. These crises had indeed thrown Nigeria into political instability at various times and had created problems of national integration and loss of confidence in democratic institutions.

Ethical norms and accountability, which are critical for every administrative system, were relegated to the background. Employment in the public service was seen as a route for accumulation of wealth rather than a means of providing services to the people. Politicians became business partners to the capitalist European businessmen. The large-scale corruption led to the first coup on January 28, 1966.

As earlier stated, Nigeria is made up of multiplicity of ethnic groups with varieties of languages, occupation and architecture and so on, yet bound together by several unifying factors such as economic and historical ties. However, the country's motto: *Unity and Strength, peace and progress*, seems to be the country's greatest problem which includes among others: marginalization, domination of political leadership by a section of the country. For instance, records have shown that the North has produced Nigeria President than any other tribe in the country. Religious bigotry, ethnicity and mediocrity have become the order of the day. The use of political thugs has put the entire society into undesirable unrest. With these factors present in the polity, the nation cannot grow in strength and unity.

Yorùbá literary writers have been addressing the theme of political oppression that often leads to various forms of undesirable unrest in their publications. They preach revolution and freedom from oppression through songs (protest or war songs), proverbs which are believed to arouse the feelings of pain, sadness and gives a stimulating factor to peoples' actions. It is a medium through which writers communicate with the readers.

The objective of this chapter is to examine and evaluate the present political system in Nigeria as presented by the selected playwrights and its consequences on the nation as a whole. It also discusses the solutions provided for freedom from oppression by the authors. In all, two Yorùbá written plays with political themes are chosen. They include Oḍúnjo's *Agbálówóọ̀mẹ̀rìí Baálẹ̀ jòntolo,* (1976) and Adeyẹmi's *Ìṣẹ̀lú Oníréké Ògè,* (2014). Our choice of texts is based on the fact that the chosen texts have political themes with elements of colonialism going by the type of governance operating at the time.

The Yorùbá traditional system of government was based on the principle of *Ọba ló nilẹ̀* meaning "the king has control over everything and he has final say in all issues" though may be seen as a form of oppressive rule, it provides checks and balance.

The chapter evaluates how Yorùbá literary writers present Nigeria's political situation in general and their views about it. The research methodology centres on text appreciation. The research employs the Marxist sociological theory of literature to put the record straight, that although Nigeria got her independence from colonial rule, yet colonialism is still noticed within the Nigerian society, and that in line with Karl Marx and his associates' opinion, the society is not folding its arms, rather, it is rising and fighting for its freedom from oppression. The chapter observes that the political administration of Nigeria has changed from what it used to be in the past. One can ask if Nigerian leaders today are truly leaders. The chapter approves protest and revolutionary actions as the best means of freeing the society from oppression. It recommends that the device should be more effectively used to add aesthetic values to the portrayal of the cultural values of Nigeria.

Scholars such as Adéléke (1986,1995), Ògúndèjì (1988, 1989, 1990, 2001, 2009), Sheba (1995), Ògúnsínà (1995), Alùkò (1993), Arohunmólàsẹ (1997), Abíólạ (2005), to mention just a few, had worked on various Yorùbá written plays, but none of them to the best of our understanding has really addressed the political administration of the Yorùbá society as presented in the selected play texts with political themes hence, the need for this chapter. The scope is limited to the examination of the two selected written plays using the Marxist's Sociological theory of literature as our theoretical framework.

Theoretical Framework: Sociological Theory (the Marxist Approach)

A theory can be described as an instrument in the hand of a literary critic used to analyse the content and form of a literary work. It gives an insight into the thinking of a literary artist. Adéyẹmí (2006, p.4) is of the view that "òtè̩ tí lítírésò̩ bá dì, ogbón lámèyító níí tú u jáde sí gbangba" meaning "the secret in a literary work is exposed by the literary critic (a theorist)". This implies that the thoughts of a

170

literary artist are best understood through the application of a literary theory. A theory exposes and publicizes the writer and his work.

A literary theory is a body of harmonized precepts needed to solve emerging questions from a literary work. A literary theory is necessary to guide the interpretation and analysis of a literary work so as to give the work associated meaning and interest. A theory helps in managing reality. Nevertheless, it has to be critically examined before it is adopted so that it would not distort reality.

Several literary theories are available to literary critics. Among them are: Formalism, Structuralism, Feminism, Post-colonialism, Marxism, New Historicism etc., but for the purpose of this study, we adopt the sociological theory of literature, the Marxist approach.

Adéyemí (2001) asserts that power tussle or power conflict between the rich, the average and the poor people is causing a lot of problem for the human race in general. Òpèfèyítìmí (1997) asserts that the few powerful, rich and highly influential people are using their positions to oppress others. This is the main focus of Marxist ideology. They are concerned with the situation of inequality within the society and this they want to find a solution to. They believe that the economic situation of a society determines her polity. Therefore, the two determine the relationship that would exist among the people of such society.

To Marx and his advocates, to put a stop to oppression and colonization, the oppressed must fight and compete with the person or groups of oppressor involved. This is the bottom line of Belbeare's (1976: 193) suggestion that:

> There must be in effect, little microcosms of a new
> society growing amidst the old. Small groups of people
> would act on it in the direction of the new and become
> different people (with evolving consciousness) as they did.
> Opèfèyítìmí (1977: 48) opines that:

> *Tíorí Marx ń fé kí òǹkòwé lo isé oná rè gégé bí agbára
> àti irinsé láti tú àsírí àwon aládàanlá láwùjo, ó sì fé kí
> òǹkòwé se akitiyan bí àwùjo se lè ra ara rè padà tí inú
> terútomo yóò fi dùn.*

Marx's theory wants writers to use their works as an instrument to expose the secret of the Capitalists in the society. It also wants writers to make effort on how the society can free itself in order to make everybody happy.

This implies that capitalist activities had been in existence long time ago. This is not restricted to African countries rather, the world in general, but in different forms. What Marxists are advocating is that wherever such situation exists, the people should join forces together and fight it, the magnitude notwithstanding.

In like manner, Dolbeare (1976: 188-265) asks:

What kind of awareness must we see? Is it one section within each group in a society that must first experience a change before others or many people will experience the changes before it actually starts? How do we take power off the hands of the authority who presently holds power? Is it forcefully with war or gently? What will the new society look like? How do we make use of the change?

Answers to the questions above shall be used as a guide to the analysis of the selected texts to prove that Marxist theory is suitable for the work. We want to see if the selected authors actually used their works to expose the secret of their society, if they actually used their work to re-awaken the poor to their responsibility to free themselves from their oppressors or not.

Nigerian Politics as presented by the selected Authors

Most Yorùbá playwrights like the traditional poets regard themselves as the conscience of the society. They do not only reflect the socio-political, cultural and economic activities of the society, they also advocate social and political change. They resist and condemn the neo-colonial order with its manifestations of corruption, violence and oppression. Examples of such plays are the ones examined in this chapter.

The selected authors in their works opine that Nigerian Politicians (which their works depict), for instance, practice politics of oppression. They use their positions to oppress the masses and to lord over the less privileged. In *Ìṣèlú Oníṛekẹ́ Ọgẹ̀*, Kòyókòyó party under the leadership of Igúnṣèyí, the incumbent president of Borípẹ́. can be described as an oppressor. As the party's name implies, they are never satisfied. No matter their wealth, they would always want more, the means notwithstanding. They are driven by the id and ego personality.

The 'id' and ego in them would not allow them to think about others. The 'id' is the original source of personality, present in the new-born infant from which the ego and the super ego later develop. It consists of everything that is inherited, including institutional drives-sex and aggression.

Characteristics of the 'id' include among others: it is closely linked to the biological processes and provide the energy source (libido) for the operation of all the three systems. The 'id' seeks immediate gratification of primitive, pleasure-seeking impulses. The 'id', like the new born baby operates on the pleasure principle.

During the party's political campaign, a member of the crowd asks Igúnṣèyí to explain to the crowd what he achieved during his first term in office and what he forgot to do that he now wants to accomplish if re-elected? Igúnṣèyí is surprised to see somebody who is bold enough to confront him with such questions. He says:

> *Págà! Lójú ayé mi náà? Láìkú ekirì, a ò gbọ́dọ̀ fawo.*
> *rè ṣe gbẹ̀du. Bí igbín ò tilẹ̀ dunbẹ̀, enu ọpọlọ́ kò là á*
> *li gbó. (o.i. 35)*
> Ha! Even when I am still alive? Nobody uses
> the skin of a living '*ekirì*', in making a drum. If
> the snail is sour in soup, it is not the frog who
> will say it. (p. 35).

To prove his oppressive ideology, Igúnṣèyí immediately gives a sign to one of his area boy, *Panápaná*, who pounced on the person, beat him mercilessly and forces him out of the campaign arena. His suspected enemies are not spared either. He is a good example of Nigerian politicians who operate and are driven by the lion archetype.

The lion archetype is characterized by selfishness, greed, misuse of power, jealousy and the like. In Yorùbá mythology, the lion is the brute, wicked and merciless king. Whenever it is hungry, it roars and catches its prey effortlessly. This best describe the average Nigerian leader and this is in line with the theme addressed by Lérè Adéyẹmí in *Ìṣèlú Onírèkè Ògè*.

During one of his confrontations with *Wọlé*, one of the leaders of '*Ẹyin nìí dàkúko*', a human activist group in *Borípẹ̀*, who he accuses of being vocal, *Òkẹkẹ* orders *Panápaná* to get rid of *Àrèmú* saying:

> *E palè ṛe ṃó ká rí nnkan míiran sẹ. Ogbón inú ọmọ*
> *nìí rán ọmọ lọ ẹyìn odi, òfun ìmòṛàn nìí yan òmòṛàn*
> *léró, ìmòṛàn àmòjú ẹnu nìí yọni. E gbé kinní jálajàla*
> *bíi námò kúrò lágbo wa. (o.i.37)*

Clear him off so that we look for other things to
do. The wisdom in a child sends the child out of
town. The throat of the wise makes the wise a
passenger, too much wisdom troubles one.
Carry that rag out of this gathering. (p.37).

Panápaná also confirms the oppressive and despotic nature of *Igúnsèyí* when he tells *Àrèmú* that Chief *Igúnsèyí* has paid for the lives of people like *Àrèmú*. He then orders *Àrèmú* to disappear if he does not want to get lost as the public money disappears from the hands of politicians.

In like manner, in *Odúnjọ's Agbálówóọmẹrìí Baálẹ̀ Jòntolo*, Agbàkànmí, the Baálẹ̀ of Jòntolo is presented as a good example of politicians who use their positions to oppress the less privileged. They resemble the lion in their handling of issues especially the ones that affect them negatively. For instance, *Agbàkànmí*, the village head, on hearing that *Aṣere*, the main character, has plenty of gold in his custody, becomes jealous and would not believe *Aṣere* even when *Aṣere* tells him everything about the said gold. *Agbàkànmí* threatens to impound *Aṣere's* main source of income (his truck) from him if he fails to disclose other items he gets from the dead blind man. He says:

*[...] Ọmọlanke ṛe tí o fi máa n ru igi yóò lọ sí ọ̀ràn yìí
nítorí emi kò rí ohun tí enìyàn lè fi iru àpótí egbére
ṛe yìí ṣe. Ìwọ tí o gbà á ni yóò máa gbé e lọ, ṣùgbọn
Ọmọlanke ṛe yóò di díẹ̀ nínú wàhálà mi yóò sì di ti
ìlú láti oni lọ. (o.i. 23).*

The truck you use to carry logs would be sacrificed.
Because I cannot think of anything useful the teetered
box you present can do. You brought it, and you are to
take it away, but your truck would pay for just a little of
my troubles and would become the community's property
from today onward (p. 23).

The use of language of threat is common among political leaders
who see political offices as their birth right or their personal property
and they do everything within their reach to hold on to their political
posts. In *Ìṣelú Oníréké Ọ̀gẹ̀*, Igúnṣeyì, the incumbent president of
Bórìpẹ́, sees the hand writing on the wall that he is losing out of the
presidential race, he employs the services of political thugs and touts
in the likes of Àlùwó, Panápaná, and Abániwákú to disrupt the
election processes by beating up electoral officers, snatching ballot
boxes and even killing a police officer without minding the negative
consequences of their actions. This gives us the impression that
Politicians use hoodlums who bear fake names probably to hide their
proper identity and possibly to escape being arrested. Such names are
dreadful and create fear in people.

It is an irony that the electoral officers collaborate with *Kóyókóyó*
party to rig the election. A police officer stumbles on an electoral
officer thumb printing on ballot papers in favour of the *Kóyókóyó*
party. The electoral officer is confident and bold to invite the police
officer to join him in the thumb printing exercise. He says: '*Ọ̀gá, ọ̀nà
kan kò wọjà sá. Ẹ̀yin náà, e bá wa di í kó kún*" meaning "Sir, many roads
lead to the market place. You can also join us in our effort to ensure
that the boxes are filled up".

The case in Nigerian politics today is not different. There have
been reported cases of missing ballot papers, ballot boxes or ballot
papers already thumb printed in the name of one political party or
the other before election days. It is however sad that no good result
emanates from any investigation on such happenings, if they are

investigated at all. Quite a number of prominent political leaders have died in the hands of their political opponents. We have heard the case of a suspect who was reminded in police custody yet he won the senatorial election of his constituency even while in custody. Who dare ask how or why?

Another peculiarity about Nigeria political system is the several attacks launched on political opponents. Through the use of foul language, proverbial and inciting songs, lies, they castigate their political rivals even when it is glaring that they have nothing useful to offer the electorate.

In *Ìṣèlú oníreké ògè,* Igúnsèyí, the presidential candidate of the *Kòyókòyó* party at a campaign says:

> ... e má fetí sí àwọn aláriwo tí ń pera wọn ní "Dádì,"
> Dádì". "Dádì" mo ọmọ tó bí. Ara wọn nìkan ni wọn ń
> dádì, wọn kìí di ire fún elòmìíràn. E má fi ìbò yín sòfò.
> Egbé wa àti ìjọba wa ṣe gudugudu méje. Ilé ńlánlá pò
> nígboro Àjùbà ju ti ayé ìgbà kan lọ. Ọkọ bọ̀ọ̀lì bọ̀ọ̀lì ni
> ìjọba wa sètò kó pò ní ìlú. Ẹyin náà mò bí ìreṣì Kútọnu
> ṣe pò lójà tó... (o.i. 34-35).

> ... do not listen to those talkatives who call themselves
> "Dádì" "Dádì". Dádì knows his children. They pack for
> themselves only but not for others. Do not waist your
> votes. Our party and our government have done wonder-
> fully well. A lot of magnificent buildings can be found
> in Àjùbà town unlike in the past. Our government has
> arranged for the provision of heavy duty vehicles. You
> all know how plenty Cotonou's rice is in our markets... (pp.
> 34-35).

In *Agbàlówóọméríì Baálè Jòntolo*, Odúnjo presents Àgbàkànmí the political head of Jòntolo town who is supposed to guide his people right, as corrupt, autocratic, oppressive, dubious and greedy. When the secret behind Aṣẹre's 'wealth' gets to Àgbàkànmí, he plans and kills those who assist him to get the truth. He even plans to kill Aṣẹre to ensure that he takes possession of all the gold found inside the mysterious tree. Kìmí Àdúgbò, the only person who follows him to the thumb where the gold is found is to be killed if not for the fact that they both perish inside the 'tree' as a result of the act of greed displayed by Àgbàkànmí.

Asẹre and Àdigún his friend have earlier advised that the quantity of gold packed is enough, more so, to save Asẹre's truck from being spoilt. Àgbàkànmí responds:

> Kí ọmọlanke má bàjé! Bí ọmọlanke bá lè bàjé kí ó
> bàjé. Mo ní kí e lo kó kinní fún mi, e ń sọrọ ọmọlanke.
> Moríyíná àti Kìmí Àdúgbò, ẹyin e jé a lo ọ jàre, kí a jo
> gbé ẹrù náà síta, ẹni tí kò bá lo, kò níi pín nínú rè. (o.i. 52-53)
> If the truck will spoil, let it spoil. I ask you to go and
> pack the thing for me you are talking about the truck.
> Moríyíná and Kìmí Àdúgbò, let's go and bring the load
> out, anyone who fails to follow us will not have a share (p.
> 52-53).

The authors also portray Nigerian politicians as liars and self-centred people. This is not different from the Westerners who pretended to bring civilization to Africa whereas they brought colonization. A clear picture of this can be seen by comparing the themes in Delano's *Lójó Ojó Un* and *Ayé Dayé Òyìnbó*.

In *Lójó Ojó Un*, the author presents the political and religious situation in Yorùbaland before the coming of the Europeans but in *Ayé Dayé Òyìnbó*, he gives an overview of the cunning methods used by the Whiteman to usurp power from the Yorùbá Traditional rulers. Before the people know this, things have fallen apart and the centre can no longer hold.

The 'id' always likes to form a mental image or hallucination of the object that will reduce tension-wish fulfilment. Anybody that is controlled by 'id' trait loves to satisfy his/her needs irrationally with no consideration of reality.

The ego develops out of the 'id' because of the necessity for dealing with the real world. The hungry man has to have food if the tension of hunger is to be reduced. Thus, the ego obeys the reality principle which requires it to test reality and delay discharge of tension until the appropriate environmental conditions are found.

Features of the ego include the following: it operates by secondary process of thinking which is realistic and logical. The 'id' seeks immediate tension reduction by such primary processes or direct gratification of impulses or wish-fulfilling imagery but the ego takes the reward into consideration. It delays gratifications until the conditions are appropriate. The ego is essentially the executive of the personality because it decides what actions are appropriate. The ego mediates between the demands of the 'id', the realities of the world and the demands of the super-ego.

The super-ego is the third party of the personality. The super-ego is the internalized representation of the values and moral of the society as taught to the child by the parents and others. The super-ego judges whether an action is right or wrong according to the standard of the society. The 'id' seeks for pleasure, the ego tests reality and super-ego strives for perfection.

Features of the super-ego include the following: it is composed of the conscience. The conscience punishes by making the person feel guilty and the ego-ideal rewards by making the individual feel proud of himself. It inhibits the impulses of the 'id' particularly those that society prohibits, such as sex and aggression. It persuades the ego to substitute moralistic goals for realistic ones. The super-ego strives for more affection. The 'id', ego and super-ego should work as a team to produce integrated behaviour. Once the 'id' dominates a person, he behaves contrary to the values of the society. This is what most Nigerian politicians of today possess.

Because they found themselves in a capitalist economy, they bulldoze their way to the top and then use their position to overlord the less privileged. This is exactly what the theory is opposed to.

During a party meeting of Ìsọ̀kan political party, Kóládé, a member of the party testifies to this in response to Apèrán's question. The conversation goes thus:

Apèrán: Sé aláàánú kò sí mọ́ nínú àwọn òsèlú wa ni?
Sé ibikan náà ni gbogbo wọn sùn tí wọn kọrísí ni?
Kóládé: Aláàánú kè, nínú àwọn olóṣèlú? Ojú àánú wọn ti
fó ní kété tí òminira ti bó sọ́wọ́ wọn tán. Eni tó gbá
ọmọ re níkòó tí orùn ọmọ fi wó, sé ó le tijú àti bẹ̀
ọmọ ọlọ́mọ lórí? Etu kìí rìn kó pàdé ọdẹ aláàánú, ejò

178

*kìí rí ọmọ ẹnìyàn kó sàánú rè ̣lọrọ ̣àwọn olóṣèlú òde
òní. Àánú ké? (o.i. 21).*

Apèrán: Are there no merciful people among our
politicians anymore? Do they all sleep and face the
same direction? Kóládé: Mercy! among politicians?
Their merciful eyes are blind as soon as they assume
office. He who knocks his child on the head and the
child's neck bends, will he hesitate to behead
another man's child? No antelope moves and meet
a merciful hunter. Snakes don't meet a man and
have mercy on him. This is exactly is the case of
politicians of today. You mean Mercy?

This is just one out of the many negative comments about
Igúnsèyi's government.

In *Agbàlówóọmérìì Baálè Jòntolo,* the author presents *Agbàkànmí* as
greedy and merciless. These traits change his name to *Agbàlówóọmérìì*
meaning somebody who forces the poor to give even the little he has.
Agbàkànmí himself confirms this when he says:

*Bí mo ti ń sa gbogbo agbára mi to, ìsọkúso ni
wón ń so sí mi káàkiri. Wón ní emi "Agbàlówóọmérìì"
Baálè Jòntolo". Wón ṣe títí, wón so ó di orúko mi
dípò Agbàkànmí tí mo ń jé. Èmi kò kúkú bìkítà fún
wọn, kí wọn máa wí. (o.i. 8).*

Despite my concerted efforts, they are talking rubbish
about me all around. They call me "*Agbàlówóọmérìì
the Baálè of Jòntolo*". They even go to the extent of
making it my name in place of *Agbàkànmí* which is
my real name. Personally, I do not care, let them
continue to say it (p. 8).

As earlier mentioned, *Agbàkànmí* cares not about the implications
of his actions on *Aṣere* or *Àdìgún* his friend, his concern is to take
possession of all the gold found inside the thumb. No wonder, he
plans to get rid of his associates in the business. This can be referred
to as "id" and ego personality which we have earlier discussed.

179

Further still, the authors describe Nigerian political system as a do-or-die affair. It is common in Africa in general that political office holders would always like to remain in power as long as they are alive even if the electorate does not want them. They would always find the means of retaining their positions even if it involves terminating another man's life. In 2011, the then Nigerian president would have gone for a third term in office if not for protest from stakeholders and various interest groups who vehemently resisted the move.

Recently, despite cries in most quarters that the political party in power has failed majority of Nigerians, they are hell bent on retaining the mantle of office. They use the media as megaphone to promote their ambitions through jingles and political propaganda which are exaggerated lies. They claim they have achieved all their electoral promises of 2011 even when they have not found a lasting solution to the Boko Haram insurgence, the abducted Chibok girls, the rising level of unemployment, bad economy and the likes.

There is no doubt that they are ready to go extra miles to stampede their opponents. When votes are counted and they lose out, they result to using their incumbency power either to reverse the election results in their favour or make the country ungovernable for the winner.

In *Ìṣèlú Oníreké Ọ̀gẹ̀,* Igúnṣeyí tries all available means to get rid of Wọlé, one of the prominent leaders of *Ẹ̀yìn níí dàkukọ* and other human right crusaders who he sees as stumbling block on his way and whom are outspoken, but all his efforts are thwarted by the youth organization. *Panápaná,* the leader of the assassin syndicate is killed.

Igúnṣeyí continues to make frantic efforts to rig the election in his favour. *Ḍẹbì, Àluwo, Ojó, Olójú Orò* are employed to disrupt the election process. It is a do-or-die affair because in the process of trying to carry out their diabolical plans, they kill a police officer but at the end, all their efforts do not materialise. They are overpowered by the combined efforts of security agents and the youth associations of Bóripẹ́. This result in the election and subsequent swearing-in of Dádì, the presidential candidate of Ìṣọ̀kan party and within his one year in office, Bóripẹ́ as a whole has changed positively.

From the foregoing, one could affirm that the authors provide ways out of political oppression in our society. When appeals, negotiations and dialogue fail, protest is the next likely option to follow. Karl Marx and his followers believe that despotic and oppressive rule of any form should be protested. They believe that the society should not fold its arms waiting for divine intervention. Yorùbá say *"enu eni ni a fi n ko mé je"* meaning: "it is with your mouth you reject what you do not want".

This is exactly what the Youth Association under the leadership of Wọlé do to remove the oppressive and despotic government of Igúnṣeyí of the *Koyókoyo* party. Even at the point of death, they defy all threats to their lives to fight the oppressive rule of Igúnṣeyí.

As earlier mentioned, a spectator who asks Igúnṣeyí to explain his achievements for four years is rough-handled by *Panápaná*. Àremú who condemns their action is also spared from rough handling. The Youth Association arrives at this point and protests with guns and other fighting instruments. Wọlé does not hesitate to confront Ọkẹkẹ when he says:

> *Alàgbà Ọkẹkẹ, ṣé ẹyin kò mọ pé ọmọ*
> *ẹgbẹ wa ni Àremú ni? E fi i sílẹ kíákíá*
> *bí e kò bá fẹ kí ilẹ ó ga jù yín lọ.* (o.i. 37)
> Mr. Ọkẹkẹ, don't you know that Àremú is
> Our member? Release him now if you don't
> want to see yourself disgraced. (p. 37).

Ọkẹkẹ requests that Panápaná should deal with Wọlé for being rude to him, but Wọlé is bold to respond:

> *Panápaná mojú iná tó lè pa. iná bíntín bí iná fìtílà*
> *ni panápaná lè pa. Bí iná bá burẹke tán, ọwọ*
> *panápaná mẹwàá kò má ràn án. Bùlà ni'ná ó bù*
> *mọ ọn lójú. Ṣé iwọ ò mọ wá nílẹ yìí ni? Òròmọdìẹ*
> *ó mawòdì, ìyáa rẹ lo masà.* (o.i. 37).

The fire fighter knows the kind of fire it is capable of putting off. The kind of fire from a local lamp is what the fire fighter can put off. If the fire kindles, ten fire fighters cannot handle it. If the fire fighter attempts to put it off, the fire will explode on his face. Don't you know us in this village? The young fowl does not know the eagle, it is the mother who knows the eagle. (p. 37).

At this point, *Panápaná* breaks a bottle with his head and attempts to stab Wọlé with the broken bottle. Wọlé also brings out an axe and before *Panápaná* knows it, the axe has landed on *Panápaná's* hand. This results into serious fracas between the two and even other members of the *"ẹyin níí dákukọ* group". The author gives the impression that the successes recorded by the Youth Association are because the protesters are united. They jointly fight the battle against the oppressive rule of *Igúnṣẹyí* despite the risks involved.

In *Agbálówọ̀ọ̀mẹ̀rìí Baálẹ̀ Jòntolo,* the people of Jòntolo jointly protest the oppressive rule of *Baálẹ̀ Àgbàkànmí* and rejected the suggestion that his heir be made to succeed him. Instead, they prefer to install *Àṣẹre* as the new *Baálẹ̀* of Jòntolo. They unanimously say:

> *A kò fẹ́ Àrẹ̀mọ Baálẹ̀ rárá. Àṣẹre la fẹ́, ẹ kò*
> *ẹrù Àṣẹre fún un, olè gégé bí Baálẹ̀ Agbàló-*
> *wọ̀ọ̀mẹ̀rìí ni Àrẹ̀mọ rẹ̀ yìí. (o.i. 70)*

> We reject *Àgbàkànmí's* heir. It is Àṣẹre we
> want. Give Àṣẹre's properties to him, *Agbà-*
> *lòwọ̀ọ̀mẹ̀rìí's* heir is a thief like his father (p. 70).

Following this joint protest, Àṣẹre is installed as the new Baálẹ̀ of Jòntolo town with the hope that he will change things for better for the people.

Findings and analysis

Our findings reveal that colonialism, oppressive rule and political domination had been in existence before the coming of the Europeans to the shores of Africa. As earlier mentioned, the inauguration of the Ọ̀yọ́mèsì council provided some freedom for the people. The Judiciary in particular was free from oppression. The Poets also served as check against misuse of power by the powerful in the society. They render poems, songs and the likes which out rightly condemn any form of oppression. The *'egúngún alárìnjó'* are prominent in this area. Their motto then was "*n ó wì, ǫba kan kìí pòkǫrin*" literally meaning "I shall say as no king kills the singer/poet".

The Yorùbá political system tagged '*Ǫba lo nílè*' meaning "the king owns the land", allows for the king's dominance and control of the judiciary, legislative and economic affairs of his domain but with adequate checks and balance. The name "*Kàbíyèsí*" (*Ká bi ó o sì*) meaning "who dare quarries you gives room for despotism. No wonder why in the Old Òyó Empire, the constitution of the '*Òyómèsì*' council of chiefs was to act as checks and balance in order to curb the excessive use of power by the executive (the Aláàfin). This implies that the political scenario experienced in Nigeria today is an archetype of what had existed in part not only among the Yorùbá but among several tribes in Nigeria.

Further still, the authors give the impression that the only language understood by political leaders at all levels of government is protest or revolution. This is the present situation in Nigeria where in some states, workers are owed up to six months salaries and when all appeals fail, they embark on total strike. Instead of paying them their salaries, government resorts to using the traditional rulers to appeal to hungry workers to resume work. This is unthinkable. They can be described as the lion archetype. Just as lions do, they endeavour to avoid pains and obtain pleasure regardless of any external considerations.

Although it is not all the time that protests work to solve problems of freedom from colonization, it is also evident that most political leaders at the Federal, State and even local levels do not respect negotiations, signed agreements, court orders and the likes. But since the oppressed cannot remain defiant to their uncomfortable situation, protest is the last option.

From the forgoing, we would like to recommend that: Nigerian politicians in particular and world politicians in general, should strive to uphold their pre-election promises. Experience has shown that only a few of them stand by their promises. They should desist from seeing the post they occupy as their birth right which should not be tampered with.

The electorate on their part should ensure that they thoroughly screen political aspirants before deciding on whom to vote for just as Dádì in *Ìṣèlú Oníréké Òghé* is scrutinized by the *Eyin níí dàkùkǫ* Youth

Association and he is found satisfactory before his candidature is supported. At the end, they are not disappointed.

As effective as protest is, its use calls for caution. This is because most protests result in loss of lives of innocent citizens and valuable properties. It may even lead to civil war. Despite the observation, and in Marx's opinion, we do not support that the oppressed should fold their arms waiting for divine intervention because the oppressors would never voluntarily surrender and give freedom to the oppressed.

It is unfortunate however that most electorates sell their conscience for money. This situation is attributed partly to the high poverty level in the society. In as much as we believe that poverty may give room for such action, it is pertinent that if the electorate cooperate and faithfully fight oppressive rules, they are likely to succeed.

Today, it is doubtful if there is any traditional ruler in Nigeria who upholds the integrity of the areas they govern. The sanctity of most religious leaders has been compromised, and they become examples of moral bankruptcy. They have all turned politicians and money mongers who sell their conscience for money and material gifts. Experience has shown that most Nigerian political leaders go through the traditional rulers by offering them money and material gifts with the promise that they would deliver their domain to a particular political party.

We have also heard of occasions when traditional rulers do collaborate with political parties to thumb print ballot papers illegally. Yoruba say: "*ẹnu bá jẹ, ojú a tì*" literally means "if you take a bribe, you cannot but do the wish of the one who gives the bribe" even if he is not the best candidate and if he is eventually declared as winner, such a person cannot complain if that candidate fails to perform. This accounts for why today, a governor appoints and deposes an *Ọba* at will. This relegates both the tradition and the people that own such tradition to the background. As long as the *Ọba* subscribes to political mismanagement, the governed would have no option than to follow suit.

Conclusion

This chapter has critically examined the Nigerian political system vis-à-vis its presentation by the selected playwrights. We have established the fact that most Nigerian politicians can be likened to oppressors and colonisers who use language of deceit, who promise heaven and earth to the electorate but as soon as they get to power, they turn their back on the electorate who vote them in. Since the only language understood by most politicians the world over, is protest, we are of the view that people should protest any form of oppression noticed on the part of their leaders because this is the only way the society can move forward. However, caution should be made to ensure that such protest do not degenerate to the level of sacrificing innocent lives and valuable properties.

References

Abíọlá, O.P. 2005. *Language of drama: Akínwùmí Ìṣọlá's plays as a case study*. Unpublished M.A. thesis, University of Ìbàdàn. Ìbàdàn.

Aderibigbe, I. S. 1993. "The moral issues in African religion". *In Studies in Religious Understanding in Nigeria*. NASR. Nigeria. Pp.292-312.

Adéyẹmi, L. 2001. Iṣẹ́ Ọ̀rọ̀ Lámèyító, Lítíréṣọ̀ Yorùbá" In Àjàyí, B. ed. *Ẹ̀kọ́ Ìjìnlẹ̀ Yorùbá: Ẹ̀dá Èdè, Lítíréṣọ̀ àti Àṣà*. Shebiotimọ Publications. Ìjẹ̀bú Òde. Pp145-166.

Adeyẹmi, L. 2001. "The Oratory Style of Láwuyì Ògúnníran in *Ọmọ Alátẹ Ìlẹ̀kẹ̀*". In *Yorùbá: A Journal of the Yorùbá Studies Association*. Ìbàdàn: YSAN.

Adeyẹmi, L. 2006. *Tịọrì lítíréṣọ̀ ní èdè Yorùbá*. Shebiotimọ publications. Ìjẹ̀búode.

Adeyẹmi, Lere. 2014. *Ìṣèlú oníreké ògè*. Villaxlnc publishers. Ilọrin.

Akanmidu, R.A. 1991. "Religion and morality" In Journal of Arabic and religious Studies.

Akanmidu, R.A. 1995. *Ethics and poverty: Inquiries in moral philosophy*. Free enterprises publishers. Ìkẹjà.

Akíntọlá, E.A. 2004. "The Nigerian nation: A historic-futuristic perspective". *In Nigerian Education Digest.* Nathadex Publishers. Ilọrin.

Alao, I.M. 2006."Democracy in Nigeria: A review. *In Journal of Arts and Social Sciences.* (IJASS). Integrity Publications. Ilọrin. pp. 248-256.

Aluko, L.O. 1995. *A comparative study of the plays of Afọlabi Ọlabimtan and Tunji Ọpadọtun.* Unpublished M.A. thesis, University of Ibadan. Ìbàdàn.

Arohunmọlaṣẹ, L.O. 1997, *Class Struggle in Yorùbá Historical and Protest Plays.* University of Ibadan, Ibadan. Unpublished PhD thesis.

Bodkin, M. 1948, *Archetypal patterns in poetry: Psychological studies of imagination.* Oxford University press. London.

Chinweizu, et al, 1985. *Towards decolonizing African literature.* KPI limited. London.

Delano, I. O. 1963. *Lọ́jọ́ Ọjọ́ Un.* Thomas Nelson and sons limited. London.

Dolbiare, C.M. and Dolbiere, P., 1976. *American Ideology, the Competing Political Beliefs of the 1970's.* Oughton Mifflin Company. USA.

Eagleton, T. 1976. *Marxism in literary criticism.* University of California Press. California.

Eagleton, T. 1996. *Literary Theory: An Introduction* (2nd edition). University of Minnesota Press. Minneapolis.

Ike, A.J. 2000. *Political discourse in social studies: An analysis.* Desvic printing and publishing company. Onitsha.

Kirk-Greene, A.H.M. 1956. *Who coined the name Nigeria? West Africa:* 22nd December.

Ọdunjọ, J.F. 1976. *Agbàlówọọomẹrìì Baálẹ̀ Jòntolo.* Longman Nig. Ltd. Ìbàdàn.

Ogundèjì, P.A. 1988. *A semiotic study of Dúró Ládiípọ̀'s mythoi-historical plays.* Department of Linguistics and African Languages, University of Ìbàdàn, Ìbàdàn, Nigeria. Unpublished PhD Thesis.

Ogundeji, P.A. 2001. Eré oníṣe Yorùbá. In Àjàyí, B. ed. *Ẹ̀kọ́ Ìjìnlẹ̀ Yorùbá. Ẹ̀dá Èdè, Lítíréṣọ̀ àti Àṣà.* Shebíotimọ Publications. Ìjẹ̀búòde. pp 167-188.

Ògúnlọlá, O.D. 2013. *"Forces against the Spirit of "ọmọlúàbí" in Selected Contemporary Yorùbá Written Plays: An Archetypal Analysis.*

Department of Linguistics and Nigerian Languages, University of Ilọrin, Ilọrin. Unpublished Ph.D. Thesis.

Ogunṣina, B. 1995. "Colonialism and the Yorùbá Writers: A Study of Ládélé's Ìgbà ló dé". In Owólabí, O. ed. *Essays in honour of Ayọ̀ Bámgbọ́ṣé.* Pp.297-310.

Ọpẹfeyitimi, A. 1997. *Tíọrì ìṣọwọloédè.* Tanímẹhìnọla Press. Ọ̀sogbo.

Posselt, B. 1935. *The Zimbabwe Culture: Origin and Decline of Southern Zambeẓian States.* Cambridge.

Sheba, O. 1995. Women and Revolution in Yorùbá Written Literature. In Adédìran, B. ed. *Cultural Studies in Ifẹ̀. Selected from 1993/1994 Seminar Papers of the Institute of Cultural Studies,* Ọbáfẹ́mi Awólọ́wọ̀ University. Ilé-Ifẹ̀. pp. 270-276.

Spierenburg, G. 2004. *Bondage of Boundaries and Identity: Politics in Post-Colonial Africa.* Cambridge.

Wellek R, and Warren, A. 1949. *Theories of Literature.* Clays limited. England.

Wilbur, S. 1962. *Five approaches to literary criticism.* Macmillan Ltd.

Chapter Eight

African Engineering and the Quest for Sustainable Development: Levelling the Ground for all Players

Munyaradzi Mawere and Gertjan van Stam

Introduction

The design, deployment and use of technical infrastructures and solutions are value-laden activities. Although engineering claims to provide for the neutral, logical answers to what is believed to be 'reasonable' challenges, any physical intervention interacts with cultural and political perspectives embedded in contemporary worldviews and paradigms (van Stam, 2012a). This is because all claims, whether social, scientific, religious or cultural, are made in context if they are to be of any relevance.

This chapter introduces African Engineering with its settings and constructs, in context. Particular attention is given to the schisms that normally to play when one tries to balance the introduction and utilisation of contemporary technologies in the African context. Often, African practitioners find technologies to be unfit for context, sometimes irrelevant, and in most cases detached from the epistemologies of the indigenous people. By indigenous people, we mean those people regarded as the traditional inhabitants of their lands prior to colonisation by foreigners (Burger, 1990). The explicit aims of engineering are "the development, acquisition and application of technical, scientific and mathematical knowledge about the understanding, design, development, invention, innovation and use of materials, machines, structures, systems and processes for specific purposes" (UNESCO, 2010: 24). Now, one questions the use and relevance of engineering when applied broadly in all contexts, including those that are foreign to the ones in which its tangibles were gestated.

In Africa, the consequence of deploying alien technological activities seems to be fostering and growing inequalities, to disempower African agency, and to create a multitude of divides, such as those with social, digital, and cultural impacts.

In this chapter, we focus on the techno-social grounding of African engineers in Africa. African Engineering is envisioned as the contextual formulation of the African technological experience. African Engineering is a distinct and empowering activity that could include, but does not focus on the contextual adaptation (or indigenisation) of imported technologies. It is an activity situated in an environment ravished by centuries of exploitation, subjugation, oppression and a legacy of colonialism. For this major reason, African Engineering has to contend with the colonial narratives historically embedded in the systems supporting the operations of the natural sciences. Maintaining space for African Engineering is a daunting, albeit crucial task (Bets *et al.*, 2013; van Stam, 2016a). The objective of this chapter is to recover the African manners of shaping the physical and psychological environments to recognise engineering systems cognisant of African culture, sociality and communality. Such reconstruction forms a basis to recognise indigenous African technical agencies.

A technology discourse unaligned with the African context

Non-Africans dominate the mainstream of discourse on technology in Africa and the world at large. The predominance of Westerners forces the conversation to conform to Western framings and a Western epistemic positionality that in many cases short-changes Africa (Grosfoguel 2011; van Greunen & van Stam 2014; Mawere & van Stam 2015). Regarding Africa, such discourse sustains an essentialistic and rhetorical argument while broadcasting a Western-specific ideological understanding of 'developmental impact'. The conversation is highly technocratic and its bifurcation sustains a colonial narrative (Dourish & Mainwaring, 2012). On this note, we argue that the dominant, Western framing of the discourse on technology is debilitating and conceals the agency and practice of African Engineering in the African context and elsewhere where its outcomes could be of use.

The dominant Western-centric discourse monopolises the thinking, behaviour, and (de)construction as well as (re)construction of epistemologies and understanding of the meaning and value of technology in Africa. The discourse assumes Western technological superiority, masks its profit motives and partnership with elites and vested interests. Meanwhile, critics are accused of ingratitude. The formats guiding technical developments relegate African input on the application of African knowledge, in both local and global realities, to the dungeons of the subaltern (Ndlovu-Gatsheni, 2013a; van Stam, 2016a). Enshrined systems and processes that facilitate the changes in technology deny an African agency and disempower African inputs (Canagarajah, 1996; Nkomo, 2009). This in itself pre-empts the efficacy of many African efforts, epistemologies and technical advancements. For a long time, African works have been consigned to the dustbin of oblivion to pave the way for hegemonic epistemologies and technologies. A critical look on the field of engineering shows that in Africa the extrinsic discourse is prevalent. This discourse continues to influence the development of techniques, skills, methods and processes used in the production of technologies, worldwide. An example is the development of the fifth generation mobile telephone systems (5G). 5G is being heralded as a fundamental change in the way of thinking about mobile networks and wireless system, and is the next step in mobile network technology, in the sequence of third generation of mobile networks (3G), standardised in 2005, and the fourth generation (4G), standardised in 2013.This evolution of mobile network systems is dominated by operators and equipment suppliers from the Global North (van Stam, 2016a). The dominance of the Global North in the evolution of technical equipment, the supplying of hardware, and the supplying of software to support network operations could be understood as an extension of colonial dominance over the Global South. Even in 5G development, there is little or no effort by the Global North to solicit African contributions to influence how the current framings, processes, and assessments of needs are being created (van Stam, 2016a). This aligns with observation by Mahmood Mamdani (2011) that Africa can only seek the crumbs as 'hunters and gatherers' of raw data, and hope to act as 'native informants' who collect and provide empirical data for processing in, and empowerment of, the Global North. Similar observations are made by Francis Nyamnjoh (2012: 1) who argues:

"In Africa, the colonial conquest of Africans – body, mind and soul – has led to real or attempted epistemicide – the decimation or near complete killing and replacement of indigenous epistemologies with the epistemological paradigm of the conqueror. The result has been education through schools and other formal institutions of learning in Africa largely as a process of making infinite concessions to the outside – mainly the Western world."

As further argued by Nyamnjoh (2012), such kind of education has tended to emphasise mimicry over creativity. It is the same education that has fostered the dominance of the Global North over previously colonised territories. There is a persistent practice to regard Africa as a geographically unified, albeit separate region. This view builds upon the racial views grounded by Comte de Bobineau and introduced and sustained by colonial powers through nefarious Eurocentric theories that were meant to caricature and subjugate the peoples of Africa and the Global South as a whole (Bernal, 2012). Such thought compartmentalises the processes of contemplation and recycles a practice that sends invitations for contributions on Africa from 'experts' residing outside of the continent. At international conferences in Africa, one often notices the main speakers being flown in from outside of the continent. At critical moments, foreign 'experts' are asked to speak about 'latest development and their impact on Africa or to Africa'! In this vein, Africa is readily designated an area 'lacking knowledge of a specific kind' (e.g. appropriate technologies). Seemingly, this links in with the idea that African borders represent boundaries of knowledge or what we call 'epistemic fronts': Africa is considered as a cold front that is inactive, therefore, incapable of effecting any meaningful change. On the other hand, 'foreign experts' represent a hot front that is more active and capable of instilling and effecting significant change. What it implies in reality is that the Global South is regarded as in need of 'technical assistance'. Such conviction sounds eerily like the colonising call at the Berlin Conference: "let's bring civilisation to Africa", which call motivated colonisers and missionaries to set-off to 'the dark continent' in the nineteenth and twentieth centuries. Within Africa, the absence of the African voice and the Western-centric orientation of technical information allows for a linking-up of the technical developments directly with imperial centres, as if Africa still is a colony (Dourish & Mainwaring, 2012). This practice perpetuates imperial dominance over the Global South.

The African context and realities are highly diverse. They are authentic and often discordant with realities encountered in Western environments. A common denominator for the African locale – which exists for substantial amounts of time – is the perception of oneself as it emerges from the joy, wisdom and knowledge of community (van Stam, 2016b). In this context, for instance, African economic behaviour does not focus on competitive segregation but aligns itself with social and communal identities. Such socio-centric cultural behaviour is embedded within Ubuntu (Metz, 2014; van Stam 2015). In daily African practice and cosmology, there exists a preference for phonocentric, oral communications (van Stam, 2013), a desire for harmonious personal relationships, and an embedded understanding that 'success' requires sharing (Sheneberger & van Stam, 2011), cheering, and long-term orientations.

Stigmatisation and the thwartilisation of the African voice

In Africa, the academic education model – both high school and tertiary level – continues to be among the key instruments and vehicles of cultural westernisation of the African continent (van Stam, 2012b). That model mistakenly regards *the start of colonialism* as *the beginning of development* and thereby human progress. These persistent narratives condition our thought processes influencing us to think that some people are intellectually more superior to others.

As being regarded (and rendered) without agency, Africa is particularly disempowered to influence the speech symbols, the legal codes, the morals, and most importantly, the values embedded in the influx of technologies that are designed in foreign contexts. This means that the conditions of their production must be carefully scrutinised. These conditions of production include *de facto* exclusion of access to participate in all aspects of (the science of) technology development, to reap direct benefits of technological advances (for example, through organic growth of scientific capacity and technical capabilities), to access the general body of knowledge, and to access

193

the related (financial) resources. In most specialisms, a relative small grouping of corporate and academic elites monopolise technological developments. A clear case is the conceptualisation and engineering of Information and Communication Technologies (ICT) that is evidently dominated by corporate interests located in the Silicon Valley of California, USA.

In the case of promising human talent, Africa is mired by open migration paths for promising human talent that is keenly absorbed and assimilated in the dominant (Western-based) technology companies. This migration yields considerable benefits for the sending communities due to remittances from the diaspora. However, most of such human talent estrange from their roots (Nyamnjoh, 2015). Only a small percentage of those migrating from Africa return to their African roots or contribute to the strengthening of African engineering capacity (Teferra, 1997; Nordling, 2015).

To understand Africa's technological agency and African Engineering, one must take into account Africa's history, the reason for current boundaries, and the long-term influence of events that ravaged the continent. On this note, we argue that one must reject the stigmatisation of African engineers as being only 'adaptors of existing technologies', and African technicians to focus on 'maintaining technologies that the West will provide'. We further argue for the need to seriously consider the contribution of those engineers hailing from the Global South and urge them to participate actively in all 'global' activities within their territory.

How imported technologies misfit Africa

From his introspections of realising conflicting observations in the Indian context, Kentaro Toyama concluded: "like a lever, technology amplifies people's capacities in the direction of their intentions" (Toyama, 2015: 28). Toyama realised and rightly understood that the social context determines the outcome of the application of any technology of which one may think. One would therefore expect that technology in Africa aligns with an African worldview, and addressing African needs, framings, and community processes. An accompanying discourse to explain 'African intentions' would provide the evidence of the African understanding of its (local) needs, and how the proposed technologies do align with the African context. Unfortunately, such discourse and technologies are absent. However, they are direly needed to close up the epistemological and technological gap between the Global North and the Global South. A superficial look on Africa and its modes of technological episteme reveals mostly imported technologies. Subsequently, Africans continue to be conditioned and constrained by the hegemonic discourse of Western engineering (and business) concepts, supported by an academy poised on dissemination of Western values and intentions (Mazrui, 2003; Ndlovu-Gatsheni, 2013b).

Given the dominance of a lopsided discourse and the denial of an African capacity, it is not a surprise that imported technologies are often misfits in the African realities. In many cases, equipment is inadequate, used in a manner that betrays the realities of the African context, or not used at all. A poignant example is reported by the World Health Organisation: only 10–30% of donated medical equipment is operational in developing countries (Petkova*et al.*, 2010). As technologies fail, there is a constant investigation of why 'the intended outcomes' are not being achieved. Technological dividends have not been forthcoming. Such investigation often falls prey to the 'failing Africa' narrative and expands on the dehumanising iterations and incarcerations of (1) condemnation ("there is lack of local capacity"), (2) brainwashing ("this is what is needed"), and (3) conditional resource provisioning ("there is need for assistance, on these conditions").

One of the effects of the mismatch of technologies and context is the growing of many divides. For example, analysis by the International Telecommunications Union, shows a digital divide that widened by a factor of 1,000 between 2001 and 2011 (Hilbert, 2011). Although such effects are recognised by various authors, the sheer foreignness of the social consequences in daily life in unfamiliar realities seems to strain understanding by affluent listeners or academics who do not reside in the African peripheral context. The result is an absence of appreciation of the significance and disempowering effect of the mismatch of many technologies in the African context for African practitioners, in both literature and practice.

Each specific philosophy of knowledge generates a different understanding of distinctions between the West and the Rest or the Global North and the Global South. The struggle for recognition of multiple forms of science – for instance, positivistic, reflexive, or African sciences – is fought in the geo-political academic realm. However, a technology-fit depends on the acquisition of an ethnographic understanding of the local contemplations. Such understanding is crucial for the translation of local intentions into the technologies that amplify them. Contextual, embedded, and embodied knowledge is crucial to inform the review and gap analysis of existing African agency.

Deconstructing Engineering in Africa

There exists a vast and unappreciated array of inconsistency when engineering and technological exploits span geographical areas with two or more world-views. In engineering practice, a particular range of processes of clinical needs assessments are followed by the methodological design of technological artefacts. Mostly, this takes place in dedicated professional environments that are removed from the communities involved. Furthermore, the contemporary design of technologies is embedded in the deliberations of Western philosophy that separate outward behaviour (in this case the act of engineering and technology creation) from an autonomous internal thought. Such philosophy is inconsistent with the worldview of African stakeholders (Bidwell, 2016). In Africa, prioritisation of autonomy can be deemed self-centric and undesirable for community cohesion (du Toit, 2009). Within Ubuntu, human interactions are focused on the convivial establishment and maintenance of harmonious relationships. The concept of engineers being parachuted into a foreign contexts to harvest information, disappear, and reappear with shiny equipment, is inconsistent with this African value and its participatory and transdisciplinary practice. In Africa, dialogue continues at appropriate moments until technology and the community are aligned and in unity (Bidwell et al., 2013). The discordance of unaligned technology is amplified by the fact that the sequence of exposure to technologies in the African socio-economic and political experience is dramatically different from the course of developments as they took shape over many years in Western contexts.

For the review of behaviour, intentions and needs in African societies, it is imperative to understand the political world that was implemented by colonialism and how that world is still in existence up to this day. In such a world, the 'settler' assumed a position of domination and the 'natives' were subdued, often by suppression or even annihilation. The colonial system implemented policies preoccupied with such binary classifications. These classifications remain compelling and confusing, even to this day (Ndlovu-Gatsheni, 2013c).

When engineering exists to produce technology that is 'an amplification of human intent', as Toyama (2015) claims, it can be expected that Western (trained) engineers build technologies that amplify a Western intent and purpose. The resulting tools, machines, structures, systems and processes are thus misfits and essentially ineffective – and possibly counterproductive - to African needs. The nonsensical narrative that large parts of Africa are culturally backward, scientifically inferior and economically incompetent, the lamentations of Africa failing to achieve Western-determined norms, and the stream of failing technologies, induce resentments and counter movements. Counter pressures mount because of growing inequalities and deteriorating living conditions; they feed upon a long history of exploitation, oppression and servitude. Such exploitation and oppression involved utilisation of imported technologies (Diamond, 2005). Counter pressures also feed upon the mismatch in the promises accompanying the import of (Western) 'appropriate' technologies and their disempowering outcomes.

The building of discontent constitutes a post-colonial engineering crisis. Such a crisis has not yet been recognised in literature. It is evident that Western-trained engineers fail to serve the needs of holistic local or national African societies (Gurstein, 2011). However, Cornel du Toit (2005) states that Africa has always known science and has always utilised technologies. In Africa, technologies are (re)constituted along the communal experience. Through such assessments, Africans relativise imported technology utilisation to link in with African customs. This counter response is triggered by an identity crisis enforced upon African communities by the growing exposure to foreign cultures through ICT and the subsequently transmitted cultural elements or systems of behaviour – memes - aligning with Africa traditional behaviour. Other counter responses are the labelling of particular techniques as 'alien' and regarding their effects as damaging. Subsequently, various groups in African society attach to certain (imported) engineering artefacts a 'settler's agency' with the result that such technologies are being rejected. Such labelling could explain the mounting rejection of 'development work' being done by Non-Governmental Organisations, and the increasing barriers to entry of foreigners involved with (engineering) research and development in various African countries.

A small portion of African engineers are academically trained in technology. Mostly, these engineers reside in urban areas and operate in the formal sectors of the African economies. These formal sectors are relatively small. For instance, in Zimbabwe, ninety-four percent of the employed persons work in the informal sector (ZIMSTAT, 2015). Naturally, the formal sectors exist by virtue of dominant discourses. They operate in modern or post-modern fashion and comply with the Western-centric engineering approaches that are enforced through exams and certifications. Formalisation processes enlist institutions linked to the nation state within the boundaries that were set during the Scramble for Africa. The first laws and regulations that defined acceptable (formal) practice were designed and implemented during colonial times by foreign powers. Many of these stipulations have remained as they were (Mbembe, 2002). The formal interest groupings and their social influence exist by virtue of political identities set by the 'settlers' without input from the indigenous population. As a result of these enshrined powers, western-centric engineering processes and practices are prioritised over the recognition and distribution of local knowledge systems in Africa. This preference represents a continuing and even strengthening the colonial practice.

By their affiliation, the Western trained engineering elites have privileged opportunities to relate with western powers. However, enticed by their privileges in urban areas, many engineers remain distant from traditional practice and have little interaction with African indigenous knowledge systems. In fact, the 'colour-bar' has been replaced by a 'power-bar', in which a privileged group of engineers act in contrast with those practising in indigenous engineering in the African society (Watson, 2013; Burawoy, 2014). It is mostly in the informal sectors of the economies where one finds the practice of, and confidence in, African Engineering. The informal context encapsulates a determined African agency, and the execution of engineering practice cognisant of African culture and the legacy of a history filled with African artisans.

Unravelling the distinctiveness of African Engineering

In African Engineering, the technologists' focus on how their endeavours align with African beliefs and customs, values and enhances social cohesion. They act cognisant of African world-views, cultures, histories, and religions. African Engineering links both artefact and people in a holistic manner. It reviews technologies on how the physical and social consequences benefit humans in their balancing act of the demands of daily life and relationships. Further, African Engineering assesses how technology helps in the comprehension of the meaning of events by all involved in interacting with it, in any stage of sensitisation, design, implementation, and operations (van Hoorik & Mweetwa, 2008). African Engineering aims to facilitate the integrity of African personhood and society, and benefits local knowledge. It does not prioritise abstract benefits or foreign (business) models and is less interested in 'cause and effect' than in the actual happenings in community. Further, African Engineering does not individualise ownership but regards everyone involved with its accomplishments as joint owners (Mukuka, 2010). In contemporary settings, in a post-scientific manner, African engineering incorporates available techniques that are beneficial in the African context and discards the rest (du Toit, 2005).

Based upon its strive for harmony and holistic integration, African Engineering has a remarkable ability to accommodate (not indigenise) divergent ideas. Thus, African Engineering does not isolate itself from the world. However, it does not subscribe to an ontological substantiation that detaches technological apparatus to existing in and for itself. Many Africans subscribe to a relational ontology where the life-facilitating agency of technology and inclusion of all stakeholders determines it value. It assures that both the rationality and the emotionality must be in balance in the technological artefact.

Any academic theory is loaded with specific concepts of human nature (Murphy, 1996). As most technologies emanate from Western thought systems, there is real danger of what Courtney Martin (2016) calls 'reductive seduction' or Chimamanda Adichie (2009) recognises as 'a single story' to explain African reality. Such a seduction and story represent a contemporary analogy to colonial practice that manipulates facts through an 'out of context' illumination. They silence the contextual, indigenous view of reality. In that manner, Western models continue to shape the general understanding of the African reality. Furthermore, implicitly, the dominant discourse regards what goes under this chapter's understanding of African Engineering as inadequate because it lacks a solid foundation in (Western) 'science'. In a globalising and connected world, this faith in the West can only steer to more and more confusion. Engineering is not a Western privilege, nor is engineering a Western prerogative. Engineers exist everywhere, and manufacture tools and shape the physical world. Facts emerge from, and must be assessed within, the lived environment and the context. Therefore, African Engineering must be interpreted from an African position. This necessitates continuous development of theoretical illuminations from the African context and not the enforcement of hegemonic thinking from the Western point of view. The limited literature describing African Engineering can be regarded as a sign that African Engineering does not depend on, or ask for, a Western acknowledgement.

Global (corporate) engineering focuses on activities in the cluster of geographical areas centring in African megalopoles like Nairobi, Accra, Johannesburg and Cape Town. This leads to a strengthening of the contemporary carving out of imperialistic bridgeheads and centres, to the detriment of the continent. Further, such focus naturalises African engineering as 'engineers in the formal economy' and strengthens the focus on Western skill sets only. With their powers consolidated in the centres, corporate engineering uses the African engineer solely as a resource in the utilitarian exploits of the *homo economicus*, bypassing the needs and dignity of the *homo situs*

(Buskens & Webb, 2009). This practice is geographically and philosophically far removed from the African reality. There is need for a critical look for ways in which the postcolonial Western needs reproduce and reinforce colonially-produced entities as the mainstream engineer. This degrades engineers as if they are natural constructs, although they are a product of an ongoing colonial history! An analogy of this thinking is the one in education, where Ken Robinson (2010) has vividly shown how the education system is purposely built to produce operators for a capitalist industry.

There remains a lopsided flow of information, with a severe information poverty affecting Africa (Graham *et al.,* 2014). This deprivation conditions Africans to accept without question the available and generic (Western) documents providing 'facts' enshrined in Western positionality. Narratives, reports, and stories from Africa do not make it to the front or else they take years to be recognised as illuminating, if they ever do. This demotes African empirics, as illumination and theory building takes place in the West. These foreign theories are used to mine for African facts and shifts focus from the necessary process of allowing African empiric evidence to provide for African theory-building. For a long time, African engineers were particularly devoid of such theory-building whilst being influenced by a continuous stream of foreign theories. There is a fundamental difference in the methods through which Africans seek to produce knowledge and the methods non-Africans employ (Mawere & van Stam, 2015).

African Engineering harvests and benefits the local empiric, and devises local theories. In the demand for justice and reciprocity in the reporting on the empiric and the derived theories, referencing of the empiric and theories from the Western settings should be attenuated. There is need to go beyond a simple critique or regurgitation of facts and to re-interpret borrowed facts. In that way, African Engineering can be recognised and Africa can be seen to innovate, based upon embodied knowledge and embedded theories that illuminate old facts and core realities in light of the previously un-revealed, and thus unconsidered, African context. This allows for an illumination in support of engineers practising within Africa, and not foreign engineering parachuted into Africa wearing colonial or so-called 'humanitarian' lenses. Thus the act of de-colonisation requires an intellectual movement to achieve.

Conclusion

This chapter has introduced a theoretical spine on African Engineering and its agency. The recognition of the African approach and practice is critical due to the prevalent African negative self-image and a mindset of dependency. African Engineering consolidates the symbolic potency of the engineering act by Africans in Africa. Although able to incorporate technologies from any source, African Engineering does not regard Western engineering as normative.

Engineers cannot ignore the growing inequalities, the poverty, exploitation and suffering of many people in the world. Colonialism and continued forms of economic and other forms of dependency from the West are threats to the African identity. However, African Engineering can be an inspiration when it has strong and long-term roots in the human connection, operates in an oral culture, is free from Western constraints, and embeds in community and represents an important critique to exclusion and aggressive competitiveness. Reliance on individual pursuits, typical within modernism, is foreign to the practise of African Engineering. African Engineering holds substantial potential for inclusive designs that incorporate shared beliefs, conventions, practices, and traditions. African Engineering addresses the question 'why' in all its pursuits and regards the symbolic value of engineering exploits at all manipulations of the physical and psychological realms.

References

Adichie, C. N. 2009. The danger of a single story. In TEDGlobal 2009. Retrieved 15 February 20016 from https://www.ted.com/talks/chimamanda_adichie_the_danger_of_a_single_story?language=en#

Bernal, M. 2012. *Black Athena: The Afroasiatic Roots of Classical Civilization, Volume One.* London: Vintage Digital.

Bets, J., van Stam, G., &Voorhoeve, A. 2013. Modeling and Practise of Integral Development in Rural Zambia: Case Macha. In K. Jonas, I. A. Rai, & M. Tchuente (Eds.), *E-Infrastructures and E-Services on Developing Countries, 4th International ICST Conference, AFRICOMM 2012, Yaounde, Cameroon, November 12-14, 2012, Revised Selected Papers* (Vol. 119, pp. 211–220). Berlin: Springer.

Bidwell, N. J., Reitmaier, T., Rey-Moreno, C., Roro, Z., Siya, M. J., & Dlutu-Siya, B. 2013. Timely Relations in Rural Africa. In *Proceedings of the 12th International Conference of the IFIP 9.4 Working Group on Social Implications of Computers in Development Countries, 19-22 May 2013, Ocho Rios, Jamaica.*

Bidwell, N. J. 2016. Moving the centre to design social media in rural Africa. *AI & SOCIETY, Journal of Knowledge, Culture and Communication, 31(1),* 51-77.

Burawoy, M. 2014. The Colour of Class Revisited: Four Decades of Postcolonialism in Zambia. *Journal of Southern African Studies, 40*(5), 961–979.

Burger, J. 1990. *The Gaia atlas of First Peoples: A future for the indigenous world,* New York: Doubleday.

Buskens, I. & Webb, A. 2009. African Women and ICTS. New York: Zed Books.

Canagarajah, A. S. 1996. "Nondiscursive" Requirements in Academic Publishing, Material Resources of Periphery Scholars, and the Politics of Knowledge Production. *Written Communication, 13*(4), 435–472.

Diamond, J. M. 2005. Guns, Germs, and Steel: The Fates of Human Societies. New York: W.W. Norton.

Dourish, P., & Mainwaring, S. D. 2012. Ubicomp's Colonial Impulse. In UbiComp'12, 5-8 Sep 2012, Pittsburgh, PA, USA.

du Toit, C. W. 2005. Implications of a technoscientific culture on personhood in Africa and in the West. *HTS Teologiese Studies/Theological Studies, 61*(3), 829–860.

du Toit, C. W. 2009. African challenges. Unfolding identities. Pretoria: Unisa Press.

Gurstein, M. (2011). The Dead Hand of (Western) Academe: Community Informatics in a Less Developed Country Context. Retrieved 15 February 2015, from https://gurstein.wordpress.com/2011/06/09/the-dead-hand-of-western-academe-community-informatics-in-a-less-developed-country-context/

Grosfoguel, R. 2011. Decolonizing Post-Colonial Studies and Paradigms of Political Economy: Transmodernity, Decolonial Thinking, and Global Coloniality. *Journal of Peripheral Cultural Production of the Luso-Hispanic World*, *1*(1), online.

Graham, M., Hogan, B., Straumann, R. K., & Medhat, A. 2014. Uneven Geographies of User-Generated Information: Patterns of Increasing Informational Poverty. *Annals of the Association of American Geographers*, *104*(4), 746–764.

Hilbert, M. 2011. Mapping the dimensions and characteristics of the world's technological communication capacity during the period of digitization (1986 - 2007/2010). In *9th World Telecommunication/ICT Indicators Meeting, 7-9 December 2011, Mauritius*.

Mamdani, M. 2011. The importance of research in a university. Retrieved July 1, 2014, from http://www.pambazuka.org/en/category/features/72782.

Martin, C. 2016. The Reductive Seduction of Other People's Problems. Retrieved February 15, 2016, from https://medium.com/the-development-set/the-reductive-seduction-of-other-people-s-problems-3c07b307732d#.o3zvsdeeu

Mawere, M., & van Stam, G. 2015. Paradigm Clash, Imperial Methodological Epistemologies and Development in Africa: Observations from rural Zimbabwe and Zambia. In M. Mawere & T. Mwanaka (Eds.), *Development, Governance, and Democracy: A Search for Sustainable Democracy and Development in Africa* (pp. 193–211). Bamenda: Langaa.

Mazrui, A. A. 2003. Towards Re-Africanizing African Universities: Who Killed Intellectualism in the Post-Colonial Era? *Turkish Journal of International Relations*, *2*(3), 135–163.Mbembe, A. (2002). At the Edge of the World: Boundaries, Territoriality, and Sovereignty in Africa. In M. R. Beissinger& M. C. Young (Eds.), *Beyond State Crisis? Postcolonial Africa and Post-Soviet Eurasia in Comparative Perspective* (pp. 53–80). Washington, DC: Woodrow Wilson Center Press.

Metz, T. 2014. Ubuntu: The Good Life. In A. C. Michalos (Ed.), *Encyclopaedia of Quality of Life and Well-Being Research* (pp. 6761–6765). Dordrecht: Springer Science and Business Media.

Mukuka, G. S. 2010. *Reap What You Have Not Sown. Indigenous Knowledge Systems and Intellectual Property Laws in South Africa.* Pretoria: Pretoria University Press.

Murphy, N., & Ellis, G. F. R. 1996. *On the Moral Nature of the Universe.* Minneapolis: Fortress Press.

Ndlovu-Gatsheni, S. J. 2013a. The Entrapment of Africa within the Global Colonial Matrices of Power. *Journal of Developing Societies*, *29*(4), 331–353.

Ndlovu-Gatsheni, S. J. 2013b. Decolonising the University in Africa. *The Thinker*, *51*, 46–51.

Ndlovu-Gatsheni, S. J. 2013c. *Coloniality of Power in Postcolonial Africa: Myths of Decolonization.* Dakar, Senegal: Codesria.

Nordling, L. 2015. Africa's Fight for Equality. *Nature*, *521*, 24–25.

Nkomo, S. M. 2009. The Seductive Power of Academic Journal Rankings: Challenges of Searching for the Otherwise. *Academy of Management Learning & Education*, *8*(1), 106–112.

Nyamnjoh, F. B. (2012). Potted plants in greenhouses': A critical reflection on the resilience of colonial education in Africa. Journal of Asian and African Studies, 47(2), 129–154.

Nyamnjoh, F. B. 2015. *"C'est l'homme qui fait l'Homme": Cul-de-Sac Ubuntu-ism in Cote d'Ivoire.* Bamenda: Langaa.

Petkova, H., Schanken, B., &Samaha, D. 2010. *Barriers to innovation in the field of medical devices.* Geneva: World Health Organisation.

Robinson, K. 2010. Changing Paradigms. London: Royal Society of Arts. Retrieved from http://www.youtube.com/watch?v=mCbdS4hSa0s.

Rodney, W. 1983. *How Europe Underdeveloped Africa.* Dar-Es-Salaam: Tanzania Publishing House.

Sheneberger, K., & van Stam, G. 2011. Relatio: An Examination of the Relational Dimension of Resource Allocation. *Economics and Finance Review*, *1*(4), 26–33.

Teferra, D. 1997. Brain Drain of African Scholars and the Role of Studying in the United States. *International Higher Education*, 4–8.

Toyama, K. 2015. *Geek Heresy: Rescuing Social Change from the Cult of Technology* (Kindle). New York: Public Affairs.

UNESCO. 2010. *Engineering: Issues Challenges and Opportunities for Development*. Paris: UNESCO Publishing.

van Greunen, D., & van Stam, G. 2014. Review of an African Rural Internet Network and related Academic Interventions. *The Journal of Community Informatics, 10*(2), online.

van Hoorik, P., & Mweetwa, F. 2008. Use of internet in rural areas of Zambia. In *IST-Africa, 7-9 May 2008, Windhoek, Namibia.*

van Stam, G. 2012a. Is Technology the Solution to the World's Major Social Challenges? In: *IEEE Global Humanitarian Technology Conference (GHTC 2012), 21-24 Oct 2012, Seattle, WA, USA.*

van Stam, G. 2012b. *Towards an Africanised Expression of ICT.* (K. Jonas, I. A. Rai, & M. Tchuente, Eds.)*E-Infrastructures and E-Services on Developing Countries, 4th International ICST Conference (AFRICOMM 2012) 12-14 Nov 2012, Yaounde, Cameroon, Revised Selected Papers.* Berlin, Heidelberg: Springer.

van Stam, G. 2013. Information and Knowledge Transfer in the rural community of Macha, Zambia. *The Journal of Community Informatics, 9*(1), online.

van Stam, G. 2014. Ubuntu, Peace, and Women: Without a Mother, there is no Home. In M. van Reisen (Ed.), Women's Leadership in Peace-Building: Conflict, Community and Care (pp. 37–54). Trenton, NJ: Africa World Press.

van Stam, G. 2016a (submitted). Techno-power in 5G, and towards a 6G that includes African inputs. In: *AfriCHI, 21-25 Nov 2016, Nairobi, Kenya.*

van Stam, G. 2016b (in press). Ubuntu, a synonym for Communal Love. Harare: The Centre.

Watson, R. T. 2013. Africa's Contributions to Information Systems. *The African Journal of Information Systems, 5* (4), 126-130.

Zimbabwe National Statistics Agency. 2015. *2014 Labour Force Survey*. Harare: ZIMSTAT.

Chapter Nine

Challenges of Integration and De-coloniality in Africa: The Nigerian Experience

Aboyeji Adeniyi Justus & Aboyeji Oyeniyi Solomon

Introduction

Nigeria, prior to its imperial mid-wifing, was a multi-national expanse of land with its plurality of states. In spite of the marriage of inconvenience and artificial imperial tinkering that coerced disparate ethnic nationalities together into a mega nation through the British administrative stance of miserliness, in the spirit of nationalism and optimism it was hoped that someday, they would either forget or understand their differences to the effect that they would accept themselves for what they really are and foster integration among the various heterogeneous groups. However, after a century of forced integration, following the 1914 amalgamation, and decades of experimented federalism, some have argued that Nigeria is still in the process of becoming or worse still, failing to become a nation. With all optimism, Nigeria is perhaps, at its best a tomorrow or futuristic nation. A century following stringent attempts at national integration, one great monster that has proved so impregnable to the problem of national integration in Nigeria is regionalism. What is more, Nigeria has become a terrorism-infested nation, having been enlisted by the U. S. A. as one of the 14 countries to be recognised as terrorist states world-wide. (Afinotan, 2010:302). Meanwhile, this same U.S. and its agencies, notably the CIA, and international banking organisations such as the International Monetary Fund and the World Bank, were set up and master-minded by the USA and its Western Allies to perpetrate all manners of malevolence against African and particularly Third World countries.

This chapter, therefore, delves into the challenges of de-coloniality and integration in Africa with particular reference to Nigeria in the light of the organised crimes, such as terrorism. The study reveals that this could not be unconnected with the activities of organisations known collectively as the **'corporatocracy'** which are behind the new global empire. It is, therefore, necessary to state that until the battle against neo-colonialism in Africa is fought and won, the attainment of a laudable integration and de-coloniality is, at best, a fool's paradise. The chapter, which adopts the historical, narrative and analytical approach, and which relies extensively on personal observation, published works and the media, attempts the trans-disciplinary approach to modern historical studies.

Conceptual Clarifications

Conceptually, *de-coloniality* is the political and epistemological movement aimed at liberation of ex-colonised peoples from global coloniality. (Ndlovu-Gatheni, 2015) It is used to depict the struggle for liberation from colonialism, imperialism and neo-colonialism. It does not only refer to the liquidation of colonialism, which most African countries celebrated in the 1950s and 1960s, but a complete disconnect from the umbilical cord of developed nations and from all forms, trends and tendencies of colonialism. This encompasses the on-going struggle for a virile economy as there can be no meaningful political freedom without economic independence (FMI, 1990:7).

Terrorism as a phenomenon is the use of violence or the threat of it to create a euphoric climate of fear in a given population. It also involves the use of organised violence in the pursuit of political, religious or socio-economic intents. It may also take the form of global structural economic violence, as well as violence in terms of structural inequalities and interventionisms by some states. These, however, are also descriptive of concepts such as guerrilla warfare, insurgency or other forms of violence. From a purely Western and liberal perspective, any group that seeks to oust any liberal democracy (Western political institution, however oppressive or repressive) through violence, will be considered a terrorist group, especially if in the process, the group resorts to unconventional forms of violence in the pursuit of their political objectives. From a purely Marxist perspective, however, such a radical or revolutionary group would simply be considered a liberation movement and the struggle seen as patriotic or nationalistic. This underscores the candour in this statement that perspective determines position just as position determines perspective. Terrorism is a universal phenomenon, not just domestic or regional. In this sense, although terrorism may occur in regions, it is not regional but also international. It is much broader than the regions within which we see the conflicts happening. Furthermore, it is not only perpetrated by the global south but also by the global north. The violence of western epistemologies on African epistemologies or what other scholars have called *epistemicide*, cultural genocide and so on constitute violence by the global north on peoples of the global south.

Mercantilism (or the mercantilist approach) first developed as a fiscal policy prevailing in Europe between the 16th and 18th centuries. This early modern European economic theory and system actively supported the establishment of colonies that would supply materials and markets, and therefore, relieve home nations of dependence on other nations. It also connotes commercialism—the principles and methods of commerce (Encarta, 2009). The word *'mercantilism'* is used here to depict the contemporary entrepreneurship of terrorism in the world. Indeed, the spate of the commercialisation of terrorism has today become increasingly nauseating.

Antecedents to De-coloniality and African Integration

E.W. Blyden (1832-1912) is reputed as the pioneer of the "Back to Africa" movement and an advocate of the Pan-African concept or the philosophy of African nationalism. W.E.B. Du Bois (1868-1963) and Marcus Garvey (1887-1940) were two other giants of Pan-Africanist thoughts whose movements held sway outside Africa from 1919 to 1927. Following the lull in the activities of Pan-Africanism between 1927 and 1945, the years 1945 to 1963 indeed marked a significant milestone in the course of the development of Pan-Africanism in Africa. The period witnessed the African continental phase and awakening of African political consciousness and the strong expression of Pan-Africanist ideas in Africa itself by young educated Africans who became the driving force for African nationalism and advocates for African integration. George Padmore, a committed Marxist and radical activist whose social outlook and orientation attracted the attention of young African students, such as Jomo Kenyatta of Kenya, Sekou Toure of Guinea, Kwame Nkrumah of Ghana, Nnamdi Azikiwe and Obafemi Awolowo of Nigeria, to mention but a few, became the source of motivation for de-coloniality—fight for liberation from colonialism and imperialism—and African integration (Oyegoke, 2002:128).

In the early 1960s, after some African states had attained independence, the moves towards African integration became intensified. Africa became polarised into two ideological power blocs. The *Brazzaville Group* of moderate states which came into existence in 1960, comprised most of the former French colonies in West and Central Africa and Madagascar. The *Casablanca Group,* formed in 1961 and led by Ghana, was a group of radical states, which included Ghana, Guinea, Mali, Egypt, Morocco and Algeria. However, by 1961, a more conservative faction dubbed as the *Monrovia Group* sprang up, led by Nigeria. It comprised Liberia, Ethiopia, Sierra Leone, Tunisia, Togo, Libya, Somalia and Nigeria, in addition to the former Brazzaville states to subsume the Brazzaville Group.

The Casablanca group which represented revolutionary Pan Africanist thought advocated for political integration which would snowball into the formation of a United States of Africa, the Monrovia-Brazzaville favoured the principles of Sovereignty, Equality and Non-interference in the internal affairs of one another. The eventual formation of the Organisation of African Unity (O.A.U.) in May 1963 recorded thirty-two independent African states. The challenges of African integration and de-coloniality had always been evident. For instance, the Brazzaville Group, which was influenced by their colonial connection and heritage with France, was still tied to the apron string of France, while African economy and states were/are still largely controlled by powers by 'remote control' far beyond the shores of Africa.

Terrorism came as a later introduction through a systematic indirect (economic) rule system. There are obvious indications of invisible matrices of global powers operating in Africa. They fuel crises, organised criminality and terrorism. Hence, as colonialism divided colonial subjects, so also neo-colonialism and European powers, with palpable fears, seek to prevent national unity and regional integration among their colonial subjects. They therefore insist on localities and other immediacies among them. It is our contention, in this chapter, that colonial authorities create and indeed benefit from different vices of divisiveness and by setting one African state against the other. This is clearly evident as demonstrated during the cold war era. On the whole, this chapter looks as de-coloniality, terrorism and other challenges of African integration with particular reference to Nigeria.

Nigeria and the Challenges of Integration

The Nigerian nation has been sitting on a socio-political gun keg and trying to patch-up with the unholy matrimony that accompanied the British amalgamation that birthed Nigeria one hundred years ago. *"If the foundation is bad, what can the righteous do?"* says the Holy Scriptures (Psalms 11:3). Diagnostically, heterogeneity, state plurality, regional sectionalism, multi-culturalism, mutual suspicion and chauvinism, among other things, form part of the foundation blocks of the Nigerian nation.

The historic statements credited to two legendary Nigerian political patriarchs may be a good starting point here. In 1953, Chief Anthony Enahoro moved for Nigeria's self-governance by 1956, to which the north amended with the words, "as soon as practicable" (Fwatshak & Ayuba, 2014:7-8). Following this, Dr. Nnamdi Azikiwe, in a rather nationalistic tone, reportedly implored: *"Let us forget our differences".* He was alleged to have been nabbed prestissimo by Sir Ahmadu Bello, the Sardauna of Sokoto, saying, *"We cannot forget our differences. We can only understand our differences. You are a Christian and a Southerner. I am a Moslem and a Northerner."* As much as one may want to applaud the candour and wit in this statement, it unravels the concealed spirit of nepotism, sectionalism and regionalism as well as the shaky foundation upon which the Nigerian federalism was built. This notwithstanding, at independence, in 1960, as revealed by General Yakubu Gowon (Rtd.) in a public lecture in 2006, Nigeria's founding fathers had a very clear vision for the Nigerian nation upon which subsequent leaders were expected to build. They saw:

...a united, indivisible nation, a melting point of cultures and religions, where everyone expressed and exploited his/her potentials without any inhibition. Nigeria, by its size and population, a Giant of Africa, taking the lead in socio-economic growth and development; a stable polity with a buoyant, rapidly developing economy; a disciplined and highly civilized society, devoid of corrupt and other social vices, a truly independent nation that is self-sufficient and able to manage her resources efficiently (Aboyeji, 2006).

One question that ensues from this is "How much has been built upon the aspirations of the founding fathers and well-meaning patriarchs?" Or better still, "How many miles from the realisation of this noble vision?"

Regionalism, Federalism and Nigeria's Plurality of States

Considering the heterogeneity of the peoples of Nigeria, and the historical upheavals in the making of the Nigerian nation, one needs to applaud the level of sacrifice, teamwork, blendings, harmonisations, reconciliations, assimilations, enculturations, etc. that have taken place to bring the heterogeneous peoples to this point of nation-building. This understanding should foster better willingness to fight for the unity of the country and to remove inhibitions such as regional sectionalism, nepotism, religious fanaticism, political gangsterism, electoral opportunism, social chauvinism and terrorism now standing like the rock of Gibraltar in the way to the actualisation of genuine nationhood in Nigeria and African continental integration (Ozumba, 1999:98-99). Indeed, an invisible matrix of global power operates on Africa. As such, crises in Africa are often sponsored by the empire and global coloniality.

Among other things, the ecological complementarity of the Nigerian vegetation zones and inter-group co-operations seemed to have prepared a conducive atmosphere for the amalgamation and knitting together of these disparate states. The ascent of Lord Lugard in 1914 as the new Governor General, with his administrative wizardry, only exploited the existing bond of political unity. However, the colonial policy of indirect rule which came more by the dictates of political convenience and imperial miserliness, than anything else, completely snubbed the question of heterogeneity and put no viable mechanism in place which could mediate in the conflicting group interests of an artificially consummated entity described by Chief Obafemi Awolowo as a mere geographical expression of the British (Fwatshak & Ayuba, 2014:5).

Subsequent British Colonial Governor–Generals built upon the Lugardian structure, thus promoting sentiment by fashioning constitutions which emphasised sectarian loyalties. For instance, between 1939 and 1946, the British decided inter alia, to restructure the country into a sort of 'tri-national' state structure (Agi, 1999:115). The Macpherson Constitution of 1951 particularly intensified this process of sectarian loyalty by dividing the country into three main regions along geo-cultural divides—Hausa/Fulani in the North, Yoruba in the West and the Ibo in the East. This particularly gave birth to *regionalism* in Nigeria. The arrangement began with three regions and subsequently the Mid-western Region. The 1953 London and 1954 Lagos conferences birthed the formal adoption of the federal principle in Nigeria, at the instance of the British authorities.

Nearly all the countries of the world practicing *federalism*, (Germany, Canada, Brazil, Nigeria, etc.) have it modelled after America; although the Americans also patterned it after that of the indigenous Iroquois whom they subsequently dispossessed, sought to extinguish, and subjugated. Benjamin Franklin had made swift to publish the translated account of the official transcript of the proceedings of the meeting of the envoys from Maryland, Pennsylvania and Virginia with delegates of the Six Nations of the Iroquois Indians in 1744. There, the Iroquois leader, Canassatego advocated the federal union of the American colonies, which their (Indian) fore-fathers had established among the [original] Five Nation, thus making them formidable (Cynthia Feathers & Susan Feathers, 2015). Today, federalism is still one of the most classic modes of political arrangement in the world. Federalism presumes that national and regional/state governments should stand to each other in a relation of meaningful autonomy resting upon a balanced division of powers and resources. The desirability of federalism hinges upon its perceived integrative propensity, which makes it capable of serving heterogeneous societies well in situations of crisis (Omotoso, 2010:141).

213

Citizens desire and actually deserve good governance. One key impetus to the adoption of the federal system in Nigeria was the colonial government's façade of amalgamating the various nationalities in a manner that would achieve higher levels of mutual, national identity and consciousness, for their own ends. As events unfolded, however, it became evident soon after independence how each region struggled to dominate the others in an attempt to gain the 'federal might' for the benefit of the region. Nigeria's federalism, at inception was bottom-heavy, with regions being apparently stronger than the centre. However, with the protracted militarisation (and politicisation) of Nigeria's federalism, it had become top-heavy by the restoration of power to the civilians in 1999. This transmogrified Nigeria's federalism to one of supremacy of the centre over the regions.

Given the concentration of resources and real powers at the centre, the competition for the control of the federal government has tended to be brutal, corrupt and politically volatile. Although dependency theorists such as Nwabueze (2010), and Walter Rodney (1971) in his *"How Europe Underdeveloped Africa"* have revealed inherent contradictions of states without civil order and colonialism's efforts towards undermining Africa's capacity for development. This unmediated brawl for power and influence at the centre has elicited the advent of a governing elite class that has elevated primordial and self-interest over and above the common good and general will of Nigerians (Omotoso, 2010:141).

Ethno-Regional Political Structures

The British had consummated a 'geo-political marriage' which already characterised the relationship of the peoples of pre-colonial Nigeria. Ever since then, political articulation has always taken on regional and sectarian colouration. Following this blazed trail, the elites who became the vanguards of nationalism had promoted primordial loyalties by appealing to egotistic sentiments in order to gain, regain or retain power. Political activities, had thus, been geared towards securing loyalty from one's own group. Little wonder therefore that political parties in Nigeria have often been shaped along regional delineations. The major political groups in the First

Republic, for instance, had no national (but ethnic-cum-regional) outlooks—Northern Peoples' Congress (NPC), Action Group (AG) and National Council of Nigerian Citizens (NCNC), for the Hausa (North), Yoruba (South-West) and Igbos (South-East) respectively.

This trend continued into the Second Republic when out of the five political parties approved out of over fifty that sought registration by the Federal Electoral Commission (FEDECO), three of them were rooted on regional grounds—National Party of Nigeria (NPN), Unity Party of Nigeria (UPN) and Nigeria People's Party (NPP) (FMI, 1990:28). Even the state-constituted political parties of the Third Republic—National Republican Convention (NRC) which had its stronghold in the north and the Social Democratic Party (SDP) which had its stronghold in the southwest did not present any significant difference. The annulment of the 1993 Presidential Election came as a result of a shift of power base from the Hausa/Fulani in the North to the Yoruba in the South. As this was perceived as a serious threat to the interests of the elite elements of the Hausa/Fulani who controlled the military, an election that was destined to foster and consolidate national integration in Nigeria was given an artificial political capsizing. Traces of the formation and composition of political parties along regional and sectarian groupings are still manifest even till date. For instance, there have been indictments against the APC as Yoruba-based, being a progeny of the Yoruba-based defunct Afenifere Group—Alliance for Democracy.

Sectarianism has always been a means to an end, not an end in itself. In most of Africa, Nigeria inclusive, the state, is thought to be the source of financial resources. The various segments of the elite class had thought that any group that captures the state power gets direct access to the resources of the state, which can be used to further their own selfish interests and that of their groups. Moreover, since its stake is considered high, the struggle for state power has been extremely fierce. It is against this background that sectarianism and regionalism have become serious impediments to national integration (Irele, 1999:104). However, drawing inferences from the neoliberal retrenchment of the state and the international tapestries of control over the African states, the real power, it could be said, lies at the global level which has overthrown the states. Obviously, with the multinational corporations, International Monetary Fund and the World Bank, states have lost their control of the source of financial resources in Africa. States cannot even sell their exploits, such as oil, or trade in their wildlife without the approval of the United States and other powers or their agents. It is thus plausible to argue that power is no longer concentrated in the states even though African states have condemnations concentrated on them.

Obiyan (2010:156) has indeed described Nigeria's Federalism with the words, "Decentralization in disarray". This has snowballed into such hysteria as sectarian militancy and terrorism almost through the length and breadth of the country. As it is with most of the African countries that emerged from colonial rule, perhaps Nigeria's foremost impediment to national integration yet remains the phenomenon of sectionalism and regionalism. This and many more complex factors such as the contradictions and anomalies in the state system brought to Africa via colonialism (Nwabueze, 2010) explain the paradox inherent within the Nigerian society whereby in spite of the immense resources (both human and material) the country yet remains stuck in the quagmire of retrogression. Nigeria has tremendous potentials for development if it could only achieve a national integration of its constituent groups. There is greater loyalty and allegiance to the sectarian groups than to the nation-state. Ever since Nigeria became an independent sovereign state on October 1st 1960, her greatest challenge has been how to weld together a unified national entity from the rather incongruent communities whose members retain primary loyalties to smaller units at the regional levels. Their leaders have more often seen these sectarian and other divisions as an advantage to themselves and their followers.

Nigeria's problem of national integration is both historical and multi-dimensional. Crawford Young's *"The Politics of Cultural Pluralism"* reflects Nigeria's political dilemma in that the country has yet to free itself from Awolowo's designation of it as being a mere *"geographical expression"*; (Agi, 1999:114) hence, still groping for a cohesive social order.

Heterogeneity is not Nigeria's bane. Irele (1999:104) contends that the organic conception of nation (that is, a homogenous nation that is bound by a common language and attached to a clearly defined territory as its material possession, invested with significance as the expression of its identity) files against historical realism. As a matter of fact, most countries of the world are multi-cultural and multi-national. As such, Nigerians need not perceive themselves rather ill-fated about their heterogeneous character or as a mere artificial legacy of European colonialism. It is our contention that nations are created; they don't come as a natural phenomenon as in the Herderian sense. Hence, a nation, as a concrete reality can only be a creation as there has never been a natural nation. Nations do not arise as a result of any instinct or experience of any culturally homogeneous set of people but as an invention in the mind. Nationhood involves feelings of affinity, shared identity and a common destiny. Nation is therefore, a community of people who feel bound together in the double sense that they share deeply significant elements of a common heritage and a common destiny for the future (Agi, 1999:110).

Plato, in his classic, *The Republic*, theorised that both the soul and city have three analogous parts: *the id* (a desiring part representing the lower class in the society); *the ego* (a spirited part, something like the will depicting the middle class) and *the super-ego* (a rational part portraying the higher class and the intellectual members of the society, typified of the thinkers, the philosophers). Plato insisted that the two non-rational classes must be administered by the rational, (i.e. the elite group), who alone can with their mental magnitude acquire knowledge of the forms—governance. The ideal state or society, he maintains, requires that the wisest and most philosophical persons rule the pleasure-seeking and passionate populace. Essentially, African societies do not have to be culturally homogenous before achieving the status of a nation. All that is required is a conscious effort on the part of the various component groups to invent the nation. The onus, in this regard, falls on the elite class.

Irele (1999:100) bemoans the fact that after some decades of independence, hardly can any nation in Africa be considered viable. Although he argued that the nation-building experiment in virtually all the African states had crumbled so tremendously, it must be argued here that Africans had for long built virile nations prior to colonisation. He contends that these elites are to blame in addressing the problem of sectionalism in Africa as it affects the issue of national integration. The elites have often frustrated the nation-building

217

efforts in Africa by exploiting propagandist sectionalism in their power fracas. The effect of the sectarian conflicts among the elite class in respect to state power has often taken the form of sectarian divisiveness, cleavages and violence (Irele, 1999:103). The problem of this *centrifugal nationalism* often arises when the principle of national self-determination is applied by all component nationalities within the state, thus greatly weakening the authority of the central government (Agi, 1999:113).

'Terrorism' and Mercantilism in Nigeria

Right from independence, Nigeria's commitment to world peace as a foreign policy objective and as an element of national interest and cherished domestic values has never been in doubt. This was demonstrated by the Obasanjo's regime (1999-2007) via his relentless combat against drugs trafficking and terrorism in all forms. Lamentably, as it has been observed, Nigeria's foreign policy and international voice rarely have been at such a lacklustre state as they were under the last two regimes. Yet, the challenges facing the nation both at home and abroad have become more self-evident. Perhaps one of such most debilitating challenges at the moment is that of terrorism and its impact on national integration and the image of Nigerians within the global society.

In Nigeria, terrorism is neither a novel nor an uncommon phenomenon. It could be traced back to the colonial era when state terrorism was employed to coerce and intimidate citizens to succumb to the unpopular policies of the colonial administration. A popular case was the Nwanyeruwa-led Women's War of 1929 in South-eastern Nigeria, often called the Aba Women Riot (God's presence 2014:21-25). The massacre of female civilians by security operatives of the colonial regime during this popular protest was one of the numerous acts of terror perpetrated against the citizenry. Hence, terror, as a political instrument, can be employed both by the oppressor and the oppressed. However, whereas the techniques used in liberation struggles may be described as creative, the use of violence in any guise and for any reason can hardly be described as humane. Meanwhile, in the real sense of it, what is seen by one as

218

liberation struggle may well be viewed by another as terrorism (Afinotan, 2010:304-309).

Afinotan (2010:310) further submits that *domestic terrorism* may be directed towards the attainment of political, religious, ideological or economic objectives. Such acts of terror include pipeline vandalisation, politically induced kidnappings, hostage taking, attacks on oil installations, bombing and destruction of public utilities, premeditated attacks on political office holders and their relatives, military coup d'état, attack on military and police personnel and politically motivated assassinations as we presently witness in the country.

If the Niger-Delta struggle in the **South-South** geo-political Zone of Nigeria had begun as a legitimate protest against state victimisation, economic deprivation or marginalisation and oppression against a sect, it did degenerate into criminality and terrorism in that geographical enclave. In the course of time, terror was unleashed upon members of other cultural groups in the region by the Ijaw. Different groups of primarily Ijaw stock were formed, popular among which are the Movement for the Emancipation of the Niger Delta (MEND), the Niger Delta Peoples Volunteer Force (NDPVF), Niger Delta Vigilantes (NDV), and the Federated Niger Delta Ijaw Communities (FNDIC). The degeneration into terrorism and criminality was thought to have been triggered off, as revealed by Asari Dokubo, by links between local militias and international terrorist organisations providing funds, arms and ammunitions to the local terrorists, like the Al-Qaeda and the Taliban Movements. The **South-East** Zone, at a time became a no-go area as some Bakassi Boys, a vigilante outfit and aggrieved unemployed folks embraced terrorism as a viable entrepreneur (The Punch, 2015[B]).

In the **Northern Region** of Nigeria, terrorism dates back to the years of the holocaust of Southerners, especially Igbos, by Northerners in Northern Nigeria between May and September 1966. The killings led to a mass exodus of Igbos from the north to their homelands in the east (FMI, 1990:15). This was among the series of events that snowballed into the Nigerian Thirty Months Civil War, from 1967 to 1970. Ever since, terrorism has been masterminded and perpetrated by members of radical Islamic movements such as the *Maitatsine* under the leadership of Mohammed Marwa against non-

219

members. This group's unwholesome activities cut across virtually all the Northern states and spanned five whole years between 1980 and 1985.

The Nigerian militant Islamic group, BOKO HARAM, founded in 2002 in Maiduguri by Ustaz Mohammed Yusuf, seeks the imposition of Sharia law throughout the thirty-six states of Nigeria. BOKO HARAM does not only abhor Western education but the entirety of Western culture and modern science. Yusuf, for instance, reportedly condemned such beliefs as the sphericity of the earth, social Darwinism and the theory that rain comes from water evaporated by the sun, as incompatible with the Islamic teaching (Afinotan, 2010:313). Besides the religious camouflage they often poise, this might have come as a counter measure to the abhorrence of Western epistemology to Islamic groups, like the Al Qaeda, ISIS and Boko Haram. It is thus apparently a mutual hatred between the West and the Islamic States.

The Nigerian Taliban emerged in the Northern State of Borno early in 2003, structured and organised along the lines of the Afghan Taliban (Afinotan, 2010:311). In July, 2009 a militant Islamic group dubbed as BOKO HARAM clashed with the Federal security forces in a sectarian violence which flared up in Wadil, Maiduguri, Potiskum and Bauchi, all in North-East Nigeria. Between 26th and 29th July 2009, over 700 deaths were recorded. Another factional upheaval broke out in Jos in January, 2010 in which people died like hordes of flies. This compelled the deployment of Federal troops to halt the terror unleashed on the people of Plateau state.

It was in the midst of this that Nigeria's image became battered internationally with the attempt of Umar Farouk Abdul Mutallib, a young Nigerian, to blow up Northwest Airline Flight 253, mid-air over Detroit, USA, in a suicide attack on the United States citizens *inter alios* on Christmas day 2009 (Afinotan, 2010:303-314). Albeit the attempt was foiled, the ripple effects therefrom have continued to be discussed in ever wider circles across the globe. Nigeria has since been enlisted by the U. S. A. as one of fourteen countries to be recognised as terrorist states world-wide. To this effect, ever since, among other things, Nigerians have to be subjected to intense and humiliating bodily search at airports all over the world. There have been both political and intellectual discourses for and against the U.S.

listing of Nigeria as a terrorist state (Afinotan, 2010:302-30) as well as its moral justification in view of the breath of terrorism in the world, today.

Odediran (2014:5) has decried how the security situation in Nigeria has today assumed a frightening and worrisome dimension. Between April 2014 and present day, he maintains that the Boko Haram terrorist group had declared a total war on the citizens through brutal killings, fatalistic maimings, and inhumane abductions. The brutality of the dastardly acts of this terrorist sect has so dazed the international community to the extent that a comity of nations such as the U.S.A., Britain, France, and China have waded in to help in the recovering of the 219 abducted school girls at the Government Girls' Secondary School, Chibok, Borno State on 14th April, 2014 (Odediran, 2014:5 & The Punch, 2015[A]). The unprecedented dimension that insecurity in Nigeria is taking through indiscriminate bomb explosions, twice in Nyanya, Abuja, in April 2014, Kano and Jos in May where over four hundred countable victims were recorded are all a pointer to the state of regional terrorism in Nigeria. Undoubtedly, the pandemic of regional terrorism has become obviously anathematic to Nigeria's survival as one nation with diverse nationalities.

In spite of America's acknowledgement of Nigeria's counter-terrorism war as documented in the 2010 American Annual Report on global terrorism, Nigeria has not been exculpated from the terrorism list. This is because apart from the cantankerous BOKO HARAM group's activities, the Niger-Delta insurgent groups in the *South-South, the Bakassi* and *MASSOB* boys in the *South-East,* the *OPC* in the *West,* and the *Maitasine, Taliban* and *Al-Qaeda* groups *in the North* are not only alive but seem to be re-gathering more explosive momentum (Afinotan, 2010:317). Lamentably today, the politico-religious crisis that has put the hitherto peaceful and serene Jos communities on the Plateau has claimed hundreds of lives and the embers are still blazing beneath the apparent calm.

The unabated wars in the creeks of the Niger-Delta has *terroristic* tendencies, especially as it affects some of the smaller nationalities in that region, as well as the international oil companies and their foreign staff. This, of course, is not unconnected with some forms of structural violence or terrorism perpetrated by these international oil companies in terms of inequalities arising from their activities and policies in Nigeria. There is also no end to the issues of internecine violence and uprisings in Northern Nigeria often camouflaged under religion. Worse still is the realisation that the existing Nigerian Laws do not specifically recognise terrorism as an offence. The Terrorism (Executive) Bill of 2006 presented to the Senate had been discarded for whatever reasons.

Among the conditionalities listed by the U.S.A. since 11th February 2010 for Nigeria to be de-listed from the global terrorists' list included the need to fast-track the legislation on terrorism before the National Assembly and the tightening of security at the nation's airports (Afinotan, 2010:318). It however behoves us to query America's moral right to enlist countries and set conditionalities when the advances of terrorism go beyond the sway of such countries but from global military industrial complex.

Rather unfortunately, Nigeria particularly and most of Africa in general have been discovered to possess all it takes to be terrorist breeding grounds: they are resource-rich but democracy-poor. Corruption is rife and almost legally, free for all. Anarchy, economic distress and criminal activities abound. What is more, the swelling populations of unemployed and underemployed youths make them easy preys to those who seek to hire resentment and despair to achieve their own ends. Regional and religious conflicts abound. Security is lacking for the civil society. Sub-Saharan Africa has often been considered almost solely as a site of poverty and conflict (Cravo 2014:1). As such, there is a sombre connection between poverty and organised crimes, such as terrorism. This could not be unconnected with the activities of organisations known collectively as the *'corporatocracy'* which are behind the new global empire— engineering, consulting, construction, accounting and banking industries and most prominent of all, oil companies. The U.S. government and its agencies, notably the CIA are the master-minders. Besides, there are also international banking organisations such as the International Monetary Fund and the World Bank, set up by the USA and its Western Allies to perpetrate all manners of malevolence against these states. Together with the big corporations and the U.S. government, they have been portrayed as the 'three pillars' of the global empire-building project (Nwabueze, 2010: 297).

The present conundrum and state of consternation the Nigerian society has been plunged into ever since her 50th Independence Anniversary in which criminality, terrorism and insecurity have become nothing more than a political game and very viable business is rather worrisome. Perhaps having seen the big life the MEND boys now live, after the Federal Government had negotiated with them, the BOKO HARAM apparently faceless monsters came on board. And is it not being foreseen, today that the Yoruba socio-political organisation, O'odua People's Congress (OPC), or another sectarian belligerent group may also consider coming up with a fresh brand or version of what seems a legitimate quest for National Cake Rights? This may come up after seeing the 'sense' in the Terrorism Business bid of the Movement for the Emancipation of Niger Delta (MEND) or BOKO HARAM sects. The Federal Government had perhaps out of frustration, openly confessed her readiness to employ any means including negotiation to appease this cruel Islamic religious sect. Today, every section of the country seems to see Terrorism not only as a potent instrument of coercively taking her portion of the 'National Cake' from the Federal Government, but also as a profitable stock-in-trade (i.e. mercantilism). The Niger-Delta experience, the on-going Boko-haram odoriferous saga, etc. are instances of recent regional terrorist tendencies which do not only threaten Nigeria's Federalism but may also spark-off other sectional reactions along the same line. Or how can one explain a situation where the security of the number one man in the country is being openly threatened by seemingly faceless folks? Is Nigeria not heading towards anarchy as well as total collapse and national disintegration?

Rumours going round the town of the involvement and role of some big Whigs of Nigerian politics in pre- and post-election crises in Nigeria are rather unfortunate (Aboyeji, 2012:7). There is an urgently dire need for an atmosphere of peace and absolute serenity for any meaningful development and genuine national integration to take place.

The *findings* of this study reveal, among other things, that Nigeria became a nation through an imperial edict which only marked the beginning of the making of Nigeria. However, the genuine and true Nigerian nation is still in the making. In furtherance, Nigeria's peregrination into nationhood was borne out of optimism and nationalism, which its heterogeneous peoples have not been able to transform into realism. Hence, with increasing criminality, intolerance for national integration, terrorism, sectional protests and agitations such as the on-going Biafran secessionist bid, the trans-mutational process which attempted to evolve different kingdoms, empires, states, caliphates and kingdoms into a united geographical entity called Nigeria, over the last century seems to have failed *abinitio* and proved a total fiasco. However, with sustained doggedness to surmount her monumental challenges, both internal and external, indications are that Nigeria is beginning to fare well with a strong capacity for sustainability. Indeed, in view of the recommendations below, Nigeria possesses a strong prospect for actualising the dream of a *Pax Nigeriana* in Africa.

Recommendations

Based on the findings of this study, the following recommendations are made as pragmatic measures out of this socio-political debacle:

i. To achieve national and regional integration in Africa, we must sink our sectarian, religious, regional, sentimental, ideological, social differences and political affiliations, which becloud our transcending national interests (Ozumba, 1999:98-99). Religious, party and ethnic divisions should be accorded with more curious avoidance.

i. Although the African states are believed to have lost effective policy space snatched by international institutions, there is yet an urgent need to rethink the idea of national integration where every component group would have a sense of belonging. The integration of the different nationalities into a nation could be achieved in Nigeria as elsewhere in Africa, through the medium of culture. The elite class should define the phenomenon of nationalism as a "civic religion" to unite together the mass society of nations (Irele, 1999:104).

ii. There must be a *will* among the people *to live together* as a nation (Agi, 1999:113). Nigerians, for instance, seem to have lost the will to live together. It took a fierce thirty months' civil war to keep the Igbo nation within the Nigerian nation till date. Yet, efforts have not yet been relented on the actualisation of the Biafran Republic. Nigeria is indeed already partitioned or fractionalised on paper into the Oduduwa, Bayajjida, Biafran Republics, etc. Whereas undoubtedly the attendant coerced unity brought some quarrels, it has become rather imperative that the artificiality of the country must be allowed to work. Hence, Africans need to stress those things that bind them together. And as such, there must be some values that must cement the unity for the welfare, good and development of the good people of Africa.

iii. The force of *Centripetal Nationalism* could be successfully harnessed to the institutions of the state to birth a single political community of enormous significance. Pan-Africanism and Nationalism constitute an explosive force which can provide a uniquely powerful instrument of integration, if positively articulated; or disintegration if wrongly employed (Agi, 1999:113).

iv. Governments at all levels should also demonstrate all astuteness in fighting crimes, terrorism and everything capable of precipitating the extinction of African nations built upon the sacrificial blood of some legendary political martyrs.

v. Concerted joint-efforts should be launched by all African and so-called Third World countries against neo-colonialism in Africa. Until this battle is fought and won, the attainment of a laudable integration and de-coloniality is, at best, a fool's paradise.

Conclusion

Sub-Saharan African has since independence, been bedevilled by enormous internal challenges and external upheavals. These include administrative problems, corruption, criminality, terrorism, neo-colonialism and other vices of divisiveness and integration, most of which are sponsored by outside forces. This chapter is therefore an attempt to deal with the historical challenges as well as the contemporary challenges and thrusts towards African integration, Pan-Africanism, African renaissance and de-coloniality with particular reference to Nigeria, the accredited 'Giant' of Africa.

From the outset, Africa had been polarised by socio-political chauvinism, religious sentimentalism and sectarian nationalism. Feelings of sectional *Afrophobia* and nostalgia have ever since become increasingly heightening. The once-upon-a-time peaceful atmosphere of this democratic dispensation has been diverted to launch national and regional violence through organised and trans-boarder crimes, since terrorism has come to be employed as profitable stock-in-trade. Is it not plausible to conclude, at this juncture, that Nigeria (and by extension, the continent) has become really dishevelled in a hysterical blight and historical blot? Nigeria might have achieved a 'strong' Nigerian state, which perhaps has won it the appellation 'Giant of Africa'; but it is yet to achieve full nationhood, going by some palpable parochial loyalties and particularistic attitudes (Agi, 1999:123).

Such was it that the "House that Lugard Built", called Nigeria, (Fwatshak & Akinwumi, 2014) grew in leaps and bounds to become the "Giant of Africa". However, in the words of Falola (1991:90), the independence granted by the colonial powers was a sham. All the colonial structures and institutions were left intact as they ensured that they handed over to politicians who guaranteed that colonial economic and other interests continued un-interfered with. Little wonder that soon after the celebrated independence, African economies were not only dominated by foreigners, but were drained by British, French and other Western countries. Following Africa's political independence, the reality that followed was one which plunged the former colonies into a new phase of economic dependency, aptly described as neo-colonialism. Its main purpose, according to Nwabueze (2010:269-271) is

> *...the maintenance of the independent country's economic dependency, of the continued domination of its economic affairs by the former colonialists...aggravated by the power and influence exerted over African economies by the three economic institutions created under the Breton Woods Agreement of 1945—the International Bank for Reconstruction and Development (otherwise known as the World Bank), the International Monetary Fund (IMF) and the General Agreement on Tariffs and Trade (GATT), which began operations in 1946, 1947 and 1948 respectively.*

Altogether, these forces, by the economic policies foisted on African governments, have been attributed by Africans, as accountable for the exacerbation of Africa's financial and economic malaise. However, other scholars such as Areoye (2002), Nwabueze (2010) and Aboyeji (2015) have argued that whereas foreign influence might have been truly very devastating and destabilising, but aroused a re-think of Rodney's (1971) *"How Europe Underdeveloped Africa"* by raising a fundamental conundrum—*For how long do we over-emphasise how Europe or foreign influence undermined Nigeria specifically, and Africa in general?*

References

Aboyeji, A. J. 2015. "Foreign Influence on Igbomina, C. 750-1900" Unpublished PhD Thesis, Department of History and International Studies, University of Ilorin, Ilorin, Nigeria.

Aboyeji, A. J. 2012. "Issues and Problems of National Development in Education (in Nigeria)" in NAKSS ELITISM, A Magazine Publication of the National Association of Kwara State Students (NAKSS), Kwara State College of Education, Oro, Nigeria.

Aboyeji, A. J. 2006. "The Third Term Question: Greatest Threat and Menace to Nigeria's Democratic Ethos" A Speech presented on the commemoration of the 7th Democracy Day Celebration in Nigeria held on 29th May, 2006, at the Multi-purpose Hall of Sapati International School, Ilorin.

Afonitan, L. A. 2010. "Nigerian Foreign Policy objectives and the Problem of Terrorism" in Omotoso, A. A., Agagu, A. A. & Abegunde, O. (Eds.) *Governance, Politics and Policies in Nigeria: An Essay in Honour of Professor Dipo Kolawole*, Editions SONOU d'Afrique (ESAF) Porto Novo, Benin Republic, pp. 302-321.

Agi, S. P. I. 1999. "Nation-Building in Nigeria: Problems and Prospects" in Ozumba, G. O., Eteng, F. O. & Okom, M. (Eds.) *Nigeria: Citizenship Education*, AAU Vitalis Book Company, Aba, Nigeria. pp. 109-127.

Areoye, O. 2002. *Black Man's Dilemma*, Revised Edition, Update of Events, 1976-2002, Board Publications Limited, Dec. 2002.

Cynthia Feathers & Susan Feathers "Franklin and the Iroquois Foundations of the Constitution" Retrieved on 29th December, 2015 from http://www.google.com.ng/search/q=American+Federalism+modelled+after+indigenous=Iroquis.

Encarta, 2009. "Mercantilism" *Microsoft Encarta* © 1993-2008, Microsoft Corporation.

Eteng, F. O. 1999. "Nigeria and Constitutional Developments" in Ozumba, G. O., Eteng, F. O. & Okom, M. (Eds.) *Nigeria: Citizenship Education*, AAU Vitalis Book Company, Aba, Nigeria. pp. 128-136.

Falola, T., Mahadi, A., Uhomoibhi, M. & Anyanwu, U. (Eds.) 1991. *History of Nigeria 3: Nigeria in the Twentieth Century*, Learn Africa Plc.

FMI, 1990. *The March to Democracy, 30th Anniversary*, Published by the Federal Ministry of Information, Lagos.

Fwatshak, S. U. & Ayuba, J. M. 2014. "Amalgamation Discourses in the "Lugardian House" During Nigeria's First Centenary" in Fwatshak, S.U. & Akinwumi, O. (Eds.) *The House that "Lugard Built" Perspectives on Nigeria's First Centenary: The Pains, the Gains and the Agenda for the Future* Historical Society of Nigeria, Nigeria.

Fwatshak, S.U. & Akinwumi, O. 2014. (Eds.) *The House that "Lugard Built" Perspectives on Nigeria's First Centenary: The Pains, the Gains and the Agenda for the Future* Historical Society of Nigeria, Nigeria.

God's presence, E. O. 2014. "Women as Agents of Social Change: A Study of Aba Women's Riot and Civil Rights Movement in the United States of America" in *Ilorin Journal of History and International Studies Vol. 4, No. 1*, (2014) Edina B. M. & Aphelion S. O. (Eds.) Department of History and International Studies, University of Ilorin, Ilorin.

Irele, D. 1999. "Nigeria and Nation-hood" in Ozumba, G. O., Eteng, F. O. & Okom, M. (Eds.) *Nigeria: Citizenship Education*, AAU Vitalis Book Company, Aba, Nigeria. pp. 100-108.

Ndlovu-Gatsheni, S. J. 2015. *Decoloniality as the Future of Africa*. History Compass, 13:485-496. See http://onlinelibrary.wiley.com/enhanced/doi

Nwabueze, B. 2010. *Colonialism in Africa: Ancient and Modern, Vol. 2—Africa's Inheritance from Colonialism* Gold Press Ltd., Ibadan, Nigeria.

Obadare, E. 2001. "Constructing Pax Nigeriana? The Media and Conflict in Nigeria-Equatorial Guinea Relations" in *Nordic Journal of African Studies 10 (1)*, pp. 80-89. See http://www.google.com.ng/url?q=http://www.njas.helsinki.fi/pdf-files/vol10num1/obadare.pdf

Obiyan, A. S. 2010. "Federal-State Relations and Nigerian Federalism: Centralization in Disarray" in Ozumba, G. O., Eteng, F. O. & Okom, M. (Eds.) *Nigeria: Citizenship Education*, AAU Vitalis Book Company, Aba, Nigeria. pp. 156-172.

Odediran, N. O. 2014. "Education for Empowerment and National Security" being a Lead Paper presented at the 5th National Conference of Kwara State College of Education, Oro from 10th-14th June, 2014.

Omotoso, F. 2010. "Federalism, Politics and Governance in Nigeria" in Omotoso, A. A., Agagu, A. A. & Abegunde,s O. (Eds.) *Governance, Politics and Policies in Nigeria: An Essay in Honour of Professor Dipo Kolawole*, Editions SONOU d'Afrique (ESAF) Porto Novo, Benin Republic, pp. 141-155.

Oyegoke, B. 2002. *An Outline History of Africa*, FootPrints Publications, Ibadan, Nigeria.

Ozumba, G. O. 1999. "Background to the Making of Nigeria" in Ozumba, G. O., Eteng, F. O. & Okom, M. (Eds.) *Nigeria: Citizenship Education*, AAU Vitalis Book Company, Aba, Nigeria, pp. 93-99.

Rodney, W. 1972. *How Europe Underdeveloped Africa,* Bogle Louverture Publications.

The Punch (2015[A]) "Chibok Girls Forced to Fight for B'Haram—Witness", *The Punch Newspaper*, 30/06/2015. See http://feedproxy.google.com/~r/punchng/NEWS/~3/1mOUZgaZUD0/

The Punch, 2015[B]. "Buhari and Terror of Ethnic Militias" *The Punch Newspaper*, 19/05/2015. See http://www.punchng.com/editorials/buhari-and-terror-of-ethic-militias/

Chapter Ten

African Traditional Religion and Representation: An Examination of Selected Yoruba Movies

Ogunbiyi, Olatunde Oyewole

Introduction

This chapter takes off from the spectrum of the symbiotic relationship that subsists between religion and movies in Nigeria. Most of Nollywood (the Nigerian Movie Industry) productions have one religious theme or the other which are often implicit or explicit in the movies. Interestingly, the technologies of production have continued to improve over the years and the avenues of access have not only increased but also cheaper. Nowadays, movies cannot only be downloaded from the internet, but can also be watched even on phones and other platforms. This opportunity has given various religions, especially African religion the chance to reach thousands of subscribers. This chapter argues that African religion of the Yoruba extraction is utilizing these variegated dynamics of technology to propagate her doctrines and practices. The resultant effect is that many people come to the knowledge of their religious dogma. Chapter concludes that the ambience of an increasing visual technology, religious representations find expression in the power of visuality.

African Traditional Religion herein referred to as ATR is the aboriginal religion of the Africans. This indigenous religious practice has been the earliest form of religion known in the African continent and practiced by all and sundry. However, with the advent of missionary religions of Islam and Christianity in Africa, ATR became the nexus from which these foreign religions struggled to make converts. Quite a number of strategies were employed by these foreign religious traditions to undermine and make the indigenous religion despicable to the African thereby gaining converts to their own side. Many scholars have appreciated these strategies and focusing on these here will amount to duplications and deviation from the subject matter of this work. However, worthy of mention here is the fact that the resultant effect of these strategies is the depiction of ATR as a religion not only worthless but also destructive. Many Africans came to detest the religion, its culture and worldview. These often relegate the religion to the background, preferring the foreign religion and above the indigenous one. The idea is that Africans cannot initiate ideas, in fact, it was Emil Ludwig who opines that God is a philosophical concept that Africans can never think about. The matters become worse when Africans themselves came to regard the religion of their forefathers as archaic, unpopular and inimical to progress. This is against the backdrop of these foreign religions, especially Christianity, that is regarded as modern, better and the true way of serving God.

Against the background of this rejection of ATR is the development of a technological advancement that is popularized and accelerated by globalization. This advancement touches virtually every area of human activities. However, the concern of this chapter is in the area of communications and its concomitant technologies on movie productions. The idea of media production is a fairly old one in Nigeria and Africa as a whole. It was part of the technologies that were introduced to Africa particularly during the era of colonial dominations of African countries. The content of these foreign films depict European life, educational and research films which were used to teach various topics on agriculture and other areas of interest to the colonialists. The films were often shown in cinema halls built solely for that purpose. African attempts at producing these celluloid films soon gained the attention of producers who also produced films for a growing audience. By the end of the seventies, and due to additional technologies from other places in the world, many Africans started viewing the films from the comfort of their homes with the video machines. Today, the availability of countless platforms has made it easier to access these films easily from different formats and cheaper forms of production.

This chapter is set to answer the following research questions of how are the evangelical religions, especially Christian movies depict ATR? How is the indigenous religion of the Africans, specifically that of the Yoruba people represented in movies emanating from

Southwest Nigeria? How do the movies of southwest Nigeria help in the revitalization and revival of the ATR? The purpose of the work is to show the roles movies play in the image laundry of ATR. A coverage of African religion will be too wide in a chapter of this nature. Therefore, the chapter examines African Traditional Religion of the Yoruba extraction and movies that are produced the in Southwest Nigeria. The reason for this anchors on the fact that the Yoruba of Southwest Nigeria are a very religious people that can be used as an archetypal representation of the traditional religion of the Africans. In addition to this, Christianity and Islam have been in the region for a long time, boasting of several adherents jostling for the conversion of worshippers of ATR. Each has laboured to present the African Traditional Religion in a bad light. Apart from the above, the Yoruba people have been in film production since the early seventies. They and the Igbo of Eastern Nigeria have made the largest production of Nollywood movies. This prolific production of movies is an indication that the movies are accepted and that the audience in the region are avid consumers of film products. Two theoretical approaches are used in this chapter. They include the mediatisation (or convergence) approach and the articulation approach based on audience used and interpretations of representations of religious themes in the movies. The methodology employed in the elucidation of this chapter is interdisciplinary, embracing Sociology, audience studies and Comparative Religion. It involves the examination and analysis of two selected movies. One of the movies, *Agbara Nla* (Ultimate Power), is a Christian movie of Mount Zion Films Productions that presents the religion from the standpoint of converting the adherents of the traditional religion. The other movie, *Apesin* (Cooperate worship) a movie from the stables of Adebayo Tijani, examines the religion from the standpoint of a believer in the dogma of the traditional religion. This will be followed by audience primary research involving interviews of focus groups, members of the clergy and those attached to movie productions. The chapter concludes on two main lines. First, movies emerge as an independent variable which religious institutions must adapt to in order make either positive or negative representation. On the second level, movies are seen as part and parcel of religion whose technology can be gainfully used in the propagation of religion

233

The religion is known by several nomenclatures including African Religion, African Indigenous Religion or sometimes these names are rendered in the plural due to the heterogeneous nature of the African continent. Much has been written about these names and their implications. Suffice it to say that the term African Traditional Religion will be used as a working term for this chapter to refer to the religious consciousness of the African. Secondly, the term is used homogenously to refer to the practice of the religion among the Yoruba. The religion is one that has existed for generations that flow from antiquity to the present in South West Nigeria. The religion has been the mainstay of the people's perception of their God. Closely allied to the religion of the people is their culture which is intertwined with their religion.

However, other religious traditions from within and outside Africa as a result of increasing globalization came to compete for the souls of the people. These traditions are Islam, mainly from Northern Africa, while Christianity came from Sierra-Leone, Liberia, Europe and America. The new religions, especially Christianity which came after Islam, vehemently attacked institutions and practices of the traditional religion of the Yoruba. The converts were taught to disregard the religion as demonic, ineffective and archaic. The resultant effect of this is that the Yoruba of South West Nigeria Christianity under its various denominations preach to their converts the evil immanent in the traditional religion. The responses of the converts include a repudiation of their culture and tradition for those of the white men. Many had to change their names believing that those names contain curses, attached to divinities and that their misfortunes are the resultant effects of the names they bear. Oha (2002) puts this binary representation between the two cultures as two opposing forms of relationship between African traditional religion and Christianity which have persisted since colonial times in Nigeria.

While this attempt to undermine the traditional religion of the people progresses, the movie industry which is another effect of the globalization thrust into Africa, started developing. Cinema came into Nigeria at inception of colonial period. Initially, the films were made to exhibit and propagate the agenda of the colonial agencies in Nigeria. Gradually, the cinema that was exhibited developed into films of representations of the white as good with the responsibilities of civilizing the black man. In the words of Haynes (2011: 68):

> Cinema arrived with colonialism and as a tool of colonialism. It was used to dazzle the "natives" with the superiority of western technology and to indoctrinate them. The British, French, and Belgian colonial authorities established film units to make propaganda and instructional films (on such topics as hygiene and farming techniques), tailored to their notion of African audiences. More ambivalently, commercial cinemas became essential features of colonial cities, powerful instances of modernity, along with electric lighting, amplified popular music, factory wages, and motorized vehicles.

Africans became avid filmgoers—gradually, most of what was shown made most things that are traditional to appear bad and everything European to be good. For example, the people's religions were depicted badly while Christianity was given a favourable representation. Eventually these depictions soon became perpetrated in the movies that were produced after the colonial period and consequently, it became stereotyped reproduced by Yoruba Christian film makers.

Theoretical Framework

Two media theories will form the structure upon which this chapter revolves. The approaches include the mediatisation (or convergence) approach. The second is the articulation approach which is based on the audience utilizations of representations of religious themes that are found in the movies under review. The basis for the use of these theories is to gauge the influence movies exert on the society and culture. Mediatisation has emerged as an important concept and theoretical framework for considering the interplay between media, culture and society (Hjarvard 2015:1). Mediatisation has been used in various and variegated contexts. Asp, Mazzoleni and Schulz (1985, 1986, 1990) have applied this concept to politics believing that political systems are influenced by the media coverage of the politics of the region. The likes of Jensen and Aalberg

235

(2007), Stromback (2007) and Cottle (2006) prefer to situate this theory in the light of conflict resolutions while Janson (2002) to interpret the theory from the perspective of marketing culture. However, more important to this chapter is the mediatisation of religion. According to Hjarvard (2006), by the help of sophisticated media technology, supernatural and metaphysical phenomena have acquired an unprecedented presence in modern societies. Today, the media is awash with expositions on religions. Incidentally, many movies often have religious themes as part of their plots. Institutionalized religion of Christianity has achieved greater coverage in movies emanating from South West Nigeria. Meyrowitz (cited by Hjarvard 2006) in his contribution to the idea of mediatisation, identified three metaphors of the media. These he referred to as the media as channel, media as language and media as environment. This division is apposite here because each of these affects religion in its own way. As a media of channel, it speaks about the content of media serving as a vehicle bearing symbols from the sender to the receiver. The second metaphor concerns the media as language. Here, the media formats and frame from the relationship between the sender, content and the receiver. The third metaphor is the metaphor of environment. This is how media systems facilitate and structure human interaction and communication. Closely related to the above is McQuail's (2005) projection of the media as connecting with reality through seven images. This includes the images of window, a mirror, a filter or gatekeeper, a signpost, a forum, a disseminator and interlocutor, insisting that each has its own purpose. Postman's (2005) position is apposite here when he employs the word metaphorically to mean: not only to speech but to all the techniques and technologies that permit people of a particular culture to exchange messages. In this sense, all culture is a conversation or, more precisely, a corporation of conversations, conducted in a variety of symbolic modes. Our attention here is on how forms of public discourse regulate and even dictate what kind of content can issue from such forms (Postman, 2005:13).

The second theory that this chapter revolves around is the articulation theory. This concerns the way the media and religion interacts with each other as they depend on the audience utilization of these variables. From the foregoing, it becomes clear that the word is a linkage between one thing and the other. The articulation theory has actually been around for a long time. As a concept, it has been used centuries ago, implying various kinds of meanings (Slack, 1996) usually relating to the sciences. Many have contributed to the concept and they include, Fairclough (1989), Dijk (1998) and Hall (1986: 53) Hall views articulation: as the form of connection that can make a unity of two different elements, under certain conditions. It is a linkage which is not necessary, determined, absolute and essential for all time.

In the light of this, articulation will refer to that which plays an intermediary role that empowering discourses of the movies with cultural interpretations. Articulation as an audience theory will affect what is watched in the movie influence audience reaction within the society. . The focus here is not only on the entertaining function of the movies, but also the role these movies play in the propagation and revitalization of African religious traditions and how they impact social behaviour in the society. The research method is interdisciplinary, embracing Sociology, audience studies and Comparative Religions. The movies were viewed and interviews were conducted on focus group assessors.

African Traditional Religion and Nollywood

As said earlier, African Religion in this work is taken as a homogenous entity rather than heterogeneous institution. Though the religion spreads across the African continent, this writer sees the religious expressions of the Africans as one, with the acknowledgements of slight variations in language, pantheon of divinities and emphasis. As a result of this, it is easy to identify various religious imaginations of the Africans from movies that are emanating from the various ethnic groups that populate the continent. In Nigeria for example, movies that are produced by the Igbo reflect the ethnic bias of their language, culture and divinities, but their world view is not very different from that of the Yoruba of South West Nigeria.

Religion is one of the dominant themes portrayed by the Nollywood industry in many of the movies that are produced. It is interesting to note that the religions of Islam and Christianity are often pitched against African Traditional Religion. This is usually done by the frequent use of their clergy in the movies. Oftentimes, Pastors and Imams are portrayed in the movies as saints and as those who provide succour and salvation to one who has been under the bondage of the machination of the African indigenous priest. On the other hand, is the portrayal of these clergies as corrupt men and women who will stop at nothing to have the good things of life. Here, they are sometimes depicted as using charms collected from African indigenous religious priests or are in consonance with their antics to develop their citadels of worship. On the other hand, these traditional priest, known as *Baba Awo* (Father of mysteries) or *Iya Awo* (Mother of mysteries) are variously portrayed by Nollywood movies. Sometimes, they are portrayed positively as honest fellows who are covenanted to the divinities to be kind to mankind or following the dictates of Orunmila to always deal favourably with everybody who seeks consultations with them. A few examples will show this. *Arugba* (2008) is a movie enacted to capture the purity of the carrier of sacrificial items for Osun goddess. *Sango* (1993) movie portrays the traditional belief of the Yoruba while *Apesin* (2006) focuses on the essence of the religion of the people. *Opon Ifa* (2006) emphasizes the necessity of knowing the destiny of a newly born child. The movies that really attack the religion are those produced by missionaries who are bent on preaching their gospel with modern technologies of the movie. On the contrary, however, many movies have sought to negatively portray them as unreliable, dishonest and evil. They want the audience to see them as people whose medical prowess is ineffective or at most counterproductive. Where they cannot deny the efficacy of their products they give the impression that whatever is collected from them cannot be good and at best will eventually destroy the end users. For example, it is relayed that whoever gets children from them will have a very sick child that will ruin the parents. Any wealth obtained from them is going to spell doom for them. In other words, efforts are made to discourage people from patronizing them. As if this is not enough, the priests are also depicted as wizards armed with weapons of destruction. They are made the authors of miseries and misfortunes in the life of the people. At other times, they present them in mortal conflict with one another, dressed with charms all over their bodies.

Apart from the above, another area worthy of mention concerning the representation of African Traditional Religion is the portrayal of spirit beings and entities. These beings are a part of the Africans' folk belief. They include *aje* (witches), *abiku* (born-to- die children), *emere* (familiar spirits) and *akudiaya* (living dead) spirit characters and other myriads of beings too numerous to mention. One of the areas that have enjoyed mass depiction especially in earlier movies is the portrayals of witches. As a matter of fact, it became stereotypes as many movies that emanated later also gave attention to these phenomena. The portrayals of witches are very prominent in the movies produced by late Ajileye whose popular productions include *Koto Aiye* (2001) *Omo Iya Aje* (2007). Other spirit beings are represented but not as popular as the coverage devoted to witchcraft scenes. Acknowledgement must also be made about the portrayals regarding Yoruba cultural display bordering on religion. There are several renditions of songs, festivals, history of the Yoruba and several other exposures.

It must however, be put on record that while there are positive portrayals of the traditional religion, strong attempts are made to caricature the religion of the forebears of the Yoruba. Representations along this line include movies that are cast in the light of modern day perceptions and the missionary religions seeking to discredit the people's religion as archaic and ineffective. Included in this category are the movies of Mt Zion Film Production which have actually made a way for other similar movies that are produced to undermine the African Traditional Religion and promote Christianity. Such movies include *Attacks from Home* (2005), *Blood on the Altar* (2005), *Ultimate Power* (1994), *The gods are dead* (2000) *and The Foundations* (2006) and *Awo Jesu* (2007) to mention only a few.

Representation of African Traditional Religion in Selected Movies

Two movies have been picked for the purpose of the elucidation of the objective of this chapter. These are *Agbara Nla* and *Apesin*. The basis for the choice of these movies anchors on the fact that *Agbara Nla* is a Christian movie that uses the African traditional religious ideological stance to project the Christian religion within the African (Yoruba) context. In the light of this, and in a bid to project the

Christian religion, a vigorous attempt was made to misrepresent the indigenous religion. The producer of *Apesin* on the other hand, posits a contrary view of the people's religious consciousness. It highlights the Yoruba worldview and metaphysical perception as believed by the Yoruba.

Review of *Agbara Nla* movie and its Representation of African (Yoruba) Religion

Agbara Nla is a production of Mount Zion Ministry, a Christian evangelical outfit dedicated to soul winning through the instrumentality of movies. The date of the production of the Yoruba movie is 1993. Mike Bamiloye is the producer and director of the movie. The movie has four parts that are shot in Yoruba language and without translation. There are other versions of this movie. They are the ones that are produced in English and in French. The aim is to reach out to non-Yoruba speakers as well as to reach the French speakers, thus reaching a wider audience with the good news.

The Yoruba in their cosmological understanding do not distinguish the physical world from the spiritual world. To the Yoruba, there is no dichotomy between the terrestrial world and that of the celestial world, in that they posit an incorporeal world affecting the corporeal existence. They believe that the spiritual world actually controls the affairs of the physical existence. It is in the light of this that in cases of dire need, the Yoruba resort to people who have esoteric abilities to reach the spiritual agencies who are believed to be vested with powers that are beyond human knowledge and comprehension. In addition to the above, the Yoruba believe in the existence of several marine and riverine spirits. It is in this respect that they speak of such water divinities like Olokun, the goddess of the ocean and Yemoja the goddess of the river. In all cases visited in the course of the field work for this chapter, the divinities held to inhabit the rivers and ocean are usually feminine with their members. They strongly believe that all the rivers have goddesses who inhabit these rivers and that these goddesses exercise dominion over and above the people. They can be either benevolent or malevolent and can be approached as long as the person knows the formulae for which they are approached. The Yoruba also believe that these goddesses live in vast habitations underneath the rivers attended to by innumerable servants. In spite of this, they also are dedicated to trapping human beings whom they use to propagate their agendas on the surface earth. Oftentimes, it is reported that they spiritually marry human beings on earth thus preventing them from having a normal life on earth. Apart from the above, and also akin to it, is the Yoruba belief of spirits living on the surface earth. These spirits often inhabit trees, mountains and even grooves. These spirits exist like the ones in the river with diverse powers and abilities. They can be approached only by and through initiates and those with esoteric powers. In addition to the mysterious beings highlighted above, there exists strange beings who also affect human beings on earth according to the postulations of the Yoruba. Some of these beings include *Emere* and the *Abiku*. The Abiku is often known by some names given to them. Such names include *Amosa*, One who is known but has run away, *Aja*, dog and a host of several other derogatory appellations. They are given derogatory nomenclatures so as to dissuade them not to torment the family again. These beings belong to the group of creatures referred to as *emi airi*, the unseen spirits. They are often associated with children[i]. According to Yoruba epistemology, these creatures exist only to torment their biological parents. These often choose where they wish to appear and may die shortly after birth, when they are about to marry or at moments that will be agonizing to their parents. Jacobs succinctly puts it like this:

> We also have the spirits of children who are regarded as "born-to- die" children. In Yoruba, we call them "Abiku" while in Igbo we call it "Ogbanje". An "Ogbanje" is a changeling; a child who repeatedly dies and returns to its mother to be reborn and retorture the mother. The acerbity created by the "Ogbanje" or the "Abiku" is indescribable. People believe that these changelings belong to a company of spirits whose task is to bring torture and mischief into the life of women that come under their sadism.

Another spiritually related being worthy of mention with regard to this film are the witches. Witches, among the Yoruba are real entities who are often devoted to wreaking havoc on their victims.

The name for witches among the Yoruba is *Aje*. They exist and belong to the *eleye* group often referred to as *iyami,* mother. The folk belief is that they are evil and must be placated to avoid their wrath. Unlike the Abiku and the emere, they are recipients of sacrifices and whenever they are angered they oftentimes give their demand and when the demand is met they are known to release their victims.

The plot is woven around the main actor, who happens to be the antagonist, in person of Isawuru whose role is acted by Mike Bamiloye. Isawuru, in connivance with the other spiritual forces ruled the people of Muwonleru. The spiritual forces include that of *Aro Meta*, (the three forces) representing the witches, *Olori Egbe* (head of the cult) and *Ayaba Oba Oluweri* (wife of the king of the river Oluweri). The people were dying and there was none to assist them. It is along these stressful times that God occasioned Kola, an Evangelist from Lagos, to take the gospel of Jesus Christ to the town. He met a stiff opposition in the wife who prefers the alluring thing of the world. When he refused the assignment against the pastors who warned him, God raised their neighbours, church members and friends to take the gospel to Muwonleru. Amidst attempts at their lives, Isawuru became a Christian, who started the work of the evangelist. Meanwhile, Kola and wife started experiencing a downturn in their business. Bose, his wife became sick with an unknown disease while he lost his job. They took up residence in the house of their pastor and the insane wife was eventually healed by Isawuru, now Paul EsuPofo, the man they were supposed to lead to Christ. Later, the Holy Spirit told the group to allow Olaboye and Olatomi to take Paul Esupofo around as he reveals the secrets of darkness. Kola and Bose were to go back to Muwonleru and continue with the work of evangelism. When the team got to the border of Muwonleru, and it was clear that they were ready to do the work, there was a miraculous healing of the eyes of Kola.

Agbara Nla's representation of African Religion is influenced focused mainly in the area of supremacy struggle between the African Traditional Religion and that of Christianity. This has become the stereotype of most Christian movies (watch for example *Ise Owo* (1997), *Kotemilorun* (2009), *Ojiji Atijo* (2002) and *You are Warned* (2009). In his elucidation of his enterprise, the producer utilizes the epistemological understanding of Yoruba spirit world. His use of these forces shows an understanding of the mechanics of the spirits world. He used three main forces in bringing home his submission of the weakness of the Yoruba spirit world. The Arometa are representative figures of the spirit of the air, while the *emere* depict the powers of the land and Omo Oba Oluweri eloquently describes the power under the rivers. Apart from this, there are other minor forces and agents that are approachable for specific assignment. His use of incantations, divinations and consultations speak powerfully of his knowledge of other matters.

One thing that can be spoken of the producer of the movie is that he demonstrates a deeper understanding of the Yoruba mysterious powers. However, it must be said that in his bid to present the Christian God superior, he undermines the capabilities of the Yoruba Olodumare. His portrayals of *emere*, and giving them obnoxious names while reflecting the folk belief, are not correct. The fact that whatever is received from the Yoruba gods will be counterproductive makes his work to be in the realms of religious intolerance.

Review of *Apesin* Movie and its Representation of African (Yoruba) Religion

Apesin movie was produced by Adebayo Tijani and directed by Muyiwa Ademola in the year 2006. Some of the *dramatis personae* include Muyiwa Ademola, Fagbuyi Bukola, Ganiyi Nafiu and Saidi Balogun. Others include Adebayo Tijani, Faithia Balogun, Yinka Quadri and Kola Oyewo. The movie was shot in various parts of Oyo State.

In everything the Yoruba are a very religious people. They are known, like other African ethnic groups to be very religious in all they do. While they acknowledge Olodumare as the Supreme Deity, they worship Him thorough the veneration of several other divinities. Apart from this, the people also venerate other spirit beings that either inhabit trees, forests or rivers. Some of the gods they venerate include Orunmila, Oya, Sango, Osun, Ogun, Ayelala and Esu to mention but a few. Often times, these gods that they venerate may be community based or may be worshipped by a family or even a particular group of people with same occupation. Taking an example from the movie under review is the Apesin that is worshipped by every member of the community, while the god of the river is the one venerated by the fishermen.

Against this background is the conflict between tradition and modernity, the old and the young. It is worthy of note to know that what is called modernity is in fact the traditions of Europe including the worship of the traditional gods of the Europeans (Nhemachena. 2015). This is a situation whereby the children of the custodians of the tradition do not wish to follow the tenets of their fathers. This is often expressed in flagrant abuse of the practices of their fathers and refusal to follow their religious principles. The worldview of the parents is regarded as archaic and must be done away with. Incidentally, the youth often prefer to change their names in reflection of their new found faith and sometimes try as much as possible to degrade their parents' religion.

The plot surrounds the story of Aworo *Osa Apesin* and his assistance the Oluode. Rogba, Aworo's only child in the film is in love with a Romade, a lady from Alawon, a town that is close to Ladidi, the town in which the *Apesin*is their tutelary divinity. The elders of Ladidi, owing to the rebellion of the fishermen, decided that they will not announce the time that *Apesin* will take its sacrificial victim, which must be a foreigner. Unfortunately, the day Rogba decided to visit her lover was the day; *Apesin* sets out to capture its victim for the year's sacrifice. She was captured and made ready to be immolated to *Apesin*. Rogba and his friends decided to rescue her. They killed several soldiers and escaped with Romade to their village in the presence of the Oluode.

Oluode lost two of his children in the ensuing struggle and on informing Aworo that his son will have to pay for the misdemeanour. They reached a compromise that Aworo must relinquish his title to Oluode. This compromise was made in the altar of Apesin divinity which therefore becomes a form of covenant. After this secret pact, the dead soldiers were buried with charms that will make them avenge their death. One after the other the friends who participated in the escape bid of Romade were mysteriously killed. When Aworo heard that his son is dead, he rescinded his decision to relinquish his title to Oluode, who had already abandoned his title in anticipation of becoming the Aworo. The inevitable happened. It was a fight.

Aworo lost the battle and cursed the land and there was an epidemic that wiped the whole of Ladidi town.

Apesin's representation of Yoruba thrust of African Religion is rich in cultural antecedents. The producer speaks of two strong pillars that hold sway in the town. One of them is the chief priest of the land while the other one is the military commander of the armed forces of the same town. It is worthy of note that both of them are steeped in the people's traditions as cult functionaries. Their personal interests affected their responsibilities as trusted servants of the town of Ladidi. As if these were not enough, many episodes that contain religious contents are tied to their roles in the movies. One of this is the role they play in the training of neophytes who were interested in understanding their religion. Here, the audience is exposed to how the Yoruba train their medicine men. Second, as a result of the ambition of Oluode and the need of the Oluwo to protect his child from death, both of them made an oath. This is another important factor in the religious perception of the Africans. Oath taking is a powerful action that is considered seriously in Yoruba land. Anyone who contravenes it will face dire consequences. The audience is treated to this when Oluwo was informed about the demise of his son.

Other representations of religion include the consequences of what can be done to the dead body of a relation who died an untimely death. The soldiers that were killed were ritually buried. This made them to pursue those who had a hand in their death. One by one, the boys who killed them were dying one after the other. Apart from the above, other religious edifices found in the movie include shrines and grooves. The people celebrate annual festivals where their relationship with their deity is renewed.

From the foregoing, it is clear that the representation of the people's religion is adequately depicted. The movie mirrors the cultic figures as mere men in spite of their esoteric knowledge. The yearly festivals speak eloquently of the people's touch with their ancestors and their divinities. However, one thing that is out of place is the fact that human sacrifice is a thing of the past. It is no longer in vogue.

Impact of the Selected Movies on the Audience

This chapter takes off from the premise that the ingenuity of the Africans is expressed in the use of western technology to produce indigenous products that announces them to the world. In addition to this, it also looked at the idea that African efforts are often classified as inferior to those of the western world. In order to arrive at a fair assessment of the audience, diverse demographic indices of location, locality, literacy level, religion and age were used. In most cases, the variables overlap, and the overarching evidence is that the audience is heterogeneous. There is a divide between the lovers of positive appreciation of depiction of African Traditional Religion in that many of those who live in urban areas and outside the shores of Yoruba land see these movies as a link to the past (Nhemachena 2015) and a source materials for the religion of the people. Whereas, the ones who abhor the religion as Christians believe that the religion should be avoided at all cost. Sesan (2013) has divided the audience on location as onshore and offshore. This writer concurs with his assessment of the audience. He maintains that Yoruba film is a medium of (re) socialization and education. Those who are outside the South west Nigeria has access to these movies through the various formats the digital technologies now present.

Conclusion

The South western Nigeria is home to the Yoruba who are made up of several dialects speaking groups. It is interesting that they have robust productions of home movies which are based on the rich cultural heritage of the people. In fact, in terms of ethnic group production of movies, they rank one of the most prolific of the Nollywood industry. The compendium of their heritage has made it possible for different institutions to use their repertoire as a tool to propagate their religious preferences to their immediate environs and to the world at large. Onuzulike (2009) captures the essence when he opines that Nigerian videofilms are deeply rooted in Nigerian cultural traditions and social texts that focus on Nigerian community life. Nigerian videofilm stories are told using African idioms, proverbs, costumes, artefacts, and the imagery of Africa and cultural displays.

It has been seen that though the foreign religions, Christianity in this context, attempt to make the traditional religion inferior, and the aesthetics of the movies still show that the people have a developed concept of their religion. This ingenuity to a large extent has shown that African Traditional Religion meets the aspirations of the people. Worthy of mention here is the fact that the movies have actually served to propagate the religion of the people either negatively or positively. While Christian movies portray African Traditional Religion as weak, the movies that are produced in its favour show that the religion is still acceptable to some people within the Yoruba and beyond.

References

Haynes, J., 2011, African Cinema and Nollywood: Contradictions. in Situations: Project of the Radical Imagination in *African Cinema and Nollywood*. Vol. 6, No 1

Hepp, A.; Hjarvard, S.; Lundby, K.; 2015. Mediatisation: Theorizing the Interplay between Media, Culture and Society. *Media, Culture and Society*. Vol 37. Issue 2.

Hjarvard, S., 2006. *The Mediatisation of Religion: A Theory of the Media as an Agent of Religious Change*. Paper Presented to the 5th International Conference on Media, Religion and Culture: Mediation Religion in the Context of Multicultural Tension. The Sigtuna Foundation, Stockholm/Sigtuna/Uppsala, Sweden.

Jansson, A. 2002. The Mediatisation of Consumption: Towards an Analytical Framework of Image Culture, *Journal of Consumer Culture*, 2 (5-31).

McQuail, D. 2005. *McQuail's Mass Communication Theory*. Sage: London.

Nhemachena, A. 2015. Indigenous Knowledge, Translation, Sublation and Conflation: Lessons from Fieldwork in Contemporary Rural Zimbabwe, In Mawere M et al, eds, *Between Rhetoric and Reality: The State and Use of Indigenous Knowledge in Post-Colonial Africa*. Langaa: Bamenda.

Nyanchoga, S. A. 2014. Politics of Knowledge Production in Africa: A Critical Reflection on the Idea of an African University in

Sustainable Development. In *Developing Country Studies*. Vol. 4. No18

OHA, O. 2002. Yoruba Christian Video Narrative and Indigenous Imaginations: Dialogue and Duelogue. *Cahiers d'étudesafricaines*1.

Onuzulike, U. 2009. Nollywood: Nigerian Videofilms as a Cultural and Technological Hybridity. In: *Intercultural Communication Studies* XVIII: 1

Postman, N. 2005. *Amusing Ourselves to Death: Public Discourse in the Age of Show Business*. USA: Penguin Books.

Sesan, A. A. 2013. Yoruba Films in the Twenty-First Century: A Critique of Genres and Audience. Paper Presented at the First International Conference of Yoruba Films. Adeleke University. Ede.

Slack, J. D. 1996. The Theory and Method of Articulation in Cultural Studies. In D. Morley and K. Chen(Eds.). *Stuart Hall: Critical Dialogues in Cultural Studies*. London: Routeledge.

Van Dijk, T. A. 1998. *Ideology: A Multidisciplinary Approach*. London: Sage Publications.

Movies Cited

Agbara Nla. 1993. Producer Mike Bamiloye. Director Mike Bamiloye. Language. Yoruba.

Attacks from Home. 2005. Producer. Mike Bamiloye. Director Mike Bamiloye. Language. English.

Apesin.2006. Producer. Adebayo Tijani. Director. Muyiwa Ademola. Language. Yoruba.

Arugba.2008. Producer. Tunde Kelani. Director. Tunde Kelani. Language. Yoruba.

*AwoJesu*2007. Producer. Oreofe Williams. Director. Oreofe Williams. Language. Yoruba.

Blood on the Altar.2005. Producer. Mike Bamiloye. Director. Mike Bamiloye and Elvon Jarrett. Language. English.

Ise Owo. 1997Producer C-sem. Director. Gbeminiyi Owoseni. Language. Yoruba.

Kotemilorun. 2009. Producer C-sem. Director. Gbeminiyi Owoseni. Language. Yoruba.

Koto Aiye. 2001. Producer. Yekini Ajileye. Director. YomiOgunmola. Language. English.

OjijiAtijo. 2002. Producer. C-sem. Director.GbeminiyiOwoseni .Language.Yoruba.

Omo Iya Aje 2007. Producer. Olatunji Balogun. Director. Muhydeen S. Ayinde. Language. Yoruba.

Omo Jesu. 2007. Producer. Bisi Ibidapo-Obe. Director Abiodun Olarewaju. Language. Yoruba.

Opon Ifa. 2006. Producer. Precious Stone Productions. Director. Laja Robert. Language. English.

Sango. 1993. Producer. Bourdillon Bodio Eyagudoor. Director. Femi Lasode. Language. English

The gods are Dead. 2000. Producer. Mike Bamiloye. Director. Elvon Jarrett. Language. English.

*The Foundations.*2006. Producer. Mike Bamiloye. Director Mike Bamiloye and Sunday Ogunyemi. Language. English.

*The Foundations.*2006. Producer. Mike Bamiloye. Director Mike Bamiloye and Sunday Ogunyemi. Language. English.

Chapter Eleven

Local Indigenous Communities and the State's Concept of Conservation in Zimbabwe

Munyaradzi Mawere

Introduction

The trouble imposed by the effects of environmental and natural resource conservation problems on already vulnerable populations and those without a voice in many rural communities of Africa calls for urgent response on what it takes to foster sustainable conservation of both natural resources and the environment. This realisation put as its centre stage obligations and responsibility of the national governments to the poor and vulnerable without compromising environmental sustainability. However, balancing obligations and responsibility to the poor while at the same time maintaining environmental sustainability has always been a challenge for many governments and conservation agents across the continent of Africa and even beyond. In many countries in Africa such as Zimbabwe, the difficulty in balancing obligations and responsibility with sustainability has allegedly been a result of lack of participation by local communities (Mukamuri 1995: 166) and the differences existent between local communities' and the state's concept of conservation. Using the case study of Norumedzo Communal Area, this paper examines the local indigenous communities and the state's concept of conservation in Zimbabwe. It was motivated by my observation that the Zimbabwean state, through its Environmental Management Agency, emphasises mono-conservation methodology (adopted from Western modernist science) instead of promoting multiple conservation methodologies (including indigenous conservation methods) in its conservation approach. The paper briefly examines conservation in both pre-colonial Zimbabwe and post-colonial periods before it focuses on Norumedzo Communal Area, one of the few cases where multiple environmental

251

conservation knowledge forms, bottom-up approaches, and concepts of conservation are employed to protect a forest known as Norumedzo *Jiri*.

Conservation in Zimbabwe

One may wonder if it is important to relook into the past conservation practices as those in pre-colonial Zimbabwe. I argue that it is in fact prudent that we understand conservation in pre-colonial Zimbabwe for two major reasons. First is the recognition that no meaningful discussion on natural resource conservation would be complete without an examination of history and the influence of colonialism in Africa. In fact, 'in-depth historical analyses *of conservation* are needed to explain the complex trajectories that have led to today's unsustainable *conservation*, and to draw lessons from earlier instances' (Hackmann and Moser 2013: 40). Second is the recognition that state-centric conservation adopted from colonial government in many African countries, including Zimbabwe, is still existent despite the fact that it is failing due to its disregard of customary systems and failure to recognise other forms of knowledge such as conservation knowledge of the locals or what is generally known as "local/indigenous conservation knowledge". While the question of what constitute indigenous (and hence indigenous knowledge) has been problematised over the years (see Altieri 1995; Mapara 2009; Agrawal 1995; Mawere 2014a; Ocholla 2007; Odora-Hospers 2001; Semali and Kincheloe 1999; Shizha 2013), in this paper, I consider indigenous to mean the original, first, native to a place or aboriginal people to an area. In view of this understanding, indigenous knowledge, which can also be known by other names as local knowledge (Warren 1991), traditional knowledge, local technical knowledge (Sillitoe 1998), folkloric knowledge, community knowledge (Kargbo 1995) or subjugated knowledge (Semali and Kincheloe 1999), would, in this paper, be interpreted as the kind of knowledge that is developed through the processes of acculturation and kinship relationships that societal groups form, and is handed down to posterity through oral tradition and other such cultural practices (see also Mapara 2009; Altieri 1995). This should not be misunderstood to mean that indigenous knowledge is static, as it is indeed dynamic, modifiable, and can be transferred from one community to another (cf. Mawere 2014a)

Conservation in pre-colonial Africa in general, and Zimbabwe in particular, was largely organic community based natural resource management (OCBNRM) (Katerere 1999; Marongwe 2004; Mawere 2014b,c) which emphasised multiple conservation epistemologies from across the society. This was opposed to CBNRM as externally initiated project, either by government representatives or non-governmental organisation (NGOs) as has been practised in southern Africa since the dawn of colonialism, which unlike OCBNRM emphasises mono-conservation epistemology. By organic CBNRM, I mean 'a strategy by which groups of people collectively manage, *on their own,* resources that cannot be managed individually because they occur in diverse and scattered configurations or are mobile, or both *such as* forests, drylands and mountain environments where individualised agriculture is ecologically difficult' (Child et al 2014: 157, emphasis original). This means that in pre-colonial Zimbabwe, protection and utilisation of resources in the countryside was initiated and executed by the communities in which the resources were found. The fact that protection and utilisation of resources was initiated and executed by the communities should not be confused to mean that the communities had no leadership that helped enforcing the protection. What should be understood is that while traditional leadership helped enforcing the "proper" utilisation and protection of resources, the restrictions enforced were communally agreed.

With the kind of conservation deployed through OCBNRM, there was no clear cut distinction between nature and culture as delineated by the modernist Western enlightenment. In fact the "indigenous" Africans or pre-colonial Africans co-existed with many other beings[1] in the environment they shared in a manner that in

---

[1] In this chapter, I prefer using the term "other beings" to Bruno Latour (1987; 1993; 2005) and others' [such as Michel Callon 1986; Dona Haraway 1991, 2003, 2008] "nonhuman" because there are some "creatures"/entities that are difficult to classify either as humans or nonhumans given that they are part human and part nonhuman. Vampire and the werewolf (see Jake Kosek 2010: 672), for example, are part human, part nonhuman becomings that result from the contagion of the battlefields. So are entities widely known in Zimbabwe as *vadzimu* (ancestors), *mhondoro* (lion spirits), and *njuzu* (mermaids/half fish half human creatures) that are not purely humans. Neither are they purely nonhumans, but are

many ways showed conviviality and interdependence: their conservation systems reflected 'the notion of humans as part of, not separate from, their environment' (Pollard and Cousins 2014; see also Iliffe 1990).

With the advent of colonialism in Africa, many changes were experienced even in the area of resource conservation. In many countries such as Zimbabwe, colonial policies such as the Land Apportionment Act of the 1930s resulted in land degradation (see Ribot 1999; Mandondo 2000). With this Act, many indigenous Zimbabweans were forced to overcrowd in poor soils which resulted in serious land degradation through over-farming and over-exploitation of resources. As Billy Mukamuri (1995: iii) observes:

> Historical interviews and records clearly demonstrate that communal life has never been sustainable since the dawn of colonialism in Zimbabwe. The communal system has always been disturbed and challenged by the colonial state's latifundialisation, that is, swallowing up the land of the poor, pauperisation and declined standards of livelihood.

Similarly, Beinart (1984: 62) cites the *Drought Commission Interim Report* which revealed that 'since the white men have been in South Africa enormous tracts of country [had] been entirely or partially denuded of their original vegetation'. As further noted by William Beinart (1984: 56):

A contributor to the *Rhodesian Journal of Agriculture* in 1913 felt that the situation in that colony was not as bad as it seemed in the semi-arid parts of South Africa. But he cited a large range of settler malpractices which were exposing precious top-soil to the rain and wind ... he bemoaned the loss of trees and burning of grass. But his list also included: overstocking; kraaling of sheep and cattle – that is bringing them home each day to a central byre near the farmer's house -which resulted in the formation of ungrassed tracks; careless construction of roads and railways; ploughing up and down the

---

simply referred to as *zvisikwa zvaMwari* (other beings created by God) (Mawere 2014). As such, throughout this chapter, I use the terms humans and other beings, the latter to refer all those entities that cannot be classified as humans both in part or in totality.

slopes of fields; clean cultivation, especially of maize, so that the soil lost all protective covering in the early rains; and intensive cultivation of vleis, shallow depressions where the soil stayed moist through much of the year, for short term economic gain (cf. Watt 1913; Weinmann 1972).

Mulwafu (2002) also observed a similar trend in colonial Malawi where state exerted more pressure in controlling land-use in areas designated to indigenous Africans neglecting that on European-owned estates. Mulwafu (2002: 25-26), thus, notes:

> Although land degradation also took place on European-owned estates, state planners presumed that estate owners knew how to manage the land and would deal with any problems that they encountered. In juxtaposition to the intense, harsh conservation campaigns imposed on African Trust Land, the colonial state virtually ignored the environmental degradation taking place on these estates. This policy of benign neglect continued throughout much of the colonial period ... Through this uneven intervention and enforcement, the colonial state racialised the environ-mental issue and made it an African problem ... The state effectively turned a blind eye toward the settlers and, even when there was evidence of substantial erosion, the state did not use its powers to enforce policy (cf: Hornby 1920s).

It is on the basis of observations such as those by Watt, Weinmann, Mulwafu, Mukamuri and Beinart (among others) that scholars such as Ribot (1999) and Mandondo (2000) argue that colonial natural resource management policies resulted in over-centralisation because they were designed in the context of conquest and subjugation. This is also why it is now generally agreed by some scholars that Europeans did not only colonise humans in Africa but also nature, that is, other beings found in the African worlds as what they did was largely contrary to the status quo (see also Plumwood 2003; Makenzie 1991; Anderson and Grove 1987).

Besides, Western modernistic science or what Nancy Jacobs call 'colonial science' despised indigenous knowledge, labelling it as unscientific, primitive and anti-development (Phimister 1974;

Mackenzie 1970; Ribot 1999; Mukamuri 1995; Mawere 2014a; Ilife 1990; Hanlon *et al.* 2013; Beinart 1984). William Beinart, for example, notes that:

> By the 1930s and 1940s, it was commonplace for both settlers and officials in southern Africa to describe African agricultural methods as careless and dangerous to the environment [...] Settlers, as has been suggested, sometimes found it in their interests to characterize peasant methods not only as inefficient, but destructive (Beinart 1984: 61).

Such perceptions on peasant methods had far-reaching impacts on the use and image of indigenous knowledge as one form of knowledge. As Nancy Jacobs (2006: 564) aptly puts it: 'We now recognise that colonial science was a highly political enterprise [...] It has been observed that the failure of *colonial* science to heed indigenous knowledge led to a "misreading" of the landscape and inappropriate intervention' (cf. Fairhead and Leach 1996). In fact there was need for the colonial government as suggested by Beinart (1984: 53) 'to disaggregate the state, to return to the ideas of the local actors and examine how they came into play when agricultural policy *and conservation* were being conceived'. Yet the failure by the colonialists to recognise indigenous conservation epistemologies should not be confused to mean that under colonialism there were no efforts at all to conserve the environment. Neither should this be interpreted to mean that all settler farmers and officials were totally against indigenous African farming practices and conservation approaches as some [settler farmers and officials] counterattacked critics of African farmers (see Beinart 1984: 62; Mulwafu 2004). Some missionaries in colonial Malawi such as Rev. Henry Rowley (1881), one of the leading members of the Universities' Mission to Central Africa (UMCA), for example, acknowledged that African land use practices were not as ecologically destructive as they had originally thought when he said:

> Yet with regard to agriculture we soon discovered that the natives could teach us more than we could teach them, and that we could offer them little inducement to grow more of anything

256

than they needed for themselves. So another part of our programme, the encouragement of agriculture, was virtually a dead letter (cf. Rowley 1881: 65).

Mulwafu (2004: 301), thus, concludes that 'while *pre*-African agriculture could not be described as the best, it could also not be dismissed as completely backward, since it was particularly suited to the conditions in which Africans operated at the time'.

The major problem with many colonialists was their misplaced thinking that only colonial science was the answer to all the problems that confronted humanity, thereby rubbishing other ways of knowing such as African indigenous knowledge. Jacobs captures this nicely when she argues that there were some non-instrumentalist sciences such as ornithology, lepidoptery, and non-economic botany that were, to a larger extent inactive in the advancement of the colonial project in Africa, yet 'the construction of authoritative knowledge in medicine, racial biology, and social science created disciplinary power over Africans' (Jacobs 2006: 564). The belief that Africans together with their indigenous knowledges were despised, caricatured and viewed as inferior to Europeans and their "science" is visible even in some of the few colonial ornithologists like George Latimer Bates who Jacobs considers to be one of the most level headed and neutral scientists yet he uses diminutive and juvenilising terms such as "Boys" referring to respectable "Black" males (see Jacobs: 2006:572). I believe, this politics of knowledge production was one reason why instead of seeking ways to integrate African indigenous knowledge with colonial science, the colonialists despised and rendered as useless all other forms of knowledge that were outside the purview of colonial science.

With the gain of national independence by most of the African states, expectations were high among the masses especially the rural folk that most of their traditional ways of life that once suffered persecution and subjugation during the colonial rule, including their indigenous conservation practices, would be recognised by the new governments. Surprisingly, this remained a tantalising dream for local communities in most parts of rural Africa. In Zimbabwe, upon independence in 1980, the new government through its representative, "National Conservation Strategy," vowed to arrest the mounting land degradation and promote sustainable land management by publishing Zimbabwe's National Conservation Strategy through the Natural Resource Board, now the Environmental Management Agency (EMA), Zimbabwe Forestry Commission, Agricultural, Technical and Extension Services (AGRITEX), and Zimbabwe Parks and Wildlife Management Authority (ZPWMA). This was partly in response to the request for all nations by the World Conservation Strategy report of the International Union for Conservation of Nature-United Nations Environment Programme-World Wide Fund for Nature (IUCN-UNEP-WWF), 1980. While this was a gesture towards the conservation of all species, I argue that the postcolonial government – like its colonial predecessor – failed the national conservation project in two respects. First, the post-colonial government, particularly through its National Environmental Policy and Strategy employed Western modernistic science as the sole tool for environmental conservation, thereby continuing to relegate local eco-knowledge to the periphery of national environmental conservation projects. William Beinart is apt when he says of farming policy in Southern Africa:

> In Malawi, colonial schemes were dropped in the years immediately before and after independence, but resurfaced in such projects as the Lilongwe Land Development Programme, a major recipient of World Bank funds since the late 1960s. In Zimbabwe, though Land Husbandry was dropped in the 1960s, programmes for rural resettlement after independence, and the Riddell Commission, offered solutions for socialist reconstruction in the countryside which bore considerable resemblance to the old planning schemes. The legacy of centralised planning and development has been powerful (see Beinart 1984: 83).

My experience during fieldwork suggests that there is a sense in which it can be argued that this stance, particularly in view of Zimbabwe blurs the possibility of different ways of thinking about relationships between people and other beings such as forest insects. I noted, for example, that even the most recent Zimbabwe National

Environmental Policy and Strategy (ZNEPS) is silent on the moral value and rights of the country's flora and fauna, which in view of the modernistic stance that ZNEPS has taken makes the silence more than just a species omission, but actually a problem of paradigm. Exclusively informed by Western science, ZNEPS (2009:7) thus discriminates against the other beings inhabiting the environment such as insects as it states: 'At species level, the country supports an estimated 4,440 vascular plant species, 196 mammal species, 672 bird species, 156 reptile species, 57 species of amphibians, 132 fish species and uncounted numbers of species in other groups. The diversity of microorganisms in particular is extremely poorly known'. The colonial government in Zimbabwe disregarded forest insects mainly on the basis that some of them such as Tsetse flies caused diseases to both humans and livestock (Mavhunga and Spierenburg 2007). The current environmental policy of Zimbabwe, therefore, has no specific clause that provides for the protection of forest insects. As is seen in the quotation above, one can see that insect species are not well recognised in Zimbabwe's environmental policy despite the contribution that most of these insects make to human livelihoods and to ecosystems as a whole. We can only assume that insects, together with other small organisms, are those being referred to as 'uncounted species in other groups' (ZNEPS, 2009:7), yet some of the insects such as *harurwa* (edible stinkbugs) are highly regarded by local communities who views them as partners in conservation and sources of livelihoods.

The discrimination of some species by ZNEPS implies that the post-independence government of Zimbabwe simply adopted the colonial government's conservation model: the colonial conservation model, thus, did not disappear with the demise of the colonial administration in the country. It was indeed more of the same person with a different jacket. Elsewhere (Mawere 2013), I have argued that at independence in 1980, the new government promised to fix all conservation problems that the colonial government left unresolved. As Murphree (1991) reported there seemed to be a paradigmatic shift from state-centred control towards alternative conservation and natural resource approaches in which local people would play a central role as exemplified by the Zimbabwean state's creation of the "National Conservation Strategy" now Environmental Management

Agency (EMA) – a government board responsible for addressing conservation problems in the country. Unfortunately, the state remained hanging on the colonial conservation methodologies. For example, to date EMA continue insisting that resettled farmers construct contour ridges – one of the colonial prescribed conservation measure – despite that they [contour ridges] have proven to accelerate soil erosion (Manjengwa 2004; see also Hanlon *et al* 2013: 178). The postcolonial government, thus, continues to employ the colonial models such as top-down approaches and science as the sole provider of environmental conservation methodologies, thereby continuing to relegate local eco-knowledge to the periphery of national environmental conservation approaches (Mawere 2013). Besides, the postcolonial erred by embarking in the farm invasions that began around 1999/2000 given that the invasions 'were characterised by the violation of the rights of both humans (especially white commercial farmers) and other beings, as well as the scandalous exploitation of natural resources and the natural environment' (ibid). Furthermore, the 'invaders' being led by the ZANU PF government paid no respect to indigenous conservation epistemologies resulting in the deepening of the environment conservation crisis in Zimbabwe.

Research methodological issues

To gain access into the Norumedzo, traditional authorities (chiefs and headmen) and government institutions (such as District Administration Office and Rural District Council) and others involved in environmental management like conservation boards (such as Environmental Management Agency [EMA]) facilitated my entry into the field site. These connections were also useful in providing me with some important information on how *harurwa* and the *jiri* have been "cultivated" and conserved over the years. Besides, entering the field site with the consent and blessings of authorities who are custodians of culture and the environment was important in gaining confidence of my respondents, in obtaining dependable results, and also for my personal security as a researcher. Otherwise, in such a politically volatile environment as that of Zimbabwe, I would have run the risk of being mistaken as a spy by any of the political party members.

Since participant observation was the primary method for this study, I was resident in my field site – Norumedzo Communal Area of south-eastern Zimbabwe – for a period of about twelve-and-a-half months. I was aware that as an ethnographic method, participant observation requires the researcher to be flexible in responding to new ideas and methods should they become necessary. As one familiar with the Shona language (used by the Varumedzo), I was able to participate in most of their daily interactions, but, of course, not all of them. I also listened to stories, observed, kept a field diary of interactions/field notes, and photograph recordings of "naturally" occurring communicative interactions with the participants in a range of everyday life activities. Stories (though they might be fiction), for example, 'succeed in giving us a vivid sense of what is at stake at any moment of being, and in introducing us to some of the ways in which existential-phenomenological thought has theorised the question of being' (Jackson 2005: xiii).

To facilitate access to community members and to ensure that data collection occurred from multiple perspectives, two key informants (interlocutors[2]), Tendai and James were recruited. Observations from multiple perspectives have merit in that they allow for patterns to be identified so that verification of data can be done before it is presented. James, having been born and grew up in the Norumedzo, assisted me with data collection, and provided additional observations and information on the social meanings and significance of some local practices. Tendai helped me in conducting structured and semi-structured in-depth interviews and informal

---

[2] In this chapter, the concepts, 'informant' and 'interlocutor' are used interchangeably to refer to research participants. However, the word 'interlocutor' is more preferred as in Zimbabwe especially during the liberation struggle, 'informants' were was a loaded term used to refer to traitors (*vatengesi*) who collaborated with the colonial enemy (see Muzvidziwa 2004: 305). Besides, the concept 'interlocutor' better reflects the exchange of ideas, collaborations, interactions and negotiations that normally take place between the ethnographer (or anthropologist) and research participants during research, and indeed the production of particular kinds of knowledge. No wonder Rene Devisch (cited in Olukoshi and Nyamnjoh 2011:16) refers to the relationship between an anthropologist and interlocutor (research participant) as ideally one of "mutually enriching co-implication".

conversations. Interviews, discussions and observations focused on: local people's beliefs and perceptions, their symbolic significance of different daily practices, their views of culture, nature, environment, personhood, interactions with *harurwa* and other beings, and aspirations as individuals and as a people. I discuss these in detail in the sections below on methodologies and later chapters. For the moment, I wish to focus on the bureaucratic government structures and traditional leadership in the Norumedzo Communal Area in order to provide a better understanding of the studied area in relation to the politically volatile context of Zimbabwe.

Norumedzo Communal Area and *Harurwa* Myth

The area in which research for this chapter was conducted is in south-eastern Zimbabwe, particularly the Norumedzo Communal Area (which includes the Norumedzo *Jiri*) in ward 15 of the Bikita District in Masvingo Province. See map 1 below which shows the seven districts of Masvingo Province including Bikita where Norumedzo Communal Area (and Norumedzo *Jiri*) is found.

The Norumedzo Community occupies an area between Chivaka, Gande and Chinyagashu Rivers in the Bikita District. The area is occupied mainly by the Varumedzo also known as Norumedzo people (as the villagers call themselves), who are also known as the Duma people of the *moyo* (heart) totem. These people are well known for their grove known as the Norumedzo *Jiri* or Norumedzo Forest. As has been highlighted in the previous sections of this paper, I chose this study area for the major reason that the Norumedzo Communal Area is one of the few communities in Zimbabwe where active local community participation and multiple indigenous conservation epistemologies are highly regarded. This makes the Norumedzo case a window through which environmental conservation issues in rural areas could be approached and humans – other beings relations grasped.

Map 1: *The seven districts of Masvingo including Bikita.*
(Source: Bikita Rural District Council, 23 July 2012).

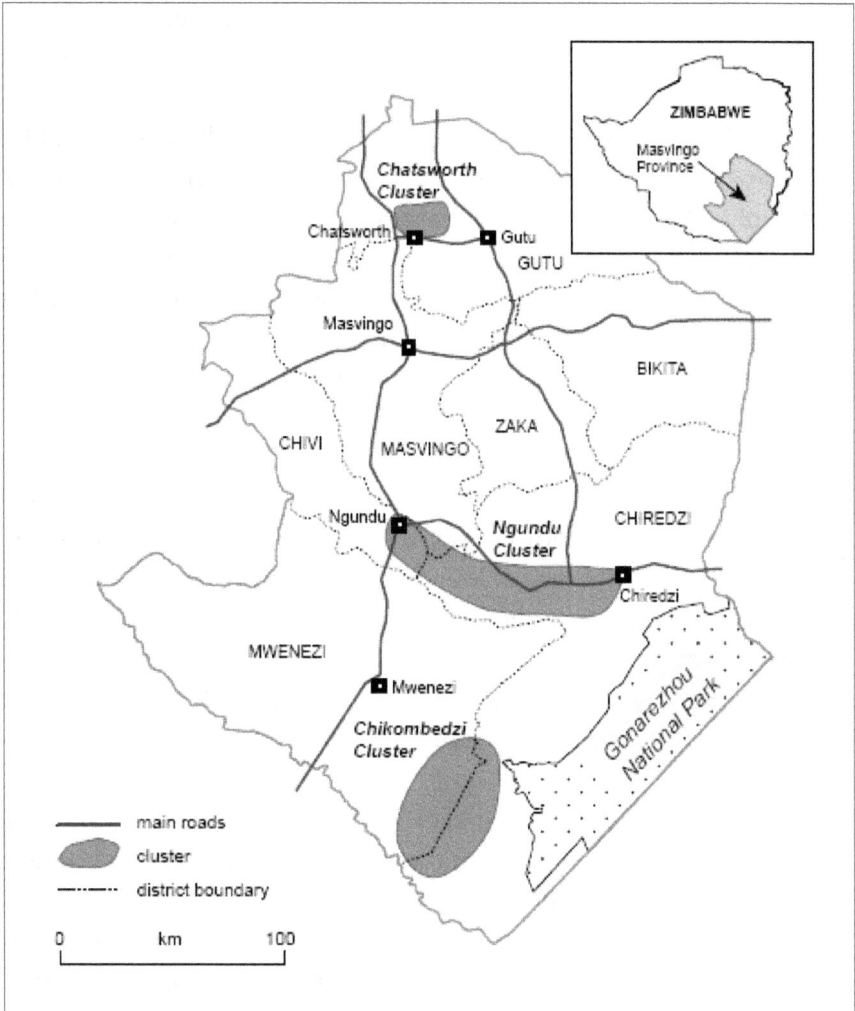

The Norumedzo Forest, locally named *jiri*, is a natural forest of about 7 km². Besides being home to riverine wetlands, rivers, honey, wildlife, and wild fruits, *jiri* is rich in edible insects locally named *harurwa* (edible stinkbugs) that are used by the Norumedzo people(VaRumedzo as they call themselves) as food and a source of income, among other uses. The origin of *harurwa* is explained in a myth about the forebears of the VaRumedzo (cf. Mawere, *et al.* 2013; Mawere 2014b). According to the myth, *harurwa* is a gift that was given to Nemeso, the forebear of the VaRumedzo, by his ancestors during the time which Nemeso and her mother suffered many tribulations and difficulties in the Rumedzo wilderness (now Norumedzo Communal Area). From what I gathered from my interlocutors such as Chief Norumedzo and other knowledgeable village elders in the Norumedzo, the myth goes:

More than a century before the coming of the Ndebele and the *vasina mabvi* (lit: those without knees) – 'white' men in south-eastern Zimbabwe, a four-eyed boy was born to a young woman, Mhepo and Chief Pfupajena of the Mazungunye ruling family (*imba youshe*). Chief Pfupajena was the eldest son of Mazungunye and was crowned as a Chief in his early twenties after the death of his father. On hearing that his wife, Mhepo had given birth to a four-eyed boy, Chief Pfupajena wanted the child to be killed. This decision was in agreement with the traditional customs of the day which dictated that any child born physically challenged or born as twins should be strangled and not allowed to live. His uncle (the younger brother of Pfupajena) by the name Mutindi Mukanganwi who was the Chief advisor of Pfupajena, however, had a dream where he was told to secretly instruct Mhepo to run away with the child to the mountains in the east called Mambiru and later on known as Rumedzo. As Chief Norumedzo recounted Mutindi's dream:

> While asleep in a dream, Mutindi saw a big lion with a shiny skin approaching him. In the dream, Mutindi was very frightened because he had no spear or an axe to fight the lion. As the lion approached and drew nearer, it immediately changed into an old man with grey hair and long white beards holding a walking stick. The old man, who appeared to be very worried, started talking: "Mutindi! Mutindi! Go and help Mhepo escape with the baby to the far-east Mountains I will show you. Mhepo should hide in the biggest cave in those mountains. You shall help feeding her and the baby. Do not worry for nothing shall befall either the mother or the baby. Do not disclose anything of what I have told you to anyone, even to your child, Pfupajena. Rise! Go immediately and deliver to Mhepo this message!" Mutindi then woke up only to find out that he was dreaming (Fieldnotes May 12, 2012).

Among the Mazungunye/Pfupajena people, dreams were highly regarded such that Mutindi could not resist the words he heard from his dream as he believed they were orders from the ancestors. He immediately went and secretly instructed Mhepo to run away with the baby, assuring her that the ancestors and he will take care of them while in exile. When Mhepo and the child who was later on given the name, Nemeso (by Mutindi) came to the mountains, they lived in a cave and drank from a perennial well at the bottom of the mountains known as *Tsime raNemeso* (Nemeso's well).

It is said that during one of the days when Nemeso was about a year and half old, his mother went out of the cave doing her domestic chores. She left her son playing inside the cave. When she came back, she saw her son seated but blowing some dust using his hands. While doing this, Mhepo was surprised to see some green insects buzzing and flying into the cave forming a large nest by Nemeso's side. Mhepo wondered what the insects were and on what might have attracted them into the cave. Surprisingly, when Nemeso stopped blowing the dust the insects stopped flying into the cave only to start again when he resumed blowing. Mhepo was greatly frightened by this occurrence and pleaded to her ancestors and ancestors of the mountains not to harm her and her child.

When night fell, Mhepo dreamt hearing a voice, 'Mhepo! Mhepo!' When she called back, she was told, 'Do not be afraid of those insects. It is relish your child's ancestors have given him and you. The insects are known as *harurwa* and are a delicacy that will make your son's name famous and always remembered in all this land and beyond'. She also saw a vision of the insects being prepared and ultimately turning golden brown. When Mhepo woke up, she couldn't see the person who was talking, but could see the *harurwa* were still in their big nest in the cave. She pondered on the dream and the vision, and wondered how such green insects could turn golden brown. With the desire to authenticate or falsify the vision she 'saw' in her dream, Mhepo prepared some of the insects and indeed saw them turning their colour to golden brown. When she tested them, they were indeed a delicacy and she and her son started feeding on the insects.

I should underscore that as stressed by Chief Norumedzo and other knowledgeable interlocutors in the Norumedzo, in the past (and even today) dreams were greatly revered and conceived as a way of knowing – what Michel Foucault (1982) calls the 'techniques of self' meaning the ways through which people develop knowledge about themselves and direction of others. And, because of this widely belief among the VaRumedzo, *harurwa* is associated with many taboos and rituals.

Harurwa and the Jiri Conservation

Given the social, cultural and economic value of the insects, the *harurwa* are cared for in the *jiri* by a caretaker team comprising *madzishe eharurwa* (*harurwa* administrators) and *mapurisa eharurwa* (*harurwa* policemen) led by one of the Norumedzo headmen selected by the chief. The *jiri* is located in a big valley bordered by two mountains, Nemahwi on the north and Rumedzo on the far southeast. The forest is at a central position of the Norumedzo Communal Area between the villages under the jurisdiction of four grandsons of Nemeso – the forefather of the Norumedzo people – three of whom are *harurwa* administrators, and one is the current chief Norumedzo. From my observations during a thirteen months ethnographic study in the Norumedzo, these grandsons, together with many other headmen as well as all other community members under the jurisdiction of Chief Norumedzo and recently the Environment Conservation Monitors (*Vanajengetavhu*), are responsible (directly or otherwise) for the conservation of the *jiri* to ensure the continued existence of *harurwa* therein (in the *jiri*). Environment Conservation Monitors are members from the Environmental Management Agency [EMA]) which is a government agency or state representative responsible for environmental conservation and management in Zimbabwe, especially in the rural areas. See picture below (figure 1) of the *jiri* from a distant.

Figure 1: The jiri *from a distance*

Besides being endowed with the edible insects, *harurwa*, the *jiri* is a source of one of the prominent rivers in Bikita District. This is where the Mukore River has its source, and it flows down through the *jiri* into the Chivaka River. See picture below (figure 2).

Figure 2: Part of the jiri *where Mukore River has its source*

Norumedzo people remain one of the few forest-dependent communities of Zimbabwe where mutual, symbiotic coexistence of humans, *harurwa* and other beings is still highly regarded. Because the Norumedzo people largely depend on the *jiri* for their livelihood, there are connections between the people and other beings in the *jiri* including *vadzimu* (ancestral spirits), *masvikiro* (spirit mediums), *mhondoro* (ancestral lion spirits), fauna and flora. The connectedness between people and other beings is normally through *miko/zviera* (taboos) that forbids people from certain behaviours that may upset other beings. This connectedness between humans and other beings should not be mistaken to mean that all beings have a spiritual nature or what other scholars refer to as soul (Ogungbemi 1997) which is sacred. Yet through *zviera*, certain plants or plant species are considered sacred and are not used for firewood. I observed, for example, that the tree species that were considered as sacred and normally reserved for use as medicines, *harurwa* habitats, for fruits, and not for firewood were these: *muroro/Annona senegalensis, munhengeni/Ximenia caffra, mukute/Syzygium cordatum, muroropasi/Annona stenophylla, muzhanje/Uapaca kirkiana, mukarati/Burkea Africana, muonde/Ficus spp., muchirara, mushozhowa/Pseudolachnostylis maprouneifolia*. Other trees such as *muunga Acacia abyssinica, muuzhe/Brachystegia glaucescens, mutondo/Julbernardia globiflora, mubvamaropa/Pterocarpus angolensis, mubvumira/Kirkia acuminata, muchirara/Pterocarpus rotundifolius*, and *msasa/Brachstegia spiciformis* were mainly reserved as *harurwa* habitats. More others such as *murwiti/Dalbergia melanoxylon, mususu/Terminalia serecea*, and *mukarati/Burkea Africana* were mainly reserved for carving, wood for furniture and also as *harurwa* habitats. All these tree species could be found both inside and outside the *jiri*, but they are found in abundance in the *jiri*, hence the *jiri* comprises different plant tree species and fauna. It is from this *jiri* richness and the dependence of the Norumedzo people on the *jiri* flora and fauna that one can safely say the Norumedzo people are still largely forest-dependent.

In terms of relations with flora, the general belief in the Norumedzo Communal Area is that for those tree species believed to be sacred, one would be followed by misfortunes such as illness and even death if s/he fails to observe traditional beliefs relating to the tree species. The same belief is held for the *jiri* itself. No one is allowed to say obscene things when walking in the *jiri*, as this is believed to anger the *vadzimu* (ancestors) who in turn may invoke a bad omen on the perpetrator. This resonates with McGregor's (2003) observation among the Tonga people of Zambezi Valley, in northern Zimbabwe, who observes that ancestral spirits mediated their (the Tonga people) relationship with the river, Zambezi.

One other important thing to note about the Norumedzo Area is that it receives low to medium but variable rainfall per annum, lacks basic infrastructure such as tarred roads, piped water and electricity, and relies to a greater extend on remittances from the Norumedzo Forest (*jiri*). It, however, shares boundaries with the Bikita highlands classified under region 3 receiving up to 800mm. The Norumedzo people, thus, largely depend on *harurwa* and other non-timber forest products found in the *jiri*.

Multiple environmental conservation in Norumedzo Jiri

As has been revealed in the sections above, there are multiple environmental actors in the Norumedzo Jiri. These multiple environmental actors allowed that in Norumedzo Communal Area, people worked productively with different approaches. While traditional leadership and the community in Norumedzo pioneered conservation in their area and are indeed in the forefront of all conservation issues to do with the *jiri*, the leadership also works hand in hand with the Environmental Management Agency (EMA) – a government agency responsible for environmental management in Zimbabwe, especially in the rural areas. From what I gathered during fieldwork, since the decade 2000 EMA intervened in conservation of the *jiri* not because traditional conservation methodologies were failing but as a gesture that the Norumedzo 'conservationists' are open to work with any agency that support conservation of their area. On the part of the Zimbabwean state, it was also a fulfilment of the government policy as is stipulated in the EMA manifesto that it actively takes part in conservation of all rural areas in the country. This gesture was indeed a change from the previous conservation initiative in Norumedzo which was largely traditional and without other actors such as EMA.

During the time of my fieldwork in Norumedzo, there were two members of EMA who, though were local members, had been trained and tasked by EMA to assist in the management of forest in the Norumedzo, including the *jiri*. These EMA members (commonly known as *Vanajengetavhu*/Environment Conservation Monitors) collaborated with traditional leadership, the *harurwa* caretaking team and the locals in conservation activities that ensured protection of the *jiri*. During the *harurwa* season, every morning one of the *Vanajengetavhu* would come to work with the *harurwa* caretaking team in the *jiri*. In the *jiri*, the *Vanajengetavhu* collaborate with the *harurwa* administrators and *harurwa* policemen, helping controlling activities in the *jiri* such as harvesting. The example of the Norumedzo *Jiri* where traditional leadership is working together with EMA's representatives – the Environment Conservation Monitors – could suggest that diverse epistemologies can, in many ways, meet and enrich each other. While traditional leadership bases its knowledge on daily practices adopted from previous generations, the Environment Conservation Monitors (ECMs) base their knowledge on modern scientific conservation approaches. In fact the ECMs unlike traditional leadership, *harurwa* administrators, and *harurwa* policemen were trained in conservation sciences by EMA. Their knowledge of environmental conservation, thus, is one that was obtained from an academy as opposed to that of the traditional leadership and community members that was adopted from previous generations and practices. This means that, in the face of the asymmetrical relations between science and indigenous epistemologies at national level (as exemplified by ZNEPS which largely employ scientific conservation methodologies in national conservation issues), humans and other beings in their interactions, the Norumedzo case offers a window of possibility for multiple conservation knowledges and a dialogue between science and other knowledge forms.

My argument on multiple conservation knowledge forms could be buttressed by what Jose David Saldivar (1997) calls 'critical border thinking' (Mignolo 2000; Grosfoguel 2008: 16). Critical border thinking is the epistemic response of the subaltern to the Eurocentric project of modernity, science included by subsuming/redefining the emancipator rhetoric of modernity (imposed by the Europeans) from the cosmologies of the subaltern, located in the oppressed and exploited side of the colonial difference (Grosfoguel 2008: 16). In other words, critical border thinking is a perspective that is critical of possible knowledge forms (whether conservation knowledge forms or otherwise) in terms of what they offer can help to improve inter – and intra-relations between humans and other beings in the world they share. When applied to conservation, critical border thinking suggests that the debates in conservational sciences and environmental management should be reframed. Reframing implies a thoroughgoing re-evaluation of the existing approaches in environment conservation and challenging them (where necessary) by suggesting new approaches as responses to the problems being faced in conservation. I have already challenged the current conservation approaches in Zimbabwe by arguing that either Science or indigenous epistemologies alone cannot solve environment conservational problems of this millennium as long as they work in isolation and mainly to undermine each other's efforts to conserve the environment. What is needed, in my view, is a holistic comprehensive approach – an approach that challenges the founding dualisms such as Eurocentric science and subaltern epistemologies and constructively addresses and reconciles understandings of contending approaches in the Science/subaltern epistemologies, Scientist/traditionalist and nature/culture binaries by offering space for diverse conservation knowledges and methodologies that complement one another or at least acknowledge the existence of the other. Such an approach mirrors the kind of conservation or rather forest protection in some rural communities in Zimbabwe such as the Norumedzo where local indigenous communities work together with the *Vanajengetavhu* (sing: *Jengetavhu*) – Environmental Conservation Monitors. I underline that such an approach – critical border thinking – in conservation has the merit that it calls for concerted action to mutual respect by appealing to both the developed and developing countries as well as western conservation science as well as other conservation knowledge forms (such as indigenous conservation knowledge) to reflect on themselves and respect each other. Besides, the approach recognises the fact that 'today's global environmental problems are shared problems that require joint effort, not only across the sciences but also between

271

science and its many stakeholders and users' (Hackmann and Moser 2013: 34).

Also, for purposes of social justice, that is, redressing injustices suffered by indigenous people in natural resource access and use as a result of colonialism, there is need for improved relationship and complementarities between community-based and state-led conservation in Zimbabwe. An improved relationship between community-based and state-based conservation would enhance collaboration between the state and local communities, and avoid the re-enactment of the historical divide in rights to resources such as wildlife that were enacted in southern Africa around protected areas such as national parks. In fact 'such prospective institutional linkages could more fully achieve biodiversity conservation in southern Africa while restoring or promoting social justice in terms of cultural renewal, governance, livelihoods and *conservation*' (Hoole 2014: 132). In this view, I argue with Marshall Murphree (2004) who proposes that genuine devolution is a necessary condition for CBNRM as he saw the most important reason for the underperformance of CBNRM systems to be "aborted devolution", that is, failure by states to devolve to local communities sufficient rights to use, manage, and benefit from natural resources around them.

Besides, it could be noted that one other reason why conservation in Zimbabwe (as in many other countries in Africa and beyond is in a state of crisis is the spirit of competition between different perspectives and conservation knowledge forms. In Zimbabwe, for example, state conservationists who widely embrace scientific-based conservation methodologies despise any conservation methodology that comes from outside the purview of science. The connoisseurs of indigenous conservation epistemologies – the so-called "traditional fundamentalists"– also do likewise. There is, therefore, more competition instead of collaborating or supporting each other, and lack of trust between conservationists from different disciplines despite the fact that they appear to be grappling and attempting to solve one and the same problem. In Zimbabwe as elsewhere, this has been largely a result of the fact that traditionally "the natural sciences have over the years become the determinant of what knowledge (*including conservation knowledge*) is and is not relevant to the question at hand" (Hackmann and Moser 2013:

38). This has promoted Western enlightenment modernistic divides (i.e. nature/culture) or what Chimamanda Adiche (2009) calls 'the danger of a single story', that is, a narrow view of the world (in this case of conservation) based on unsubstantiated prejudices. There is in fact the promotion of mono-conservation (from science) *yet* as Adichie (2009: 5) warns us 'a single story creates stereotypes. And the problem with stereotypes is not that they are untrue, but that they are incomplete. They make one story become the only story" by rejecting all other possible ways of telling the same story. It is on this pretext that I argue that avoiding the danger of a single story would entail advocacy of "multiple conservation epistemologies' (Mawere 2014b: 3) as opposed to the current 'mono conservation knowledge' being promoted by the Zimbabwean government (since the colonial era) in its national conservation projects. In fact, relying on the idea of a 'single story" of conservation where science is considered the sole provider of conservation knowledge, the Zimbabwean government has in many parts of the country initiated externally driven community-based natural resources management as opposed to organic community-based natural resource management which is conservation as was always practised (and is still practised elsewhere) by some local communities. I, therefore, argue in this chapter that as long as the spirit of competition between different conservation knowledge forms (and even disciplines concerned with conservation) is unresolved to the extent that the spirit of competition overrides that of collaboration and support then distrust will continue and conservation crisis also persists. To deal with this problem, I propose the need to appreciate and embrace multiple conservation epistemologies that are complementary and supportive of each other's conservation strategy. The challenge, may however, be how this could be made possible but once such a break-through is made, multiple governance in issues of conservation will become a possible solution to the problems of conservation that Zimbabwe and the world over are facing.

Conclusion

This chapter has discussed the local indigenous communities and the Zimbabwean state's concept of conservation. It revealed that the local indigenous communities' concept of conservation differs greatly from that of the state such that there seem to be more of mistrust and competition instead of collaboration between indigenous conservationists and state conservationists (also known as conservation scientists). It has been argued that such mistrust and contestations between different conservation knowledge forms will always betray the success of sustainable conservation in Zimbabwe. In view of these realisations, the chapter has argued for multiple conservation epistemologies, that is, collaboration among different conservation knowledge forms (for example, those represented by the state and those by local communities) to foster social justice and sustainable conservation.

References

Adichie, Chimamanda N. 2009. "The danger of a single story", talk filmed July 2009. Accessed June 17, 2013. http://www.ted.com/talks/chimamanda_adichie_the_danger_of_a_single_story.html.

Agrawal, Arun. "Indigenous and scientific knowledge: Some critical comments." *Indigenous knowledge and Development Monitor*, 3.3 (1995): 3-6.

Altieri, Miguel A. 1995. *Agro-ecology: The science of sustainable agriculture*, 2nd Edition, IT Publications: London.

Anderson, David and Grove, Richard. 1987. The scramble for Eden: Past, present and future in African conservation, In Anderson, David and Grove, Richard, (Ed), *Conservation in Africa: People, policies and practice*, Cambridge University Press: Cambridge.

Arnold, David. (Ed), 1988. *Imperial medicine and indigenous societies*, Manchester University Press: Manchester.

Beinart, William. 1984. Soil erosion, conservationism and ideas about development: A Southern African exploration, 1900-1960, *Journal of Southern African Studies*. Vol. 11 (1): 52-83.

Beinart, William. 2000. African history and environmental history, *African Affairs*. 99 (395): 269-302.

Beinart, William and McGregor, Joan. 2003. *Social history and African environments*. Ecology and History Series, Ohio University Press, USA.

Callon, Michel. 1986. Some elements of a sociology of translation: Domestication of the scallops and the fishermen of St Brieux Bay, In *Power, action and belief: A new sociology of knowledge?* (Ed), Law, John, p. 196-229, Routledge and Kegan Paul: London.

Child, Brian., Mupeta, Patricia., Muyengwa, Shylock., and Lubilo, Rodgers. 2014. Community-based natural resource management: Micro-governance and face-to-face participatory democracy, In: Sowman, Merle. and Wynberg, Rachael (Eds), *Governance for justice and environmental sustainability: Lessons across natural resource sectors in sub-Saharan Africa*, Earthscan Publishers, London, p. 156- 179.

Claassens, Aninka. 2011. Contested power and apartheid tribal boundaries: The implications of 'living customary law' for indigenous accountability mechanisms, *Acta Juridica*, p. 141- 174.

Digby, Anne. *Diversity and divisions in medicine: Health care in South Africa from the 1800s.* Peter Lang International Publishers, USA, 2006.

Dowie, Mark. 2009. *Conservation refugees: The hundred-year conflict between global conservation and native peoples*, MIT Press, Cambridge and London.

Fairhead, James and Leach, Melissa. 1996. *Misreading the African landscapes: Society and ecology in a forest-savanna Mosaic*, Cambridge University Press: Cambridge.

Feierman, Steven and Janzen, John. (Eds). 1992. *The social basis of health and healing in Africa*, University of California Press: Berkeley.

Foucault, Michel. 1982. *The subject and power*, University of Chicago Press: Chicago.

Grosfoguel, Ramon. 2013. Transmodernity, border thinking and global coloniality, *Eurozone*, 2008. Accessed April 10, 2013. www.eurozine.com.

Hackmann, Heide and Moser, Susanne. 2013. Social sciences in a changing global environment: General introduction, In *World Social Science Report, 2013: Changing Global Environments*, UNESCO Publishing, Paris.

Hanlon, Joseph, Manjengwa, Jeanette, and Smart, Teresa. 2013. *Zimbabwe takes back its land*, Jacana Media (Pty) Ltd, Johannesburg: South Africa.

Hara, Mafaniso, Turner, Stephen, Haller. Tobias, and Matose, Frank, 2013. Governance of the commons in southern Africa: Knowledge, political economy and power, *Development Southern Africa*, 26 (4): 521: 537.

Haraway, Donna. 1991. A cyborg manifesto: Science, technology, and socialist-feminism in the late twentieth century, In Haraway, Donna. *Simians, Cyborgs and Women: The Reinvention of Nature.* Routledge: New York, p.149-181.

Haraway, Donna. 2008. *When species meet,* Minneapolis, University of Minnesota Press: MN.

Haraway, Donna. 2003. *The companion species manifesto: Dogs, people, and significant otherness,* Chicago, IL: Prickly Paradigm.

Hoole, Arthur. 2014. Community-based conservation and protected areas: Commons perspectives for promoting biodiversity and social justice in southern Africa, In: Sowman, Merle and Wynberg, Rachael, (Eds), *Governance for justice and environmental sustainability: Lessons across natural resource sectors in sub-Saharan Africa.* Earthscan Publishers, London, p. 131-155.

Hornby, Arnold. 1924. 'The erosion of arable soil in Nyasaland and methods of prevention,' In F. Dixey, J. B. Clements and A. Hornby, *The destruction of vegetation and its relation to climate, water supply, and soil fertility*, Zomba, Government Printer. Bulletin No.1 (1924): 10-16.

Ilife, James. 1990. *Famine in Zimbabwe*, Mambo Press, Gweru: Zimbabwe.

Jackson, Michael. 2005. *Existential anthropology: Events, exigencies and effects*, Berghahn Books: Oxford.

Katerere, Yemi. 1999. Overview of CBNRM in the region, *Paper presented at the workshop: CBNRM and its contribution to economic development in Southern Africa*, 3-5 June 1999, Chilo Safari Lodge, Mahenye: Zimbabwe.

Kargbo, Abdul. 2005. Managing indigenous knowledge: What is the role for public libraries in Sierra Leone? *The International Information and Library Review 37,* Sierra Leone.

Jacobs, Nancy. 2006. Intimate politics of ornithology, *Society for Comparative Study of Society and History*, 48 (3): 564-603.

Kosek, Jake. 2010. Ecologies of empire: On the new uses of the honey bee, *Cultural Anthropology* Vol. 25 (4): 650-678.

Latour, Bruno. 1987. *Science in action: How to follow scientists and engineers through society*, Cambridge, MA: Harvard University Press.

Latour, Bruno. 2005. *Reassembling the social: an introduction to actor-network-theory*, New York, NY: Oxford University Press.

Latour, Bruno. 1993. *We have never been modern*, Cambridge, MA: Harvard University Press.

Mackenzie Walter, E. 1970. Colonial labour in the chartered company period, *Rhodesian History*, Vol. 1 (1970): 43-58.

Mandondo, Alois. 2000. Situating Zimbabwe's natural resource governance systems in history, CIFOR: Bogor, *Occasional Paper* No. 32.

Manjengwa, Jeanette. 2004. Local environmental action planning in Zimbabwe: An analysis of its contribution to sustainable development, *PhD Thesis*, Institute for Development Policy and Management, University of Manchester.

Mapara, Jacob. 2009. Indigenous knowledge systems in Zimbabwe: Juxtaposing postcolonial theory, *Journal of Pan African Studies*, 3 (1): 139-155.

Marongwe, Nelson. 2004. Traditional authority in community-based natural resource management (CBNRM): The case of Chief Marange in Zimbabwe, In Dzingirai, Vupenyu and Breen, Charles, (Eds), *Confronting the crisis in community conservation-Case studies from Southern Africa, Centre for Environment,* Agriculture and Development, University of KwaZulu-Natal.

Mawere, Munyaradzi. 2013. A critical review of environmental conservation in Zimbabwe, *Africa Spectrum*, 48 (2): 85-97.

Mawere, Munyaradzi. 2014a. *Environmental conservation through Ubuntu and other emerging perspectives*, Langaa RPCIG Publishers, Bamenda: Cameroon.

Mawere, Munyaradzi. 2014c. *Culture, indigenous knowledge and development in Africa: Reviving interconnections for sustainable development*, Langaa RPCIG Publishers: Bamenda.

Mawere, Munyaradzi. 2014b. *Forest insects, conservation and the environment: Harurwa (edible stinkbugs) and conservation in south eastern Zimbabwe*, PhD diss., University of Cape Town: South Africa.

Mawere, Munyaradzi, Mukombe, Cosmas, and Mabeza, Christopher. 2013. *Memoirs of an Unsung Legend, Nemeso*, Langaa RPCIG Publishers: Cameroon.

Mavhunga, Clapperton and Spierenburg, Marja A. 2007. Finger on the pulse of the fly: Hidden voices of colonial anti-Tsetse science on the Rhodesian and Mozambican Borderlands, 1945-1956, *South African Historical Journal*, 58 (2007): 117-141.

Mignolo, Walter. 2000. *Local histories/Global designs: Essays on the coloniality of power, subaltern knowledges and border thinking.* Princeton University Press: Princeton.

Mulwafu Oliver, Wapulumuka. 2002. Soil erosion and State intervention into Estate production in the Shire Highlands economy of colonial Malawi, 1891-1964, *Journal of Southern African Studies* Vol. 28 (1): 25-43.

Mulwafu Oliver, Wapulumuka. 2004. The Interface of Christianity and Conservation in Colonial Malawi, c. 1850-1930, *Journal of Religion in Africa* Vol. 34 (3): 298-319.

Murphree, Marshall. 2004. 'Communal approaches to natural resource management in Africa: From whence to where?' *Keynote address to the Brslauer Symposium on Natural Resource Issues in Africa*, University of California, Berkeley CA, 5 March 2004.

Murphree, Marshall. 1991. *Communities as Institutions for Resource Management*, University of Zimbabwe, Centre for Applied Social Sciences: Harare.

Neumann, Rod. 2002. *Imposing wilderness: Struggles over livelihood and nature preservation in Africa*, University of California Press: Berkeley.

Ocholla, Dennis. 2007. Marginalised knowledge: An agenda for indigenous knowledge development and integration with other forms of knowledge, *International Review of Information* 7. (9): 1-10.

Odora-Hosppers, Catherine. 2001. *Indigenous knowledge and the integration of knowledge systems: Towards a conceptual and methodological framework*, HSRC: Pretoria, South Africa.

Ogungbemi, Segun. 2011. An African perspective on the environmental crisis, In: Ojomo, P. A. *Environmental ethics: an*

African understanding, 2011. Accessed February 16, 2014. http://www.readperiodicals.com/201103/ 2323094941.html.

Okoth-Ogendo Hastings Winston, Opinya. 2008. The nature of land rights under indigenous law in Africa, In Claassens, Aninka, and Cousins, Ben. (Eds), *Land, power and custom: Controversies generated by South Africa's Communal Land Rights Act.* University of Cape Town Press: Cape Town.

Olukoshi, Adebayo and Nyamnjoh, Francis. 2011, "Introduction", In: Rene Devisch and Francis Nyamnjoh, (Eds), *The post-colonial turn: Re-imagining anthropology and Africa.* Langaa RPCIG Publishers: Bamenda.

Phimister Ian, R. 1974. Peasant production and underdevelopment in Southern Rhodesia, *African Affairs,* Vol. 73 (291): 217-228.

Plowden, Charles. 1968. The District Commissioner's meeting with Chiefs Norumedzo and Mazungunye, Chigumisirwa, *District Administration Archives,* Bikita, Zimbabwe.

Plumwood, Val. 2003. Decolonising relationships with nature, In Adams, William and Mulligan, Martin (Ed), *Decolonising nature: Strategies for conservation in a post-colonial era,* Earthscan, London.

Pollard, Sharon and Cousins, Tessa. 2014. Legal pluralism and the governance of freshwater resources in southern Africa: Can customary governance be embedded within the statutory frameworks for integrated water resources management? In Sowman, Merle and Wynberg, Rachael (Eds), *Governance for justice and environmental sustainability: Lessons across natural resource sectors in sub-Saharan Africa.* Earthscan Publishers, London.

Ribot, Jesse. 1999. Decentralisation, participation and accountability in Sahelian Forestry, Legal instruments of political-administrative control, *Africa,* Vol. 69 (1): 23-65.

Rowley Harold, Henry. 1881. *The Story of the Universities Mission to Central Africa,* London.

Salvadiar, Jose. David. 1997. *Border matters,* University of California Press, Berkeley.

Semali, Ladislaus and Kincheloe, Joe. 1999. Introduction: What is indigenous knowledge and why should we study it? In Semali, Ladislaus and Kincheloe, Joe. (Ed). *What is indigenous knowledge? Voices from the academy,* Falmer Press: New York.

Shizha, Edward. 2013. Reclaiming our indigenous voices: The problem with postcolonial sub-Saharan School curriculum," *Journal of Indigenous Social Development*, 2 (1): 1-18.

Sillitoe, Paul. 1998. What know natives? Local knowledge in development, *Social Anthropology*, 6 (2): 203-220.

Timberlake, Lloyd. 1991. *Africa in crisis: The causes, the cures of environmental bankruptcy*, Earthscan Publishers, London.

Warren Morland, D. 1991. Using indigenous knowledge in agricultural development, *The World Bank Discussion Paper No. 127*, Washington DC.

Watt, Martin. 1913. The dangers and prevention of soil erosion, *Rhodesia Agricultural Journal*, X, 5.

Weinmann, Henry. 1972. *Agricultural research and development in Southern Rhodesia under the rule of the British South Africa Company*, Salisbury.

Western, David. 2002. *In the dust of Kilimanjaro*, Island Press, Washington DC.

Wicomb, Wilmien and Smith, Henk. 2011. Customary communities as 'peoples' and their customary tenure as 'culture': What we can do with the Endorois decision, *African Journal of Human Rights Law*, Vol. 11 (2011): 422-446.

Zimbabwe Ministry of Environment and Natural Resources Management. 2009. *Zimbabwe National Environmental Policy and Strategies (ZNEPS)*, Ministry of Environment and Natural Resources Management, Harare: Zimbabwe.

Chapter Twelve

Education and Religion as Sociological Tools for Sustainable Development in Nigeria

Amali, I. O. O.

Introduction

Sustainable development is paramount to the existence of any nation. Education and religion have significant roles in the directions of sustainable development. They have influenced the lives of all Nigerians, where educational institutions and places of worship are on the increase daily.

In Nigeria, it is assumed that most Muslims, Christians and African Indigenous and traditional worshippers are devoted to their religious beliefs with great passion (Dopamu, 2009). Ekanem and Ekefre (2013) asserted that Nigerians view every aspect of their lives on religious prism and that particularly for a good Muslim there would be no difference between religion, culture and education. Further, that religion has become the basic social element through which societies are grouped. Thus, a disagreement relating to any aspect of society is viewed as a disagreement on religious views or belief among Nigerian multi-cultural and religious society. Education on the other hand has its cardinal philosophy. Ukeje (1988) using Johann Frederick Herbert (1776 – 1834) conception, stated that, the ideal man or the educated man is one who achieved the highest moral character through the development of moral, physical , emotional and intellectual powers that enables the individual to contribute to social reforms and to development of his environment or society.

Thus, Education and Religion in Africa ought to be the two social institutions that would sustain the basic principles of security, freedom and other fundamental human rights as enshrined in the Nigeria Constitution (FGN, 1999) and the National Policy on Education (FGN, 2013). In this regard, education and religion in Africa call for synergy in teaching, learning with overall goal that integrates the principles, values and practices of sustainable development into all aspects of education and religious practices. In this respect, the basic principles of security, freedom and other fundamental human rights enshrined in the Nigeria Constitution (1999) and the National Policy on Education (2013) appeared to have addressed the challenge of education and religion in Nigeria toward sustainable development.

Conceptual Clarification of Terms

Education and Religion
Fafunwa (2004) stated that in Nigeria before the advent of Western or Islamic education, education was functional in nature and served as guiding values upheld by elders that ensured an enduring society. That education in whatever form, was used to train the young and adult members of the society. To him education was a tool for disseminating or transmitting social values, knowledge and cultural heritage from one generation to another. This was why the Federal Government of Nigeria (2004) posited that:

> *Education is an instrument for national development. To this end, the formulation of ideas, their integration for national development and the interaction of persons and ideas are all aspects of education. Education fosters the worth of development of the individual for his sake and for the sake of the general development of the society (pp. 6-7).*

Education ensures that there exists a vivid understanding of the concept of sustainable development. The interdisciplinary nature and practical issues of education and religion will bring to fore their relationship with regards to the challenges of sustainable development. It would be through education that an effective evaluation and effectiveness of a broad range of methods, theories, perspectives, and frameworks relating to religion and sustainable development could be assessed.

Religion
Religion is man's belief which centred on the sacred, and believed by many Africans as the supernatural power (Davis, 1988; Dopamu,

2009; Dzurgba, 2009). Dzurgba (2009) noted that Durkheim showed how religious beliefs and practices had shaped the course of human civilization and social life. Thus, he referred to Durkheim's Social theory of religion as functionalism. Fafunwa (2004) observed that Traditional, Islamic as well as Christian religions have the same functionalist prerequisite. Like Mahutta (2011) asserted, if education and religion are accorded their well-deserved values and places, they would mean a lot to the society especially for ensuring social solidarity and cooperation amongst people.

Sustainable Development

In this study, sustainable development is used as paradigm which intertwined in the thinking about the future of education and religion in Nigeria multi- cultural and religious society. This is because, education and religion hold a pride of place in environmental and economic consideration in the pursuit of approved quality of life needed by the citizenry for sustainable development. Thus, as posited, by Dzurgba (2009), education and religion are fundamentally optimistic human endeavour characterized by aspiration for progress and betterment of societies. They are both understood by many to be means of overcoming human difficulties, achieving greater human equality and social status. They are both social institutions where children can develop according to their unique needs and potentials. They both connote the idea of pasture-ship that would lead to the development of the Nigerian societies and the nation. Both invoke enlightenment and training as means to achieve the end.

Theoretical framc of reference

Fafunwa (2004) and Dzurgba (2009) acknowledged Durkheim's social theory of education and religion as functionalism, this creates the belief that any form of education (traditional, western or Islamic) have functionalist prerequisite. The same could be said for any other form of religion. In the content of this view, this study submits that all curricula, taxonomies of education and religion including environmental education are subsumable under Education for Sustainable Development (ESD) which equips individuals and societies with knowledge, values, and skills to live and work in an equitable, secure and sustainable manner needed for economic wellbeing of the people. This study thus, recognizes the model for Virtuous Cycle of Education for Sustainable Development (VCESD). This is important for Africa or Nigeria's transformation, sustainable development and global competitiveness; since Nigeria and many other Africa countries are still classified in the Human Development Index (HDI, 2010) and ranked as low Human Development Nation (http://hdr.org/en/stastical/). The Virtuous Cycle of Education for Sustainable Development (VCESD) model requires that educational policies, programmes and actions should promote, sustain and have as deliverables outcomes; economic growth, human development, environmental protection and sustainability for the benefit and interest of present and future generations. In this respect, educational enterprise or system that fails to achieve these outcomes ceases to be virtuous, having deepening poverty and underdevelopment which impedes sustainable development and competiveness (Jenkins, 2010). Adopting the VCESD model presupposes that human rights approach to quality education at all levels, science and technology, research and innovation, environmental education, indigenous culture, language education and achieving the Millennium Development Goals (MDGs) (now framed as Sustainable Development Goals) are the functional prerequisites for ESD. Thus, the assumption in this study is that VCESD model is the critical pathway to Africa/Nigeria sustainable development and global competitiveness.

In this regard, education and religion should be used as catalysts for sustainable development. This calls for national and international initiatives to address the problems we face in African/Nigeria today as the indigenous value systems have been eroded and destroyed through years of African colonization and neo-colonization coupled with the ever increasing social decadence and strife such as the so-called 'ethnicism,' unbridled corruption, favouritism, lawlessness, religious bigotry, 'ethnic' wars, political unrest etc. agonizing Nigeria and Africa continent. These are antithetical to the hospitality and communalism of the Africa culture (Orlu-orlu and Nsereka 2014).

Based on these views as expressed above, education and religion have been viewed in conformity to Jean Henrich Pestalozzi (1746-1847) conception expressed in Ukeje (1988) to be the necessary instruments of social reforms through individual development.

Relatedly, the conception of Herbert Spencer (1820-1903) also expressed in Ukeje (1988), addressed the general problems of life and the right rating of conduct in all directions, under all circumstances in what way to treat the mind and how to use all our faculties to the greatest advantages to ourselves and others. It is about how to live well completely. Thus, in this conception education and religion should be the process of teaching and learning toward living well completely.

Again, sustainable development, in the argument of McKenzie (2005), puts into consideration that the majority of the world's populations are adherents to a religious belief of some kind. Johnson (2010) asserts that in all major religions are ideas about the responsibilities of the individual toward the environment and toward other people, and agendas for achieving sustainability may fruitfully draw on these ideas. Thus, religion is introduced into sustainable development discourse as the Nigerian society is increasingly faced with issues that border on what is worth sustaining and what sustains them. Answering them invites reflection on the totality of what sustains the individual. For many Africans and Nigerians, a good answer must reach toward the quality of education and religious—belief which encompasses the spirit, the sacred, God, love and faith. Education, at least provides a parameter for addressing questions for sustainable development.

The Parity between Education and Religion in Nigeria

The National Bureau of Statistics (NBS) portrayed 50.48% of Nigerians as Muslims, 48.2% as Christians while 1.4% were members of other religions. This typified Nigeria as a good example of two major religious societies where the bulk of the Muslims are in the North and the bulk of the Christians reside in the South. Education in this respect is to serve each society the freedom to practice their religion and to educate their young ones the practice of such religion. This has been spelt out in the Federal Republic of Nigeria Constitution (1999) where freedom of worship is enshrined and guaranteed for the citizenry, making Nigeria a secular state. Even though African epistemologies of worship and places of worship are excluded in the formal education curricula of Nigerian schools, the teaching and learning of African traditional religion has been included for educational programme at the territory level in most Nigerian territory institutions. Thus, education and religion are intended to cultivate and prepare individuals towards tolerance and cooperation which would facilitate freedom of worship and the promotion of peaceful co-existence among Nigerian.

Basically, the teaching of religion in Nigeria is faith oriented. In Nigeria schools, it is a means of getting people to embrace Christianity or Islam. This is why Christian and Islamic religious studies remain the only two religions of study in schools particularly at the lower levels of Nigerian educational system. In this respect, education and religion have brought together, Nigerians from diverse socio-cultural, 'ethnic' and linguistic groupings to promote social integration. For example, Nigerian public schools have been known for promoting social solidarity by admitting Nigeria children without bias to socio-cultural, 'ethnic,' religious and linguistic considerations.

Education is thus the panacea for settling problems created by religion as it equips people with better understanding of the dynamics of religion. To this end, Achunike (2008) asserted that better education will equip religious adherents with better understanding of the dynamics of religion, making the individual to compromise or give up some religious or doctrinal rights for the sake of social change.

According to Akinpelu (1981) and Cobb (1997), it is within the realm of philosophy to raise fundamental issues and to question certain beliefs. Thus, in Nigeria, the interface between education, religion and culture cannot be ignored. At the cultural level, the family and the indigenous communities had provided the young ones (even before he got to know religion) education. But nowadays, when people talk about religion, their minds go to school education where the institutionalization of religious life precedes that of education for most societies. As such, religious institutions as asserted by Cobb (1997) had contributed to the development of education systems. This was true of Northern and Southern parts of Nigeria where the Mosques and the Churches spawned the early Western and Islamic schools (Dopamu, 2008). This was so because parents would like their children to adopt their values. The schools in this case provided personal development of pupils where the ethos of civil religious education continues to affect the overall personality of many youth in Nigeria schools.

Again, education and religion in Nigeria have become centres for impartation of fresh ideas that create values for civic responsibility and civil order. This indicates that there exist epistemological relationship between education and religion which create the required awareness in the citizenry towards social and moral values needed for sustainable development. Therefore, the parity of education and religion is that of mutuality. This is because, the more education and religion work together and borrows the values of another, the more values that people shared together would affect their social life needed for sustainable development. In this way religious education will continue to influence the overall climate of social life of many schools in Nigeria.

Implications of Education and Religion as Designs for Sustainable Development in Nigeria

Education and religion ought to serve as the instrument of social solidarity for any society. But in Nigeria, religion has at times caused insecurity due to either lack of understanding and misinterpretation of the various religious doctrines that have been sometimes fuelled due to religious rivalry or dogma. The issues of religious conflict have become common phenomena in the country, especially in the last three decades. The rivalry existing between Islam and Christianity sometimes lead to religious conflict, violence and terrorism. The latest ravaging the country is a sect known as Jama'atul Ahlus sunnab haddla'awati wal Jihad (Brethren unite in the pursuit of holy war), also known as Boko Haram; a group that sees western education as an extension of colonialism and imperialism Omotoye, 2012). Thus there have been accentuations of regional and 'ethnic' distinction attributed to religion differences in Nigeria (Dopamu, 1993; Achunike, 2008).

Further, Islam and Christianity are missionary in nature, who through education tried to disconnect people from their traditional religion that have been handed down from generation to generations of Africans (Dopamu, 1993). But today, religion as much as education has becomes one of the important weapons which selfish elites and leaders use in manipulating and dividing the people (Lemu, 2012). Consequently in Nigeria, access to education and religion has become the dominant force used to control the lives and rights of groups and individuals. This has led to multiplicity of religious sects and educational institutions across Nigeria. This has implications for education, since education attempts to liberate the minds and remove all forms of mental cobweb gathered through cultural and religious activities and beliefs either for local or foreign interests. Sometimes, these have been exploited by local or foreign religious bigots and fanatics in Africa and Nigeria in preference to social values needed for sustainable development (Lemu, 2012).

Again the interactive forces of Education and Religion have created unhealthy atmosphere for social and national development. This is because religion has become a very emotive issue among Africa and Nigerians, particularly in the institutions of learning where there are occasional break down of law and order due to religious differences (Alana, 1993). Amali (2009) attested that the opportunities created by the establishment of exogenous religious influences (Christianity and Islam) provided a new pattern of challenge to teaching and learning in multi-religious society. That, it is on the basis of this scenario that teaching and learning of religious tenets in schools are accorded a high premium and recognition in the life of the Nigerian people which are included in Nigeria educational curricula. The Nigeria Constitution (FGN, 1979) and the National Policy of Education (FGN, 2013) took cognizance of the values of education and religion and make legislative provisions to regulate and control the behaviour of the citizenry.

Thus, educational institutions in African and indeed Nigeria stand the chance of reawakening and resuscitating the conscience of other African and Nigerian people for positive endeavour. Religious education plays a crucial role in this respect. This has implication for teaching and learning, particularly in Nigeria where the consequences of religious teaching have sometimes negatively influenced the social wellbeing of the citizenry leading to ordeal, disorder, wanton destruction of lives and property. Similarly, Lemu (2012) observed that education and religion are the causes of the disparity that entrenched marginalization in terms of sustainable development in Nigeria. Achunike (2008) has asserted that the several religious

288

conflicts in Nigeria have assisted in the accentuation of regional and 'ethnic' distinction due to the pattern of education where there were differences between the North and South. Thus institutions of learning ought to stand as crop fertilization grounds for ideas about religious belief to various religious adherents.

The Way Forward

The National Policy of Education and Religious curriculum did not spring from nowhere. They evolved as a reflection of the need, perceptions and historical development in Nigeria for Nigerians. Multiplicities of religions and strict corporate compliance to religious dogma have become a challenge to cooperative existence of people in Nigeria. Education would serve to curtail excesses in the behaviour of individuals. The essence of education and religion for sustainable development thus revolve around the interface between education and religion as presented as a recommendation in the paradigm below:

Recommended Paradigm on Required Interface between
and Religion for Sustainable Development

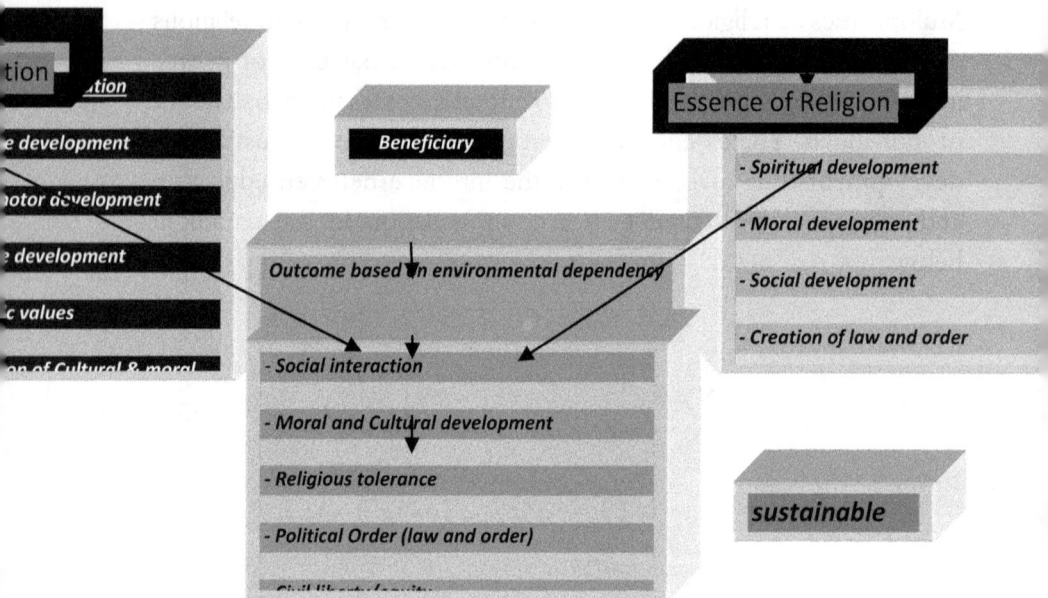

tion

..tion

e development

..otor development

e development

.c values

..on of Cultural & moral

Beneficiary

Essence of Religion

- Spiritual development

- Moral development

Outcome based in environmental dependency

- Social development

- Creation of law and order

- Social interaction

- Moral and Cultural development

- Religious tolerance

sustainable

- Political Order (law and order)

..urce: *Amali (2014)*

As shown in figure I, there would be need for national initiative to address religious challenges using Nigerian institutions of learning as forerunners to address excesses of individual behaviour through dialogue, religious discourse, symposia, conferences, spiritual and moral development, social development etc. This would employ constructive education based on sound philosophies of education and religion that would recover the minds and souls of those behind religious bigotry that at times result into rivalry which creates problems for Nigerian sustainable development.

This would also address the challenges posed due to low level of enlightenment of religious adherents in Nigeria. Ekanem and Ekefre (2013) pointed out that what has been taken as philosophy of education in Nigeria, are policy statements and objectives of education. That there would be need for the creation of department of philosophy particularly for the interest of Northern part of Nigeria where they noted that no Federal and State universities teach philosophy as a course of study, except University of Abuja. Again a combination of physical and spiritual dimensions that would help to develop sustainable development is needed. In this regard, education would help to re-educate and eradicate those vices that tend to retard the development of Nigerian people and the Nation.

Education and religion should jointly help to promote peace, sound and appropriate meaningful social order required for national development. Thus Nigerians would use education and religion to enhance their living side by side as long as they do not insult or cast aspersion on one another's sanctities. Education and religion should not conflict in social responsibility. Religious adherents should be taught how to discuss popular misconceptions about their beliefs without taking it as an offence or with the aim not to convert but to develop a better mutual understanding that encourages social solidarity needed for national development.

Also education could be used in the re-direction of misuse of religion for selfish ends. This would require correct teaching of religion that would facilitate common values for all persons irrespective of their religious differences.

Recommendations

The following recommendations are drawn for this study:

1. There should be a promotion of education and religious philosophy that would bring about understanding, cooperation among communities with multi-religious background.

2. Education should encourage the publication and distribution of books about different religions that should be used in the various tiers of educational systems in Nigeria.

3. Teachers of religion in Nigeria schools should be well grounded in philosophies of education and religion to enable them understands the essence of education and religion in Nigeria.

4. Government at all levels should be involved in the funding of education to promote and monitor religious activities in Nigeria.

5. Liberalism should be promoted both in religious and educational spheres of Nigerian national life. Components of Christianity should be included in Islamic syllabus and vis-a-visa. Thus teachers should realistically and objectively explain the basic principles of the religion they teach to promote social justice and national consciousness.

6. Education should discourage poor theological education in Nigeria and encourage inter-religious dialogues, interactions and discussions between two or more different religious groups with a view to bring about an atmosphere of social harmony needed for social and national development.

Conclusion

Basing on the findings of this study, it is concluded that an application of education and religion as sociological tools in examination of societal values can help fostering sustainable development. This is because sociological tools such as religion are normally viewed from prisms of belief as a discipline while education and religion are viewed as institutions for facilitating social wellbeing for sustainable development. Since the need for sustainable development is paramount to the existence of any nation, the collaborative roles of education and religion in Nigeria is essential because they would help to ensure unity, peace (within Nigeria religious diversity) required for social solidarity and sustainable development. This has been enshrined in the Nigeria Constitution (1999) and in the National Policy on Education (FGN, 2013).

References

Achunike, H. C. 2008. Religious practices in Nigeria as a source of conflict, *Journal of Liberal Studies*, 12(1 & 2), 286-295.

Akinpelu, J. A. 1981. *An introduction to philosophy of education*, Ibadan: Macmillan Company Ltd.

Alana, O. E. 1993. 'The relationship between Christians, Muslims and Afrolists in History with particular reference of to Nigeria,' In R. D. Abubakre (ed), *Studies in religion understanding in Nigeria*, Ilorin: Christy-David Printers.

Amali, I. O. O. 2009. The challenges of teaching and learning in a multi-religious society, *Nigeria Journal of Sociology of Education*, III: Nigeria.

Cobb, J. B. 1997. *Religion and education*, Lecture one: California Claremont School of Theology, USA.

Davis, D. 1988. The study of religion; In R. P. Bearer (ed.), *The World's Religions* (10-11), Hert, England: Lion Publishing.

Dopamu, P. A. 1993. African religion in Nigeria society: Past, present and the future in Studies in religion understanding in Nigeria. R. D. Abubakre (ed) *Studies in religion understanding in Nigeria*, Ilorin: Christy-David Printers.

Dopamu, A. T. 2009. Religious' pluralism in Nigeria: the example of the Yoruba. In A. P. Dopamu (ed), *Dialogue: Issues in contemporary discussion*, Akure: Big Small books.

Dzurgba, A. (2009). An introduction to sociology of religion, Ibadan: John Archers.

Ekanem, S. A., & Ekefre, E. N. 2013. Education and religious intolerance in Nigeria: The need for essencism as a philosophy, *Journal of Educational and Social Research*, 3(2).

ESD- Education for sustainable development available http// www.esdtoolkit.org/discussion/whatisesd, (2009).

Fafunwa, B. A. 2004. *History of education in Nigeria*. Ibadan: NPS Educational Publisher Ltd.

Federal Republic of Nigeria 2013. *National policy on education.* Abuja: Ministry of Education.

Federal republic of Nigeria, FRN 2006. MDGs- Millennium Development Goals. Report, Abuja National planning Commission.

Federal Republic of Nigeria 1999. *Constitution of the Federal Republic of Nigeria,* Lagos: Federal Ministry of Justice.

Helen, K. and Meyer, F. 2008. *Education for Sustainable Development: Exploring theoretical and practical challenges,* The Hague University of applied sciences, The Hague in Netherland.

Jenkins, W. 2010. Sustainability theory, *Berkshire Encyclopaedia of Sustainability: The Spirit of Sustainability,* 106(10), 100.

Johnston, L. 2010. The religious dimensions of sustainability: Institutional religions, civil society, and international politics since the turn of the twentieth century, *Religion Compass,* 4(3), 176-189.

Lemu, B. A. 2012. *Religious education in Nigeria – A case study,* Nigeria: Islamic Education Trust.

Mahutta, M. G. 2011. Education for morality: A panacea for rebranding the Nigeria society, *Nigeria Journal of Sociology of Education,* 5(1).

McKenzie, S. 2005. Social sustainability, religious belief and global ethics: Outlines for research, *Working Paper Series, No 30.* Magill, South Australia: Hawke Research Institute for Sustainable Societies, University of South Australia.

NBS - National Bureau of Statistics

Omotoye, R. 2012. Inter-religious dialogue as a panacea for National development in Nigeria, Centre Point 15(1).

Orlu-Orlu, H.C. & Nsereka, B.G. 2014. Social media as a bastion for correcting moral ills in Nigeria. A focus on educational decadence, new media and mass communication, 22, 38-49. http://www.iiste.org/journal/indexphp/NMMC/article/view/1078.

Prothero, S. 2007. *Religious literacy: What every American needs to know about religion – And doesn't,* New York: HarperCollins.

Tikjoeb, S. A. 2004. Mainstreaming religion in sustainable development: A casual layered analysis, *Journal of Future Studies,* 8(4), 47-60.

Ukeje, B. O. 1988. *Education for the survival of the Nigerian nation,* an inaugural lecture delivered at the University of Port Harcourt.

VCESD- Virtuous cycle education for sustainable development/ HDI (human development index. Source UNDP (2010). http//hdr.org/en/statistical

WCED (World Commission on Environment and Development) (1987). *Our common future.* Oxford: Oxford University Press.

Chapter Thirteen

A Fading Liberation Heritage Legacy: Reflections on Gonakudzingwa Detention Camp in Southeastern Zimbabwe

Tapuwa Raymond Mubaya and Munyaradzi Mawere

Introduction

The road to the independence of Zimbabwe was marred and loaded with many political struggles and obstacles meant to derail and rob the peace and wealthy of the indigenous people. As such struggles needed men and women of valour, high integrity, discipline and dedication to liberate the country from the whims and shackles of colonial oppression. The colonial oppressors tried their all-out efforts to dampen the indigenous masses' will, desire, aspirations and determination to set free their birthright. Undeniably, independence came into force after a gruesome, bitter and protracted liberation struggle that entailed a lot of self-denial, sacrifice, misery, and suffering. The 1950s and early 1960s saw a boom in the radicalisation of nationalism in the then Rhodesia (now Zimbabwe). From the late 1960s to 1979, political imprisonment in colonial Zimbabwe was a consequence of the colonial Rhodesian authorities' high-handed response to Africans' nationalist and liberation struggles, whose foremost agenda was to dislodge white settler colonial rule (Munochiveyi 2014). During this period, African nationalists engaged in a protracted guerrilla war which seriously affected the repressive systems of the colonial government. The settler regime responded by imprisoning a large number of activists and those whom it suspected of being aligned with the guerrillas (Munochiveyi 2008).

Although the Rhodesian colonial authorities had always used imprisonment as part of colonial repression since the establishment of Rhodesia as a colony in the 1890s, widespread political imprisonment, detention, and intensified state repression of Africans (see also Ibid: 2014) occurred between the 1960s and 1970s, the period of the nationalist and liberation struggles. Despite the iron fisted rule of the colonial government, nationalists moved from a posture of negotiation and participation in political institutions to an aggressive demand for self-rule. To this end, trained guerrillas started entering the country in 1963, in small groups of two, four or six (Ibid). These men were unarmed and most of them headed for urban areas which later became vibrant centres for nationalist movements and trade unions. On 11 November 1965, Ian Smith formed his Unilateral Declaration of Independence Cabinet (UDI) and the Rhodesia Front (RF) leader declared that there would be no African nationalist rule in his lifetime. This was a myopic, racist utterance from an arrogant and repressive regime that intended to cling to power at all costs in defiance of the winds of change and the inevitable dawn of a new era of black majority rule. As a way of suppressing and thwarting efforts and initiatives spearheaded by nationalists' parties, the Rhodesian Front Government declared a State of Emergency in the Highfields African township of Salisbury now Harare. 'Black' nationalist organisations that had been employing strategies of non-violent civil disobedience since the 1950s began advocating violent struggle to achieve an independent Zimbabwean nation. In this respect, two rival organisations vied for control of the Zimbabwean people against each other and the Rhodesian government. The Reverend Ndabaningi Sithole (succeeded by Robert Mugabe) led the Zimbabwean African National Union (ZANU) and its armed wing, ZANLA consisted primarily of Shona speaking tribes. The Zimbabwean African People's Union (ZAPU) and its armed wing ZIPRA was led by Joshua Nkomo and consisted primarily of Ndebele ethnic groups. To worsen the situation, Ian Smith's Government also banned ZANU and ZAPU and arrested the leaders of these two political parties.

The ZANU leaders were sent to Sikombela camp in Zhombe District of Kwekwe while ZAPU leaders went to the Gonakudzingwa camp in the south-eastern part of the country. To date, Gonakudzingwa and Sikombela are some of the known remaining few places associated with the liberation history of Zimbabwe. Undeniably and undoubtedly, they are living testimonies of the arduous suffering that people went through in the quest to liberate Zimbabwe. These historical places despite being part and parcel of the country's cherished cultural heritage are very important in as far as they explicitly and vividly show the brutality of the colonial government in trying to quell and silence the masses who felt short changed by the unjust and discriminatory minority rule. That said, the colonial government conceived an idea of separating the 'fish' from the 'water' through the creation of detention camps. Specifically, the creation of detention camps was meant to separate prominent nationalists from the masses and by so doing psychologically robbing them of their political think tanks and strategists. Rhodesian authorities anticipated that arresting and detaining the most vocal and active African political figures would work to intimidate African communities into submission and thus eradicate political dissent (Ibid). The social composition of people who were imprisoned by Rhodesian security forces during the liberation struggle was quite diverse. Those detained ranged from guerrilla militants, political organisers, and ordinary men and women who were suspected of sympathising or collaborating with the liberation movement (Munochiveyi 2008).

The Rhodesian regime designed this form of confinement specifically for the holding of political activists who had not been charged of any crime in the Rhodesian courts, but whom the authorities wished to isolate from their communities. Detention was particularly meant to isolate known African political activists to remote and inaccessible parts of the country and thereby render political activists and supporters of the struggle for liberation politically, intellectually, and socially dead. By cutting prisoners off from the outside political world by limiting visitations and withholding radios, newspapers, and other communication Rhodesian authorities hoped that detention would short-circuit the circulation of anticolonial politics and ideas. This category of prisoners was not convicted of any crime. Instead, detention was "preventive": detainees were held on grounds of their potential to endanger public safety or public order (Feltoe 1978). To detain a person without trial is to do him/her gross injustice. At Gonakudzingwa the African nationalist leaders were purposefully cut off from any contact with the outside world. Nothing could be worse than this. It was indeed the worst mental torture of its own kind.

The chapter argues that far from being centres of isolation, detention spaces failed to completely isolate and cut off activists from the political world of Rhodesia. We argue that despite Rhodesian authorities' concerted attempts to physically isolate African political activists to remote detention spaces such as Gonakudzingwa, Sikombela, and WhaWha, detention centres were spaces in which detainees actively negotiated their incarceration and challenged rules of detention. For example, instead of conforming to the dreary and disempowering monotony of detention life, African detainees took advantage of their captivity to empower themselves through academic and political education, political debate, and to developing powerful critiques of colonial rule through writings that were smuggled out of prison. Thus, although being detained was a major infringement on the personal and political freedoms of African political activists, African detainees were more than defenceless and weak victims of Rhodesian repression. Oral histories of detention suggest that political detainees were protagonists who rejected the subordinate status to which Rhodesian authorities relegated them, and were capable of playing a role in the struggle for liberation.

In this chapter, we are particularly interested in the dearth of literature on the significance of detention and restriction camps in post independent Zimbabwe. Yet, the history of Zimbabwe is incomplete without the inclusion of these historic and iconic places that by and large made the independence of this country possible. Unfortunately, the importance and contribution of detention and restriction camps such as Sikombela and Gonakudzingwa to the freedom of the country have been overshadowed by massacre sites such as Chimoio, Nyadzonya and Freedom Camp among several others in and outside the country. In view of this, we may not be wrong in arguing that the histories and lived experiences of African political detainees and prisoners whose experiences and contributions towards the liberation struggle have been rendered invisible by dominant historical and state narratives. The later sites have fairly received commendable attention and media coverage as compared to the former. The majority of sites in the former category with the exception of Sikombela which was fortunate to be proclaimed a national monument are yet to be publicised let alone receive legal protection. Notwithstanding their unparalleled socio-political values, some of these sites such as Gonakudzingwa are gradually disappearing. It is sad to note that there is lack of political will and commitment to recognise the significance of such places in national development discourses as has happened to neighbouring countries such as South Africa which have transformed such sites into formidable generators of income while at the same time conserving their priceless liberation heritage. The major argument being advanced in this chapter is that Zimbabwe should draw lessons from other countries and start developing and giving priority to the rehabilitation and protection of its detention and restriction camps.

It is pathetic to note that 35 years after attaining independence, nothing worth noting has been done to nominate Gonakudzingwa on the National Monuments Register as a national monument. The proclamation of Sikombela as a national monument exacerbates matters as this gives an impression that former ZANLA restriction camps are more important than the ZIPRA ones. We however, strongly recommend that something must be done to salvage this important cultural heritage site from neglect and extinction and also to present a balanced picture of the true history of the liberation struggle. Recognising Sikombela and neglecting Gonakudzingwa presents and invites more questions than answers. This may also be considered as fertile ground by some political opportunists to criticise the 1987 Unity Accord that brought together the two parties into a strong force. Seemingly, uplifting Sikombela and neglecting Gonakudzingwa is like removing the glue that binds the two parties. Albeit, Sikombela was proclaimed a national monument, more effort should be put in developing the place to match its huge contribution to the development of this country. In the process, dominant state narratives have rendered invisible and inaudible the histories, lived experiences, and significant contributions of other historical subjects, such as those who were incarcerated by the colonial state (Munochiveyi 2014).

Locating Gonakudzingwa Detention Camp

Gonakudzingwa lies at the end of the Gonarezhou National Park on the Zimbabwe/Mozambique Border. It was established in the early 1960s as a detention camp for the ZIPRA Forces during the struggle for independence (NMMZ File 2009). The site is in the south eastern part of the country on the Sango border post, the border between Zimbabwe and Mozambique. Gonakudzingwa is about 176km east of Rutenga Growth Point and the road to the site follows the Zimbabwe-Mozambique railway line, transcending through the Gonarezhou National Park.

The Camp covers an area of 500 square meters and currently the site consists of house remains particularly floors and some poles made of steel. Sango Border Post (Immigration and Zimbabwe Revenue Authority (ZIMRA) offices and staff houses are to the east while to the south there is the Sango Police Post (NMMZ File 2011). The former detention camp is right on the border and on its western bound is the Gonarezhou National Park. Gonakudzingwa was a place in the wilderness, and its environment was very harsh since it was unbearably hot and inhospitable. The area was populated with wild animals including lions and elephants, subject to extremes of heat and cold, expensive and difficult to access, and had virtually no infrastructure save for the tin huts, roads and boreholes put in for the detainees. The restriction area was run by police rather than the prison service, and it held the largest number of detainees by a considerable margin, with over 3,000 residents at some points.

Establishment of Gonakudzingwa

Gonakudzingwa was established in 1964 as a detention camp for ZAPU nationalists as Sikombela was for ZANU. The site was a place of incarceration for prominent politicians such as Cde Joshua Nkomo among other luminaries were detained during the liberation struggles. The first people to be dumped at Gonakudzingwa with Joshua Nkomo were Joseph Bruno Msika, Josiah Chinamano, Daniel Madzimbamuto and Mrs Ruth Chinamano. These were held at Camp Number One. These nationalists are believed to have come at Gonakudzingwa sometime in February 1964 and stayed alone for about six months before being joined by other nationalists like Cde Jane Ngwenya who became the second woman to be detained at Gonakudzingwa, John Landa Nkomo, and Chenjerai Hunzvi among others (NMMZ File 2011). The site is in a very remote area that is generally dry and hot thereby creating hard living conditions. The nearest settlement on the Zimbabwean side is about 60km west, so the detainees were completely alienated from the rest of the people (NMMZ File 2006). The camp was a death site, it was very hot for human habitation and engulfed by dangerous animals such as lions and elephants and this would have discouraged any attempts to flee the camp.

From an interview that was carried out by one of the researchers while he was working for National Museums and Monuments of Zimbabwe during a visit to the site, there was a consensus among the ex-detainees that before the creation of Gonakudzingwa, Whawha was used as a political detention camp to those who were regarded as threats to the Rhodesia Government. As time lapsed, Whawha could no longer accommodate the ever increasing numbers of nationalists who continued to speak against the government and end up being detained. Cde Jane Ngenya one of the ex-detainees narrated that before Gonakudzingwa was established all political activists were detained at Whawha regardless of being either affiliated to ZAPU or ZANU. However, tension was always building up between members of the two revolutionary parties (Interview with Jane Ngwenya 2011). As a result, Gonakudzingwa and Sikombela were established for ZAPU and ZANU cadres respectively. The concept of detaining political activists is believed to have been coined by Sir Godfrey Huggins as a strategy to alienate nationalists from influencing the general population.

Gonakudzingwa was made up of five sub-camps. The first camp known as camp 1 or Main Camp was where the first nationalists were detained. The Main Camp comprises of three barracks and ten huts. One of the huts served as a storeroom for food whilst the rest were used by women who were residing two in each hut. Camp 1 is located on the eastern side and as the number of detainees increased, other 4 sub camps were built stretching to the western side. Camp 2 was there for our meetings with visitors. Thus, the last camp, number 5 is about 2.5km west of camp 1. In between these two camps were camps 2, 3 and 4. Unfortunately, these three camps are not accessible due to the threats of landmines that continue to haunt the place. Camp 5 was an exceptional camp where the Indians and Coloured people who were regarded as threat to the Rhodesian Government by sidelining with the African nationalists were detained namely the likes of Thomas Fore, Joseph Necks and Patel (NMMZ File 2011).

On his arrival in Gonakudzingwa, Joshua Nkomo immediately set about establishing what he called a "government" in the wilderness. As he explained in his memoir,

> Our prison became a centre for political education, both for us prisoners and for our visitors. The government had evidently not thought what the effect would be of putting us away in that remote place, almost without supervision. We took control of our own lives, set up our own camp government and ran it as a practical course in democratic administration. The camp was run by the central committee, whose members acted as the chairmen of specialised committees for education, reception, hospitality and so on. The committee secretaries ran the day-to-day business, carrying out policy and reporting back on the people's reactions to it (Nkomo 1984:124).

Nkomo's hut, where he received visitors, dignitaries and journalists, was called "State House".

The detainees lived in five separate camps, each with its own administration. At first communication among the camps was relatively easy, but with restrictions on movement and visitors and the fencing of the camps, they were forced to function more autonomously, with consultation through the circulation of written messages (Ncube 2008). Newcomers with party posts were assigned to administrative roles and set about gathering the sort of information about resources and population on which bureaucratic states depended to make their citizens visible and to establish a normative basis for claims to legitimacy. Victor Kuretu, an early entrant into Gonakudzingwa, describes how Nkomo, told us at our arrival that we had to run the detention camp along the lines of a "government". "This meant keeping track of its citizenry." We kept intricate records of every inmate, with details about their names, places of origin and so forth. We generated a number of records that filled books (Munochiveyi 2008). While he was resident in Gonakudzingwa, R. K. Naik served as treasurer for the overall administration. He kept meticulous records of party funds, and the funds and goods brought into the camp by well-wishers and visitors: "I had a receipt book and everything. We had to. How can I justify what I've done otherwise? Everything is recorded" (Naik 2008). The committee structure was specialised and expert, "so as to reflect government" as another detainee put it (Nyathi 2009). The orderliness, specialisation and record-keeping was something of which many detainees were and still are extremely proud; this was the "proper" basis of authority. John Mzimela explained, "we had order and discipline. We had a register of our own [...]. We had a pure administration laid out" (Mzimela 2009). Jane Ngwenya exclaimed, "We had committees; we were organised; we could run a government!" (Ngwenya 2008).

Figure 1: ZAPU Leaders at Gonakudzingwa

Insights from Ex-Detainees

On 6 September 2011, one of the researchers had the privilege to accompany six ex-detainees to Gonakudzingwa. The major purpose of the trip was to conduct an on-site interview with them since they have first-hand information about the site. The other aim of the visit was to record the history of the place for posterity. The trip was a

305

follow-up to another one which was conducted on the 16th of June 2011 and was criticized by the general public for not being granted fair media coverage. The first visit to Gonakudzingwa was initiated by Mr. Mazorodze, a Voluntary Social Worker who also coordinated the second trip. The six ex-detainees interviewed include, Cde N. Ndlovu, Cde Jane Ngwenya, Cde I. Chakanyuka, Cde T. Macharaga, Cde K. Kayenda and Cde D. Hunda. The information gathered shaded more light on different knowledge gaps that existed concerning the history of the site (NMMZ File 2011). Albeit, the researcher remained conscious about the challenges and limitations of oral information and to counter this, a cross examination of information among ex-detainees was done. From the interviews carried out, it emerged that ex-detainees wanted Gonakudzingwa to be nominated on the National Register List as a national monument taking into cognizance its role in the liberation of the country. They highlighted that the liberation history of the country is incomplete without mentioning Gonakudzingwa. Besides, they echoed the need for the site to be properly protected and rehabilitated so that future generations will be able to know the bitter history of Zimbabwe. Apart from that, they reiterated the fact that the government should be proactive in protecting and marketing this priceless heritage.

Adding to that, the ex-detainees lamented the need to clear the other parts of the site from landmines so that the whole area can be fully rehabilitated with a view to promote and develop the site for purposes of tourism as is happening in neighbouring countries such as South Africa. In South Africa, Robben Island where the late President Mandela was detained has been developed and turned into a vibrant tourism centre currently generating money for the country while at the same time preserving their rich cultural heritage. More so, they also voiced the need to engage some of the surviving people who were working at the site during its functional period with a view to interview them and record their experiences. It was noted that some of these people are residing in the nearby contemporary local communities.

Gonakudzingwa today

Today Gonakudzingwa stands out mainly as house remains, particularly floors and a few standing walls. These remains are scattered over an area of about 2 square kilometres. The southern part of the camp has modern buildings. These buildings include houses and offices for ZIMRA, ZINWA, Immigration Officials as well as a Police Camp. The northern part of the camp is in a thick forest. Generally most of the buildings have collapsed. The southern section has a number of new buildings that have been built on remains of the camp. It is in this area that floors are visible. On the northern edge of the camp are remains of houses. There is only one building that still has standing walls but the walls are ridden with bullet holes. The site is currently protected and managed by the Sango Border Post Police Camp. It also receives attention from the Zimbabwe National Army who carries out occasional demining operations of anti-personnel landmines which were planted at the height of the liberation struggle. The landmines remain a serious potential hazard within the vicinities of the site. The site is virtually in a state of neglect. There is no regular monitoring of the Gonakudzingwa Detention Camp site that takes place besides sporadic visits which are made by NMMZ Officials from its Southern Region and these are normally carried out upon specialised requests from interested quarters of the society.

Figure 2: Concrete slabs at Gonakudzingwa, being all that remains of the camp in 2011

Beyond the Gonakudzingwa edifice: Some recommendations

The ex-detainees recommended that the history of Gonakudzingwa should be recorded and published for present and the future generations. It was noted that the liberation war heritage of Zimbabwe is incomplete if important places such as Gonakudzingwa are not put on the limelight. They were not happy about the way the place is being preserved as it is not being given fair attention in terms of maintenance and protection (NMMZ File 2011). In view of this, they recommended that the place be spruced and uplifted in order to portray a correct image of the liberation heritage. Add to that, the ex-detainees noted that funds permitting the place should be developed for purposes of tourism drawing lessons from Robben Island in South Africa. Equally important is the need to construct a shrine on the site to remind the present and future generations about the struggle towards the freedom of Zimbabwe. It was suggested that a statue of Joshua Nkomo can also be erected on the site and during historical national commemoration days such as the Independence Day and the Heroes Day people from Chiredzi District and others across the country will converge and celebrate at the shrine. It is also recommended that the stories, histories, and contributions of ex-political detainees to the freedom of Zimbabwe as well as the places they resided such as Gonakudzingwa should be properly recorded and archived for posterity.

Conclusion

Liberation heritage sites are highly contested hence they can be very divisive if not properly managed. As such, the government through the National Museums and Monuments of Zimbabwe must be very careful when it comes to issues of nominating such politically and emotionally sensitive places as detention camps. An objective reflection on the past political imbalances as well as a critical introspection of the current political terrain in the country should be seriously taken into account before undertaking such actions. Such issues may be particularly controversial in societies challenged by divisions based on ethnic and or linguistic backgrounds such as the case in Zimbabwe. Nominating Sikombela on the National Monument Register and overlooking Gonakudzingwa tantamount to inflicting pain on a healing wound. The chapter has shown that detention camps played a crucial role in the liberation of Zimbabwe hence, there is urgent need to rehabilitate them for posterity. If properly managed, detention camps can be used as centres of fostering national unity and identity.

References

Feltoe, G. 1978. Law, Ideology and Coercion in Southern Rhodesia, *MPhil Thesis*, University of Kent.

Munochiveyi, M.B. 2008. 'It was a difficult time in Zimbabwe': A history of imprisonment, detention, and confinement during Zimbabwe's liberation struggle, 1960-1980'', PhD Thesis, University of Minnesota.

Munochiveyi 2014. Prisoners of Rhodesia, Palgrave Macmillan, New York.

Mzimela, J. 2009. Interview, 4 February 2009, Bulawayo in Alexander, J. n.d. Nationalism and Self-Government in

Rhodesian Detention: Gonakudzingwa, 1964-1974, University of Oxford.

Ncube, F. D. 2008. Interview, 1 October 2008, Bulawayo in Alexander, J. n.d. Nationalism and Self-Government in Rhodesian Detention: Gonakudzingwa, 1964-1974, University of Oxford.

Ngwenya, J. 2008. Interview, 14 October 2008, Bulawayo in Alexander, J. n.d. Nationalism and Self-Government in Rhodesian Detention: Gonakudzingwa, 1964-1974, University of Oxford.

Nkomo, J. 1984. *Nkomo: The Story of My Life,* London, Methuen.

NMMZ File. 2006. Great Zimbabwe National Monument, National Museums and Monuments of Zimbabwe.

NMMZ File. 2009. Great Zimbabwe National Monument, National Museums and Monuments of Zimbabwe.

NMMZ File 2011. Great Zimbabwe National Monument, National Museums and Monuments of Zimbabwe.

Nyathi, T. P. 2009. Interview, 29 September 2009, Bulawayo in Alexander, J. n.d. Nationalism and Self-Government in Rhodesian Detention: Gonakudzingwa, 1964-1974, University of Oxford.

Chapter Fourteen

Colonial Land Husbandry Measures and African Responses: A Case Study of the Mutasa Chiefdom in Rhodesia, 1941-1975

Fidelis P. T. Duri

Introduction

This chapter examines African responses to environmental conservation measures imposed by the Rhodesian (colonial Zimbabwean) government. With reference to the Mutasa Chiefdom of Manyika in eastern Rhodesia, it explores how the British administration enforced environmental conservation measures from the early 1940s until 1975 when the programme was suspended owing to the intensification of the national armed struggle for independence. The colonial government wrongly assumed that Africans lacked environmental management strategies and failed to acknowledge its involvement in aggravating land degradation through annexing land from Africans and resettling them in mountainous, semi-arid, unproductive and overcrowded conditions. The Natural Resources Act, Chapter 20, of 1941 and the Native Land Husbandry Act, Chapter 9, of 1951, for example, imposed various conservation measures such as destocking, resettling Africans in a spatially linear residential pattern and compelling them to erect contour ridges in farmlands (Birmingham and Martin 1983; Murray 1970).

Contrary to the discourses of Afrocentricity, this chapter argues that African responses to particular aspects of colonial rule were varied and far from being homogenous. They largely depended on the extent to which various sections of the African population, together with their socioeconomic livelihood dynamics, were equitably accommodated by the colonial order. It should be noted that colonial land husbandry measures were not a major grievance for some sections of the African population. These included wealthy

Africans who had bought large tracts of land and some labour migrants who had sought alternative means of livelihood away from their rural areas. Other colonial husbandry policies such as destocking tended to antagonise those Africans who owned large herds of cattle than those who did not. In the case of Africans who were negatively affected, there was no uniformity in terms of resistance but that specific sections of the population tended to direct their concerns at particular environmental measures that severely eroded their livelihoods. The African elite capitalised on these localised but widespread concerns and packaged them into a nationalist collectivity that became a critical mobilisation resource in the struggle against colonial rule.

Given that environmental management was an important aspect of life in pre-colonial Africa, most colonial husbandry measures were not a peculiar or drastic development. Most provisions of the Land Husbandry Act, for example, were not very different from pre-colonial African environmental management systems. In actual fact, most colonial environmental preservation measures could have been favourably received by many Africans were it not for the Land Apportionment Act, Chapter 6, of 1930 and other statutes that had deprived them of the most productive land and its natural resources. The resistance by sections of the African population to colonial environmental measures, therefore, should not be viewed as a nostalgic reaction to modernity.

This chapter makes a significant contribution to the 21st century development debates on global environmental sustainability. It informs that the success of externally-initiated and elite-driven natural resource management programmes largely hinges on the extent to which they create a sustainable balance between the proposed outcomes of the development agenda and the socioeconomic complexities and livelihood dynamics of local communities.

African indigenous environmental management systems in pre-colonial Zimbabwe

As was the case in the greater part of the African continent during the pre-colonial period, land tenure formed the basis of environmental management in many Shona chiefdoms in Zimbabwe such as Manyika under the Mutasa dynasty. Shona chiefs and their administrative subordinates, who included ward heads (headmen and headwomen) and village heads, had the power to distribute land and regulate its use in terms of settlement, grazing and hunting. The chiefs also controlled the exploitation of resources such as vegetation, game and minerals. The political leadership allocated individual land rights for settlement and growing crops although hunting grounds and pastures were communally owned and utilised by people from specific villages or wards (Beach 1984; Bourdillon 1976).

Some pre-colonial African chiefs sometimes encouraged their subjects to migrate into less densely populated areas in order to reduce pressure on natural resources (Duri and Mapara 2007). When the population of the Mutasa Chiefdom shot up to over 14 000 between the years 1750 and 1800, for example, the chiefs allowed their subjects to move into the Nyanga Plateau (Bhila 1982).

Most colonial administrators believed that Africans were "irresponsible and reckless with the environment to the extent of jeopardising their existence and that of future generations" (Duri and Mapara 2007: 98). African land rotation cultivation, for example, was regarded as "slash-and-burn" to give the impression that it was environmentally destructive (Palmer 1977: 15). What the colonial observers failed to appreciate was that this farming technique was "a concession to the nature of the soil" than "a relic of barbarism" (Hailey 1957: 819). This cropping mechanism was "very adaptable to areas with low population densities and extensive tracts of land that permitted other unoccupied areas to be fallowed for long periods" (Duri and Mapara 2007: 102). It was not that destructive considering that the ashes from the burnt vegetation in specific places enriched the soil with nutrients (Jackson and Jackson 1996). In addition, the burning was controlled and destroyed weeds and pests (Booth, McCullum, Mpinga and Mukute 1994).

Contrary to the views held by most colonial administrators, many pre-colonial African societies employed various measures to prevent soil erosion. By the 15th century, for example, Africans in the mountainous areas of the Mutasa Chiefdom and the neighbouring Nyanga region constructed stone terraces along hill slopes to reduce soil erosion (Bhila 1982). In this area, noted Bulpin (1968: 61) there were "countless miles of contour terracing where man struggled to cultivate the steepest of slopes." Similar pre-colonial structures are found in other parts of Africa such as the Kainam Hills in Tanzania (Booth, McCullum, Mpinga and Mukute 1994) and the Jos Plateau in Nigeria (Faniran and Ojo 1980).

Since cattle were symbols of wealth in pre-colonial Zimbabwe, Mutasa traditional leaders allocated each village or groups of villages land pastures where cultivation was prohibited (Bhila 1982). Transhumance grazing, with advantages similar to modern padlocking, was an ecologically sustainable practice by most African pastoralists to prevent overgrazing (Beach 1984). Wealthy people sometimes loaned or sold cattle to those from other areas in order to guard against overstocking and overgrazing. In the Mutapa state during the 18th century, the cattle owned by rulers were so many that they loaned some to their subjects as far away from the capital city as 150 kilometres (Mudenge 1988). Among the Manyika people of Chief Mutasa, wealthy individuals often loaned some of their cattle to relatives and friends residing in distant areas (Bhila 1982). During the early 1890s, the Ndebele king, Lobengula, loaned more than 50% of his cattle to subject people in Mashonaland who hired them in return for utilising their manure and milk (Stigger 1980). Being symbols of wealth, cattle were rarely slaughtered for food. There is, however, no record of overstocking or overgrazing in pre-colonial Zimbabwe largely because of the sustainable indigenous livestock management systems that were put in place. It is, however, prudent to avoid romanticising the African past and its dynamics as a collectivity (Adeleke 2009). The number of cattle one possessed was one of the ways of distinguishing between the rich and the poor in most pre-colonial African societies. Cattle possession can actually constitute one of the analytical criteria for defining the relations between the rich and the poor. During the early 1890s, for example, King Lobengula raided some Shona subject chiefs after they had refused to return the cattle he had loaned them (Ranger 1967).

Some African traditional authorities strictly enforced wildlife conservation strategies in their societies. This was largely because of the critical role played by wildlife resources in people's livelihoods during the pre-colonial era. Game meat, insects and fruits, for example, were an important part of the diet. The preservation of ecological zones such as forests and wetlands was therefore absolutely necessary since they provided food and habitat for wild animals. In addition, trees were important for firewood and timber while grass was used for thatching. Several plant species were important herbs while vegetative cover protects the water cycle and reduces soil erosion (Duri and Mapara 2007).

Chiefs also crafted institutional prohibitions such as taboos to safeguard the environment. In the Mutasa Chiefdom, for instance, it was taboo to cut the *muchakata* tree (*parinari curatellifolia*) on grounds that it provided shed during most traditional rituals. The reality on the ground was that its fruits were an important source of food for both people and wild animals such as monkeys and baboons (Bulpin 1968).

Certain species of vegetation were also preserved because they were habitat and food for some insects that were important to the human diet. Since the 18th century, Norumedzo, a 50-hectare forest in the Bikita District in south-eastern Zimbabwe, for example, has been a habitat of edible stink bugs (*Encosternum Delegorgue*) known as *harurwa* by the local Karanga people. This mini-livestock was critical to the livelihood of the indigenous people as a delicacy, staple and an item of trade. Since the pre-colonial period, chiefs, with the support of their administrative hierarchies and local communities, declared the Norumedzo Forest a protected area and supervised its preservation, owing to the importance of the insects to people's livelihoods. The harvesting of the bugs was regulated by the traditional leaders in an attempt to protect vegetation. The cutting down of trees and smoking in the area were strictly prohibited. Indigenous epistemological mechanisms were also crafted to mythologise the forest in order to make it taboo for people to cut trees in the area for firewood and other uses (Dzerefos 2014; Makuku 1993; Mapendcmbc 2004; Maredza 1987; Mawere 2013, 2014; Schabell 2010). This community habitat stewardship illustrates the importance of indigenous institutions in maintaining a sustainable balance between consumption needs and the conservation of natural resources.

Other vegetative species such as the *mubvamaropa* tree (*pierocarpus angolensis*) and the *zumbani* plant (*Lippia javanica*) were specifically

315

preserved for their medicinal properties (Duri and Mapara 2007). The sustainable utilisation of the vegetative environment by most pre-colonial African societies shows that they were "very much, men of trees, living so close to nature that they sought no way to alter it ..." (Bulpin 1968: 15).

The preservation of game was another important aspect of life in most pre-colonial African societies. As is the case with modern national parks, pre-colonial African chiefs set aside certain lands for the hunting of wild animals where cultivation was prohibited. Attempts were made to ensure that hunting was done in a systematic and sustainable manner. In an effort to take stock of animals hunted in their areas, some Shona chiefs in pre-colonial Zimbabwe demanded one tusk for every elephant killed (Beach 1994; Bourdillon 1976). Some Shona chiefs were also entitled to certain parts of game such as hearts and skins of lions and leopard skins while pangolins were wholly surrendered (Garbett 1966; Holleman 1951). Indiscriminate hunting was strictly prohibited. The killing of young animals and female ones, particularly those that were pregnant, was discouraged (Booth, McCullum, Mpinga and Mukute 1994). The use of traps during hunting and fishing was also discouraged since it resulted in the indiscriminate killing of animals such as the females, the pregnant, the young and even those that were not part of the human diet (Booth, McCullum, Mpinga and Mukute 1994; Duri and Mapara 2007; Tatira 2000). Totemic taboos were also instituted in most Shona societies to prevent the depletion of game animals. According to Bourdilllon (1976), it was taboo for one to eat his or her totem animal. Since most Manyika and other Shona societies have totem animals such as elephant, buffalo, zebra, eland, fish and birds, such taboos played a critical role in wildlife conservation (Duri and Mapara 2007).

Various measures were also taken to protect water bodies from pollution. There were Shona taboos specifically meant to prevent the contamination of water bodies. One taboo was that water sources would dry up if people cleaned pots and linen near them. Another cautioned that a well dried up if people sought fish from it. The other warned that one would become sterile after urinating in a well (Tatira 2000). These taboos were environmental management strategies meant to protect water bodies.

It should be noted, however, that African indigenous environmental systems had their own challenges. The existence of such community taboos did not in any way suggest the existence of a homogenous and utopian pre-colonial African society. People of the elephant totem, for example, could wipe out the number of buffalo herds in their area. In addition, as Beach (1984) notes, some Shona subjects, driven by the profit motive, breached hunting regulations in the same manner as poachers operate in the contemporary world. The high demand for ivory by the Portuguese traders during the early 16th century, for instance, intensified elephant hunting by the Shona. As a result, the elephant population "gradually disappeared" and by the late 18th century, one European traveller noted that "there are no elephants in the country and therefore, there is no ivory" (Bhila 1982: 34). In addition, taboos that were meant to preserve various animal and plant species were sometimes violated by some people as they sought livelihoods (Duri and Mapara 2007). Again, most, if not all, of the indigenous knowledge systems associated with environmental management were not written and could be interpreted differently by future generations and other communities (Mukwindidza 2008). Such challenges, however, do not in any way discredit the efforts of Africans to preserve their environment during the pre-colonial era.

This discussion, therefore, falsifies the views of most Rhodesian colonial environmentalists that African agricultural practices were not environmentally sustainable and that they were generally hesitant to accept European land husbandry standards. Gale (1960:151-152) for example, said, "The African peasant has an instinctive distrust of instructors whose colour differs from his own, and the instruction has to be done by his fellow Africans. Nor is it sufficient merely to instruct. The new ways must be demonstrated and the instructor must stay on the job to see that the lessons have gone firmly home." It is now quite apparent that, contrary to the assumptions of most colonial apologists, African societies in Africa in general and Zimbabwe in particular employed a surfeit of strategies to utilise the environment in a sustainable manner. As will be noted in the next section, colonial land policies actually triggered an environmental catastrophe.

Colonial land husbandry policies could not have dismally failed had its administrators integrated some of the indigenous knowledge systems and factored in the involvement of African communities as willing participants in a dispensation free of racial discrimination in the access to natural resources. It should be noted, however, that some African indigenous environmental management systems were rather localised to be applicable to the 21st century world, given the changing dynamics associated with urbanisation, globalisation and cosmopolitanism, among others. Despite these developments, some of the indigenous environmental knowledge systems can be positively modified and utilised to address contemporary global challenges. Natural fertilisers from the immediate environment, for example, can be used as substitutes for chemical fertilisers which contaminate water with phosphates and nitrates. Herbs from the natural environment can also provide affordable alternative medicines that can alleviate the contemporary global health challenges related to HIV/ AIDS, among others.

Colonial land policies and environmental degradation prior to the mid-1930s

Massive annexation of African land in Rhodesia, particularly in the province of Mashonaland, by Europeans began with the arrival of the British South Africa Company (BSAC)-sponsored Pioneer Column in 1890. Having defeated the Ndebele in 1893, the BSAC displaced the Ndebele from their land and resettled them in the unproductive Gwaai and Shangani reserves (Palmer 1977). The Southern Rhodesia Order-in-Council of 1898 officially robbed the traditional leaders of powers to allocate land to their subjects. This policy document approved the annexation of land by white farmers and miners and recommended the creation of African reserves in Mashonaland (Bratton 1978; Rifkind 1968). It also empowered Native Commissioners to allocate land for African huts, gardens and pastures and specifically forbade traditional leaders from organising fresh villages or allocating land to people (Palley 1966).

By the year 1900, many portions of land within the Mutasa Chiefdom had been turned into European mining areas, estates and commercial farms leaving many Africans overcrowded in mountainous areas. In July 1899, for example, Little of Penhalonga Proprietary Mines Limited successfully requested the Native Commissioner for Umtali to relocate all people under Ward Head Nyakuwanikwa resident within the vicinity of the mines (NAZ, N3/1/19: 23 August 1899). By the year 1901, Headman Muchena's ward had been swallowed up by Coldstream Farm owned by Cocknell (NAZ, NUA1/1/1: 16 April 1901). During the same year, Headman Saungweme suffered the same fate after being evicted from the Penhalonga area to pave way for the establishment of St Augustine's Farm (NAZ, NUA2/1/4: 21 February 1901). While some of Chief Mutasa's ward heads, village heads and their subjects were forced to move out of their lands, some remained as tenants on the newly-established commercial farms, estates and mining areas (Bhila 1982; NAZ, NUA1/1/2: 26 August 1903).

In 1902, the process of setting up reserves in Mashonaland Province, in which the Mutasa Chiefdom was located, began (Rifkind 1968). As similar developments took place countrywide, the dispossession of Africans from their original lands and the subsequent resettlement exercise resulted in the overcrowding of people and livestock in the reserves. By 1910, for example, Africans and more than 700 000 of their cattle were crowded in reserves about 8.7 million hectares in extent across Rhodesia (Chitiyo 2007).

With the appointment of the Native Reserves Commission by the Secretary of State for Colonies in 1914, further annexation of land took place and more reserves were set aside for African settlement in the whole of Rhodesia (Haw 1965). A direct result of the 1914 Commission was the establishment of the Mutasa North Reserve in the Honde Valley in the northern part of the Mutasa Chiefdom in 1917 (NAZ, NUA2/1/10: 1917 Umtali District Annual Report).

The Land Apportionment Act, Chapter 6, of 1930 institutionalised the racial division of land in terms of both quality and quantity (Chivandi, Fushai and Masaka 2010; Mukwindidza 2008). It allocated 50.8% of land in the country to the whites, 30% to the Africans in the reserves while the remaining 20% was owned by the government and companies or set aside as conservation areas (Chivandi, Fushai and Masaka 2010). This allocation was grossly inequitable considering that there were about 1 081 000 Africans and 50 000 Europeans in Rhodesia in 1930 (Mupfuvi 2014).

Environmental degradation resulting from overcrowding worsened in the reserves since Africans, who constituted the majority of the population, were allocated less land as compared to the minority whites. In addition, most of the reserves were located in the mountainous and semi-arid Agro-Ecological Regions Four and Five that were relatively unproductive and vulnerable to soil erosion (Chivandi, Fushai and Masaka 2010). The Act also created 'Native Areas,' which could be purchased by Africans and worked on an individual basis. With the introduction of Native Areas, many African peasants were displaced and resettled in the already existing and newly created reserves (Palmer 1977; Rifkind 1968). The displacements and subsequent resettlement exercises overcrowded the reserves resulting in massive land degradation. By December 1930, nearly all the annual reports of Native Commissioners countrywide complained that African reserves within their districts were heavily congested (Rifkind 1968).

As Native Purchase Areas were established, new reserves were created while the existing ones became overcrowded (Ranger 1960). In 1933 the colonial administration began surveying land in order to open up Mutasa North, Mutasa South and Jenya reserves (NAZ, S235/511/3: 1933 Umtali District Annual Report), owing to the overcrowded conditions in other reserves within the Mutasa Chiefdom such as Manga and Manyika (NAZ, S235/511/3: 1933 Inyanga District Annual Report). It can be noted that colonial land annexation resulted in serious environmental degradation countrywide.

Imposition of colonial environmental conservation in the Mutasa Chiefdom, 1941-1974

From the mid-1930s, the Rhodesia Agricultural Union became very concerned about soil and water conservation in both European and African areas. The Natural Resources Board was established in 1941 to look into the condition of land in the reserves (Murray 1970). The Natural Resources Act, Chapter 20, of 1941 made Native Commissioners responsible for soil and water conservation in their districts. They were given authority to reduce the numbers of livestock and give orders on methods of cultivation, prohibit cultivation of certain lands and the control of water (Birmingham and Martin 1983; Murray 1970). The Natural Resources Board appointed Land Development Officers to implement the provisions of the Act and ensure that Africans constructed contour ridges in their fields and covered up galleys in their areas to prevent soil erosion, among other things (Artkinson 1972). In 1943, the Destocking Regulations Act was passed to get rid of excess cattle (Mupfuvi 2014). In line with the provisions of the Act, the government identified 49 reserves in the country that were overstocked by 29 December 1944. In the Mutasa Chiefdom, the Jenya, Mutasa South and Manyika reserves were considered overstocked. Jenya was reportedly overstocked by 266 cattle (184%), Mutasa South by 675 cattle (52%) and Manyika by 2110 cattle (67%) (Mupfuvi 2014). The Government Notice of 1944 introduced compulsory destocking in 40 reserves countrywide (Murray 1970).

Ezekiel Makunike (1998), an African journalist, whose home area was Nyakatsapa Village close to Chief Mutasa's headquarters, recalled how colonial destocking policies were implemented. Every household in the village was ordered to have not more than four head of cattle. His father had more than 25 beasts. The African cattle-dipping superintendent at each dipping tank would announce ahead of time about the pending visit of buyers of 'excess' livestock. Most of the cattle-buyers were whites who owned butcheries in urban areas. On the day when the buyers were coming, every African cattle-owner was supposed to come with the whole herd to the dipping tank. Makunike (1998: 3) lamented how his father lost more than 25 cattle in one day in 1944:

> Cattle were weighed on an industrial scale and the price depended on the weight of each animal. Cattle owners had no hand in determining the rate per pound. There was no mutual bargaining. I will never forget the anger I had at seeing the many huge and impressive fat oxen we had in our stock just being herded away. They went and disappeared just like that, and while we watched in despair.

Makunike's father was particularly pained because cattle, which had been a symbol of wealth during the pre-colonial period, had assumed new income-generating roles for innovative Africans in the colonial dispensation. Ox-drawn wagons had become important sources of wealth through transporting maize, beans and other goods for African producers to the nearby markets in the towns of Penhalonga and Umtali. His father had bought two four-wheeled wagons and used to span 16 oxen (eight pairs) to pull each wagon, sometimes loaded with up to 50 bags of maize. The micro-business collapsed as a result of colonial destocking measures (Makunike 1998).

These environmental conservation efforts did not bear much fruit as African reserves increasingly became overcrowded owing to the continuation of land seizures in order to create space for Native Purchase Areas, Second World War ex-servicemen and the rising number of white settlers and businesspeople during the 1940s. In 1944, Muponda, Chief Mutasa's headman, and his people were forced out of their traditional home around Mount Ruunji when Meikle bought the farm from the Manhattan Syndicate (NAZ, S2985/LAN/1: August 1952, Umtali Native Commissioner's Minutes). Muponda and a number of his people were resettled in the Mutasa North Reserve in the Honde Valley while some of his followers were resettled in the Zongoro area, near Manyika Bridge, and Mafararikwa in Bocha. On arrival in the Honde Valley some of Muponda's subjects opened up areas of settlement in the Mupotedzi ward. The subsequent overcrowded conditions resulted in conflict between Muponda and Mupotedzi ward heads (NAZ, S2985/LAN/1: August 1952, Umtali Native Commissioner's Minutes).

With the establishment and expansion of the Tsonzo Native Purchase Area close to Chief Mutasa's village, many African families were evicted from the area. In 1948, for example, more than 200 families that had been displaced were moved to the Mahwemasimike area in Holdenby Reserve (NAZ, S2807/4. 30 May 1949: Provincial Native Commissioner, Manicaland, to Chief Native Commissioner). In 1956, some families 'illegally' occupying the Tsonzo Native Purchase Area were ordered to move to the Marange Reserve which was located outside the Mutasa Chiefdom (NAZ, S2807/4, 1956: Southern Rhodesia Government Notice, Number 41). The displacement of Africans led to overcrowded conditions and massive environmental degradation in the reserves. The Government Notice, Number 612, of 1944 declared that 49 African reserves countrywide were overstocked (Weinmann 1996).

Environmental degradation became rampant as African reserves became congested (Ranger 1960). In 1949, the Danziger Commission noted that the combined area of African reserves in Rhodesia could not adequately accommodate Africans (Rifkind 1968). In June 1950, W.E. Winterton, the Minister of Native Affairs, revealed that African reserves in the country were accommodating 286 405 families against a recommended carrying capacity of 266 405 families (Rifkind 1968).

The Native Land Husbandry Act, Chapter 9, of 1951 was largely meant to address the environmental catastrophe in the African reserves. It was "one of the most progressive measures attempted in Africa" (Rifkind 1972: 59) and "one of the most far-reaching land-reform measures in Africa" (Yudelman 1964: 117), given that the "deterioration of African areas had reached alarming proportions by 1950" (Kay 1971: 88). The Act imposed farming methods on Africans and ordered that all land in rural areas, with the exception of pastures, be individually owned and worked on a peasant-farmer basis (Murray 1970; Rifkind 1968). On the average, the Act reduced arable land holding to 3.2 hectares and a maximum of five cattle per family (Makanyisa, Chemhuru and Masitera 2012). Traditional leaders were also stripped of powers to allocate land (Murray 1970; Steele 1973). The allocation of farming and grazing land was now done by Native Commissioners and their subordinates such as Land Development Officers and Assessment Committees. The Assessment Committee for the Mutasa South Reserve in 1952, for example, was headed by R.L.D. Herbert, the Native Commissioner for Umtali. He was assisted by D.R.C. Thomas, the Land Development Officer (LDO) for Watsomba Station (NAZ, S2808/1/20: 1954-1960). In October 1952, the colonial administration instructed African traditional leaders in Mutasa North Reserve to forbid their subjects from ploughing on steep slopes and not to open up new lands until a Native Commissioner (NC), LDO, Demonstrator or Land Assessment Committees had authorised them to do so (NAZ, S2985/ LAN/ 1, LDO Watsomba, to NC Umtali, 18 October 1952). The Land Development Committees also compelled the Africans to rearrange their dwellings in a linear pattern to distinguish between pastures and land for cultivation. Many Africans came to call the village *raini*, the vernacular term for a line, because of the linear arrangement of their homesteads (Garbett 1960).

Chiefs and ward heads were forced to supervise the conservation of land yet they no longer had any authority to allocated land to their subjects. In 1952, for example, the Land Development Officer for Watsomba instructed ward heads of the Mutasa North Reserve to ensure that their subjects would not plough on steep slopes and not to open new lands which had not been recommended by a Demonstrator (NAZ, S2985/LAN/1, LDO, Watsomba, to NC Umtali: 18 October 1952).

The colonial administration ordered traditional leaders to supervise the destocking of their areas as African reserves increasingly became overcrowded. Mayika and Manga reserves, for example, were declared overstocked by 3 219 and 404 cattle respectively in December 1951 (NAZ, S2827/2/2/1, Inyanga District NC's Annual Report: 1951). During the course of 1952, Assessment Committees for various reserves within the Mutasa Chiefdom recommended the maximum number of animal units a village could possess and traditional leaders were tasked with ensuring that this regulation was not violated (NAZ, S2403/ 2682, Inyanga District NC's Annual Report: 1952). In the Manyika Reserve, destocking was carried out for the first time in 1952 during which Africans were sometimes forced to sell each head of cattle to the whites for as low as £2-10 (NAZ, S2403/ 2682, Inyanga District NC's Annual Report: 1952; Nyado, Interview: 5 August 1998). During early March 1952, 267 head of African cattle were sold out to Europeans in a single day in Mutasa South Reserve (NAZ, S1618, Umtali Native Commissioner Quarterly Report: 31 March 1952). During the same year, Manga Reserve was also declared overstocked by about 600 cattle (NAZ, S2403/ 2682, Inyanga District NC's Annual Report: 1952). Throughout the year 1952, destocking was carried out in various reserves in the Mutasa Chiefdom such as Mutasa North and Mutasa South where pressure on land was declared as serious by colonial administrators (NAZ, S2403/ 2681, Umtali District NC's Annual Report: 1952). In 1955, the Assessment Committee for the Jenya Reserve decided to reduce the number of animal units (cattle) per African household to six and that five goats would equal one animal unit (NAZ, S2808/1/20, Jenya Reserve Assessment Committee Meeting: 20 May 1955). Compulsory destocking in the Masukume Village in Jenya Reserve resulted in the reduction of African cattle from 600 in 1946 to 151 in May 1955 (NAZ, S2808/1/20, Jenya Reserve Assessment Committee Meeting: 20 May 1955).

Colonial Demonstrators and teams of peggers also assisted the Assessment Committees in deciding specific lands which were to be cultivated. During the year 1952, for example, a soil conservation group comprising Africans operated in the Manyika Reserve in the western part of the Mutasa Chiefdom (NAZ, S2403/ 2682, Inyanga District NC's Annual Report, 1952).

Ward heads were also compelled to assist Demonstrators, usually by supplying pegs and additional manpower. On 21 March 1962, for example, a land inspectorate team visited Headman Fezayi Zindi and told him that his present lands and those he wished to plant the following season had to be pegged before cultivation took place. He was also instructed to be responsible for the conservation of his area. For the pegging, he was ordered to supply the pegs and the necessary labour to assist the peggers (Mutasa District Administrator Per 5/1 Files: 23 March 1967).

Ward heads were also ordered to set up courts where violators of land conservation measures were tried. Native Commissioners and Land Development Officers usually convened meetings with individual ward heads to decide on punitive measures to be applied. The table below shows the court fees and charges stipulated for the Zindi and Samanga wards in 1971 for violating land conservation measures (Mutasa District Administrator Per 5/1 Files: 1971).

Table 1: Court fees and charges for violating the land husbandry measures in Zindi and Samanga wards, 1971

	CHARGES ZINDI	CHARGES SAMANGA
Hearing Fee.	$2.00	$1.00
Messengers' Fee.	75c	50c-75c
Conservation Work not up to standard.	$2.50	$1.00
Not completing Conservation Work on time.	$4.50	$4.50
Use of Sleighs.	$5.00	$5.00
Removal of Conservation Beacons.	$8.00	$4.00
Cultivation of land without permission from Kraalhead and Tribal Land Authority.	$10.00	$3.00
Cultivation of new land without permission from farmer.	$4.50	$10.00
Insult to Tribal Land Authority members on duty.	$10.00	$10.00

African responses and the failure of colonial environmental measures in the Mutasa Chiefdom

African responses to colonial environmental measures were varied and far from being homogenous. The varied responses tended to be generally localised and determined by the extent to which the livelihoods of specific social groups were affected by particular colonial environmental measures. The middle-class Africans, for example, could afford to buy relatively large tracts of land in the Native Purchase Areas and were less aggrieved than their subaltern counterparts who resided in the overcrowded reserves where colonial conservation measures such as destocking were strictly enforced.

The establishment of Native Purchase Areas created a class of small African landowners whose class position became a threat to the power of traditional rulers. About 52 farmers from the Tsonzo Native Purchase Area held a meeting on 23 December 1953 at St Mathias School to form the Tsonzo Native Council. Council members were elected during the meeting but Chief Chimuriwo Mutasa was not part of the Council. In 1955, the colonial government officially approved the establishment of the Tsonzo Native Council. During the same year, the council went on to draft its own by-laws which were later approved by the government (NAZ, S2797/2636, Minutes of Tsonzo Native Council: 30 December 1955). With the establishment of the Native Purchase Area in his chiefdom, Chief Mutasa no longer had any authority over the Tsonzo area. This was confirmed by the Chief Land Officer in 1949 when he said, "Landowners in the Native Purchase Area have never been considered as coming under the jurisdiction of a chief" (NAZ, S2807/4, Chief Land Officer to CNC: 31 May 1949). Chief Chimuriwo Mutasa complained on 6 July 1958 that he was unable to exercise traditional control on land holders (NAZ, S2807/4, PNC to CNC: 30 May 1949). In 1949, the Chief Native Commissioner had also expressed Chief Mutasa' discomfort: "What Mutasa really wants is to have Tsonzo as a Native Reserve, to add to his own power and prestige, and he seems to regard any of his followers who apply for land in Tsonzo area as disloyal to him" (NAZ, S2807/4, CNC to Ian Wilson: 4 June 1949).

Colonial conservation measures were very unpopular among the ordinary African people especially in conditions of land alienation (Kwashirai 2006; Makanyisa, Chemhuru and Masitera 2012). As Chitiyo (2007: 1) noted, "Impoverished, alienated and landless, peasants have traditionally opposed state interventions through 'silent' violence." One strategy of resistance was the refusal to cooperate with colonial conservation officials. On 4 June 1949, for example, the Chief Native Commissioner reported:

> The Director of Native Agriculture tells me that the people in the area (Mutasa Chiefdom), especially the Chief (Mutasa) and his followers, have never, during the past 18 years, shown any inclination to profit by the visual lessons taught by the Demonstrator, and have always regarded him with dislike and distrust... (NAZ, S2807/4, CNC to Ian Wilson: 4 June 1949).

The resistance, mostly by the severely marginalised sections of the African population, to colonial environmental measures should not be interpreted as a nostalgic reaction to modernity. It has been demonstrated earlier on in this chapter that Africans employed various environmental conservation strategies during the pre-colonial Africa. In actual fact, most colonial husbandry measures were not a peculiar or drastic development. Contour ridging which was enforced by colonial environmentalists, for example, was not very different from terracing which was undertaken by some Africans in mountainous regions during the pre-colonial period. In addition, individual land tenure which was a central provision of the Land Husbandry Act was a common practice in pre-colonial Africa. In actual fact, most colonial environmental preservation measures could have been favourably received by many Africans were it not for the Land Apportionment Act of 1930 and other statutes that had deprived them of the most productive land and its natural resources. In addition, the dismissal of indigenous knowledge systems by colonial officials dampened the enthusiasm of Africans from implementing land husbandry measures (Kwashirai 2006). The colonial environmental project largely failed because it failed to sustainably accommodate the socioeconomic complexities and livelihood dynamics of local African communities.

Arbitrary instructions, arrogance and bullying by land conservation officials caused widespread resentment among African peasants (Kwashirai 2006; Pendered and Memerty 1955). At times, Demonstrators took their time to come and allocate land for Africans to cultivate. In 1952, for instance, most Africans in Umtali North Reserve did not do winter plough because Demonstrators did not come. This made Headman Pote and nine villagers from his area and another two from Headman Sahumani's Ward to raise their concerns with the Native Commissioner (NAZ, S2985/LAN/1, LDO Watsomba, to NC Umtali: 18 October 1952). Some disgruntled Africans opened up new lands for cultivation in defiance of colonial conservation orders. In October 1952, for example, the LDO for the Umtali North Reserve reported that a group of peasant farmers comprising Tapfumangei, Zuze, Makina, Tarirakunzwa, Gera, Fesi, Juwawo, Mutseyekwa and Chesanyi had illegally allocated themselves lands for cultivation and that some of them had been influenced by Headman Sahumani to do so (NAZ, S2985/LAN/ 1, LDO Umtali North Reserve to NC Umtali: 7 October 1952).

There were also generational dimensions in the protests against colonial conservation measures. The younger generation, especially the boys, were concerned about the loss of cattle by their parents. What was particularly worrying about the loss was that they would have problems to raise the required number of cattle to pay bride price when they married (Ngwende, Interview: 10 August 1998). Ezekiel Makunike (1998: 4-5) recalled that during the 1940s, when he attended Old Umtali Boarding School on the southern part of the Mutasa Chiefdom, older boys used to express their anger at destocking through songs one of which lamented:

> We are sold by the white people to sell off our cattle yet the country is ours. Day after day, we carry our belongings after eviction and scatter. We have been made landless when the country is ours. Now, what shall we do father? Now, what shall we do? It began with poll taxes, then fencing, then roads. Our country is finished! Our cattle are finished!

Gender dynamics were also conspicuous in the resistance to colonial conservation measures. This was largely due to the fact that peasant women bore much of the brunt of colonial conservation measures since the majority of African men were migrant labourers at European labour markets such as mines, farms and towns. On 15 November 1960, for example, a group of 100 angry African women, comprising a significant number of widows, from the Mutasa North Reserve besieged the Native Commissioner's office in order to present complaints related to colonial land seizures and conservation measures. The women were from villages in the Honde Valley which included Samaringa, Ragu, Mukanda Mupotedzi, Saruwaka, Baradza, Mutsaka, Ngwende, Manyonho, Gwandi, Hambira, Kamutsamba, Mutetwa and Nyabadza. Having failed to see the Native Commissioner who was away, the women reconvened on 18 November 1960 numbering 106. The Native Commissioner advised them to elect three spokeswomen to present their grievances. The issues raised by the representatives included the unfair distribution of land to Africans which resulted in poor yields and hunger and harassment by Demonstrators. The Native Commissioner reported afterwards that the situation in Mutasa North Reserve soon deteriorated and "peggers have had to work in pairs for fear of assault, and one complainant to the police said he was actually beaten up and driven away by some women." He charged that the women were being influenced by political agitators, mostly those returning from work in the towns (NAZ, S2808/1/20, NC Umtali to PNC Manicaland: 19 November 1960).

The exclusive colonial environmental policies and other forms of subjugation were gradually exploited by the African nationalist elite to mobilise the ordinary people in the struggle against colonialism. As early as 1930, for example, the Young Ethiopian Manyika Society was formed. It soon opened branches in Bulawayo, Salisbury and Cape Town (Maxwell 1999). In 1948, a leaflet was circulated amongst Manyikas resident in Salisbury. Its title was 'Manyikaland: Memorandum to the Government.' It attacked colonial land policies and conservation measures. The memorandum began by clearly identifying its source as "the people and chiefs of Manyikaland..." and continued:

> The people of Manyikaland are definitely suffering from a sense of frustration. They have in another respect lost all allegiance to their hereditary chief, Mutasa. Owing to this removal, they have been forced to live under completely new conditions which have destroyed all tribal and family life as such (Maxwell 1999: 112-113).

In addition, as Fifkind (1968: 170) noted, African hatred of colonial conservation measures resulted in "an unofficial alliance" between some chiefs and African nationalist political parties. On 10 March 1949, there was a large meeting of the British African National Voice Association (BANVA) in Bulawayo. It was attended by chiefs from Manicaland and Matebeleland. Chief Chimuriwo Mutasa was present. At the meeting, Benjamin Burombo, the Association's leader, attacked colonial land policies. After the meeting, the delegates marched to the Provincial Commissioner's office. As they marched, they sang the revolutionary song 'God Bless Africa' (Ranger 1999: 162).

On 28 August 1951, the Mutasa Branch of the BANVA held a meeting at Chief Mutasa's residence at Bingaguru. It was attended by over 300 Africans. The meeting's agenda included African grievances against the Land Apportionment Act and complaints that African cattle were being destocked while the same was not happening with European herds (NAZ, S1012/ SBV1-6, Minutes of the Mutasa Branch of the BANVA: 28 August 1951).

From 1957, early African nationalist political parties such as the Southern Rhodesia African National Congress (SRANC), National Democratic Party (NDP) and the Zimbabwe African People's Union (ZAPU) capitalised on the widespread disillusionment against the land husbandry policies to gain nationwide support. The Land Husbandry Act, as George Nyandoro, a SRANC leader, later stated "was the best recruiter Congress ever had" (Rifkind 1972: 34). In March 1958, Joshua Nkomo, the President of the Southern Rhodesia African National Congress (SRANC), for example, expressed misgivings about the Land Husbandry Act:

> Any law, act or measure whose effect is to undermine the security of our small land rights, dispossess us of our little wealth in the form of cattle, disperse us from our ancestral homes in the reserves and reduce us to the status of vagabonds and a source of cheap labour, will ultimately turn the African people against society to the detriment of peace and progress...Nobody is against good husbandry. No one is against soil preservation. No one quarrels with that aspect of the (Land Husbandry) Act. But the African needs more land today and conditions of tenure similar to other people. Only then can you teach good husbandry and soil conservation (Fifkind 1968: 162-163).

In March 1959, an African man from the town of Umtali in the southern part of the Mutasa Chiefdom explained why he had joined SRANC:

> Because I was not allowed to have enough cattle nor land enough to plough. Because my cattle were not allowed to walk on the contour ridges [...] Also my sons who work in towns, if they wish to come back to the reserve, they are not allowed to have cattle or any land. I expect Congress to give more cattle and more land (Mupfuvi 2014: 177-178).

With the formation of African nationalist parties in Rhodesia from the late 1950s, resistance to colonial conservation measures became widespread in the Mutasa Chiefdom. In March 1961, there were fierce clashes between Land Development Officers and angry African villagers in the Honde Valley in the north-eastern part of the Mutasa Chiefdom. In other parts of the country such as Buhera District in March and April 1961, there were riots involving more than 400 African peasants against colonial conservation measures during which officials were assaulted and their cars stoned. In one of the incidents, a Land Development Officer was thrown into a stream (Rifkind 1968). In 1962, the Rhodesian government abandoned the Land Husbandry Act amid of fears of arousing further antagonism and nationalist activities among the Africans (Rifkind 1968).

In 1965, Chekecheke, a Hakuziwi Village Head, was imprisoned for beating Mupatsi, the Headman of Mandeya Ward, who had succumbed to colonial orders to reduce the number of livestock owned by African families (Nyaumwe, Interview: 3 August 1998). Mafi, who succeeded Mupatsi in 1965, openly defied colonial orders and declared that destocking was unfair to Africans. Consequently, he was detained at Inyanga Prison by the colonial police (Nyado, Interview: 5 August 1998).

In November 1966, the Extension Officer for Holdenby Reserve complained that Headman Zindi had been resisting the pegging of his lands by failing to make available the necessary manpower and pegs. The officer wrote to the DC for Inyanga on 17 November 1966:

> Zindi will have to be treated with considerable firmness if this conservation plan is to be carried through. He is a master of delaying tactics. There has already been argument about the digging of demarcation banks. If he fails to get these done on time I suggest he be prosecuted (Mutasa District Administrator Per 5/1 Files: 17 November 1966).

On 8 August 1970, the Provincial Commissioner for Manicaland reported to the Secretary for Internal Affairs that he had instructed all chiefs and ward heads in the province to issue conservation orders to their subjects and be responsible for enforcing these orders through local courts but "(Headman) Muparutsa has seen it fit to disregard this instruction" (Mutasa DA Per 5/1 Files: 8 August 1970). He accused Headman Muparutsa of refusing to deal with those who refused to dig their contours and recommended that his salary be reduced (Mutasa DA Per 5/1 Files: 8 August 1970). Even though colonial conservation measures were abandoned during the mid-1970s as a result of the armed struggle for independence that became widespread in Rhodesia, they had largely failed as a result of resistance particularly from the ordinary sections of the African population.

It can be noted that Rhodesian environmental conservation measures could not succeed in a colonial dispensation where land was disproportionately apportioned, in terms of quality and quantity, in favour of the whites resulting in overcrowding and depletion of natural resources in most African areas. Resistance was, however, more protracted in the overcrowded reserves where the measures were strictly enforced on the colonially marginalised sections of the population as compared to the relatively more spacious Native Purchase Areas which could only be afforded by middle class Africans. The African elite capitalised on several grievances of the ordinary people against colonial rule such as the arbitrary land husbandry measures for mobilisation purposes in the struggle for independence.

Conclusion

This chapter makes a significant input to the contemporary development discourse on global environmentalism by highlighting the need for externally-initiated and elite-driven natural resource management agendas to seriously consider sustainable capacity building efforts that cater for the socioeconomic and livelihood needs of the local communities. With reference to land husbandry measures in the Mutasa Chiefdom in Zimbabwe during the colonial period, this chapter has demonstrated that prescriptive or top-bottom approaches to development often face various forms of resistance from local communities whenever their livelihood options are not adequately catered for. Thus, the goals of externally-initiated and elite-driven development projects need to be harmonised with the interests and livelihood dynamics of local communities to guarantee their success.

This chapter has also illustrated that development projects should be carefully planned in a manner that seriously considers local communities as active participants and beneficiaries. Rhodesian administrators wrongly assumed that Africans lacked environmental management strategies and sought to impose land husbandry measures upon them. This paternalistic approach provoked African resistance. To make matters worse, the colonial government exacerbated environmental degradation by continually seizing land from Africans and overcrowding them in mountainous, semi-arid and unproductive areas. It therefore becomes apparent that the resistance by sections of the African population to colonial environmental measures was not a nostalgic reaction to modernity. Peasant resistance was directed against colonial impositions that severely eroded their livelihoods through land alienation and destocking while the same was not happening for Europeans and some middle-class Africans who owned relatively large tracts of land.

It should be noted that African responses to colonial land husbandry measures were far from being homogenous. Contrary to Afrocentric sentiments, this chapter has shown that African responses were largely determined by the extent to which the livelihoods of particular sections of the population were jeopardised or accommodated by the colonial order. As far as some sections of the African population were concerned, colonial land husbandry measures were not a major grievance. These included some relatively wealthy Africans who had bought large tracts of land and some labour migrants who had sought alternative means of livelihood at European labour markets such as farms, mines and towns. Resistance was actually widespread in the overcrowded reserves. Within the reserves, colonial land husbandry measures policies such as destocking negatively affected those Africans who owned large herds of cattle than those who did not. In addition, significant numbers of rural African women, most of whose husbands were away as migrant labourers, were conspicuous in resistance as they shouldered much of the burden of implementing colonial land husbandry measures. Many traditional leaders were also disgruntled because they were ordered to supervise environmental conservation yet they had been deprived of powers to allocate land. Some sections of the African elite capitalised on these grievances and formulated them into a nationalist package that became a vital mobilisation tool in the anti-colonial struggle.

References

Adeleke, T. 2009. *The case against Afrocentrism*, Jackson: University Press of Mississippi.

Artkinson, N. 1972. *Teaching Rhodesians: A history of education policy in Rhodesia*, London: Longman.

Beach, D.N. 1984. *Zimbabwe before 1900*, Gweru: Mambo Press.

Beach, D.N. 1994. *The Shona and their neighbours*, Oxford: Blackwell.

Bhila, H.H.K. 1982. *Trade and politics in a Shona kingdom: The Manyika and their Portuguese and African neighbours, 1575-1902*, Essex: Longman.

Birmingham, D. and Martin, P.M. 1983. *A history of Central Africa Volume 2*, London: Longman.

Booth, A. McCullum, J, Mpinga, J. and Mukute, M. 1994. *State of the environment in Southern Africa*, Harare: Southern African Research and Document Centre.

Bourdillon, M.F.C. 1976. *The Shona peoples: An ethnography of the contemporary Shona with special reference to their religion*, Gwelo: Mambo Press.

Bratton, M. 1978. *From Rhodesia to Zimbabwe: Beyond community development*, *Gwelo:* Mambo Press.

Bulpin, T.V. 1968. *To the banks of the Zambezi*, Cape Town: Books of Africa.

Chitiyo, T.K. 2007. 'Land violence and compensation: Reconceptualising Zimbabwe's land and war veterans' debate,' www.africarcsource.com, Accessed 15 November 2015.

Chivandi, E, Fushai, F. and Masaka, J. 2010. Land ownership and range resource management in Zimbabwe: A historical review, in: *Midlands State University Journal of Science, Agriculture and Technology*, Volume 2, Number 1, pp.13-24.

Duri, F. and Mapara, J. 2007. Environmental awareness and management strategies in pre-colonial Zimbabwe, in: *Zimbabwe Journal of Geographical Research*, Volume 1, Number 1, pp.98-111.

Dzerefos, C.M. 2014. 'The life history, use and socio-economics of the edible stinkbug *encosternum delegorguei* (*hemiptera: tessaratomidae*), in South Africa,' PhD thesis, Faculty of Science, University of the Witwatersrand, Johannesburg, May 2014.

Faniran, A. and Ojo, O. 1980. *Man's physical environment: An intermediate physical geography*, London: Heinemann.

Gale, W. D. 1960. *Deserve to be great: The story of Rhodesia and Nyasaland*, Bulawayo: Stuart Manning.

Garbett, G.K. 1960. 'Growth and change in a Shona ward,' Occasional Paper Number 1, Salisbury: University College of Rhodesia and Nyasaland.

Garbett, G.K. 1963. The Land Husbandry Act of Southern Rhodesia, in: D. Biebuyck, ed. *African agrarian systems: Studies presented and discussed,* London: Oxford University Press.

Garbett, G.K. 1966. The Rhodesian chief's dilemma: Government officer or tribal leader? In: *Race*, Number 2, pp.113-129.

Hailey, W.M. 1957. *An African survey*, London: McGraw-Hill.

Haw, R.C. 1965. *Land Apportionment Act Rhodesia,* Salisbury: Rhodesia Information Service, Information Paper Number 1.

Holleman, J.F. 1951. Some Shona tribes in Southern Rhodesia, in: E. Colson and M. Gluckman, eds. *Seven tribes of British Central Africa*, London: Oxford University Press.

Jackson, A.R.W. and Jackson, J.M. 1996. *Environmental science: The natural environment and human impact*, Essex: Longman.

Kay, G. 1971. *Rhodesia: A human geography*, London: University of London Press.

Kwashirai, V.C. 2006. 'Dilemmas in conservationism in colonial Zimbabwe, 1890-1930,' in: *Conservation and Society*, Volume 4, Issue 4, pp.541-561.

Makanyisa, I. Chemhuru, M. and Masitera, E. 2012. The land tenure system and the environmental implications on Zimbabwean society: Examining the pre-colonial to post-independent Zimbabwean thinking and policies through history and philosophy, in: *Journal of Sustainable Development in Africa*, Volume 14, Number 6, pp.175-183.

Makuku, S.J. 1993. Community approaches in managing common property forest resources: The case study of Norumedzo community in Bikita, in: G.D. Pearce and D.J. Gumbo, eds. *Proceedings of an international symposium on ecology and management of indigenous forests in southern Africa,* Victoria Falls: Zimbabwe Forestry Commission, pp.86-96.

Maredza, C. 1987. *Harurwa: The amazing but true mystery of Norumedzo in Zimbabwe,* Harare: Longman Zimbabwe.

Mawere, M. 2013. A critical review of environmental conservation in Zimbabwe, in: *Africa Spectrum,* Volume 48, Number 2, pp.85-97.

Mawere, M. 2014. 'Forest insects, personhood and the environment: *Harurwa* (edible stinkbugs) and conservation in south-eastern Zimbabwe,' PhD thesis, Faculty of Humanities, School of African and Gender Studies, Anthropology and Linguistics, Department of Social Anthropology, University of Cape Town.

Maxwell, D. 1999. *Christians and chiefs in Zimbabwe: A social history of the Hwesa people, C 1870s – 1990s,* London: Edinburgh University Press, London.

Mudenge, S.I.G. 1988. *A political history of Munhumutapa, c1400-1902,* Harare: Zimbabwe Publishing House.

Mukwindidza, E. 2008. 'Implementation of environmental legislation in the Mutasa District of Zimbabwe,' Master of Public Administration thesis, University of South Africa.

Mupfuvi, B.M. 2014. 'Land to the people: Peasants and nationalism in the development of land ownership structure in Zimbabwe from pre-colonialism to the Unilateral Declaration of Independence (UDI) period,' PhD thesis, Salford Business School, University of Salford, United Kingdom.

Murray, D.J. 1970. *The governmental system in Southern Rhodesia,* Oxford: Clarendon Press.

Mutasa DA Per 5/1 Files, Court fees and charges for Headmen Zindi and Samanga: 1971.

Mutasa DA Per 5/1 Files, Extension Officer, Holdenby, to DC, Inyanga: 23 March 1967.

Mutasa DA Per 5/1 Files, Extension Officer, Holdenby, to District Commissioner (DC), Inyanga: 17 November 1966.

Mutasa DA Per 5/1 Files, Provincial Commissioner, Manicaland, to Secretary for Internal Affairs: 8 August 1970.

Mutasa District Administrator (DA) Per 5/1 Files, Native Commissioner (NC), Inyanga, to Provincial Native Commissioner (PNC): 16 February 1948.

National Archives of Zimbabwe (NAZ), N3/1/19 Little to Chief Native Commissioner (CNC): 23 August 1899.

NAZ S2797/2636, Minutes of the First Meeting of the Tsonzo Native Council held at St Mathias School: 30 December 1955.

NAZ, NUA1/1/1, Cocknell to NC, Umtali: 16 April 1901.

NAZ, NUA1/1/2, NC, Inyanga, to NC, Umtali: 26 August 1903.

NAZ, NUA2/1/10, Umtali District Annual Report: 1917.

NAZ, NUA2/1/4, Acting NC, Umtali, to CNC: 21 February 1901.

NAZ, S1012/ SBV1-6, Minutes of the Mutasa Branch of the BANVA: 28 August 1951.

NAZ, S1618, Umtali NC's Quarterly Report: 31 March 1952.

NAZ, S235/511/3, Inyanga District Annual Report: 1933.

NAZ, S235/511/3, Umtali District Annual Report: 1933.

NAZ, S2403/ 2681, Umtali District Native Commissioner's Annual Report: 1952.

NAZ, S2403/ 2682, Inyanga District Native Commissioner's Annual Report: 1952.

NAZ, S2807/4, Chief Land Officer, Salisbury, to CNC: 31 May 1949.

NAZ, S2807/4, CNC to Ian Wilson: 4 June 1949.

NAZ, S2807/4, PNC, Manicaland, to CNC: 30 May 1949.

NAZ, S2807/4, Southern Rhodesia Government Notice, Number 41 of 1956

NAZ, S2808/1/20, Jenya Reserve Assessment Committee Meeting: 20 May 1955.

NAZ, S2808/1/20, Land Husbandry Act: Mutasa, Umtali and Jenya Reserves, 1954-1961.

NAZ, S2808/1/20, NC Umtali to PNC Manicaland: 19 November 1960.

NAZ, S2827/2/2/1, Inyanga District NC's Annual Report: 1951.

NAZ, S2985/LAN/ 1, Land Development Officer (LDO) Umtali North Reserve to NC Umtali: 7 October 1952.

NAZ, S2985/LAN/1, LDO, Watsomba, to NC, Umtali: 18 October 1952.

NAZ, S2985/LAN/1, Umtali NC's minutes of a meeting to resolve boundary dispute between Headman Muponda and Kraal Head Mupotedzi in Mutasa North Reserve: August 1952.

Ngwende, D. 10 August 1998. Interview: Domborutinhira Business Centre, Mutasa District.

Nyado, C. 5 August 1998. Interview: Chipagura Ward, Mutasa District.

Nyaumwe, S. 3 August 1998. Interview: Sherukuru Ward, Mutasa District.

Palley, C. 1966. *The constitutional history and law of Southern Rhodesia, 1888-1965, with special reference to imperial control,* Oxford: Clarendon Press.

Palmer, R. 1977. *Land and racial domination in Rhodesia, London:* Heinemann.

Pendered, A. and Memerty, W. 1955. The Native Land Husbandry Act of Southern Rhodesia, in: *Journal of African Administration,* Volume 7, Number 3, pp.99-109.

Ranger, T.O. 1960. *Crisis in Southern Rhodesia,* London: Heinemann.

Ranger, T.O. 1967. *Revolt in Southern Rhodesia, 1896-7: A study in African resistance,* London: Heinemann.

Ranger, T.O. 1999. *Voices from the rocks: Nature, culture and history of the Matopos Hills of Zimbabwe,* Harare: Baobab.

Rifkind, M.L. 1968. 'The politics of land in Rhodesia: A study of land and politics in Southern Rhodesia with special reference to the period 1930-1968,' Master of Science thesis, University of Edinburgh.

Rifkind, M.L. 1972. Land apportionment in perspective, in: *Rhodesian History,* Volume 3, pp.53-62.

Schabel1, H.G. 2010. Forest insects as food: A global review,' in: P.B. Durst, D.V. Johnson, R.N. Leslie and K. Shono, eds. *Forest insects as food: Humans bite back,* Proceedings of a workshop on Asia-Pacific rcsources and their potential for development, 19-21 February 2008, Chiang Mai, Thailand, Bangkok: Food and Agriculture Organisation of the United Nations, pp.37-64.

Steele, M.C. 1973. Review Article: Community development in Rhodesia, in: *Rhodesian History,* Volume 4, pp.105-112.

Stigger, P. 1980. The Land Commission of 1894 and cattle, in: *Rhodesian History,* Volume 11, pp.20-44.

Tatira, L. 2000. *Zviera zvaVaShona*, Gweru: Mambo Press.

Weimann, J. 1996. *Zimbabwe's land crisis: A reassessment*, Berkeley: University of California Press.

Yudelman, M. 1964. *Africans on the land*, Massachusetts: Harvard University Press.

Chapter Fifteen

Impact of Religion on Socio-Political and Economic Development: A Case of Religious Crisis in China and Nigeria, 1990-2015

Lemuel Ekedegwa Odeh & Afolabi Opeyemi Glory

Introduction

China is a country located in East Asia, which has the largest population in the world (about 1.3 billion persons), while Nigeria is located in West Africa and it is the largest Africa Country with a population of about 160 million persons. Although, China and Nigeria are located on different continents, both countries have a lot of commonalities which have helped to strengthen their relationship which was established on 10th February, 1971. However, one unique similarity between both countries is the presence of religious conflict which pose great threats to the process of modernization and nation building going on in both countries. China and Nigeria have a profusion of religions which could have been used to foster socio-political and economic development in both countries, in that, religious value systems play very significant role in collective self-awareness and identity, which draw together individuals, families and regions, and pull them towards greater self-consciousness needed to build and animate a nation from within. However, religion is been manipulated by some unscrupulous elements in both countries, as an instrument of destruction and disintegration, which threatens the peace, stability and security of both countries.

Religious crisis in China and Nigeria can be attributed to the rise in the Islamic activism of the Uyghurs in China and Boko Haram sect in Nigeria from the 1990s up till 2015. The Uyghurs (who are the Turkic minority Muslim who live primarily in the Xinjiang region of Western China) have been perpetrating a lot of religious crisis as a result of religious restrictions and human rights abuses which they are subjected to by the Chinese government. Also, the Boko Haram

Islamic sect in North-East Nigeria, carry out a lot of terrorist attacks in the country because of their hatred for Western education and influence, which in their view, is responsible for the high rate of poverty in their region. Both the Uyghurs and Boko Haram adopt extreme measures to achieve their goals, which culminate in the loss of lives and properties.

Against this backdrop, this chapter seeks to look at the religious revival in China and Nigeria, noting specifically, the activities of the Uyghurs in Xinjiang China, and the Boko Haram in North-East Nigeria. The linkages of these religious conflicts on the socio-political and economic development of China and Nigeria shall also be examined.

Conceptual Clarification

Religion

Several definitions of religion abound as a result of the variety of religious beliefs and organizations. In view of this, only the definition which portrays the essence of this work shall be conceptualized. Religion is a collection of cultural systems and views that establish symbols that relate humanity with spirituality and sometimes to moral values. Religion deals with shared beliefs and practices; it is pre-eminently social and is found universally in every society, from the most simple and isolated, to the most complex and urban. In all established societies, religion is one of the important institutional structures which constitute the total social system. It is a product of culture and an outgrowth of mans' activities since man is the only culture bearing creature. Religion is a cultural tool which enables a man to accommodate himself to his experience and his environment (Adega, *et al*, 2009:59). H.L. Tiscler conceptualizes religion as a system of beliefs, practices and philosophical values shared by a group of people (Okau, 2003:19). O.T. Oshadare *et al*, posited that religion as a social factor emphasizes cohesion and collective actions among members in a unified system of beliefs and practice relating to sacred things which unite adherents into a single moral community (Oshadare, *et al*, 2005:71).

Religious value systems play very significant role in collective self-awareness and identity, which draw together individuals, families and regions, and pull them towards greater self-consciousness needed to build and animate a nation from within. However, religion can be manipulated as an instrument of destruction and disintegration, which threatens the peace, stability and security of a nation (Ethel, 2010:26). This is exactly the case in China and Nigeria, in that, religion is being manipulated by the Uyghurs and Boko Haram for the purpose of achieving their aims. This however, culminates into the destruction of lives and properties which has greatly impeded the socio-political and economic development of both countries.

Religious Revival in China

China (officially known as the Republic of China) is a country in East Asia, which has one of the oldest civilization in the world. The name China was given to it by foreigners and it's probably based on the corruption of Qin (pronounced as "chin") a Chinese dynasty that ruled during the 3rd century BC. According to the 2008 estimate, one-fifth of the world's population (1.3 billion people) live in China. Of the country's inhabitants, about 92 percent of these are ethnic Han Chinese. The Han are descendants of people who settled on the plains and plateaus of Northern and Central China more than 5,000 years ago, and of people in Southern China who were absorbed by the Northerners more than 2,000 years ago and gradually adopted a shared culture with them. The remaining 8 percent of China's population consist of minority nationalities, such as: Tibetans, Mongols, Uyghurs, Zhuang, Miao, Yi and many smaller groups, who inhabits the sparsely settled areas of Western and South-Western China. China has one of the largest land mass (measuring about the same size as the United States). Beijing, which is located in the North is China's capital, as well as its cultural, economic and communication centre (Clunas, 2008).

Prior to the Maoist era, the traditional religions of China were Confucianism, Daoism and Buddhism. People often practiced and adhered to traditions of all three religions as well as incorporating variety of local beliefs into their religious practice. Islam and Christianity were among the more formal and organized religions practiced in China, but these faiths had few adherents. After gaining control in 1949, the Chinese Communist Party officially eliminated organised religion. The CCP's move received little resistance because Confucianism is largely secular and because most Chinese adhered to aspects of all three major faiths; thus they lacked strong allegiance to any single religion (Clunas, 2008). However, this situation changed following the death of Mao Zedong in 1976. The post-Maoist China witnessed the emergence of diverse, encompassing, official, unofficial, underground and folk religions. The catalyst for these was the Chinese constitution of 1982 which allowed citizens freedom of religious belief and protected legitimate religious activities as defined by the state. The growth of religious activities in China can be attributed to modernization. A large body of literatures on modernization suggests that this process could transform and disrupt the existing class structure, ethnic and tribal relations, political power structure, and even the value system religions (Lai, 2003). This was the case in the post-moist China, and consequently, people embraced religion because it met their needs for psychological comfort and spiritual fulfilment, especially in confronting a variety of problems inherent in the modernization program, including increasing marketization, rapid social transition and emerging social problems.

The five major officially recognised religions in China includes: Buddhism, Daoism, Islam, Catholicism and Protestantism. Following recent studies on China's religion, this chapter leaves out Confucianism from the discussion, largely because in present-day China it exists primarily in form of ethical teachings, rather than religion *per se*. In 2005, the State Council passed new Regulations on Religious Affairs, which allows state–registered religious organizations to possess property, publish literature, train and approve clergy and collect donations, but religious freedom is still not universal in China (Albert, 2015). All religious activities in China are regulated by the state authority, for instance, the administration of religious affairs, including establishment of official places for worship (mosque, church, and temple, amongst others), training of religious clergy, and management of religious activities such as: membership registration, service organization, and preacher certification (Lee, 2014:6).

Although religious belief in China is protected by the constitution, all evidence of religious restriction proves otherwise. For instance, Article 36 of the constitution states that "citizens of the

People's Republic of China enjoy freedom of religious belief. No state organ, or public organization or individual may compel citizens to believe in, or not to believe in, any religion; nor may they discriminate against citizens who believe in, or do not believe in, any religion..." (Albert, 2015). Nevertheless, the Chinese government reserves the right to refuse equal protection to any religious group. The Uyghur Muslims are the worst hit by this situation, in that they are treated more unfairly than other Islamic groups in China. The Chinese government tighten their grip on religious activities of the Uyghur Muslims because of their ethnic and religious affiliations with neighbouring Islamic countries whom the Chinese government accuse of supporting religious extremism in the Xinjiang region. This situation, amongst others, is the motivating factor for the religious conflicts that is being perpetrated by the Uyghurs in Xinjiang province of China from the 1990s till date, which culminates in the loss of lives and properties. The Chinese government also carry out military reprisals against the protesting Uyghur Muslims as a way of curtailing their uprising.

Against this backdrop, the preceding paragraphs seek to examine Islamic activism in Xinjiang, as well as, its impact on the socio-political and economic development of China.

The Rise of Islamic Activism in Xinjiang, Uyghur Province of China

The Uyghurs are a Turkic minority Muslim who live primarily in the Xinjiang region of Western China (Corradini, 2010:29). Xinjiang is a Western province that makes up one-sixth of China's landmass with a population of 20 million. It is rich in mineral and natural resources and is home to the Uyghurs, the largest ethnic minority group in the province, with over 8 million people (Gorrie, J). The region now known as Xinjiang came under Chinese rule in the 18th century, when the Qing dynasty conquered the Xinjiang province and incorporated it into China. Uyghur nationalists organized several uprisings against the dynasty, which ruled China until the early 20th century. An East Turkistan State was briefly declared in 1949, but independence was short-lived later that year as Mao Zedong's forces thwarted Uyghur's aspirations by imposing total control over

Xinjiang, setting off protracted tensions that have characterized the Uyghur - State relations till date (Siddiqui, 2015). However, after the death of Mao, the Chinese Constitution of 1982 gave official support to religious freedom of the five official religions in China. Thus, the Uyghur Muslims intensified their religious activities and resumed their clamour for an autonomous state. This was a catalyst for the ethic, cultural and religious tensions between the Uyghurs and the Chinese leadership. Although article 36 of the Chinese constitution explicitly allows "freedom of religious belief", the Chinese government continue to put harsh restrictions on Uyghurs. Most Uyghurs are Muslims, and Islam is an important part of their life and identity (BBC News, 26th September 2014). Recent religious revival among the Uyghur population developed through unofficial channels to avoid state control. These unofficial religious organizations are very capable to attract followers and build mobilizing power through underground religious preaching. The records of recent 'violent incidents' suggest that many attacks were associated with these underground organizations and networks (Lee, 2014:6). However, a resurgent Islamic cultural and religious identity is a force which China's officially atheistic government cannot cope with, and this factor has been responsible for the religious crisis between the Uyghurs and the Chinese government from the 1990s till date.

Xinjiang is an area of special concern because of the region's ethnic and religious ties to neighbouring states. Xinjiang is a "designated autonomous region" in China and it's also known as East Turkistan, with historical and religious ties to several central Asian nations. In fact, it shares borders with Mongolia, Russia, Kazakhstan, Kyrgyzstan, Tajikistan, Afghanistan, Pakistan, and India, as well as with Tibet. Uyghur populations are found in some of these countries, who in recent years, has been providing greater levels of support to the Uyghurs' separatist's movement in Xinjiang (Albert, 2015). The Uyghurs view China's presence in Xinjiang as imperialism and identify themselves as belonging to the central Asian Islamic Republic more than they do with China. An independence movement has been in existence since the early 1990s, when Uyghur separatists staged numerous attacks against Chinese rule over the region. In response to those attacks, China maintained a demographic policy in Xinjiang of migrating ethnic Han Chinese (which is about 92 percent of the Chinese population) as a means of displacing Uyghurs and minimizing their disruptive influence (Gorrie, J). The Han Chinese then took up the control of the government in Xinjiang, and this was also part of the grievances of the Uyghurs, who felt side-lined in the politics of their region. The "Uyghur problem" is viewed by China as highly inflammatory since the province borders five Muslim countries with a history of supporting Islamic militants. Since the September 11, 2001, attacks in the United States, China has increasingly portrayed its Uyghur separatists as auxiliaries of al-Qaeda, saying they have received training in Afghanistan (BBC News, 30th April 2014). Thus, Uyghur Muslims are placed under the watchful eyes of the Chinese government and the United States and many of them are also being arrested.

The Uyghurs are in two groups: those who want an independent Uyghur state and those who realize that it is easier to conform to traditional Chinese culture. This is probably because, the Uyghur youths want to be able to practice their religion without worrying about persecution, but they also believe that going to Chinese schools, wearing traditional Chinese clothing, and living comfortably with Han Chinese in Xinjiang is more acceptable than constantly being targeted by the Chinese government. This situation has undoubtedly reinforced the Chinese government's efforts to continue its political and cultural pressure on the Muslim minorities in Xinjiang. As more Uyghurs conform to the traditional Chinese way of life, the government believes that its restrictions are working and the Uyghur independence movement is getting smaller (Corradini, 2010:29). However, that is not to say the Chinese government has been able to quell the uprising totally. Religious conflicts characterises East Turkistan Islamic Movement (ETIM), who according to the US state Department in 2006, are "the most militant of the ethnic Uyghur separatist groups" (BBC News, 26th September 2014). Although most Uyghurs do not support ETIM, they are frustrated with the Chinese government because they face discrimination for having a different culture than the typically wealthier Han Chinese.

China's problems with the Uyghurs have culminated into numerous outbreaks of rioting and protracted violence with death tolls in the hundreds. Tensions and instability remain high due to killings carried out by armed Uyghurs Muslims, on ethnic Han Chinese in the province, and a meeting of 200 Uyghurs – hosted by Japan – to publicize their demand for independence, which was met with condemnation by China (Gorrie, J). Several terrorist attacks which led to the loss of several lives and properties have been traced to the Uyghurs. For instance, in 2009 following a large-scale ethnic rioting in the regional capital, Urumqi, some 200 people were killed, and most of them were Han Chinese. Security was increased and many Uyghurs detained as suspects. In June 2012, six Uyghurs reportedly tried to hijack a plane from Hotan to Urumqi before they were overpowered by passengers and crew. There was bloodshed in April 2013 and in June that year, 27 people died in Shanshan County after police opened fire on what state media described as 'a mob armed with knives attacking local government buildings'. An October 2013 incident where a car plunged into a crowd and burst into flames in Beijing's Tiananmen Square was blamed on Xinjiang separatists. At least 31 people were killed and more than 90 suffered injuries in May 2014 when two cars crashed through an Urumqi market and explosives were tossed into the crowd. In July, Chinese authorities said a knife-wielding gang attacked a police station and government offices in Yarkant, leaving 96 dead. The Imam of China's largest mosque, Jume Tahir, was stabbed to death days later. This and many more riots were blamed on the Uyghurs (BBC News, 26th September 2014). Although these attacks are tragic, they are attempts by the Uyghurs to seek the religious freedom forbidden by the Chinese government.

The Uyghurs' religious intransigence is a challenge that China's leaders have so far been unable to address successfully, even though it has resorted to drastic measures to quell the rise of Islamic activism. From teachers, force-feeding Muslim children candy during Ramadan, to bans on religious expression throughout Xinjiang, such measures have not produced the desired outcomes, rather, it has only succeeded in provoking more violence in the province and increased separatists' sentiment. For instance, the ban on fasting of Muslim civil servants in July 2014, was followed by a lot of attacks on the public which was traced to the Uyghur extremists. This situation also worsens China's relations with Pakistan, which it suspects of supporting Islamic radicalism in the province. China is also trying to bring the Xinjiang's orbit closer to Beijing, to quell the unrest of its Islamic population by force, migration and accommodation, but it's yet to realize success. In fact, it has achieved just the opposite. There is no doubt that as economic conditions continue to deteriorate and Beijing's oppression of the province escalates, Xinjiang will seek further involvement and deeper ties with its Muslim neighbours and grow more distant from CCP's authority (Gorrie, J).

It should be noted that, much of the conflicts which were attributed to the Uyghurs might have been highly exaggerated by the Chinese government. This is because the Chinese government is known for its human rights abuses and one cannot ascertain the authenticity of the information that is being dished out to the world by the Chinese government because they control the media. The world only hears China's side of the story, but there are always two sides to a coin. That notwithstanding, the Uyghurs insurgency has a very devastating effect on the Xinjiang region, as able bodied men who ought to develop the economy are being slaughtered by this Islamic extremists. The destruction of properties made several persons homeless. Also, the resources of China which are supposed to be utilized for the socio-economic development of China are being diverted to quell this uprising.

Religious Revival in Nigeria

Nigeria is a country in West Africa and it is the largest black African country. The Name 'Nigeria was coined by Flora Shaw (later Flora Lugard). It refers to the people who inhabit the Niger Area. Nigeria is a multi-ethnic and multi-religious country with about 160 million people cutting across the divides of ethnicity and religious beliefs. Nigeria has three major religions which are: Christianity, Islam and African Religion. These religions, with an exemption of African Religion, proliferated into the country from foreign countries. Christianity for instance, came into the country through the activities of the European missionaries who were on a mission to preach the gospel of Jesus Christ to the inhabitants of Africa which they labelled as a "dark continent", and in which Nigeria belongs to. On the other hand, Islam (the religion of Prophet Mohammed) proliferated into the area now known as Nigeria from the Middle-

East, during the trans-Saharan trade. However, Islam gained much prominence and attracted a lot of adherents in Nigeria as a result of the Sokoto Jihad of 1804 which was championed by Uthman Dan Fodio. Both Christianity and Islam are monotheist religions and the activities of their adherents have impacted in one way or the other, the process of nation building in the country.

African religion was the main religion of those living in the present day Nigeria, prior to the coming of the European missionaries. However, modernity has posed acute challenges on traditional religion in Nigeria, and it is gradually going into oblivion, in that, it has just few adherents today. This can be attributed to the activities of the European missionaries who viewed African religion as evil and did everything possible to eradicate it. This was done through the preaching of the word of God, and by making people believe that if they died they would go to hell fire if they did not repent and convert to Christianity. The efforts of the missionaries were consolidated by the British colonialists (colonial rule started in 1900 and ended in 1960) who destroyed the shrines of African worshippers and erected churches on those sites. Not only did the British colonialists suppress African religion, they also introduced Western education which in turn helped to erode the African belief systems and customs in Nigeria.

However, after the attainment of independence in 1960, the religious persecution by the colonialists ended and all the three religions were given the right to carry out their religious activities. The monotheistic religions of Islam and Christianity enjoyed special government protection during the post-colonial era. However, each claim superiority over and seek to outdo each other in the unfolding competition in the number of converts and influence in national policies. Both religions also experience internal squabbles between adherents of various denominations or sects. Religious tensions sometimes lead to serious crisis and disruption of public order, which threatens the peace, stability and security of the country (Ethel, 2010:26). However, the most extreme cases of religious crisis are those perpetrated by the Islamic Sect "Boko Haram". From the 1990s to 2015, the Boko Haram sect carried out terrorist attacks which claimed a lot of lives and properties in Nigeria. Although, the Nigerian government put in place strict security measures to curb this menace, the situation persists and it has a negative impact on the socio-political and economic development of Nigeria. Against this backdrop, the following paragraphs seek to examine the Rise of Islamic Activism in North-East Nigeria, as well as, its effects on the socio-political and economic development of the country.

The Rise of Islamic Activism in North-East Nigeria

Although, Nigeria has over the years faced a lot of religious crisis, the one caused by the activities of the Islamic sect, Boko Haram, remains quite unique in all ramifications. The Boko Haram insurgency in the North-East geo-political zone of Nigeria, that originally took the form of sectarian religious violence, have escalated into terrorist activities with international linkages and affiliations making it a relatively difficult nut for the Nigerian government to crack (Awortu, 2015:213). The Boko Haram is a dreaded Islamic sect known as "Jama'atu Ahlis Sunna Lid da'awati Wal-Jihad" (Congregation of the People of Tradition for Proselytism and Jihad) (Shuaibu, *et al*, 2015:254). The Hausa appellation 'Boko Haram' signifies its ideology which forbids Western education and any culture that is Western. Since 1995, the Boko Haram has been operating under the name Shabab Muslim Youth Organization with Mallam Lawal as the leader. However, the leadership of the group shifted to Mallam Mohammed Yusuf, following Mallam Lawal's departure to Saudi Arabia for further studies (Babatunde, *et al*, 2014:61).

Boko Haram grew out of a group of radical Islamic Youths who worshipped at the Al-Haji Muhammadu Ndimi Mosque in Maiduguri, capital of Borno State, in the 1990's. Its leader, Mohammed Yusuf, began as a preacher and leader in the youth wing of Shababul Islam of Ahl-Sunnah, a Salafi group. His literal interpretation of the Quran led him to advocate that aspects of Western education he considered contradictory to the Holy Book be forbidden. While critical of the government, Yusuf was involved in official efforts to introduce and implement Sharia in several Northern states in the early 2000s. The failure to achieve this fully helps to explain Muslim Youths' anger with government deception and insincerity and the call for a full blown Islamic Revolution. Boko

351

Haram's principal goal is to create a strict Islamic state in the North that it believed would address the ills of society, including corruption and bad governance. Abu Qaqa, the group's best known spokesman, explained that the group's agenda is to destabilize Nigeria and take her back to the pre-colonial period when the Sharia law was practiced (Awortu, 2015:214).

However, the movement did not become militant until 2009 when its leader, Mohammed Yusuf, was captured by the men of Nigerian security forces and was later found dead. Consequently, Abubakar Shekau who assumed the leadership of the group, applied a more radical approach to the activities of the group. To buttress this point, BBC online, on 22nd June, 2012, stated that the sect's level of radicalization and terrorism is perhaps, a function of the death of its initial leader and the subsequent clampdown by the state, the taciturn psychopath, Abubakar Shekau, a Kanuri native who once boasted "I enjoy killing any one that Allah commands me to kill-the way I enjoy killing chickens and rams". Gilbert posited that the new leadership turned to the use of lethal weapons such as: rocket propelled grenades (RPGs), anti-tank missiles, Improvised Explosive Devices (IEDs), surface-to-air missiles, armoured tanks, A-K 47, as well as machetes and daggers for the purpose of meting out mayhem to the Nigerian state, which adversely affects her economy considering the high rate of loss of lives and properties (Awortu, 2015:214).

Although the Boko Haram insurgency is a religious crisis, it also has some level of socio-economic and political undertones. Considering the high level of poverty in Nigeria, it can be rightly asserted that the Boko Haram menace emerged as a result of poverty in the North. Nigeria is naturally endowed with mineral resources and naturally blessed with fertile land that is good for both cash and food crops and its high potential for industrial and economic development. The discovery of crude oil is an additional advantage to the country as it serves as her major foreign exchange income, making Nigeria the sixth largest oil producing country in the world. However, despite Nigeria's huge resource endowment, majority of her population wallow in abject poverty (Onuoha, et al, 2015). For instance, many Nigerian citizens are living below the poverty line of $1 a day. Statistically, poverty distribution in Nigeria shows that

Northern Nigeria is worst hit by this situation. For instance, North-Central records 67%, North-West records 71.1% and North East records 72.2%. Thus, it is not out of turn to say that the high level of poverty in the North-East, gave rise to the Boko Haram insurgency in the region. The Boko Haram sect attributes the high level of poverty in the North-East to the Nigerian government who imposed Western education on them and failed to manage the resources of the country to their benefits. Thus, in their view "Western Education is a sin". To support this claim, Ahokegh, observed that "if one thinks deeply about the rejection of Western education by this Islamist group, a sense will be deduced. Western education and Christianity were introduced forcefully in Nigeria through colonialism as instruments of economic exploitation and socio-cultural transformation. Since the exit of colonialism in Nigeria, the citizens continue to suffer its legacies of economic exploitation and socio-cultural transformation through the existence of an indigenous exploiting class". Thus, the resentment of the Boko Haram sect against the corrupt elites who are products of Western education became the foundation of the Boko Haram insurgency (Ahokegh, F).

Furthermore, the Boko Haram sect took advantage of the Nigerian government's inability to provide basic welfare schemes to criticize Western education and drum up support for their false Islamic teachings. They exploited the lacuna created by the high level of unemployment, non-availability of basic infrastructure and the general high poverty level in the area to their benefit through the strategy of providing some welfare package to the citizenry. For instance, they used food and employment to attract youths to their fold and created the impression that their fundamental Islamic viewpoint of society organization is better than the Western capitalist mode of production (Awortu, 2015:215). These strategy paid dividends, in that, the Boko Haram gained the support of youths whom they recruited as suicide bombers and fighters.

Another catalyst for the rise in the Islamic activism of the Boko Haram sect is the inability of Northern politicians (who used the sect to achieve their selfish goals) to keep to their own side of the bargain. There were attacks and counter attacks by political supporters which gradually resulted in divisions within the sect. The death of Mohammed Yusuf provided an impetus for those opposed to his non-violent approach to use their proposed violent approach to achieve their aims. It should be noted that, the death of Yusuf gave rise to different violent sect groups who constructed "a state within a state" with a cabinet and its own religious police, and attracted more and more people. Most of those attracted by the group are refugees from the wars over border in Chad and jobless Nigerian Youths domiciled in Northern Nigeria, as well as other Islamic sects in the Middle-East who gives technical, moral and financial support to them.

The Boko Haram has claimed responsibility for several terrorist attacks which claimed a lot of lives and properties, and attracted the attention of the international community. From the year, 2009 till date, the Boko Haram in pursuit of their ideology, engage in arson, kidnap, bombing and sporadic shooting with disdain and impunity, targeting important national events, public institutions, markets, churches and even mosques. Since 2009, Boko Haram has constituted a serious security threat in the Northern part of Nigeria. However, until June 16, 2011, the onslaught was restricted to the North-East geo-political zone. The first attack outside the zone was the bombing of the Nigerian Police Headquarters in Abuja. That attack was triggered off by the utterances of Hafiz Ringim, the then Inspector General of Police who threatened to smoke Boko Haram out in a press statement on his duty tour in Maiduguri, where the sect launched an attack. The attack on the Police Headquarters was followed up with the bombing of the United Nations Office in Abuja on 26th August, 2011 (Babatunde, et al, 2014:61). These and many more attacks which were carried out by the Boko Haram sect, has an adverse effect on the socio-political and economic development of Nigeria. Since stepping up its activities in 2009, the group has killed over 18,000 people and displaced about 1.5 million people. Killings by Boko Haram since 2009 are largely responsible for Nigeria's decline from 7th of 115 countries in 2012 to 4th of 121 countries in 2014 in the Global Terrorism Index (Onuoha, 2015).

A Comparative Analysis of the Activities of the Uyghurs and Boko Haram

From the forgoing discussion, it is clear that China and Nigeria have been experiencing a lot of religious conflicts which have destabilized the socio-political and economic landscape of both countries. At this juncture, therefore, it is imperative to briefly juxtapose the activities of the Uyghurs in Xinjiang Province of China, with the activities of the Boko Haram in North-East Nigeria.

Firstly, both the Uyghurs and the Boko Haram, adopt Islamic activism to achieve their aims. Secondly, while the Uyghurs are fighting for religious recognition and the establishment of an autonomous state, the Boko Haram are fighting for the establishment of an Islamic state that is free from Western influence. Thirdly, both the Uyghurs and the Boko Haram sect adopts guerrilla tactics to further their cause; they make use of weapons of mass destruction which leads to the destruction of lives and properties in both countries; and they carry out their arson and bombings in public places which culminates in heavy casualty.

Fourthly, both sects get moral and financial support from neighbouring Islamic countries, especially from the Middle East, as a result of their ethnic and religious affiliations with those countries. Also, these Islamic countries gladly give their support to Islamic insurgents all over the world because of their anti-West posture. Lastly, while the Boko Haram claim responsibility for their actions, the Uyghurs don't.

Linkages of religious conflicts on the Socio-Political and Economic Development of China and Nigeria

There is no gainsaying that the activities of the Uyghurs and Boko-Haram from the 1990s till date, have greatly impeded the process of modernization and nation building in China and Nigeria, in that, it has dealt a big blow on the socio-political and economic development of both countries. In the social spheres, the activities of the Uyghurs and Boko Haram leads to palpable fear among the citizenry and high sense of insecurity due to regular loss of life and damage of properties and infrastructures on account of bombings and reported cases of assassination. Many people are displaced as a result of this crisis and they become refugees in other communities. In Nigeria for instance, the Nigerian government established camps for the Internally Displaced Persons (IDPs) who lost all they had during the Boko Haram destruction. There is no doubt that the migrants will put additional pressure on the host communities in terms of infrastructure usage and might also act as security threat to their host communities. Also, the psychological effect of this crisis cannot be underestimated. The survivors of those attacks are always traumatised as a result of the shock which they experienced, as well as the pain of seeing people being blown into pieces by bombs.

Economically, the religious conflicts in China and Nigeria have a lot of negative impacts on the development of both countries. In the first instance, some of the able bodied men and women, as well as intellectuals who are supposed to help in the development of the economy of both countries are being murdered by the day. Also, the resources which are supposed to be utilized for the development of both countries are being diverted towards solving the menace of this religious insurgency. The destruction of government properties makes it impossible for development to take place in those regions because the more the government put in place infrastructural facilities, the more it gets damaged. Furthermore, the Islamic activism of the Uyghurs and Boko Haram in Xinjiang, China and North-East Nigeria scare away investors who could have invested in key areas of the economy (since no investor prefer to invest in a crisis ridden nation). In Nigeria for instance, most of the foreign investors are scared of investing in the country because they believe they might lose their investments to the attacks of the Boko Haram terrorists, as well as their lives. The curfews which are imposed by the government as a result of the incessant terrorist attacks, prevents people from going about their daily activities, therefore, causing a decline in economic development of this regions.

Politically, the insecurity situations in Xinjiang, China and North East Nigeria have dented the image of both countries in the international arena, in that people are scared of travelling to these regions for fear of death. Also, it has helped to worsen the diplomatic relationship between the government of these regions and their international counterparts. For instance, most foreign countries view all Nigerians as terrorist and they treat them as such. Nigerians are always subjected to strict security checks whenever they are travelling to other countries. Also, the Chinese government accuse some neighbouring countries of supporting Islamic activism in Xinjiang, and this situation has worsened China's relationship with those countries. It is imperative to note that, in Nigeria, some greedy politicians make use of the Boko Haram sect for the selfish interest and they also provide financial support for the sect. This factor is responsible for the inability of the Nigerian government to be able to properly quell this insurgency, thereby, making them look incompetent.

It is imperative to stress that one of the factors responsible for the inability of the Nigerian government to put an end to the Boko Haram insurgency is corruption. Most of the officers, who are charged with the responsibility of purchasing arms and ammunitions for the military, use the situation as conduit pipe for fraud and misappropriation of fund. They siphon the money meant for the purchase of arms, and purchase cheap and substandard weapons which cannot match the sophisticated weapons being used by the Boko-Haram sect (Egana, 2015)

All the aforementioned salient issues are the socio-political and economic impact of the religious crisis of the Uyghurs in Xinjiang, China and the Boko Haram of North-East Nigeria, on the development of China and Nigeria. Although, the Chinese and Nigerian governments have tried their best to suppress these uprising, the situation persists till date. However, if this scourge is not checkmated, it will have a devastating effect on the economy of both countries.

Conclusion

From the forgoing discussion we can deduce that, religious conflicts in China and Nigeria was a "frustration aggression hypothesis" on account of religious restrictions and the influence of Western education in China and Nigeria respectively. In view of this, rather than religion being used as an instrument of socio-political and economic development in China and Nigeria, it was manipulated by the Uyghurs and Boko Haram as an instrument of destruction and disintegration, which threatened the peace, stability and security of both countries from the 1990s up till 2015. This chapter asserted that religious conflicts in China and Nigeria can be attributed to ethnic rivalry, religious bigotry and poverty and these has greatly impeded the socio-political and economic development of both countries. This crisis which culminates in the loss of lives and properties is the bane of underdevelopment in Xinjiang, Uyghur province in China and North-East Nigeria, in that, no sustainable development can thrive in a crisis ridden environment. Despite the measures put in place by the Chinese and Nigerian governments to curtail this crisis, the situation persists and if no concrete measure is put in place to revamp this situation, the crisis will act as a canker worm that will eat deep into the fabrics of the national economies of both countries. It is instructive to stress that, the current high level of religious crisis in China and Nigeria is not insurmountable. The situation can be revamped if the governments of both counties adopt the following recommendations:

Firstly, the government of the People's Republic of China and the Federal Republic of Nigeria should extend their bilateral relations to include security cooperation, so that both countries can consolidate their efforts in the fight against insurgency and insecurity in China and Nigeria, so as to achieve quick and concrete result, since "two good heads are better than one". Also, they should put in place pro-active security measures that will help to eradicate this menace once and for all.

Secondly, the Chinese and Nigerian governments should put in place measures that will help to improve the standard of living of their citizens. Poverty has been attributed to be one of the causes of ethno-religious crisis, since "a hungry man is an angry man". Therefore, the governments of both countries should look for ways to eradicate poverty and create employment opportunities for the youths because an "idle mind is the devil's workshop".

Thirdly, religious leaders should stop the wrong interpretation of religious texts and Holy Books, so as not to spark up excessive patriotism, which in turn culminate into religious extremism. Also, religious leaders should preach religious tolerance to their adherents so that they can live peacefully amongst themselves.

Fourthly, the government of both countries should create a forum for the leadership of the various religions to meet and discuss ways in which religious crisis can be abated and propose ways in which all the various religions can live peacefully amongst themselves. Furthermore, the Chinese government should try and improve their human rights record and grant the Uyghurs more participation in the government of their region, as well as religious freedom. Also, the Nigerian government should always pay close attention to security issues in the country, because if they had tackled the Boko Haram menace before it escalated, the country wouldn't have experienced incessant killings and destruction of properties.

Lastly, all culprits must be severely punished to act as deterrents to others irrespective of their societal status. In Nigeria, corrupt public officials who are involved in corruption and politicians who are sponsors of the Boko Haram sect should be punished, so as to rid the country of those who are agents of underdevelopment and security threats.

References

Adega, P. *et al*, (2009). "Religion and Anti-Corruption Campaign in Nigeria: Any Impact?" *Journal of Research and Contemporary Issues*, Vol.5, No.182.

Ahokegh, F. "Boko Haram: A 21st Century Challenge in Nigeria", *European Scientific Journal*, Vol.8, No.21. <eujournal.org/index.php/esj/articleFile/334/363> Retrieved on 13th October, 2015.

Albert, E. 2015. "Religion in China", *Council on Foreign Relations*. <http://www.cfr.org/China/religion-China/p16272> Retrieved on 15th October, 2015.

Awortu, B. 2015. "Boko Haram Insurgency and the Underdevelopment of Nigeria", *Research on Humanities and Social Sciences*, Vol.5, No.6.

Babatunde, M. *et al*, 2014. "Historical Antecedents of Boko Haram Insurgency and its Implications for Sustainable and Educational Development in North Central Nigeria". *Journal of Education and Practice*, Vol.5. No.22.

BBC News, "Who are the Uighurs", 30th April, 2014. <http://www.bbc.com/news/world-asia-China-22278037> Retrieved on 15th October, 2015.

BBC News, "Why is there Tension between China and the Uighurs?" 26th September, 2014. <http://www.bbc.com/news/world-asia-China-26414014> Retrieved on 15th October, 2015.

Clunas, C. *et al*, 2008. "China", *Microsoft® Encarta® 2009* [DVD]. Redmond, WA: Microsoft Corporation. Retrieved on 14th October, 2015.

Corradini, K. 2010. "Uyghurs under the Chinese State: Religious Policy and Practice in China", *Tropical Research Digest: Human Rights in China.*

Egana, E. 2015 "Buhari Orders Arrest of Dasuki, others over $2.9b Arms Deal", <dailytimes.com.ng/buhari-orders-arrest-of-dasuki-others-over-2-9b-arms-deal/>

Ethel, M. *et al*, 2010. "Place of Religion in Nation Building and Security in Nigeria: A Historical Survey of Aro Expedition on 1901", *African Journal of History and Culture*, Vol 2(2).

Gorrie, J. "The China Crisis: How China's Economic Collapse will lead to a Global Depression" <https://books.google.com.ng/books?id=A5eO4XalbglC&pg=PT153&lpg=PT153&dq=religiour+crisis+in+China&source=bl&ots=Vj1gjNxNGQ&sig=TpycAR4hWsJEMtTs2km5cu2T_qg&hl=en&sa=X&ved=oCBUQ6AEwATgkahUKEwjP8JrDqt71AhUBuxQKHXauBxg> Retrieved on 19th October, 2015.

Lai, H. 2003. "The Religious Revival in China", *Copenhagen Journal of Asian Studies*, No.18.

Lee, R. 2014. "Unrest in Xinjiang, Uyghur Province in China", *Al Jazeera Center for Studies*, Report for 9th February.

Onuoha, F. *et al*, 2015. "Political, Economic and Security Challenges facing President Buhari", *Al Jazeera Center for Studies*, Report for 21st September.

Oshadare, T. *et al*, 2005. *Perspectives on Nigerian Peoples and Culture*, Makurdi: Aboki Publishers.

Shuaibu, S. *et al*, 2015. "The Impact of Boko Haram Insurgency on Nigeria National Security", *International Journal of Academic Research in Business and Social Sciences*, Vol.5, No.6, 2015.

Siddiqui U. "The Ethnic Roots of China's Uighur Crisis" <America.aljazeera.com/opinions/2015/7/the-ethnic-roots-of-Chinas-uighur-crisis.html> Retrieved on 15th October, 2015.

Tiscler, H. "Introduction to Sociology"; cited in, Okau, A. *et al*, 2003. *Readings in Current Sociology*, Makurdi: Aboki Publishers.

www.ingramcontent.com/pod-product-compliance
Lightning Source LLC
Chambersburg PA
CBHW060022030426
42334CB00019B/2145